# RACE AND GENDER
# IN ELECTRONIC MEDIA

This volume examines the consequences, implications, and opportunities associated with issues of diversity in the electronic media. With a focus on race and gender, the chapters represent diverse approaches, including social scientific, humanistic, critical, and rhetorical. The contributors consider race and gender issues in both historical and contemporary electronic media, and their work is presented in three sections: content, context (audiences, effects, and reception), and culture (media industries, policy, and production). In this book, the authors investigate, problematize, and theorize a variety of concerns which at their core relate to issues of difference. How do we use media to construct and understand different social groups? How do the media represent and affect our engagement with and responses to different social groups? How can we understand these processes and the environment within which they occur? Although this book focuses on the differences associated with race and gender, the questions raised by and the theoretical perspectives presented in the chapters are applicable to other forms of socially-constructed difference.

**Rebecca Ann Lind** is an Associate Professor in the Department of Communication at the University of Illinois at Chicago.

ELECTRONIC MEDIA RESEARCH SERIES
Sponsored by the Broadcast Education Association
*Robert K. Avery and Donald G. Godfrey, Series Editors*

MEDIA MANAGEMENT AND ECONOMICS
RESEARCH IN A TRANSMEDIA ENVIRONMENT
*Edited by Alan B. Albarran*

MEDIA AND THE MORAL MIND
*Edited by Ron Tamborini*

MEDIA AND SOCIAL LIFE
*Edited by Mary Beth Oliver, Arthur A. Raney*

DIGITAL TECHNOLOGY AND THE
FUTURE OF BROADCASTING
*Edited by John V. Pavlik*

# RACE AND GENDER IN ELECTRONIC MEDIA

## Content, Context, Culture

*Edited by*
*Rebecca Ann Lind*

Routledge
Taylor & Francis Group

NEW YORK AND LONDON

First published 2017
by Routledge
711 Third Avenue, New York, NY 10017

and by Routledge
2 Park Square, Milton Park, Abingdon, Oxon, OX14 4RN

*Routledge is an imprint of the Taylor & Francis Group, an informa business*

*Library of Congress Cataloging in Publication Data*
A catalog record for this book has been requested

ISBN: 978-1-138-64010-8 (hbk)
ISBN: 978-1-315-63680-1 (ebk)

Typeset in Sabon LT Std
by Swales & Willis Ltd, Exeter, Devon, UK

# CONTENTS

# CONTENTS

CONTENTS

# CONTRIBUTORS

**Alan B. Albarran** (PhD, The Ohio State University) is Professor of Media Arts at the University of North Texas. His research and teaching interests revolve around the management and economics of the media and communication industries. The author of 14 books, he served as the founding Director of the Center for Spanish Language Media at UNT from 2006–2011.

**Jace K. Allen** (BA, University of Montana) is a graduate student in the Communication Studies Department at San Francisco State University. His research focuses on sexuality and communication; representations of non-normative sexual identities in video games and new media; and gay male identity in cross-cultural settings, especially in Japan, Korea, and the United States, within and outside of various forms of media. His work has been published in several anthologies on gender, sexuality, and intercultural communication.

**Kim Baker** (MA, Auburn University) is a doctoral candidate in the College of Communication and Information Sciences and an Institute for Communication and Information Research Fellow at the University of Alabama. She is also an assistant professor of multimedia journalism at Alabama State University. Recent studies include analyzing the ways in which people acquire knowledge and form beliefs of public issues and policies, collaborating with colleagues in developing and testing a cultural visual literacy instrument, and considering how new media and technologies affect health-related attitudes and behaviors.

**Andrew C. Billings** (PhD, Indiana University) is the Ronald Reagan Chair of Broadcasting and Director of the Alabama Program in Sports Communication at the University of Alabama. His research frequently examines the intersection of sport, media, and issues of identity. He is the author of over 120 journal articles and book chapters, along with 10 books, including *Olympic Media: Inside the Biggest Show on Television* (2008) and *Sports Media: Transformation, Integration, Consumption* (2011).

**Robert Alan Brookey** (PhD, University of Minnesota) is a Professor of Telecommunications at Ball State University where he also serves as Director of the graduate program in Digital Storytelling. His books include *Reinventing the Male Homosexual: The Rhetoric and Power of the Gay Gene*, *Hollywood Gamers: Digital Convergence in the Film and Video Game Industries*, and *Playing to Win: Sports, Video Games and the Culture of Play*. His articles have appeared in *Critical Studies in Media Communication*; *Convergence, Games and Culture*; and *Text and Performance*.

**Carolyn M. Byerly** (PhD, University of Washington) is Professor and Chair, Department of Communication, Culture and Media Studies, Howard University. She is a feminist critical scholar who conducts research on gender and race in media. Her recent research in political economy of women's employment in newsrooms around the world was published in the *Global Report on the Status of Women in News Media* (2011) and *The Palgrave International Handbook of Women and Journalism* (2013). She is co-author of *Women and Media: A Critical Introduction* (2006) and co-editor of *Women and Media: International Perspectives* (2004). Her book chapters and articles have appeared in *Critical Studies in Media and Communication*, *Journalism: Theory and Practice*, *Feminist Media Studies*, and others.

**Christopher P. Campbell** (PhD, University of Southern Mississippi) is a Professor in the School of Mass Communication and Journalism at the University of Southern Mississippi, where he served as the school's director from 2005 to 2014. He previously led mass communication and journalism programs at Xavier University of Louisiana, the University of Idaho, Hampton University, and Ithaca College. He is the author of *Race, Myth and the News* (1995) and the co-author/editor of *Race and News: Critical Perspectives* (2012). He is currently editing *The Routledge Companion to Race and Media*, scheduled for publication in 2016.

**Nicholas T. Chivers** (MA, San Francisco State University) is a Lecturer in Speech and Communication Studies at San Francisco State University and Ohlone College in Fremont, CA. His work focuses on bringing social justice issues and critical theory into the community college classroom. He is a popular presenter in the Ohlone College Speech Colloquium series with his lectures on current issues in the social construction of identities and their relationships to power and privilege. He is also a lover of ska music and distance running.

**Charisse L'Pree Corsbie-Massay** (PhD, University of Southern California) is an Assistant Professor of Communications at the S. I. Newhouse School of Public Communications at Syracuse University. Her research investigates the relationship between media and identity to understand how media affect the way we think about ourselves and others, and how we use media to construct and reaffirm positive identities.

**Travis L. Dixon** (PhD, University of California, Santa Barbara) is the Communication Alumni Professorial Scholar and Associate Professor of Communication at the University of Illinois at Urbana-Champaign. His research interests include the presence of stereotypes in the mass media and the impact of stereotypical imagery on audience members. Much of his work has focused on racial stereotyping in television news.

**Charles Ecenbarger** (MA, Ball State University) is a PhD student in the Department of Communication, Rhetoric, and Digital Media at North Carolina State University. His research interests include virtual reality, video games, the video game industry, and critical theory. He has published in journals such as *Well Played: Video Games, Value, and Meaning* and the *International Journal of Gaming and Computer-Mediated Simulations*. He also sits on the editorial board of *Press Start*, an open access peer-reviewed journal for graduate students and new faculty.

**Stine Eckert** (PhD, University of Maryland) is an Assistant Professor in the Department of Communication at Wayne State University. Her research interests include the intersections of social media, minorities and gender as well as the democratic potential of social media. She has published articles in the *International Journal of Communication*; *Media, Culture and Society*; the *Journal of Communication Inquiry* and *Journalism: Theory, Practice and Criticism*. She co-founded the Wikid GRRLs project to teach online skills to teenage girls. Find out more on stineeckert.com and follow on Twitter @stineeckert.

**Bruce W. Finklea** (PhD, University of Alabama) is an Assistant Professor of Mass Communication at the University of Montevallo. His research and teaching interests include gender representations in children's media, media effects, newscast production, social media, and multimedia journalism. His recent publications include an invited entry on comprehensive theories of media effects in the *International Encyclopedia of Media Effects* and a co-authored chapter on Muted Group Theory in Pixar films in *Communication Theory and Millennial Popular Culture: Essays and Applications*. He also co-authored *Fundamentals of Media Effects* (2nd ed.) with Jennings Bryant and Susan Thompson.

**Sarah Florini** (PhD, Indiana University) is an Assistant Professor in the Department of English at Arizona State University. Her research focuses on the intersection of emerging media and race. She is currently working on a monograph titled *Blackness. There's an App for That: Racial Politics and Black Digital Networks*.

**Ben Light** (PhD, University of Salford) is Professor of Digital Society at the University of Salford, United Kingdom. He engages science and technology studies bringing it to research questions of the sociocultural in digital society. Themes of his work relate to everyday digital (non)consumption practices, digital methods, and gender. He is author of *Disconnecting with Social Networking Sites* (2014) and, with Kylie Jarrett and Susanna Paasonen, he is currently working on the book, *Not Safe for Work*, for MIT Press.

**Rebecca Ann Lind** (PhD, University of Minnesota) is an Associate Professor and Director of Undergraduate Studies in the Department of Communication and an Associate Dean in the College of Liberal Arts and Sciences at the University of Illinois at Chicago. Her research interests include race, gender, class, and media; new media studies; media ethics; journalism; and media audiences. Her most recent book is *Produsing Theory in a Digital World: The Intersection of Audiences and Production in Contemporary Theory, 2.0. Volume 2*, and she is working on a fourth edition of *Race/Gender/Class/Media: Considering Diversity Across Audiences, Content, and Producers.*

**Adrienne L. Massanari** (PhD, University of Washington) is an Assistant Professor in the Department of Communication at the University of Illinois at Chicago. Her research centers on the social and cultural impacts of new media, gaming, information architecture and user-centered design, crowdsourcing, youth culture, and digital ethics. In her recent book, *Participatory Culture, Community, and Play: Learning from Reddit*, she analyzed the culture of the social news and community site Reddit.com. Her work has also appeared in *New Media and Society*, *First Monday*, *Journal of Computer-Mediated Communication*, and *Journal of Information Technology and Politics*.

**Dana Mastro** (PhD, Michigan State University) is a Professor in the Department of Communication at the University of California, Santa Barbara. Her research documents depictions of Latinos in English and Spanish language U.S. media and empirically examines the range of intergroup and identity-based outcomes associated with exposure to these portrayals.

**Leigh M. Moscowitz** (PhD, Indiana University) is an Associate Professor in the School of Journalism and Mass Communication at the University of South Carolina. Her research examines the cultural production of news and the politics of media representation. She is the author of *The Battle over Marriage: Gay Rights Activism through the Media* (2013) and *Snatched: News Coverage of Child Abductions in U.S. Media* (2015, co-authored with Spring-Serenity Duvall at Salem College). Other research projects include news coverage of gay athletes, the impact of feminist media literacy initiatives, and the televisual production of class and gender in popular reality programs.

**Philip M. Napoli** (PhD, Northwestern University) is the James R. Shepley Professor of Public Policy in the Sanford School of Public Policy at Duke University, where he is also a Faculty Affiliate in the DeWitt Wallace Center for Media & Democracy. His research interests include media institutions and media policy. His most recent book is *Audience Evolution: New Technologies and the Transformation of Media Audiences* (2011).

**Jonathan A. Obar** (PhD, Penn State University) is an Assistant Professor of Communication and Digital Media Studies in the faculty of Social Science and Humanities at the University of Ontario Institute of Technology. He also serves as a research associate with the Quello Center for Telecommunication Management and Law at Michigan State University. His research has been published in a variety of academic journals and addresses the impact digital technologies have on civil liberties, civic engagement, and the inclusiveness of public culture.

**Kristin M. Peterson** (MA, University of Colorado Boulder) is a doctoral candidate in media studies at the University of Colorado Boulder where she is also a research fellow for the Center for Media, Religion and Culture. Her research focuses on Islam in North America, specifically examining how young Muslims engage with online media as spaces to explore different discourses, aesthetic styles, and affects. Her other research interests include the use of Arabic in social media, Islamic fashion, feminism and religion, the racialization of Islam, social media celebrities, and discourses around authenticity.

**Sage E. Russo** (MA, San Francisco State University) is a graduate student from the Communication Studies Department at San Francisco State University. Her current interests include exploring the intersection of critical theory and performance studies as a methodological investigation into gender and sexuality, specifically queering academic conceptualizations of flirting. Her research has appeared in *Boyhood Studies: An Interdisciplinary Journal* as well as several (inter)disciplinary anthologies.

**Nancy Signorielli** (PhD, University of Pennsylvania) is Professor of Communication at the University of Delaware. She has conducted research on images in the media and how these images are related to people's conceptions of social reality (cultivation analysis) for the past

45 years. An original member of the Cultural Indicators Research Team, she has published extensively on gender role images, television violence, and health-related images on television. Recent studies include Morgan, M., Shanahan, J., & Signorielli, N. (2015). Yesterday's new cultivation, tomorrow. *Mass Communication & Society, 18*, 674–699.

**Alexander Sink** (MA, University of California, Santa Barbara) is a PhD student in the Department of Communication at the University of California, Santa Barbara. His research interests are focused on the role of media in issues of stereotyping, prejudice, and discrimination.

**Linda Steiner** (PhD, University of Illinois) is a Professor in the College of Journalism at the University of Maryland. Her research interests include media ethics; citizen participation in journalism; feminist theorizing; roles of women working in alternative, feminist, and mainstream media; and war reporting. Her co-authored or co-edited books include *Women and Journalism* (2004); *Key Concepts in Critical-Cultural Studies* (2010), *Routledge Companion to Media and Gender* (2013), and *The Handbook of Gender and War* (2016). She is editor of *Journalism and Communication Monographs* and has published 100 book chapters and journal articles.

**Tammy Swenson-Lepper** (PhD, University of Minnesota) is a professor and internship director in the Communication Studies Department at Winona State University. Her research interests include communication ethics, ethical sensitivity, pedagogy and communication ethics, organizational communication, and service learning. Her most recent publication, for which she was lead author, "Communication ethics in the communication curriculum: United States, Canada, and Puerto Rico," was published in *Communication Education*.

**Alisa Valentin** (MS, Northwestern University) is a doctoral student in the Communication, Culture and Media Studies program at Howard University. She is also a teaching assistant in Howard's principles of speech program, a graduate assistant for the *Howard Journal of Communications*, and a member of the Howard Media Group, a faculty–student research collaborative focused on communication policy. Her research interests include communication policy and social media in social movements. She is a former broadcast journalist specializing in urban affairs reporting.

**Mary Douglas Vavrus** (PhD, University of Illinois) is an Associate Professor and Donald V. Hawkins Professor of Communication Studies in the Department of Communication Studies at the University of Minnesota. A feminist media researcher, her interests include media postfeminism, electoral politics, various forms and practices of media militarism, and feminist satire and parody. Her work focuses on intersections between media political economy and gender, race, class, and sexuality. She is the author of *Postfeminist News: Political Women in Media Culture* and is currently completing a book on women in the media-military-industrial complex.

**Nicole Warncke** (BA, Temple University) is an MFA candidate in Documentary Production and Studies at the University of North Texas. Her work has been driven primarily by interests in education, social equity, media literacy, youth development, and civic engagement. She has worked in nonprofit, academic, and television production industries, taking on online and offline pursuits. She holds degrees in Sociology and Broadcasting, Telecommunications, and Mass Media, and conducts research that blend the two fields.

**Yiyi Yang** (MA, University of Alabama, 2014) is a doctoral student in the College of Communication and Information Sciences at University of Alabama. Her research interests include health communication, sports communication, and social media studies.

**Gust A. Yep** (PhD, University of Southern California) is Professor of Communication Studies, Graduate Faculty of Sexuality Studies, and Faculty in the EdD Program in Educational Leadership at San Francisco State University. His research examines communication at the intersections of culture, race, class, gender, sexuality, and nation, with a focus on sexual, gender, and ethnic minority communities. In addition to three books and a monograph, he has authored more than ninety articles in (inter)disciplinary journals and anthologies. He is recipient of numerous academic and community awards including the 2011 San Francisco State University Distinguished Faculty Award for Professional Achievement (Researcher of the Year) and the 2015 Association for Education in Journalism and Mass Communication (AEJMC) Leroy F. Aarons Award for significant contributions to LGBT media education and research.

# SERIES EDITOR'S FOREWORD

Since its inception in 1948, the Broadcast Education Association has fostered a serious commitment to scholarly research, though that commitment became more formalized with the publication of its first scholarly journal, *Journal of Broadcasting* (later *Journal of Broadcasting & Electronic Media*) in 1957. Over the Association's rich intellectual history, BEA's annual meetings have afforded both academics and professionals with a wide range of opportunities for the presentation of important scholarship focusing on broadcasting and the electronic media.

In 2008, BEA launched a new series of programs designed to advance original research initiatives under the direction of the Association's Research Committee. The name of this new scholarly venture within the framework of the annual conference is the BEA Research Symposium Series, and over the past eight years it has served to advance the research agendas of our discipline and provide a forum for some of the leading scholars and latest ground-breaking research in our field. The first Research Symposium in 2008 was orchestrated by Professor Jennings Bryant with a focus on Media Effects. This was followed in 2009 with a Research Symposium on the subject of TechnoPolitics, under the direction of Professor Linda Kaid.

In response to these two highly successful symposia, discussions began in 2010 between BEA and the Taylor and Francis Group of Routledge to form a partnership to enable the publication of an annual volume resulting from the yearly BEA Research Symposium. That new scholarly publication venture is the Electronic Media Research Series, and is intended to serve as cutting edge seminal publications that offer an in-depth cross section of significant research topics. The 2010 Research Symposium Chair was Andrew C. Billings and hence the first volume in the new series edited by Professor Billings was *Sports Media: Transformation, Integration, Consumption* published in 2011. The 2011 Research Symposium Chair, Ron Tamborini, edited the second volume, *Media and Morality*, released in 2012. The third volume growing out of the 2012 Research Symposium, published in 2013, was edited by Alan B. Albarran and is titled *Media Management and Economics Research in a Transmedia Environment*.

The fourth volume, *Media and Social Life*, was co-edited by Arthur A. Raney and Mary Beth Oliver and was published in 2014. The fifth volume, titled *Digital Technology and the Future of Broadcasting: Global Perspectives*, edited by Professor John V. Pavlik, Rutgers University, was released in 2015.

The present volume, titled *Race and Gender in Electronic Media: Content, Context, Culture*, resulted from the 2015 Research Symposium chaired by Professor Rebecca Ann Lind, University of Illinois at Chicago. This volume has been edited by Professor Lind and contains both selected papers from the Symposium and essays written especially for this collection. Together, the chapters contained in this volume offer a unique perspective on questions about a wide range of issues on race and gender in both historical and contemporary media contexts. The chapters address the intersections of race and gender with other important sociological and political issues from both social science and humanistic perspectives. The Broadcast Education Association and Routledge are proud to make this important volume available to scholars across the entire communication discipline and beyond.

Robert K. Avery
BEA Research Committee Chair
Symposium Series, Executive Editor

# ACKNOWLEDGMENTS

I keep hearing nightmarish tales about editing a collection such as this: contributors will flake out; the work won't be up to snuff; people will miss deadlines; and so forth. You can even buy a t-shirt that says "Being an editor is easy. It's like riding a bike except the bike is on fire you're on fire everything is on fire and you're in hell."[1] But other than wanting to edit that statement (it could use some punctuation) I can't relate to this— or to the nightmarish tales—at all.

My greatest thanks are to the contributors to this volume. We've had, by any measure, a wonderful collaboration. They've shared many intriguing ideas in these pages, and throughout they have been responsive, understanding, and willing to engage with an active editing process. I hope they are pleased with the outcome.

I owe thanks, also, to the Broadcast Education Association for suggesting this topic and for nominating me to edit this volume. Along the way, it has been a pleasure to work with Linda Bathgate and Routledge. Paul Couture has also been a consistent asset in helping my work come to fruition.

As always, many thanks are due to my colleagues in the Department of Communication at the University of Illinois at Chicago, and to the College of Liberal Arts and Sciences, for their support.

Grateful acknowledgment is made to the following for permission to use copyrighted material:

Cover image *Difference* by Chuck Sabec (2015). Reprinted with kind permission of the artist and Studio Eight Fine Art (www.StudioEightFineArt.com). All rights reserved.

*To my parents and my students.*

## Note

1 https://www.sunfrog.com/Being-an-Editor-Its-Like-Riding-A-Bike-Purple-Ladies.html

# 1

# RACE AND GENDER IN ELECTRONIC MEDIA
## Perennial Challenges and Opportunities

### *Rebecca Ann Lind*

The average person aged 18 and above in the US spends just four minutes shy of 12 hours per day with electronic media (Nielsen, 2015). Close to five hours per day is spent with television; in addition, we spend just under two hours per day with radio and close to another two hours per day online via PCs or smartphones. Given these figures, it is clear that for the average American adult nothing else can approximate the time we spend with electronic media. Using this average, people who get a minimal six hours of sleep per night spend two-thirds of their waking lives with electronic media. For people who get eight hours of sleep, this average represents three-quarters of their waking lives. Concerns about this can't be alleviated by saying "most of this is probably multitasking"; the fact remains that most of us are spending the vast majority of our waking hours with the electronic media. We have long been concerned about the effects of such media use. Fears of how audiences are affected by entertainment (and other) content extend at least as far back as the fourth century BCE to Plato, who argued, as Heins put it, "that the government should censor unsavory or unpatriotic messages" (2001, p. 2). These concerns are hardy perennials,[1] indeed.

## Constructing and Responding to Difference

At its core, this volume is concerned with issues of difference. How do we use media to construct and understand different social groups? How do the media represent and affect our engagement with and responses to different social groups? How can we understand these processes and the environment within which they occur? Although this book focuses on the differences associated with race and gender, the questions raised by and the theoretical perspectives presented in the chapters are often applicable to other forms of difference. Indeed, the primary focus on race and gender is complemented in this book at times by chapters which also incorporate other differences such as social class, able-bodiedness, or appearance.

Considering race and gender in the context of difference is important for two main reasons: these differences are socially constructed, and these socially constructed groups experience very different realities. One need not look farther than arrest and sentencing records or healthcare disparities (such as presented by the Agency for Healthcare Research and Quality, n.d.; Federal Bureau of Investigation, n.d.; United States Bureau of Justice, n.d.) or employment and salary data (such as presented by the United States Department of Labor, n.d.) for evidence of the latter. The former is less amenable to statistical verification, but the socially constructed nature of raced and gendered differences nonetheless remains significant.

According to Boas (1945/1969), "the existence of any pure race with special endowments is a myth, as is the belief that there are races all of whose members are foredoomed to eternal inferiority" (p. 20). Boas further argued that "the belief in organic differences between [races] has come to appear as so fundamental that social and political relations are determined by it," and that we do not "demand any careful examination of the reasons for the feeling of difference, but accept it" (1945/1969, p. 20). Thus, Boas challenged biological theories of race, foregrounding the reality of race as a social rather than a biologically meaningful construct. Sixty years later, however, Smedley and Smedley (2005) said that "recent advances in the sequencing of the human genome and in an understanding of biological correlates of behavior" (p. 16) have reinforced the conflation of biology and race. They argued that these developments "have fueled racialized science, despite evidence that racial groups are not genetically discrete, reliably measured, or scientifically meaningful" (p. 16). They stated that "race as biology is fiction, racism as a social problem is real" (p. 16) and advocated instead for approaching race as a socially constructed phenomenon. The race-based social and political determinations originally noted by Boas in 1945 continue in the new millennium. According to Omi (2001, p. 254), "the idea of race and its persistence as a social category is only given meaning in a social order structured by forms of inequality—economic, political, and cultural—that are organized, to a significant degree, by race."

As with race, considerations of gender have evolved from what were once primarily biological understandings into a recognition of the importance of the social context in which gender functions, and seeing "gender as systems of status and power relations" (Shields & Dicicco,

2011, p. 496). In a special anniversary section in *Psychology of Women Quarterly*, Shields and Dicicco reviewed some of the "massive transformations" that have occurred in our understanding of gender, and introduced a set of retrospectives highlighting "turning points in the social psychology of gender" (2011, p. 491), which include a focus on gender in a social context.

The social context was powerfully highlighted by Berger and Luckmann (1967), who in *The Social Construction of Reality* argued that "social order exists *only* as a product of human activity" (p. 52, emphasis in original). Our actions—no matter how mundane—are both the genesis of social order and the impetus by which it continues to exist. In short, through our interactions, we create our world. Our actions generate and perpetuate shared mental representations; reality and knowledge are socially relative and contextually situated. Subjective meanings become objective facticities. As we engage with others in processes of reciprocal habitualized activity, we create and maintain institutions which ultimately serve to control us by "setting up predefined patterns of conduct" (1967, p. 55). As Lind interpreted Berger and Luckmann,

> Even as we create our world, therefore, we create, recreate, and legitimate institutions, and we begin to see these socially constructed institutions—which restrict, limit, and inhibit us—as objective realities. Institutions are continually reified, the symbolic universes (belief systems) underlying them reinforced, and their supposed objective status augmented as they are passed on to subsequent generations.
>
> (2015, p. 2)

Equally important is Berger and Luckmann's concept of typification. Typifications are knowledge structures, cognitive frameworks, or sense-making structures that we use to help us understand and respond to the world around us. As we approach our interactions and dealings with others, we are guided and affected by typificatory schemes; as Berger and Luckmann put it, "I apprehend the other as 'a man,' 'a European,' 'a buyer,' 'a jovial type,' and so on" (1967, p. 31). However, Berger and Luckmann acknowledged that only face-to-face interactions provide direct evidence regarding a particular person's actions and attributes; further, they argued that "the typifications of social interaction become progressively anonymous the further away they are from the face-to-face situation" and, further, that "every typification . . . entails incipient anonymity" (p. 31). During face-to-face interactions, our always potentially anonymizing typifications are, as Berger and Luckmann described it, "'filled in' by the multiplicity of vivid symptoms referring to a concrete human being" (p. 32). In the process, the person with whom we are interacting—despite continuing to be seen as a member of the potentially anonymous and anonymizing category or group being typified—becomes less anonymous and less typical, that is, unique and individualized.

Typifications are similar to what have been called schema, schemata (Bartlett, 1932), or social schema, defined by Fiske and Taylor as "knowledge about a concept or type of stimulus, including its attributes and relations among those attributes" (1991, p. 98). Pennington (2000) argued that social schemas are important in understanding stereotyping, even though they are conceptually distinct. According to Dovidio and Gaertner, stereotypes contain information about qualities such as social roles [and] traits," and "reflect beliefs about the qualities that distinguish a group from others, that characterize the typical member of a group, and that indicate the consistency with which members of a group share a quality" (2010, p. 1084). As several of the chapters in this book will show, stereotypes are alive and well in the mass media.

The chapters in this volume, as mentioned above, are concerned with how difference is constructed and responded to in an electronically mediated environment. Several chapters use social scientific methods to document the under-representation or stereotypical representation of minorities in media or to build theory or taxonomy to guide research investigating the effects of those representations on audiences. These are complemented by chapters engaging rhetorical or critical perspectives to analyze how raced or gendered media texts serve to perpetuate or challenge the dominant ideology—whether these texts are produced by media conglomerates, independent media producers, or the users themselves. Yet another approach is represented by authors who investigate the impact of regulatory, legal, and policy decisions on the extent to which different socially constructed groups have access to media.

## Media Content, Context, and Culture

The two main pleasures in compiling a collection such as this are working with the contributors in developing and expressing their arguments, and organizing the resulting fruits of the authors' labors into a coherent whole. How best to arrange these individual stories?

One option is to arrange the contributions according to whether they consider race, gender, or a combination or intersection thereof. For example, the contributions by Dixon (Chapter 10), Brookey and Ecenbarger (Chapter 11), Campbell (Chapter 12), Napoli and Obar (Chapter 17), and Albarran and Warncke (Chapter 20) focus on issues related to race and ethnicity in electronic media. The works by Billings, Moscowitz, and Yang (Chapter 3); Finklea (Chapter 6); and Light (Chapter 14) focus on issues related to gender. The rest of the chapters—the majority—study both race and gender. Of these, some focus more on race than on gender (Mastro & Sink, Chapter 9; Florini, Chapter 19), whereas others focus more on gender than on race (Baker, Chapter 7; Steiner & Eckert, Chapter 13; Byerly & Valentin, Chapter 16; Massanari, Chapter 18; and to a lesser extent Vavrus, Chapter 5). Still others consider race and gender equally: Signorielli (Chapter 2); Yep, Russo, Allen, and Chivers (Chapter 4); Corsbie-Massay (Chapter 8); Peterson (Chapter 15); and Lind and Swenson-Lepper (Chapter 21).

Another option is to arrange the chapters according to the type of media being considered. For example, both Vavrus (Chapter 5) and Finklea (Chapter 6) study films (either documentary or fiction) to learn more about gender in our society. A number of authors study broadcast television to interrogate race or gender (or both): Signorielli (Chapter 2); Billings, Moscowitz, and Yang (Chapter 3); Yep, Russo, Allen, and Chivers (Chapter 4); Baker (Chapter 7); Byerly and Valentin (Chapter 16); and Albarran and Warncke (Chapter 20). Some chapters are not medium-specific: Corsbie-Massay (Chapter 8); Mastro and Sink (Chapter 9); Lind and Swenson-Lepper (Chapter 21). The largest subset of chapters is that investigating what may be called new media, emerging media, or social media, as enabled by digital communications technologies: Dixon (Chapter 10); Brookey and Ecenbarger (Chapter 11); Campbell (Chapter 12); Steiner and Eckert (Chapter 13); Light (Chapter 14); Peterson (Chapter 15); Napoli and Obar (Chapter 17); Massanari (Chapter 18); and Florini (Chapter 19).

The chapters could also be organized according to whether they primarily considered entertainment media or news/public affairs media, by theoretical paradigm employed, or by some other potentially equally interesting metric. Ultimately, I have used none of these possible organizational schemes, although I have presented them to facilitate alternate approaches to the material in this volume.

The chapters herein are grouped into three main sections, which represent three of the major components of our complex contemporary media environment. Part I covers media content, or the messages which are disseminated via mass media; Part II considers the media context, including audiences, effects, and reception; and Part III looks at media culture, including media industries, policy, and production.

As I have argued elsewhere (Lind, 2013), an organizational scheme based on audiences, content, and the production environment is consistent with both social scientific and critical models of communication. Social scientists have long been informed by the work of Laswell (1948) and Shannon and Weaver (1949), and many empirical studies of mass media can be understood as addressing (at least in part) questions of who says what to whom and with what effect. The work of critical/cultural studies scholars can be organized similarly around what is being said to whom, by whom, and with what effect, although these studies take a more overtly political stance and approach these focal points as what can be called "points of intervention": text, audience, and production. Thus the tripartite division of this book aligns well with multiple paradigms, and allows for a rich confluence of perspectives from the social scientific to the humanistic to the historical to the critical.

In this book, questions of "who says," or message production as a point of intervention, are in the *media culture* section (Part III), which focuses on how, by whom, and in what sort of culture (including organizational culture and policy/regulatory culture, and historical as well as contemporary perspectives) mediated messages are crafted. Questions of "what" is said, or the media text as a point of intervention, are in the *media content* section (Part I), and include content analysis, framing analysis, narrative analysis, and critical analysis. Questions of "to whom and with what effect," or reception as a point of intervention, are in the *media context* section (Part II), which includes how individuals receive, use, understand, and are affected by mediated messages; this section contains research employing experiments, discourse analyses, analyses informed by actor network theory, and more.

Despite the value of organizing this book according to the works' focus on content, context, or culture, it is important to acknowledge that some chapters cross the content-context-culture boundaries. At times they span the boundaries because even though there is a predominant focus on one or another of the three main sections, the authors have taken a wide enough view of their topic that they expand beyond that section. For example, Mastro and Sink (Chapter 9) and Dixon (Chapter 10) bridge content and context by describing how minorities are represented in media before they turn to the effects of such exposure on audiences; Billings, Moscowitz, and Yang (Chapter 3) bridge content and culture by interviewing journalists to inform their analysis of media coverage; and Florini (Chapter 19) bridges culture and content by considering how an independent media organization's content reflects the organizational mission. At other times, chapters span boundaries because the authors study mediated messages which by their very nature exist in what Lind (2015) called the interstices—the intersections between audiences and content enabled by social media or Web 2.0 technologies, involving produsage (a portmanteau of production and usage; Bruns, 2008) and user-generated content. I including these chapters with other audience-centered works in the context section (Part II) to highlight the active role held by the participants in these communicative acts.

## *Media Content (Part I)*

The six chapters in Part I emphasize the mediated messages themselves: what they present, and how; what is included, and by implication, what is excluded. The content under investigation varies widely, ranging from a near half-century retrospective of prime time television, to sustained multi-channel coverage of a prominent sporting event (the Olympics), to multiple seasons of television series (*Glee*; *The Walking Dead*), to a defined set of films, whether animated fiction (released by Pixar) or documentary (about servicewomen).

Chapter 2, written by Nancy Signorielli, is informed by cultivation theory and social cognitive theory, and describes continuing patterns of under-representation of women and different minority groups. Analyzing nearly 50 years of prime time television content, Signorielli found that Blacks in prime time only reached parity with their numbers in the U.S. population when the schedule included situation comedies with mostly minority characters. When those programs disappeared Blacks again became under-represented. Women and minorities continue to be younger than men, and until the beginning of the twenty-first century women were less likely than men to be seen working outside the home or in prestigious occupations. Signorielli argues that these patterns provide problematic, narrow lessons about race relations and gender expectations, and that they reinforce racial isolation.

In Chapter 3, Andrew Billings, Leigh Moscowitz, and Yiyi Yang combine framing and political economy in their analysis of journalistic discourses surrounding Russia's anti-gay policies both before and during the 2014 Sochi Winter Olympics. Their mixed-method study incorporates textual analyses of newspaper and television coverage leading up to and during the 18-day event and interviews with lead journalists from *USA Today* regarding how they treated the story. Prior to the Games, the authors find, news stories emphasized controversial themes relating to Russia's legislation and whether the US should push for reform, but during the Games the issue largely disappeared. Billings, Moscowitz and Yang posit that the pre-Olympics coverage used gay rights issues to titillate and amplify public interest in the Games rather than to encourage policy reform or enhance equality for LGBTQ citizens. Once the Games began, such issues may have diverted attention from the inherent drama of the competition, and overall, the coverage seemed to silence human rights issues in favor of covering the global spectacle of Olympic sport.

Gust Yep, Sage Russo, Jace Allen, and Nicholas Chivers, in Chapter 4, explore the intersection of race and gender and the representation of non-normative gender identity by conducting a close reading of the character Unique in the television show *Glee*. The authors use transing as a theoretical framework, and find that Unique's representation works to conflate genders and sexualities, reify boundaries, maintain unintelligibility, and essentialize authenticity. They argue that representations of intersectional gender identities are problematic, and that subjectivities are dangerously overlooked. Despite *Glee*'s apparent attempts to present contemporary social issues and to raise visibility of marginalized identities, the show reifies the structures it may seek to challenge. Thus, normative power relations are maintained and reinforced.

In Chapter 5, Mary Douglas Vavrus conducts a feminist intersectional analysis of six recently released documentary films about U.S. servicewomen, informed in part by Judith Butler's concepts of grievability and recognizability. Vavrus argues that these documentaries constitute a regime of representation she calls the Warrior Women regime. This regime illustrates not only a growing recognition of women's value to military service, but also that the meanings of gender, race, and military life are discursively constructed, intensively managed, and negotiated in and through media. Her analysis reveals that the Warrior Women regime of representation exhibits a mixture of resistance and capitulation to patriarchy and racism, and that it obscures the violence and destruction that accompany militarism.

Bruce Finklea (Chapter 6) presents a narrative analyses of 13 Pixar films, exploring the films' narratives about masculinities in Pixar's feature films, focusing particularly on the New Man model of masculinity. He discusses the typical narrative pattern reflecting characters' transformations into New Men (emasculation, relational bonding, and emergence as New Man). He found that most transformations are catalyzed by homosocial (male–male) rather than heterosocial (male–female) relationships. Further, homosocial narratives resulted in the emerging New Men learning a much wider variety of messages about masculinity than was the case with heterosocial narratives. Heterosocial bonds focus primarily on the men's roles as fathers or family men. In essence, male catalysts result in one becoming a better, fuller New Man; although women can instigate change in men, such change is tied to the family, a traditionally female domain. Ultimately, Finklea concludes, although the films may appear to challenge normative gender roles, the characters and their actions work to reinforce patriarchy and hegemonic control.

Chapter 7, by Kim Baker, analyzes the television show *The Walking Dead* (*TWD*), in which the appearance of zombies leads to the sudden collapse of society and ensuing chaos. Baker is guided by McKerrow's principles of critical discourse analysis and Foucault's conceptualizations of power, and considers both initial power relations and attempts to reestablish institutionalized structures and symbolic power (which, as simulations, ultimately fail). She argues that *TWD* represents a world in which social structures and hegemony are exposed and old prejudices discarded. An egalitarian system emerges through necessity, and those who cling to beliefs about racial and gender stereotypes become examples of how not to survive. Her analysis reveals how *TWD* and its use of power symbols reflects society, and proposes that the characters eventually adopt a freed gaze among the blind gaze of the zombies, thus recognizing and confronting stereotypical gender and racial roles.

## Context: Audiences, Effects, Reception (Part II)

Part II contains eight chapters, focusing on the people who engage, consume, or interact with mediated messages: how they use the media, what sense they make of media content, and how they are affected by the media. The section includes two new models for approaching the study of media effects from a social scientific perspective: the Media FIT Taxonomy, and the Social Mediated Stereotyping Model. It contains a comprehensive review of how both Latinos and non-Latino audiences are affected by the portrayal of Latinos in the media. The context section also features a wide array of studies of user-generated content created as audience members become what Axel Bruns (2008) called produsers of media: racist and xenophobic discourse among online video game players, social media as a site of postmodern media criticism, the democratic potential of feminist Twitter, using digital networks to produce sexual cultures and pseudonymous publics, and Islamic fashion images on Instagram.

In Chapter 8, Charisse L'Pree Corsbie-Massay conducts a methodological review of how media effects researchers have manipulated the variables of race and gender. In the process, she has created what she calls the Media FIT Taxonomy. The taxonomy allows scholars to define and categorize media content according to three dimensions: Format (e.g., text, images, video), Industry (e.g., journalism, advertising, entertainment), and distribution Technology (e.g., analog, electronic, digital). Using her taxonomy, Corsbie-Massay found previously undetected patterns in the field of media effects studies that highlight areas in need of attention. She also found that assumptions about race and gender are often deployed as fact—for example, many studies manipulating gender use names that can be assumed to reflect Whiteness, and potential confounds of race are not addressed. Corsbie-Massay concludes that the Media FIT Taxonomy reveals methodological patterns which limit our understanding of race and gender in media. However, researchers can use the taxonomy as a tool to help expand the range of media effects studies.

Dana Mastro and Alexander Sink, in Chapter 9, present an analysis of the portrayals of Latinos across the media landscape (television, film, and video games) to lead into their consideration of the effects of exposure to such content on Latino and non-Latino audiences. Their review of the quantitative media effects research reveals that although individual attributes of the audience members moderate the effects, the effects are wide ranging and powerful. On the positive side, research has demonstrated that exposure to favorable messages can improve social perceptions and encourage more auspicious interethnic dynamics among Latinos and non-Latinos. However, even short-term exposure to a small number of unfavorable Latino portrayals in the media can influence non-Latinos' cognitions about and attitudes toward Latinos; among Latinos, exposure to negative representations of Latinos can prompt a range of harmful psychological and social consequences. Mastro and Sink address the significance of both the quantity and the quality of media messages for interethnic relationships, and suggest that continued research could help us understand how to enhance positive outcomes and diminish negative outcomes.

In Chapter 10, Travis Dixon (as did Mastro and Sink) looks at the representation of minorities in news before turning his primary attention to the effects of such exposure on audiences. He notes the increasing importance of the Internet in news distribution, and proposes a model to help guide our thinking about the effects of stereotypical content in socially mediated contexts. As users curate and share news from a multitude of sources, various psychological theories might suggest an increased likelihood of racism and stereotyping. Dixon's Socially Mediated Stereotyping Model (SMSM) is a synthesis of several existing theories, capitalizing on the strengths and ameliorating the weaknesses of those theories in the Internet context. It contains two propositions: that dominant themes make stereotypes more accessible, but are shaped by agenda setting and media diets; and that social utility will moderate the effects of social media on stereotyping via selective exposure. Dixon's theorizing supports a consideration of a social media environment in which the accessibility of stereotypes is mediated by users' specific social media diets, and the effects of social media are driven by social utility and selective exposure, but in which social media also provide the affordances that activists can use to counter stereotypes.

Robert Alan Brookey and Charles Ecenbarger (Chapter 11) incorporate the constructs of xenophobia and racism into their critical rhetorical analysis of *League of Legends* players' discourse regarding Spanish-using players. *League of Legends* (*LoL*) is one the most popular online games in the world, but prior to the introduction of Spanish language servers, English-using *LoL* players complained vigorously about Spanish-using players ruining the game. Brookey and Ecenbarger analyze the comments posted by English-using *LoL* players about Spanish-using players—players they perceived to be from Mexico and other countries in Central and South America. The arguments reflected both racism and xenophobia, and were similar to those found in discourse surrounding illegal immigration. Brookey and Ecenbarger found that language operated as a marker for race and national identity, and that Spanish-using players were considered a foreign threat and should be removed from North American soil. However, the authors also found that many participants challenged the racist and xenophobic arguments. Thus, they argue, the *LoL* discourse reflects a debate in which domination is both asserted and challenged.

In Chapter 12, Christopher Campbell examines the #IfTheyGunned MeDown social media posts following the 2014 fatal shooting of Michael

Brown, an African American, by a White police officer. Young African Americans posted positive and potentially negative photographs of themselves, asking which would be used by the media should they be shot by police. Campbell argues that the posts reflect keen insight into the notion of media representation, and that people using the hashtag perceptively and concisely identified the problems with journalistic representations of Black people as pathological criminals. He explores these posts as a form of postmodern media criticism, further informed by Stuart Hall's politics of signification. With #IfTheyGunnedMeDown, critiques of problematic racial representations moved into the popular culture, and were then addressed by traditional news organizations—in the process increasing their impact as news coverage reached larger and older audiences. Campbell asks whether social media and other elements of contemporary media could significantly advance the discussion of race in America.

In Chapter 13, Linda Steiner and Stine Eckert reflect on the democratic potential of feminist Twitter. Grounded in the theory of fluid public clusters, and also informed by intersectionality, the authors conducted a textual analysis of the #FemFuture report, several major essays on the so-called "toxicity" on Twitter among feminists, and the comments posted to those essays. Steiner and Eckert argue that although feminism is often understood as a singular movement, intended to counter all oppressions, the notion of a single feminist movement was challenged by disagreements over the #FemFuture report. Women of color—who seem not to feel welcomed by or included in the feminist movement—are establishing distinct online spaces to provoke discussion of intersectionality. The authors argue that multiple feminisms are fueling current forms of activism, using social media to fight oppressions of various kinds that are consistent with feminism's overarching goals but doing so in ways that are not neatly aligned. They suggest that the emergence of a Black feminist Twitter suggests a problem for and within feminism—and that perhaps feminists must self-consciously work on the intersectionality that may otherwise merely be assumed.

In his actor network theory-informed analysis of the hook up site Squirt, Ben Light (Chapter 14) demonstrates how networked media and digital devices inform and allow for the co-existence of a broad spectrum of sexual politics, sexual preferences, and sexual practices. His analysis leads to critically reflexive interpretations of the potentials of networked publics, as well as the assumptions of publicness that can be attached to them when they become interwoven with discourses of the real name web. Light extends our theoretical understanding of networked publics into what he calls pseudonymous publics. He argues that pseudonymous publics display the characteristics of networked publics, and hold the potentials for connection and disconnection with physical worlds, but do not demand an engagement with the heteronormative assumptions of the real name web.

11

Kristin Peterson, in Chapter 15, analyzes Islamic fashion images on Instagram and the visuality of Muslim women. She argues that the online spaces of social media offer young female Muslims in Western countries the opportunity to present their identities in ways that contrast the dominant discourses and visualities of Muslim women as veiled and oppressed. Peterson examined the Instagram pages of three prominent Muslim fashion gurus to see how these women use the style of Islamic fashion and the affordances of social media to present the complexities of their lives and to resist over-simplified representations. She found that these Muslim women create images that represent themselves as independent, creative and assertive; they present their beauty in ways that are fashionable but still modest. Still, the pressures of postfeminism were evident in these women's Instagram pages, which at times reflected the idea of women's liberation through consumption, entrepreneurship, and constant self-work. The Instagram pages of these women, Peterson argues, illustrate the intersecting demands and ambivalences that are specific to Muslim women in the West.

### Culture: Media Industries, Policy, Production (Part III)

The six chapters in Part III focus on the cultures associated with producing media content. Production involves anything having to do with the creation and distribution of mediated messages: how the messages are assembled, by whom, in what circumstances, and under what organizational, policy, legal, or other environmental constraints. The section begins with a pair of pieces considering the impact of law and policy on people engaging with media (the first from a regulatory standpoint regarding ownership of and employment in broadcasting, and the second from a policy standpoint regarding the digital divide). It then presents a trio of chapters looking into the cultures associated with the production of various types of media content: gaming culture and games journalism, an independent digital media company which foregrounds Blackness, and Spanish language television broadcasting in the US. The section ends with a chapter presenting a tool to help journalists (and other media professionals) become more sensitive to ethical issues involving racial and gender intolerance.

In Chapter 16, Carolyn Byerly and Alisa Valentin argue that media access is an important condition for women's equality and represents an important aspect of women's right to communicate, but few women have owned or controlled major media companies. Their feminist analysis explores women's structural relationship to the news and communication media in the US by examining laws, federal communication policies, lawsuits and court rulings related to women's media access. Besides tracing women's efforts to gain greater access to jobs in media and to own media companies, they also examine women's agency in challenging exclusion and discrimination. A further contribution to the discipline is the table presented by Byerly and Valentin—a compilation of the policies, lawsuits, and so forth that were key in the development of the events they discuss. They note that women's progress was often influenced by analogous efforts by racial minorities, hence their analysis (and table) also address key developments in racial minorities' quest for media access.

Philip Napoli and Jonathan Obar (Chapter 17) study how access to media via the mobile Internet differs from access via personal computers, and find that in many ways, the former is considerably inferior to the latter. They note that race has long been a key dimension of the digital divide, that policies have been implemented to address such disparities, and that increasing minority populations' access to mobile devices is often seen as a positive development. The authors offer a counterpoint to the popular discourse about how mobile diffusion is helping to alleviate the digital divide, and highlight the potentially negative implications of the relative prominence of mobile natives and mobile onlys in minority populations. Although mobile Internet diffusion may effectively address the basic issue of getting individuals online, they say, the differences between mobile and PC-based forms of Internet access can reinforce inequities in digital skill sets, online participation, and content creation, potentially resulting in a mobile Internet underclass. Napoli and Obar argue that policy dialogue should incorporate a comprehensive and nuanced recognition of the socially, economically, and politically significant shortcomings associated with the transition to mobile-based forms of Internet access, particularly for mobile-only users.

In Chapter 18, Adrienne Massanari interrogates how geek masculinity often marginalizes women and people of color in the gaming community. She uses the ongoing harassment of Anita Sarkeesian (a response to her *Tropes vs. Women in Video Games* series) as a case study to reveal how what she calls toxic technocultures coalesce around and are implicitly supported by the politics of new media platforms. Harassment campaigns using the hashtag #GamerGate claimed, in part, to be a response to ethical shortcomings in games journalism; many Gamergaters criticized what they call "social justice warriors" in the gaming industry and among games journalists, whom they see as pushing a feminist agenda in terms of how games are made and covered. Massanari argues that these misogynistic, anti-feminist movements reflect a particular form of entitlement felt by a certain segment of the gaming community (mostly White men) who perceive the increasing diversity of gaming content and audiences as fundamentally threatening their social identity as gamers.

Sarah Florini, in Chapter 19, presents an in-depth analysis of This Week in Blackness (TWiB!), an independent media company. She argues that the dominant racial discourse in the US is colorblindness, which

13

conflates the erasure of difference with the attainment of racial equality; further, she says, dominant cultural logics construct Black Americans as a homogenous, undifferentiated mass, a monolith to which recursive racist archetypes can be attached. TWiB! was deliberately designed as a space to challenge these notions, and Florini presents how TWiB! approaches what she offers as the seemingly irreconcilable demands of both foregrounding and interrogating the construction of Blackness. TWiB! rejects discourses of colorblindness, emphasizing the centrality of race and reasserting race as a central axis of social life. In addition, Florini shows how TWiB! highlights the diversity of Black people, rejecting reductive understandings of Blackness and prioritizing the intersectionality of social identities such as race, class, gender, and sexuality.

In Chapter 20, Alan Albarran and Nicole Warncke reflect on the problems and prospects of Spanish language television broadcasting in the US. They review the state of the industry, its ownership, and its audiences, followed by a discussion of the problems and prospects facing this dynamic sector of the media landscape. Relatively few outlets are Latino-controlled, which (as did Byerly & Valentin in Chapter 16), the authors argue is a long-term problem and a major concern. Further, Spanish language television is prone to the same issues of under- and poor representation as documented by other contributors to this volume (e.g., Signorielli, Chapter 2; Mastro & Sink, Chapter 9; Dixon, Chapter 10). Albarran and Warncke note that many Spanish-language broadcasters focus on their audiences as consumers rather than as citizens, which has clear implications for the democratic processes in the US. On the other hand, Spanish language broadcasters may benefit from increased revenue based on the growth and expansion of Latinos in the US; these revenues may support measures to counteract some of the challenges facing the industry. Further, the increasingly bicultural nature of the audience, coupled with the deployment of new and emerging media technologies, may afford multiple opportunities for Spanish language broadcasters.

Chapter 21, by Rebecca Ann Lind and Tammy Swenson-Lepper, considers an aspect of the media industry which bears further scrutiny: the training of future journalists and the ongoing professional development of media workers. The authors apply the concept of ethical sensitivity (ethsen) to media coverage of ethical issues related to socially constructed difference, such as race, ethnicity, and sexual orientation. They argue that the assessment of ethsen can function as an important pedagogical tool in journalism and media education. Approaching issues of diversity, difference, and intolerance as ethical issues is consistent with prior literature, which further makes a strong connection between professional practice (exemplified in professional codes of ethics) and moral behavior. Lind and Swenson-Lepper discuss how sensitivity to issues involving socially constructed difference might be assessed and used in both educational and research contexts.

## What Next?

As you read this book, you will no doubt notice from the recurrence of several powerful examples that it has been written in a particular moment. Of course, all books are written in particular moments, but this one was born during a time of escalating racial tension and violence in the US. The years leading up to and including 2016 have made their mark on these pages, and indeed we must remember Michael Brown, Eric Garner, Laquan McDonald, Feminism's Toxic Twitter Wars, racist anti-immigration discourse, the racism and sexism of the 2016 presidential campaigns, #GamerGate, and hashtags or rallying cries such as #IfTheyGunnedMeDown, #BlackLivesMatter, #ICantBreathe, and #HandsUpDontShoot. If there were ever any doubts as to the relevance of addressing race and gender in the media, they cannot remain in the light of these and other events. These and other examples underscore the importance of directing our attention to issues of socially constructed difference both in the electronic media context and beyond.

Yet even as many of what are at the moment contemporary examples shine a spotlight onto crucial contemporary challenges, they also function to support theoretical evolution and advancement of our understanding of relevant concepts in the realm of media and the social construction of difference. The theoretical and conceptual vitality of the chapters in this volume means that they will be able to inform research into race and gender in electronic media for many years to come. What will Spanish language media mean for and to Latinos in the future? When, if at all, will the underrepresentation of minorities, and the stereotypical portrayal of minorities and women, end? Might representation become more equitable if broadcast facilities were owned by women or minorities? Have we inadvertently created a mobile Internet underclass, and if so, how can that be rectified? How can we create a culture where we constructively debate important issues instead of generating toxic technocultures? How can we best manipulate race and gender in experimental studies? How do the extensions of theory here guide our understanding of race and gender in media? Can future media content and discussions about media coverage of race and gender be improved if we make an overt effort to educate our students and future media professionals to become more sensitive to ethical issues regarding socially constructed difference? What forms of activism will work best to help us create the culture in which we would most like to live? What can hashtag activism do to bring real change? And of course, how will theory continue to evolve to shine light onto a rapidly changing media environment?

The authors and I have enjoyed creating this volume. I hope you enjoy what follows, that you find the chapters interesting and informative, and that what you read here stimulates you to pose even more intriguing, important and rewarding questions.

## Note

1 I borrow the term used in the classroom by Donald R. Browne, a mentor and friend, for whom I served as a teaching assistant at the University of Minnesota.

## References

Agency for Healthcare Research and Quality (n.d.). *Topic: National Healthcare Disparities Report (NHDR)*. Retrieved November 29, 2015, from http://www.ahrq.gov/health-care-information/topics/topic-national-healthcare-disparities-report-nhdr.html.

Bartlett, F. A. (1932). *Remembering: A study in experimental and social psychology*. New York, NY: Cambridge University Press.

Berger, P. L., & Luckmann, T. (1967). *The social construction of reality: A treatise in the sociology of knowledge*. New York, NY: Anchor Press.

Boaz, F. (1969). *Race and democratic society*. New York, NY: Biblo and Tannen. (Original work published 1945.)

Bruns, A. (2008). *Blogs, Wikipedia, Second Life, and beyond: From production to produsage*. New York, NY: Peter Lang.

Dovidio, J. F., & Gaertner, S. L. (2010). Intergroup bias. In S. T. Fiske, D. T. Gilbert, & G. Lindzey (Eds). *Handbook of social psychology* (5th ed.) (Vol. 2, pp. 1,084–1,121). Hoboken, NJ: John Wiley.

Federal Bureau of Investigation (n.d.). *Uniform crime reports*. Retrieved November 29, 2015, from https://www.fbi.gov/about-us/cjis/ucr.

Fiske, S. T., & Taylor, S. E. (1991). *Social cognition* (2nd ed.). New York, NY: McGraw-Hill.

Heins, M., (2001). Violence and the media. In M. Heins, with J. Cantor, H. Jenkins, D. Niehoff, J. Savage, R. Corn-Revere, R. A. Smolla, & R. M. O'Neil (Eds). *Violence and the media: An exploration of cause, effect and the First Amendment* (pp. 1–18). Nashville, TN: First Amendment Center. Retrieved November 28, 2015, from http://www.firstamendmentcenter.org/madison/wp-content/uploads/2011/03/violenceandthemedia.pdf.

Lasswell, H. D. (1948). The structure and function of communication in society. In B. Lyman (Ed.). *The communication of ideas* (pp. 37–51). New York: Harper & Row.

Lind, R. A. (2015). Produsing theory in a digital world: Life in the interstices. In R. A. Lind (Ed.) *Produsing theory in a digital world: The intersection of audiences and production in contemporary theory, 2.0. Volume 2* (pp. 1–18). New York, NY: Peter Lang.

Lind, R. A. (2013). Laying a foundation for studying race, gender, class, and the media. In R. A. Lind (Ed.), *Race/gender/class/media 3.0: Considering diversity across audiences, content, and producers* (3rd ed., pp. 1–12). Boston, MA: Pearson.

Nielsen, A. C. Co. (2015). *The Total Audience Report, Q2 2015*. Retrieved November 28, 2015, from http://www.nielsen.com/content/dam/corporate/us/en/reports-downloads/2015-reports/total-audience-report-q22015.pdf.

Omi, M. A. (2001). The changing meaning of race. In N. J. Smelser, W. J. Wilson, & F. Mitchell (Eds.), *America becoming: Racial trends and their consequences* (Vol. 1, pp. 243–263). Washington, DC: National Academies Press.

Pennington, D. C. (2000). *Social cognition*. Modular psychology series. London, UK: Routledge.

Shannon, C., & Weaver, W. (1949). *The mathematical theory of communication*. Urbana, IL: University of Illinois Press.

Shields, S. A. & Dicicco, E. C. (2011). The social psychology of sex and gender: From gender differences to doing gender. *Psychology of Women Quarterly, 35*, 491–499.

Smedley, A., & Smedley, B. D. (2005). Race as biology is fiction, racism as a social problem is real: Anthropological and historical perspectives on the social construction of race. *American Psychologist, 60*(1), 16–26.

United States Bureau of Justice (n.d.). *Bureau of Justice statistics*. Retrieved November 29, 2015, from http://www.bjs.gov/.

United States Department of Labor (n.d.). *Data and statistics*. Retrieved November 29, 2015, from http://www.dol.gov/wb/stats/stats_data.htm.

# Part I

# CONTENT

# 2

# RACE AND SEX IN PRIME TIME

## Five Decades of Research

*Nancy Signorielli*

This chapter focuses on portrayals of leading/major character in five decades of network prime time programming, examining images of men and women as well as of Whites, Blacks, and other minorities overall and in relation to age, violence, and occupational status. My goal is to discuss what previous research has told us about the portrayal of minorities, to supplement and extend this information with new analyses, and to ascertain what changes, if any, have occurred since the 1960s.

The portrayal of minority groups on television has been a consistent and important research focus. Some of the early research was fueled by government funding; in the late 1960s the Kerner Commission, appointed by President Johnson to investigate racial disturbances in many U.S. cities, charged that these disturbances could be traced to the U.S. mass media industry's failure to serve and adequately represent minority interests. The Kerner Commission (1968) found that the media seemed to encourage racial conflict by presenting Black Americans in negative and limited ways and suggested that the industry and its regulating agencies prioritize improving coverage related to minority groups. In the mid-1970s studies conducted for the United States Commission on Civil Rights (1977, 1979) found that minorities continued to be both under-represented and stereotypically portrayed in network prime time programming.

Most research initiatives, however, come from the ongoing research programs of communication scholars. Some of our knowledge about minority representation comes from studies conducted during the 1970s and 1980s focusing on network broadcast programming, the venue then most readily available to viewers. Today, however, the way we receive television and how we watch has changed, specifically the proliferation of sources such as Netflix and changes in the platforms upon which we view. Network broadcast programming, although no longer the sole viewing option, remains an important component of the average person's viewing (Nielsen, 2015). Many viewers still turn to network TV, and because it remains an important source of entertainment its images continue to play an important role in the socialization process.

## How It Works

There are two theoretical perspectives relevant to racial portrayals on television: social cognitive theory and cultivation theory. Social cognitive theory (Bandura, 2002) posits that the media provide images and role models that viewers, particularly children, may use to develop scripts or schemas about different types of people and how they behave.

Social cognitive theory suggests that through observing others, individuals can develop rules to guide their subsequent behavior. Bandura (2009) articulated four subprocesses of vicarious learning: attention, retention, production, and motivation. First, one must attend to the actions or behavior of a model, which is often influenced by the attractiveness of the model. Second, an individual must retain the information, which is dependent upon symbolic coding, cognitive organization rehearsal, and cognitive skills (Pajares, Prestin, Chen, & Nabi, 2009). Third, the symbolic representation of an observed behavior must be translated into a behavior, and fourth a person is motivated by rewards or punishments (Bandura, 2009). Social cognitive theory is also highly dependent upon findings from content analyses because these findings illustrate the types of schemas viewers may see on a regular basis.

Cultivation theory argues that television is a collective symbolic environment of messages with an underlying pattern or formulaic structure and posits that those who spend more time with television have views that reflect what they see on television (Morgan, Shanahan, & Signorielli, 2009). Due to commercial constraints, television cultivates a common world view and common stereotypes through a relatively restrictive set of programs, images, and messages. Cultivation studies continually find that television content has little diversity and frequently recurring features (Morgan et al., 2009).

This perspective suggests that television is a primary contributor to people's conceptions of social reality through the cohesive and cumulative stories it tells, most of which are developed with similar underlying formulaic structures. The main hypothesis of cultivation theory is that individuals who spend more time with television are more likely than those who view less television to view the real world as congruent with the portrayal of reality presented on television (Morgan, Shanahan, &

Signorielli, 2009). Consequently, if television presents distorted images of reality, those who watch more television—the heavy viewers—may have conceptions of reality based on what they have seen on television.

Critical to cultivation analysis are Shrum's (2002) principles of (1) heuristic/sufficiency and (2) accessibility. These principles indicate that television viewing may play an important role in how people see the world and the judgments they make about the world. The heuristic/ sufficiency principle, for example, notes that when we form judgments we typically retrieve the information most readily available to us (sufficient) rather than try to reconstruct everything we know about a topic. In addition, the information typically retrieved is that which is most readily available or easiest to remember (accessibility).

Both perspectives postulate that judgments about people of color rely upon the images seen on television. In addition, we know that television's images may be particularly relevant for those who do not regularly encounter people of color in their day-to-day activities (Greenberg & Brand, 1994). Consequently, if the television landscape segregates racial groups, viewers' conceptions about their own interaction or lack of interaction with people of color may be cultivated or reinforced by what they experience when viewing.

### Representation of Minorities

One of the most interesting and perhaps telling findings of research on minorities in prime time entertainment programs is how their representation relates to their numbers in the U.S. population. In the 1970s and 1980s studies found that the numbers of Blacks on television had begun to reflect their proportion in the U.S. population (Greenberg, 1980). Analyses of programs from the 1990s found an even greater degree of parity. Mastro and Greenberg's (2000) and Glascock's (2001) analyses of samples of 1996 prime time network programs found that Blacks' prime time representation reflected their numbers in the U.S. population. Similarly, Harwood and Anderson (2002), in an analysis of spring 1999 prime time programs, found that although Whites were overrepresented, Blacks were at parity when compared to the U.S. population. Moreover, a study of 2001 prime time programs found that Blacks were overrepresented in relation to their numbers in the U.S. population (Hunt, 2002). Parity in representation, however, has changed in the twenty-first century. Signorielli (2009a) found a statistically significant decreasing linear trend in the representation of Blacks in prime time between fall 2000 and fall 2008. Interestingly, this decrease in representation was due to the decrease in the number of situation comedies.

Other minority groups (e.g., Latinos and Asians) are nearly invisible (Mastro & Greenberg, 2000). In samples from the late 1970s, Greenberg

23

and Baptista-Fernandez (1980) found that Latinos were usually concentrated in one or two programs. This pattern has not changed in 20 years. In 1996, Mastro and Greenberg (2000) found 30% of the Latinos in their sample appeared in a single program. Glascock (2001) found Asians and Latinos under-represented on the newer networks, and Harwood and Anderson (2002) found Latinos under-represented in the entire prime time lineup. Similarly, Signorielli (2009a) found, between the fall of 2000 and the fall of 2008, that Latinos made up only 5% of the prime time major character population compared to 16% of the U.S. population.

Besides the overall frequencies of representation, the genre of programs in which characters are cast is another way to examine program diversity. For example, research has shown that Blacks are less diversified because they appear most frequently in situation comedies and in programs with predominantly Black characters (Greenberg, Mastro, & Brand, 2002; Signorielli, 2009a). Signorielli (2009a) found a high degree of segregation for both White and Black characters in major/leading roles, with large percentages of Blacks, particularly Black women, in programs (typically sitcoms) with mostly minority characters and most White characters found in programs with all White or mostly White characters. On the other hand, the portrayal of other minority groups is more diversified because they are seen in more genres, including crime/action or drama programs. Greenberg and Baptista-Fernandez (1980) found that Latinos (usually Mexican Americans and Puerto Ricans) were often involved with gangs or barrios in crime/action programs, and Mastro and Greenberg (2000) found that 77% of Latino appearances were on crime programs.

The early studies show a high degree of consistency in television's demography, with consistent images of men and women and under-represented minority groups. Blacks were generally portrayed in stereotyped roles and as less powerful and less important than Whites (Gerbner, Gross, Morgan, & Signorielli, 1982). Some of these early studies found that Black characters were younger, funnier, and flashier than White characters and that minority characters were poorer, jobless, or in less important jobs. Blacks were rarely cast as bad or as villains and it seemed as though television writers went out of their way not to cast minorities in negative roles (Baptista-Fernandez & Greenberg, 1980; U.S. Commission on Civil Rights, 1977, 1979). More recent studies have found that crime dramas and reality programs typically show Whites as offenders thus avoiding an abundance of racial or ethnic minorities in these roles (Entman & Rojecki, 2000). In addition, programs such as the *Law and Order* series tend to minimize minorities through under-representation and do not demonize them as offenders or even show them as victims of violence (Britto, Hughes, Saltzman, & Stroh, 2007). Similarly, in programs such as *Law & Order* and *NYPD Blue*, Whites tend to be over-represented compared to crime statistics from New York City (Eschhoz, 2004). However,

Blacks are considerably more likely be shown in restraining devices such as handcuffs, and overall are more likely to be seen as offenders than as victims or lawyers. Interestingly, the research also found that prime time network series often include communication practices that inhibit close cooperation, intimate relationships, or deep friendships between Blacks and Whites (Auletta & Hammerback, 1985).

Age is another important way in which both women and minorities are differentiated. Signorielli (2004) found that women tend to be younger than men although they age faster. On average women are four years younger than men and are proportionally more often cast as young adults. Yet, once women on television reach 50, they are often shown with diminished capabilities and are often categorized as elderly rather than as middle aged. Men, on the other hand, are usually not categorized as elderly until they reach 65 or older; men between 50 and 64 are usually categorized as middle aged and still seen working and often involved romantically. In terms of age, minority characters more closely resemble women. Minorities are judged as younger than White characters but interestingly Signorielli (2004) found that they do not age faster than White characters.

### Occupational Portrayals on Television

Television is an important source of information about occupations, and research has provided good information about what occupations are seen on television and how they are portrayed (Elasmar, Hasegawa, & Brain, 1999; Greenberg & Collette, 1997; Signorielli, 1993; Vande Berg & Streckfuss, 1992). Yet only a few content analyses have extensively analyzed television's portrayal of occupational roles, particularly in relation to biological sex and racial stereotypes (Signorielli & Bacue, 1999; Signorielli & Kahlenberg, 2001).

The world of work on television is dominated by men, and more women than men lack an identifiable occupation (Signorielli, 1989; Signorielli & Bacue, 1999; Vande Berg & Streckfuss, 1992). In the 1990s, for example, Signorielli and Bacue (1999) found that 4 out of 10 women either did not work (20.3%) or their occupation was unknown (19.2%); by comparison, fewer than 1 in 4 men did not have an occupation (12.4%) or did not work (12.3%). Early studies found that men were frequently cast in a diverse number of high-status, professional or law enforcement jobs. Women, on the other hand, were cast in a narrower range of occupations often perceived as less prestigious, glamorous, or interesting: secretaries, nurses, teachers, and household workers (Greenberg, 1982; Signorielli, 1993; Vande Berg & Streckfuss, 1992). In comparison, in the past 25 years, changing societal mores and financial constraints have resulted in more than half of the women in the U.S. becoming part of the civilian labor force (http://www.census.gov/prod/2004pubs/04statab/labor.pdf).

Other content analyses have found somewhat more equal representations of men and women in professional occupations (Signorielli, 1993; Vande Berg & Streckfuss, 1992). For example, Atkin (1991), in an analysis of television series broadcast between 1966 and 1990, found more single women in professional and managerial positions and less in secretarial jobs. Similarly, Elasmar et al. (1999) found, in a sample of prime time programs broadcast in 1992–1993, about one-fourth of the women in professional and white-collar jobs (including entertainment) and one-fifth in blue-collar positions. Yet Greenberg and Collette (1997), in an analysis of a season's new programs using *TV Guide* synopses, found that men were often portrayed as professionals, managers, and police officers whereas women were often cast as homemakers, home care workers, and unskilled laborers.

Race adds another dimension to occupational portrayals. White men were more likely than women and nonwhites to be portrayed as professionals and white-collar workers. Nonwhites, on the other hand, were found in less prestigious, blue-collar jobs. For instance, Northcott et al. (1975) found that Black men and women were often cast in service occupations and as students, homemakers, or involved in illegitimate activities. Nonwhites, regardless of gender, were most frequently cast in service or clerical positions.

Signorielli and Kahlenberg (2001) found that more White than minority characters were characterized as working. In addition, minorities were less likely to be cast as professionals when compared with Whites, with a higher proportion of people of color than Whites holding law enforcement and blue-collar jobs. More White men than men of color were criminals, whereas fewer White women than women of color were so categorized. Moreover, White men were more likely to be cast as professionals than were men of color, White women, or women of color. Hunt (2005), in an analysis of 2002 programming, also found that Black and White television characters often had high-status occupations such as doctors and lawyers and that Blacks and Latinos were often also cast as police officers. Similarly, a study of 2003 prime time programs by Children Now (2004) found that more Whites and Blacks, compared to Latinos, were cast as high-status professionals, with Blacks and Latinos again likely to be seen as police officers. Although characters of all races were cast as criminals, Middle Eastern characters were the most likely to be cast in these negative roles.

During the first part of the twenty-first century there were differences in occupational portrayal that essentially reflected program genre, especially for characters of color. Dates and Stroman (2001) found that African Americans were often cast in more successful occupations in situation comedies than in other genres.

Signorielli (2009b) found that occupational prestige is tied to the racial makeup of a program and the sex of the characters. Men in programs with a cast of only White characters and programs with a cast of mostly minority characters were rarely seen in non-prestigious jobs. Women were more likely found in non-prestigious jobs when in a program whose cast was mostly or all White characters. Women in programs with mostly minority characters, on the other hand, typically have jobs best categorized as neutral in terms of occupational prestige. Overall Signorielli (2009b) found that women, especially Black women in programs with mostly minority characters, had the least diversity and prestige in terms of the jobs in which they were cast. Men's occupations, on the other hand, were equally diverse in all types of programs except for the lack of law enforcement jobs in programs with mostly minority characters. This distinction makes sense because most programs with mostly minority characters are situation comedies where the presence of law enforcement officers is not relevant.

Television's portrayal of occupational roles is governed by dramatic considerations rather than educational ones. Only jobs that serve a dramatic or useful function in a story or are part of the programs' action are regularly portrayed on prime-time. The work of law enforcement officers, doctors, and lawyers is often more exciting, suspenseful, interesting, and prestigious than that of farmers and laborers. Consequently, television consistently over-represents these types of occupations while it under-represents blue-collar occupations (Greenberg, 1982; Signorielli, 1993). These images may ultimately serve to influence negatively the types of scripts or schemas young girls and minorities develop in relation to their eventual socialization into an occupation role.

The following analysis will focus on one overarching question—how have the sexes and the races (White, Black, other people of color) been represented in network prime time programs during the past five decades, particularly in terms of images relating to program genre, age, violence, and occupations? Although of interest, the analysis will not examine the portrayals and representations of Latinos because only a few samples in this data set (all collected after the turn of the century) isolated these groups. The data reported here came from the analysis of 46 week-long samples of prime time network entertainment programs and were generated in two waves of data collection. Data from the fall of 1967 through the fall of 1992 were collected as part of the Cultural Indicators Project at the Annenberg School for Communication at the University of Pennsylvania. Data from the fall of 1993 through the fall of 2013 were collected as a research component of an upper level communication course at the University of Delaware. I oversaw the collection of data in both sources of data, thus ensuring consistency throughout the 46 years of data collection.

The variables used identical coding schemes in each of the samples. Genre classified the programs as situation comedy, crime/action, drama, or reality (added in the middle of the 1990s). The race of the program's

27

cast (added in the mid-1990s) originally consisted of five categories: all White, mostly White, mixed, mostly minority, and all minority. For this analysis the mostly minority and all minority categories were combined to increase the number of programs in this category. Characters were coded by biological sex and race. Race was coded as unknown, White, Black, American Indian, Asian, and other characters of color; the analyses focused on three categories: White, Black, and a combined category of people of color (Asian, Native Americans, and Other). Latinos were not included in this coding because they were not considered a racial category by the Census Bureau. A separate variable coding Latinos was added to the recording instrument in 2004 but the data set lacks an adequate number of characters for this chapter's decade by decade analysis.

Age was coded in two ways: social age, a description of where characters were in the life cycle (child/adolescent, young adult, middle aged, elderly); and chronological age. The analysis in this chapter focuses primarily on chronological age. The examination of violence in relation to characters looked at two variables—committing violence (hurting or killing another character) and victimization (being hurt or killed)—that were combined to form a variable, involvement in violence, that indicated whether each character was involved in violence as either a perpetrator or a victim.

The detailed coding scheme for occupation was added in 1973 and required several steps. Coders first described each character's occupation (which included some dramatic occupations such as criminal and superhero) and placed it in one of the 67 categories. Occupations were further categorized by job prestige into four classifications: (1) not prestigious (household or service workers), (2) neutral in prestige (secretary, social worker, nurse, teacher, household worker, clerical, etc.), (3) prestigious jobs (doctors, lawyers), and (4) unknown (did not work, could not tell). Overall, 17 different occupations were classified as not prestigious, 17 as prestigious, and 30 as neutral. The analyses for occupation included characters 16 and older.

Most of the programs (three-quarters or more) in each of the samples were coded by two independent coders to provide a test of reliability. Reliability was measured for each variable in each sample by Krippendorff's alpha. All of the variables used in this analysis met Krippendorff's (1980) standards of reliability. The statistical analysis used cross-tabulations, testing for statistical significance by Chi Square.

## Images Over Time

Aside from a small percent of news/information and game programs (which are excluded from this analysis), the prime time lineup is divided into four main genres: situation comedies, action adventures, dramas, and (since the mid-1990s) reality shows. During these five decades of programs the number of situation comedies rose from 40% of the programs between the late 1960s and the end of the 1980s, to more than half during the 1990s, but decreased to a third at the beginning of the twenty-first century and to a quarter between 2010 and 2013. Reality programs concomitantly increased. Beginning in the mid-1990s, programs were categorized by the racial makeup of the cast. In the 1990s about one in ten had a predominantly or totally minority cast, but by 2010–2013 that number had fallen to only 2%.

The representation of major/leading characters has undergone one major change from the late 1960s to the fall of 2013: the increase in the percentage of female characters. Table 2.1 shows that in the 1960s–1970s women made up less than 30% of the major characters and in the 1980s about a third of the major characters. Since the 1990s about 40% of the characters in each sample have been women. Although this increase is statistically significant and shows some change from the late 1960s to the 1990s, women are still under-represented and not at parity with their numbers in the U.S. population (49% male and 51% female).

Similarly, the representation of race in prime time network programs does not accurately reflect race in the U.S. population (see Table 2.2). Whites are consistently over-represented; Blacks and other people of color are under-represented. Moreover, looking at the intersection of sex and race, we see even more under-representation. The five decades of prime time programming analyzed here contain only two decades when the population of the television world was at parity with the U.S. population. During the 1990s and 2000s the racial distribution of female characters in prime time programs was similar to that of the U.S. population. The racial distribution of males, however, has never been at parity with the

Table 2.1 Representation of Major Characters by Sex by Decade (TV vs. U.S. Population)

| | Men | | Women | | ChiSq |
|---|---|---|---|---|---|
| | TV | U.S. | TV | U.S. | |
| 1960s–1970s | 71.2 | 48.7 | 28.8 | 51.3 | 512.9*** |
| 1980s | 65.7 | 48.6 | 34.3 | 51.4 | 238.5*** |
| 1990s | 59.1 | 48.7 | 40.9 | 51.1 | 134.4*** |
| 2000s | 58.0 | 49.1 | 42.0 | 50.9 | 99.4*** |
| 2010s | 60.0 | 49.2 | 40.0 | 50.8 | 62.3*** |

Notes: Census data through the 1990s obtained from http://www.census.gov/compendia/statab/2011/tables/11s0007.pdf; for 2000 and 2010 from http://www.census.gov/prod/cen2010/briefs/c2010br-03.pdf.

*** $p < .001$

*Table 2.2* Representation of Major Characters by Sex and Race by Decade (TV vs. U.S. Population)

| | White | | Black | | Other Races | | ChiSq |
|---|---|---|---|---|---|---|---|
| | U.S. | TV | U.S. | TV | U.S. | TV | |
| *All* | | | | | | | |
| 2010 | 79.6 | 85.7 | 12.9 | 8.4 | 7.5 | 5.8 | 32*** |
| 2000 | 81.1 | 80.9 | 12.7 | 14.4 | 6.3 | 4.7 | 18.1*** |
| 1990 | 83.9 | 81.9 | 12.3 | 14.0 | 3.8 | 4.1 | 9.52** |
| 1980 | 83.1 | 88.1 | 11.7 | 8.9 | 5.2 | 3.1 | 38.23*** |
| 1960s–1970s | 87.6 | 89.7 | 11.1 | 8.2 | 1.3 | 2.2 | 35.33*** |
| *Men* | | | | | | | |
| 2010 | 80.0 | 85.7 | 12.5 | 9.5 | 7.5 | 4.9 | 16.52*** |
| 2000 | 81.5 | 80.9 | 12.3 | 14.8 | 6.2 | 4.4 | 19.18*** |
| 1990 | 84.2 | 81.0 | 12.0 | 14.5 | 3.8 | 4.5 | 14.27*** |
| 1980 | 83.3 | 87.3 | 11.4 | 9.4 | 5.3 | 3.3 | 17.78*** |
| 1960s–1970s | 87.9 | 88.8 | 10.9 | 9.0 | 1.2 | 2.2 | 21.86*** |
| *Women* | | | | | | | |
| 2010 | 79.1 | 86.3 | 13.3 | 6.7 | 7.6 | 6.9 | 21.11*** |
| 2000 | 80.7 | 81.1 | 13.1 | 13.9 | 6.2 | 5.0 | 3.59 |
| 1990 | 83.6 | 83.6 | 12.7 | 13.3 | 3.7 | 3.1 | 1.58 |
| 1980 | 83.0 | 90.4 | 12.0 | 7.9 | 5 | 1.7 | 29.6*** |
| 1960s–1970s | 87.4 | 92.1 | 11.4 | 6.3 | 1.2 | 1.67 | 19.81*** |

*Notes:* Census data through the 1990s obtained from http://www.census.gov/compendia/statab/2011/tables/11s0007.pdf; for 2000 and 2010 from http://www.census.gov/prod/cen2010/briefs/c2010br-03.pdf.

*** p<.001
** p<.01

U.S. population. Further, since the end of the first decade of the twenty-first century, the racial distribution of major characters in prime time programs has become less and less reflective of the U.S. population.

The data from these analyses indicate that changes in the representation of Blacks in prime time programs are most likely due to changes in the number of situation comedies: when there are more situation comedies, there are more Black characters. Similarly, minority representation is also due to the sheer number of programs with mostly minority characters. The decrease in minority representation in the last four samples is a direct result of the decreased number of programs with mostly minority casts. In the most recent samples just about a third of the programs have a cast containing almost equal numbers of people of color and Whites whereas more than half of the programs had mostly White casts (with one or two seemingly token major characters of color) and there were almost no programs with mostly minority casts.

Overall, there have been very few children and older characters throughout these five decades of programs, and except for the larger percentage of young adult women the distribution is similar across racial groups. Chronological age, however, differentiates characters both by sex and race. During the past 45 years, women have always been presented as younger than men, typically by at least 4 years. Similarly, except for the most recent decade (2010–2013), Blacks are also presented as younger than Whites and characters of other races. In the most recent decade Blacks and Whites represented the same chronological age, with characters of other races about three years younger.

Throughout the five decades, although both men and women were involved in violence, men were more likely than women to be so involved. Men were sometimes more likely to commit violence than be a victim of violence, and women were always somewhat more likely to be victims of violence than to have committed violence. There are few differences by race; until the most recent samples, major characters of other races were more likely to be involved in violence than either Whites or Blacks.

One of the most interesting elements of portrayal across sex and race is whether major/leading characters are cast as working and if so, the prestige level of their jobs. Throughout these five decades women have always been less likely than the men to be seen as working outside the home. Typically about a fifth to a quarter of the female characters, compared to less than one in ten male characters, were not cast in a specific job. Until the most recent samples, a woman's occupational status was more difficult to ascertain than a man's. In terms of race, major characters of other racial groups are more likely to be seen working than either Whites or Blacks. Moreover, until the start of the twenty-first century, Blacks in major roles were less likely to be seen as having a job than Whites or characters of color.

Until the last decade of this analysis (2010s) there were differences in whether men or women were found in prestigious, neutral, or non-prestigious jobs, with men more likely than women to be cast in prestigious jobs. Although this pattern was reversed in the samples from the most recent decade these differences were not statistically significant and hence warrant continued examination.

The occupations of Black major characters represent interesting differences for men and women. Until the most recent decade, Black women in major roles were considerably and statistically less likely than Black men to be seen working; however, in the most recent samples, the groups are comparable. Until the most recent samples, Black women consistently were cast in non-prestigious occupations. In the most recent samples, more Black male than Black female major characters held non-prestigious jobs, and Black women were more likely than Black men to be in neutral or prestigious jobs. None of the analyses for occupational prestige for major characters of other races were statistically significant.

## The More Things Change the More They Stay the Same

The decade by decade analysis shows that women have increased their presence in prime time network programs somewhat, but have not yet reached parity with their numbers in the U.S. population. For the past 25 years, women have made up about 40% of the major/leading television characters, but are more than half of the U.S. population.

Blacks and other characters of color also lack parity with their numbers in the U.S. population. During the first decade of the twenty-first century Blacks reached proportional parity on television because they were cast in situation comedies whose casts were mostly minority characters. This was a tenuous parity; if we removed the so called "minority" programs from the sample, Black characters would no longer achieve parity with their numbers in the U.S. population. Today, however, Blacks are again under-represented because the prime time lineup contains fewer situation comedies and almost no programs with mostly minority casts. Characters in other racial groups (e.g., Asians), although under-represented, are seen in more diverse types of programs. They are more likely to be seen in crime/action and drama programs than Black characters. On the whole, White characters continue to be over-represented during prime time.

It is important, however, to consider what this actually means. Is it optimal for race relations and socialization when Blacks reach numerical parity but are cast primarily in situation comedies or relegated to programs that have all or mostly minority characters? The television lineup has few programs showing characters of all races working together. Consequently there are continued issues of racial parity and White characters seemingly given more screen time than minorities. Also these program constellations make it difficult for viewers to see situations in which characters of different races work together in harmony.

The representation of age has been consistent for the past 45 years with few major or leading characters who are either children or elderly. Also, women and Black characters are typically younger than men, White, or characters of other races. Violence is prevalent in prime time, involving men more often than women. Further, for the most part, men were more likely to commit violence than be victims of violence, whereas women have always been somewhat more likely to be victims of violence than to commit violence. During the past five decades, race has not differentiated major and leading characters in terms of violence.

The occupational portrayals of major and leading characters provide interesting differences by sex and race, but again, few changes over time. Throughout these five decades, women have been less likely than men to be cast as holding a job. On the other hand, recent years have seen an increase in the numbers of minorities portrayed as working. During the last part of the twentieth century, the portrayal of Black characters was similar to that of women: they were less likely to hold a particular job. In the more recent samples, however, Blacks and Whites were equally likely to be cast as holding a particular job. The prestige level of characters' occupations has also undergone interesting changes during the past five decades. Women's and Blacks' jobs have become more prestigious over time and are now similar in prestige level to men's and Whites' jobs.

Overall, except for the prestige level of jobs, characterizations have changed very little during the past five decades. Importantly, prime time programming was less diverse in the middle of the second decade of the twenty-first century than it was at the beginning of the twenty-first century and was similar to distributions found in the late 1960s and 1970s. The percentage of White characters increased, and the percentage of Black characters decreased in the most recent samples of network prime time broadcast programs. Coupled with the decrease in the number of situation comedies and programs with segregated minority casting practices in the most recent samples, the gains made by Blacks in terms of parity have disappeared. Moreover, as the prime time network landscape continues to change to schedule more economically viable programs, such as reality shows, the fate of other characters of color may also be changing. These trends also reflect that reality programs often cast specific types of characters and/or stereotypes so as to provide the most conflict and/or interesting interpersonal interactions

This study shows that, except for the first decade of the twenty-first century, prime time programs typically under-represented minority characters, and isolated characters of different races. These images tend to provide relatively few opportunities for viewers to observe all races mingling and working together. Consequently, from the perspectives of both social cognitive (Bandura, 2002) and cultivation (Morgan et al., 2009) theories, prime time provides very narrow lessons about race relations for viewers, particularly children. Thus, the messages and lessons for viewers whose only exposure to people of color comes from watching television reinforces the racial isolation in which they live. These results are particularly compelling because they span 45 years of programming, dating from the late 1960s to the beginning of the second decade of the twenty-first century. What is perhaps most interesting is that although the platforms of viewing and our viewing behavior (binge-viewing, for example) have changed exponentially, the basic demography of what is available for us to view has remained, for the most part, extremely stable, limited, and reflective of the status quo of the twentieth century. Remembering that most broadcast programming is created by a relatively few number of multinational corporations and increasingly must appeal to wider audiences, it is most prudent economically to continue to provide what has drawn an audience in the past.

These images of race and biological sex are not without potential effects, but unfortunately there is not a large body of studies examining how images relating to race, in particular, relate to viewers' conceptions about women and people of color. Signorielli (1989) found in the late 1980s that women were often perceived in sex stereotyped roles that tended to maintain the status quo. There is some—but again, not much—data showing how televised images of aging influence people's conceptions about age and the aging process. Gerbner, Gross, Signorielli, and Morgan (1980) found that those who watched more television in the early 1970s had more negative images of the elderly and believed that women became old earlier in life than men.

There are few studies looking at how racial images on television affect viewers' conceptions of minorities. Some studies found that watching negative racial images had an adverse effect on how viewers evaluate minorities (Ford, 1997; Gilliam & Iyengar, 2000). Mastro (2003), for example, using a social identity theory framework, found that entertainment programming, particularly for Whites, may influence attitudes about outgroups (other races and/or ethnic groups). Interestingly, most of these studies about the potential effects of minority images focus more on the effects of images of violence in the news than in entertainment programming (Mastro, Lapinski, Kipacz, & Behm-Morawitz, 2009; Dixon, 2008).

Images about minorities have undergone few changes in the past 45 years. Under-representation still looms as a significant and telling component of how minorities are portrayed. Indeed, except for the decade in which there was an overabundance of situation comedies, many of which had casts of mostly minority characters, minorities do not come close to reaching parity with their numbers in the U.S. population. We know that those who create these programs are a fairly static group of people, mostly White men, and according to the Writers Guild of America (Robb, 2015) the numbers of women and, particularly, minorities hired as writers has decreased over the past few TV seasons. Consequently, because those who write the stories may be likely to write about people with whom they are comfortable—presumably people like themselves—it is no surprise that the world of television continues to under-represent both women and people of color.

# References

Atkin, D. (1991). The evolution of television series addressing single women, 1966–1990. *Journal of Broadcasting & Electronic Media, 35,* 517–523.

Auletta, G. S., & Hammerback, J. C. (1985). A relational model for interracial interactions on television. *The Western Journal of Speech Communication, 49*(4), 301–321.

Bandura, A. (2002). Social cognitive theory of mass communication. In. J. Bryant & D. Zillmann (Eds.). *Media effects: Advances in theory and research* (2nd ed.) (pp. 121–154). Hillsdale, NJ: Erlbaum.

Britto, S., Hughes, T., Saltzman, K., & Stroh, C. (2007). Does "special" mean young, white, and female?: Deconstructing the meaning of "special" in Law & Order: Special Victims Unit. *Journal of Criminal Justice and Popular Culture, 14*(1), 39–57.

Children Now. (2004). *Fall colors: Prime time diversity report (2003–2004).* Oakland, CA: Author.

Dates, J., & Stroman, C. (2001). Portrayals of families of color on television. In J. Bryant & J. A. Bryant (Eds.). *Television and the American Family* (pp. 207–225). Mahwah, NJ: Erlbaum.

Dixon, T. L. (2008). Crime news and racialized beliefs: Understanding the relationship between local news viewing and perceptions of African Americans and crime. *Journal of Communication, 58,* 106–125.

Elasmar, M., Hasegawa, K., & Brain, M. (1999). The portrayal of women in U.S. prime time television. *Journal of Broadcasting & Electronic Media, 43,* 20–34.

Entman, R., & Rojecki, A., (2000). *The Black image in the White mind.* Chicago: The University of Chicago Press.

Eschholz, S., Mallarad, M., & Flynn, S. (2004). Images of prime time justice: A content analysis of "NYPD Blue" and "Law & Order." *Journal of Criminal Justice and Popular Culture, 10*(3), 161–180.

Gerbner, G., Gross, L., Morgan, M., & Signorielli, N. (1982). Charting the mainstream: Television's contribution to political orientations. *Journal of Communication, 32*(2), 100–127.

Gerbner, G., Gross, L., Signorielli, N., & Morgan, M. (1980). Aging with television: Images on television drama and conceptions of social reality. *Journal of Communication, 30*(1), 37–47.

Gilliam, F., & Iyengar, S. (2000). Prime suspects: The influence of local television news on the viewing public. *American Journal of Political Science, 44,* 560–573.

Glascock, J. (2001). Gender roles on prime-time network television: Demographics and behaviors. *Journal of Broadcasting & Electronic Media, 45*(4), 656–669.

Glascock, J. (2003). Gender, race and aggression in newer TV networks' primetime programming. *Communication Quarterly, 51*(1), 90–100.

Greenberg, B. S. (Ed.) (1980). *Life on television: Content analysis of U.S. TV drama.* Norwood, NJ: Ablex Publishing.

Greenberg, B. S., & Brand, J. E. (1994). Minorities and the mass media: 1970s to 1990s. In J. Bryant & D. Zillmann (Eds). *Media effects: Advances in theory and research* (pp. 273–314). Hillsdale, NJ: Lawrence Erlbaum Associates.

Greenberg, B. S., Mastro, D., & Brand, J. E. (2002). Minorities and the mass media: Television into the twenty-first century. In J. Bryant & D. Zillmann (Eds.), *Media effects: Advances in theory and research* (2nd ed.) (pp. 333–351). Hillsdale, NJ: Lawrence Erlbaum Associates.

Greenberg, B. S. (1982). Television and role socialization: An overview. In D. Pearl, L. Bouthilet, & J. Lazar (Eds.), *Television and behavior: Ten years of scientific progress and implications for the eighties* (Vol. 2: Technical Reviews, pp. 179–190). Rockville, MD: U.S. Department of Health and Human Services.

Greenberg, B. S. & Collette, L. (1997). The changing faces on TV: A demographic analysis of network television's new seasons, 1966–1992. *Journal of Broadcasting & Electronic Media, 41*, 1–13.

Greenberg, B. S. & Baptista-Fernandez, P. (1980). Hispanic Americans: The newest minority in television. In B. S. Greenberg (Ed.), *Life on television: Content analysis of U.S. TV drama* (pp. 3–12). Norwood, NJ: Ablex.

Harwood, J., & Anderson, K. (2002). The presence and portrayal of social groups on prime-time television. *Communication Reports, 15*(2), 81–97.

Hunt, D. (2005). Making sense of blackness on television. In D. Hunt (Ed.), *Channeling blackness: Studies on television and race in America* (pp. 267–302). New York, NY: Oxford University Press.

Kerner Commission (1968). *Report of the national advisory commission on civil disorders*. Washington, DC: Government Printing Office.

Krippendorff, K. (2004). *Content analysis*. Thousand Oaks, CA: Sage.

Mastro, D. E. (2003). A social identity approach to understanding the impact of television messages. *Communication Monographs, 70*(2), 98–113.

Mastro, D. E., & Greenberg, B. S. (2000). The portrayal of racial minorities on prime time television. *Journal of Broadcasting & Electronic Media, 44*(4), 690–703.

Mastro, D., Lapinski, M. K., Kopacz, M. A., & Behm-Morawitz, E., (2009). The influence of exposure to depictions of race and crime in TV news on viewer's social judgements. *Journal of Broadcasting & Electronic Media, 53*(4), 615–635.

Morgan, M., Shanahan, J., & Signorielli, N. (2009). Growing up with television: Cultivation processes. In J. Bryant & M. B. Oliver (Eds). *Media effects: Advances in theory and research* (3rd ed.) (pp. 34–49). Hillsdale, NJ: Lawrence Erlbaum Associates.

Nielsen, A. C. Co. (2015). *The total audience report: Q4-2014*.

NAACP (2001, August 15). NAACP television report shows diversity remains unfulfilled goal. *NAACP News*.

Norcott, H. J., Seggar, J. F., & Hinton, J. C. (1975). Trends in TV portrayal of blacks and women. *Journalism Quarterly, 52*(4), 741–744.

Pajares, F., Prestin, A., Chen, J., & Nabi, R. L. (2009). Social cognitive theory and media effects. In R. L. Nabi & M. B. Oliver (Eds.), *The Sage handbook of media processes and effects* (pp. 283–296). Thousand Oaks, CA: Sage.

Robb, D. (2015, March 3). WGA study: Most jobs go to white guys in their 40s. *Deadline Hollywood*. Retrieved June 13, 2015, from http://deadline.com/2015/03/women-minority-older-tv-writing-jobs-fewer-wga-report-2014-1201385425.

Shrum, L. J. (2002). Media consumption and perceptions of social reality: Effects and underlying processes. In. J. Bryant & D. Zillmann (Eds.), *Media Effects:*

*Advances in theory and research* (2nd ed.) (pp. 69–96). Hillsdale, NJ: Lawrence Erlbaum Associates.

Signorielli, N. (2004). Aging on television: Messages relating to gender, race, and occupation in prime time. *Journal of Broadcasting & Electronic Media, 48*(2), 279–301.

Signorielli, N. (2009a). Minority representation in prime time: 2000 to 2008. *Communication Research Reports, 26*(4), 323–336.

Signorielli, N. (2009b). Race and sex in prime time: A look at occupations and occupational prestige. *Mass Communication and Society, 12*(3), 332–352.

Signorielli, N. (1993). Television and adolescents' perceptions about work. *Youth & Society, 24*, 314–341.

Signorielli, N. (1989). Television and conceptions about sex-roles: Maintaining conventionality and the status quo. *Sex Roles, 21*(5/6), 341–360.

Signorielli, N., & Bacue, A. (1999). Recognition and respect: A content analysis of prime-time television characters across three decades. *Sex Roles, 40*(7/8), 527–544.

Signorielli, N., Gross, L., & Morgan, M. (1982). Violence in television programs: Ten years later. In D. Pearl, L. Bouthilet, & J. Lazar (Eds.), *Television and behavior: Ten years of scientific progress and implications for the eighties* (Vol. 2, Technical Reports, pp. 154–174). Washington, DC: U.S. Government Printing Office.

Signorielli, N. & Kahlenberg, S. (2001). Television's world of work in the nineties. *Journal of Broadcasting & Electronic Media, 45*(1), 1–19.

U.S. Commission on Civil Rights. (1977). *Window dressing on the set: Women and minorities in television.* Washington, DC: Government Printing Office.

U.S. Commission on Civil Rights. (1979). *Window dressing on the set: An update.* Washington, DC: Government Printing Office.

Vande Berg, L. R., & Streckfuss, D. (1992). Prime-time television's portrayal of women and the world of work: A demographic profile. *Journal of Broadcasting & Electronic Media, 36*, 195–208.

# 3

# FRAMES OF THE OLYMPIC HOST

## Media Coverage of Russia's Anti-Gay Legislation

*Andrew C. Billings,*
*Leigh M. Moscowitz, and Yiyi Yang*

On the opening day of the 2014 Sochi Winter Olympic Games, four protesters representing the gay rights group All Out unfurled a banner quoting the Olympic Charter's ban on any form of discrimination, before quickly being detained by police. The Olympic stage has always been seen as a platform for stories about culture, politics, and human rights, which percolate through the predominant coverage of athletes. Sochi was no different. Orwall and Terlep noted that, "the perennial Olympic debate— whether sports and politics should be mixed—[was] burning for weeks, long before the Olympic flame reached Sochi" (2014, p. A10). Although myriad concerns were prevalent in the weeks and months before the Games, the issue receiving the most attention was Russia's newly adopted anti-gay legislation, which banned the "propaganda of nontraditional sexual relations to minors" (Grekov, 2013) and outlawed verbal and symbolic proclamations of gay rights—making everything from pro-gay signage to rainbow symbols to participation in gay pride parades a punishable crime. Although the Olympic charter prohibits any form of political propaganda at an Olympic site, Whiteside asserted that, "The Olympics are often remembered for iconic gestures, such as the black-gloved salute on the medal stand at the 1968 Mexico City Games. Whether it be rainbow-painted fingernails or a same-sex kiss on the medal stand, the Sochi Games might be remembered for such a gesture" (2013, p. 1C).

Some writers seized the controversy as an opportunity to discuss larger concerns about the Olympics, whereas others focused on issues such as the possibility of boycotts and other manners in which solidarity for LGBTQ athletes and citizens could be demonstrated. Jenkins wrote that "if the Olympics hadn't come to Sochi, there wouldn't have been such a tough but needed dialogue over whether the International Olympic Committee needs to stop awarding the Games to countries that commit human rights violations" (2014, p. D1).

Yet, in the months preceding the Games, other issues competed with the anti-gay legislation for coveted media space. Such concerns ranged from the readiness of the Sochi facilities to the possibility of terrorist attacks— and, of course, the need to preview and profile Olympians and events likely to provide memorable moments during the 18 days of Olympic competition. Gay summarized the confluence of events: "This is ordinarily a moment in which all pre-Games panic cedes to a genuine enthusiasm about the athletic events and athletes themselves. Instead there is a broad anxiety" (2014, p. R10).

In this chapter, we consider how that general broad anxiety interfaces with news outlet realities related to time, space, and primacy. Focusing specifically on how coverage of the anti-gay legislation debate unfolded before and during the 2014 Sochi Winter Games, we employ the dual lenses of framing and political economy to establish how the debate was shaped, amplified, and/or stifled via various systemic needs of U.S. news media. We then use interviews we conducted with two prominent journalists, Christine Brennan and Kelly Whiteside from *USA Today*, to increase our understanding of how certain aspects of the debate were highlighted, bolstered, or diminished. However, before exploring the theoretical underpinnings of this work, we first discuss the rapidly evolving visibility of lesbian, gay, bisexual, transgender, queer, and otherwise non-gender normative (LGBTQ) representations.

## LGBTQ Representations in News, Entertainment, and Sport

A growing body of work in media and cultural studies since the 1990s has studied the increased visibility of gay and lesbian people and issues in mainstream media and popular culture over the past two decades (Alwood, 1996; Becker, 2006; Gross, 2001; Moscowitz, 2013; Sender, 2004; Walters, 2001). Gay rights issues, considered unfit to print a mere 60 years ago by America's most widely read newspapers and magazines, now routinely make headlines (Alwood, 1996). In the 2000s, issues such as the U.S. military's Don't Ask Don't Tell policy, same-sex marriage, and the Employment Non-Discrimination Act received unprecedented media coverage in print, web, and broadcast news (Barnhurst, 2003; Leibler, Schwartz, & Harper, 2009; Moscowitz, 2013; Schwartz, 2011). Moreover, since Ellen DeGeneres portrayed the first openly lesbian lead character on television in 1997, gay and lesbian characters and themes have become mainstreamed into hits such as *Glee, Grey's Anatomy*, and *Modern Family*; gay, lesbian, and transgender storylines dominate new media series such as Netflix's *Orange is the New Black*.

Although gay rights issues have become more prominent in news coverage, and gay and lesbian themes more marketable in entertainment media, commercial and critical media success has not eradicated homophobia or confronted heterosexual privilege (Clark, 1995; Dow, 2001; Landau, 2009; Moscowitz, 2013; Sender, 2004; Walters, 2014). The increase in media visibility has coincided with considerable progress on gay civil rights issues both in the U.S. and abroad—at least in terms of greater inclusion into mainstream social institutions such as military service and marriage equality. However, these contemporary media depictions of gay and lesbian identity have been crafted to attract niche markets and win the approval of straight audiences rather than to challenge heterosexist values. Media visibility can be a false substitute for cultural acceptance and inclusive citizenship (Walters, 2001, 2014). In a consumerist media marketplace, only particular versions of gay and lesbian identity are marketable and, thus, visible: White, upper-class, and anchored to dominant notions of masculinity and femininity.

Thus, although gay rights issues have attracted more widespread media attention, LGBTQ communities and issues are covered in ways that "don't challenge hegemonic notions of gender and sexuality, and [do so] by employing frames that privilege heterosexuality" (Leibler, Schwartz, & Harper, 2009, p. 256). Analysis of news framing shows how standard journalistic devices polarize gay rights issues, favoring frames of controversy and conflict; silence alternative perspectives; provide a platform for homophobic (oftentimes religious) rhetoric; amplify the voice of anti-gay sources; and conform coverage to official institutions of power that have historically criminalized and marginalized the gay community (Barnhurst, 2003; Leibler, Schwartz, & Harper, 2009; Moscowitz, 2013; Schwartz, 2011). Although gay and lesbian sources are more likely to be cited or quoted in news stories after the early 2000s, these LGBTQ spokespersons have become increasingly professionalized and privilege "hegemonic ways of seeing" (Barnhurst, 2003, p. 670).

Organized sport remains a "highly homophobic institution" in which gay identity is cast as incompatible with athleticism (Anderson, 2002, p. 860; see also Butterworth, 2006; Nylund, 2004). Outing, especially of gay male athletes, remains controversial, and only a handful of major-league sports team athletes are openly gay. The media spectacle surrounding the coming out announcements of the NBA's Jason Collins and the NFL's Michael Sam fueled heated debates about whether American team sport leagues were ready for a gay player and to what extent a player's sexual orientation would distract from team play (Billings, Moscowitz, Rae, & Brown, 2015). Likewise, during the 2008 Beijing Olympics, NBC broadcasters came under fire when they appeared to bury the sexual orientation of out gold-medal winner Matthew Mitcham, neglecting to show his same-sex partner watching in the stands.

These examples highlight how the world of sport remains a mainstay of hegemonic masculinity, heterosexism, and homophobia. As Anderson (2002, p. 862) argued, sport is the leading definer of "orthodox masculinity and patriarchy" in a mass culture that has lost its male initiation rituals. In this arena, hegemonic masculinity is defined as exclusively heterosexual and physically powerful. Gay men perceived as effeminate or queer are positioned as the antithesis of masculinity, athleticism, dominance, and power (Hekma, 1998).

Collectively, the body of work on sport and sexuality has shown how journalistic standards reinforce normative gendered and sexual boundaries, construct coming out as an *individual* choice/problem, and deny the institutional nature of homophobia in sports. Overt homophobic statements are no longer readily accepted, and blatant verbal and physical abuse is decried. Sports reporters valorize the world of sport as an equal playing field, mischaracterizing it as an open, democratic civil rights battleground that paves the path toward greater inclusion in all walks of life, a place where racism, sexism, and homophobia are inconsequential once the game begins (Billings, Moscowitz, Rae, & Brown, 2015; Butterworth, 2006).

Significantly, then, the discussion of Russia's anti-gay legislation took place on the stage of the world's largest international sporting event, offering scholars an opportunity to analyze how U.S. media cover gay rights issues in the contexts of sports reporting and a non-American setting. As such, this study drew from both media framing and political economy perspectives to interrogate how the debate was framed both leading up to and during the Olympic Games, and to understand how the political economy of everyday news both guided and constrained the journalistic practice of reporting on bummer topics during the Games.

## Theoretical Underpinnings: Framing and Political Economy

With underpinnings from Goffman (1974), framing theory can be expanded to explain the tripartite manner in which "media frames are persistent patterns of cognition, interpretation, and presentation, of selection, emphasis, and exclusion, by which symbol-handlers routinely organized discourse, whether verbal or visual" (Gitlin, 1980, p. 7). Thus, frames are far more than a binary distinction of present/not present, offering instead a ratio-sense of presence, ranging from heavy focus to complete silence about different concepts, themes, and ideas. As such, framing can

41

often be combined with notions of agenda-setting (McCombs & Shaw, 1972) to explain how issues become more or less prominent in media settings (see Scheufele, 2000).

Moreover, Gitlin noted that frames frequently involve "persistent patterns of cognition, interpretation, and presentation of selection, emphasis, and exclusion" (1980, p. 7). These forms of framing inevitably interact with news dissemination realities. For instance, the same news story could be constrained by a medium ranging from a tweet (140 characters) to a column (600 words) to an Internet post (potentially unlimited space). However, even the seemingly infinite spaces have limitations, necessitating framing choices. For example, a web-based story about Sochi could have greater impact if the piece is on a news outlet's main Web page, or, it could be relatively hidden if not directly linked from the most easily-accessed Web pages.

In this chapter we are not only concerned with the framing of the story itself, but also with the production of news content, or how individual, organizational, and professional factors influence journalists' decision-making. Understanding the process of newsmaking is part of an overall political economic approach focusing on the production and distribution of media content (Garnham, 2011; Herman & Chomsky, 1988; Meehan, 2013; McChesney, 2008; Schiller, 2006), which examines the relationships between ownership, economics, labor, consumers, advertisers, and the state, and how those relationships in turn influence content. Research on the production of news has uncovered factors influencing news content, including organizational constraints, professional norms, journalistic routines, and the social, ideological and demographic make-up of individual journalists (Beam, 2008).

Building on framing theory and political economic perspectives, we employed a two-prong methodological approach that combined interviews with leading sports reporters and textual analyses of newspaper and television Olympic coverage. Political economy perspectives are valuable in examining how everyday constraints (deadlines, word count) and professional values (neutrality, objectivity) shape how journalists gather and report information, select sources, and define as newsworthy stories considered controversial, novel, dramatic, and unusual (Gans, 1979; Schudson, 1982; Tuchman, 1978). First, because much scholarly investigation of media framing and the role of political economy takes the form of exploring media content, a core element of this chapter is to interrogate how those journalistic selections then influenced U.S. media coverage leading up to the Sochi Olympics, and in particular, the host network's treatment of the Games during the 18 days of coverage. We then interviewed select reporters in order to understand how journalists made overt choices regarding the selection, emphasis, and exclusion of given aspects of the Sochi anti-gay legislation controversy.

## Frames Before the Games

Focus on the anti-gay legislation was fairly heavy in the months preceding the Sochi Opening Ceremonies. Initial Lexis-Nexis results (search terms "Sochi," "Olympics," "same-sex legislation," and "gay rights") yielded more than 800 articles pertaining to the legislation specifically within the realm of the Sochi Olympics in the six months before the Games. In this coverage, three overarching themes emerged, all of which were at least tinged by the question of whether the American team should boycott the Sochi Olympics: (1) orientation, which provided readers a general overview of the legislation, (2) American exceptionalism, in which Russian and U.S. laws regarding LGBTQ rights were compared, and (3) boycott, reflecting direct stances on whether the United States should withdraw from the Sochi Games, including a subtheme related to celebrity/Olympian spokesperson perspectives on a potential ban.

The orientation theme introduced and explained the tenants of Russia's "gay propaganda law" to readers—typically to indicate why one should oppose it in various forms, including a potential boycott. In this theme, journalists described the legislation in detail and informed readers of its reach. Many articles contrasted the new Russian laws with other nations' prohibitions on non-heterosexual sex acts, noting that Russia's laws extended into speech and rights even in private situations. As You Can Play founder Patrick Burke noted: "The laws are absurd, insulting and shameful. You are talking about laws that are in a culture in Russia right now where gay people are being beaten in the street. They are being arrested. Gay parents can lose their children. You are talking about draconian laws" (Allen, 2013).

Journalistic concerns about the legislation were bolstered by media coverage that compared Russian laws to current American legislative protections for LGBTQ citizens. These articles tended to focus less on the Russian laws than on congratulatory sentiments about U.S. progressiveness toward gay rights. Topics ranging from the coming out of the NBA's Jason Collins to the increasing number of states legalizing gay marriage were used to tacitly make a core argument: the United States is advancing on LGBTQ issues while Russia is regressing. As such, these frames reflected a tone that was both progressive and nationalistic, arguing that while the U.S. was advancing the gay rights movement, nations like Russia were thwarting progress.

These themes were used collectively to advance the most prevalent topic in pre-Olympic coverage, the debate over a potential boycott. Many articles made the simple query: Should the U.S. attend the Winter Games? The boycott seemed to be generally dismissed by most journalists and athletes, as our interviews with reporters indicated, leading many of the articles to focus on alternate paths for showing support. This was

43

especially true when President Barack Obama named three openly gay athletes to the U.S. delegation. Obama had been critical of the laws, as were many others using the boycott discussion as impetus to argue that speaking freely about gay rights in sport was the best approach. Some articles reported on other nations' plans to protest the laws while still participating in the Games. For example, Finland's Sports Minister, Paavo Arhinmaki, announced that although Finland would compete, he personally would boycott the Opening Ceremony because of "human rights violations, restrictions to freedom of speech and the oppression of sexual minorities" (Williams, 2014).

The boycott theme also included reports on Russian attempts to quell concerns about the laws, with many stories about the public protest zones that would be available as a result of international pressure. However, some articles also gave voice to the Russian mitigators trying to spin the legislation in a positive light, as a rallying point for national solidarity. As one Russian Olympic volunteer noted: "With the anti-gay law and the [possibility of terrorist bombings] there has been much negative press. But I had the same feeling about London, everyone saying, 'We'll never make it good.' But when it started, people got involved and it became positive, rather than negative" (Harris, 2014).

Additionally, a prominent subtheme of this boycott theme that emerged was the use of former and current athletes (sometimes as surrogates, other times as spokespersons) to assess the debate, often employing their celebrity voice and presence as an *alternative* to boycotting the Games altogether. This coverage included out athletes such as Ashley Wagner, Billie Jean King, and Johnny Weir overtly declaring the legislation horrific, yet making the case that a boycott would be unnecessary and ineffective. Former track star Diane Jones Konihowski was quoted as saying "It's unfortunate. Boycotts don't do anything, really, other than bring attention to a political situation. They certainly don't move sport forward, and they only hurt the athletes. [The 1980 boycott of the Moscow Olympics] didn't prove anything" (Gillespie, 2013).

Other athletes were used to make an argument that the brunt of the harm of a boycott would be directed at athletes who have very few opportunities to compete in an Olympics. U.S. hurdler Ryan Wilson received coverage for his outspokenness when he argued: "This is our livelihood. It's easy for people sitting behind desks to say, 'You guys should boycott.' I've been training 20 years to do this" (Rosen, 2013). Wilson went on to query whether other options were particularly useful, while placing the boycott in a context of larger atrocities: "What gesture are we supposed to make that's really going to have an impact—wear a ribbon? There are worse things going on in the world. Our whole uniform could be filled with ribbons if we wanted to make a public gesture. Some legislation vs. mass genocide or child soldiers" (Rosen, 2013). In addition, some comments pertained to athletes planning to compete in the Sochi Games and then, after the competition is over, making a statement. Australian snowboarder Belle Brockhoff exemplified this theme: "After I compete, I'm willing to rip on [Putin's] ass. I'm not happy and there's a bunch of other Olympians who are not happy either" (Nichols, 2014).

Thus, through the predominant frames of orientation to the legislation, comparisons between U.S. and Russian same-sex rights, and the debate over whether to boycott, the stage was set to alert fans of the Olympics to watch how the controversies would unfold throughout the Games. As such, the overall strategies appeared to rationalize (why the boycott would be a bad idea) and to mitigate (offering alterative actions to a boycott).

## Frames During the Games

Because this study also sought to understand how journalists reported on the anti-gay rights legislation once the Games began, a different method was used to capture the major frames the host network, NBC, employed to cover the issue. We accessed 18 days of broadcast coverage from February 6, 2014, through the Closing Ceremony on February 23, 2014. Over 1,500 hours of televised coverage was tracked across all four NBC networks covering the Games: NBC, NBC Sports, MSNBC, and CNBC. Combined, these four networks aired a total of 1 hour, 59 minutes, 42 seconds to discussion of Russia's anti-gay legislation. This finding demonstrates the overall lack of coverage and airtime dedicated to the anti-gay legislation as the issue faded from the media spotlight once medals were at stake. The most coverage NBC networks dedicated to discussing gay rights or LGBTQ issues was 26 minutes, occurring the day of the Opening Ceremonies. However, subsequent days featured scant attention to these issues: most days had less than five minutes of airtime dedicated, and several days had none.

Additionally, much of the discussion that did take place was neither in the main sports coverage nor in primetime, instead relegated to smaller market programs such as NBC's *The Today Show*, NBC's *Access Hollywood*, MSNBC's *Now with Alex Wagner*, MSNBC's *Politics Nation with Al Sharpton*, MSNBC's *The Rachel Maddow Show* and MSNBC's *Weekends with Alex Witt*. The network sidelined what the *Washington Post* (Farhi, 2014) referred to as "bummer topics," including human rights violations, national security threats, terrorism risks, the condition of the Olympic facilities, and the instability in the Ukraine, once the opening ceremonies ushered in the start of the Games.

When gay rights were discussed as part of Olympic coverage, four key themes emerged, including (1) unfounded fears, (2) non-existent protests, (3) sport as a social justice equalizer, and (4) the de-politicization of sport. Consistently, these frames worked together to produce narratives that downplayed the violations of LGBTQ rights in Russia and skated around host-country controversies. Each will be discussed in subsequent sections, in no hierarchical order.

First, media commentators framed fears about Russian's anti-gay policies as unfounded because athletes themselves had not faced discrimination, unwittingly denying the situation LGBTQ Russians face. Although a concern prior to the games, the issue became much ado about nothing, citing out gay athletes, commentators, and broadcast reporters who appeased audiences through reports that the host country's anti-gay campaign had no material impact on their lives. For example, on day 16 of the Games, Bob Costas asked out Olympic skater and NBC commentator Johnny Weir, "How have you been treated in Russia?" Weir responded that, "There is no weirdness. The actual practice of this stuff hasn't touched me or affected me and I think I've brought in a very gay way to Sochi so if there ever was going to be problem it would happen to me and I've just been absolutely fine" (Costas, 2014, February 21). Similarly, when Costas asked Russian journalist Vladimir Pozner what practical effect the anti-gay legislation would have on athletes and visitors, he responded, "Zero. No effect at all. I don't see anything happening" (Costas, 2014, February 6).

In addition to dismissing gay rights concerns and other "bummer topics" as irrelevant to Games coverage, another related theme that emerged focused on the overall *lack* of protests both in the U.S. and abroad, or the "protest movement that wasn't." As indicated earlier, questions of whether the U.S. should boycott were largely dismissed before the Games began, and a handful of reporters began to ask instead: Why haven't we seen any public protests? The Human Rights Campaign's Brian Moulton was asked on MSNBC's *Andrea Mitchell Reports* why, despite the "hype" before the Games, there was "no fist raised," or "no rainbow moment" (Mitchell, 2014, February 11).

Likewise, MSNBC's Alex Wagner compared the outcry over China's human rights violations during the Beijing Olympics in 2008 to the lack of concern in Sochi, asking whether the activist community had "given Russia a free pass." In her view, "Ordinary Americans don't seem to care" (Wagner, 2014, February 18). The answer to these queries was two-fold: First, as Moulton explained, because the risks of protesting in Russia were too high and the current legislation too severe, the activist community expected that demonstrations would take place in other countries with comparatively more freedoms. Relatedly, sources argued the protests had become largely symbolic ones through the election of gay and lesbian U.S. delegates such as Brian Boitano and Billie Jean King. The visibility of these representatives sent a strong message of intolerance toward Russia's anti-gay policies. Billie Jean King told MSNBC, "Visually, we're going to send a very strong message just by being there" (Witt, 2014, February 15).

As a result, a scant number of news reports covered any sort of protest movement over LGBTQ rights in Russia. Only Rachel Maddow reported on the LGBTQ activists arrested on opening day for unfurling part of the charter on a sign (2014, February 7). Two other symbolic protests received minimal coverage: an Italian gay activist was detained by Sochi police for carrying a rainbow flag, and a transgendered activist was removed from the Games when she tried to enter with a rainbow-themed outfit. MSNBC's Alex Witt briefly covered a protest in Australia, where thousands of athletes and fans held the hand of a person of the same sex in a protest against Russia's new law (2014, February 8). In another symbolic gesture, Google marked the Winter Games by flying the rainbow colored flag Thursday on its search page. Despite concerns that aired prior to the start of the Games, NBC gave little attention to the protests about gay rights.

A third theme that emerged in coverage, consistent with prior coverage of LGBTQ issues in sport, framed the world of athletics as a great equalizer, systematically denying the heterosexism and homophobia institutionalized in the world of sport. As President Barack Obama told NBC's Bob Costas, "The wonderful things about the Olympics, you are judged by your merit, how good you are, regardless of where you come from, what you look like, or who you love" (2014, February 6). Focusing on principle 6 of the Olympic Charter ("The practice of sport is a human right"), news reports valorized the ability to practice sport without discrimination. In interviews with politicians, out gay athletes at the games, and Olympic delegates, the locker room was celebrated as "the last closet" and "the last wall in sports" for LGBTQ citizens.

Sports reporters used the story of NFL prospect Michael Sam's coming out as a news hook to draw connections between anti-gay policies in Russia and Sam's upcoming entrance into the NFL as the first out gay male player. Sam's announcement came during day 5 of the Olympics, and MSNBC commentators drew parallels between the spotlight on Russia's anti-gay laws and the "somewhat appropriate" announcement that "All-American college football player Missouri's Michael Sam came out of the closet" (Melvin, 2014, February 10).

Paradoxically, a fourth theme emerged claiming that sports and politics don't mix, that any concerns about LGBTQ rights should be considered apart from Game play, because they distracted from the main event. For the seven openly gay athletes from the U.S., once the Games began, the focus centered on the sport, not on the "politics" of their social identities. During coverage of the opening ceremonies, even Rachel Maddow quipped, "Nobody wants politics mixed in with their Olympics." Likewise, Janet Napalatano told MSNBC's Andrea Mitchell, "If you're a [gay] Olympic athlete, you are focused on your event . . . It's not a time or place for them for focusing on the politics of the moment. It's about the sport of the moment." Bisexual Dutch speed skater Ireen Wust said she wasn't interested in being an activist but in being treated just like "any other athlete." On MSNBC Live, former U.S. Olympian Michael Eruzione advised athletes to stay out of politics: "I think the athletes are there to perform. They're there to represent their country. What your opinions are on political stuff is something that should stay away from the arena" (Melvin, 2014, February 15).

## Journalistic Perspectives

In light of the differences in themes before and during the Games, we interviewed two journalists from the U.S. newspaper having the most comprehensive Olympic coverage: *USA Today*. Christine Brennan and Kelly Whiteside were selected because they have covered many Olympic Games, including Sochi; moreover, both have written on issues of human rights, both within the Olympics and beyond.

Both journalists revealed that they felt positive about how their coverage of the issue unfolded, but conceded that even more could have been written. Whiteside noted that the issue did not immediately garner mass media attention, but rather unfolded relatively organically, with layers naturally revealed over the course of time. She noted that she "didn't feel pressure either way" in terms of writing about the anti-gay legislation, and although Brennan concurred, she also felt public interest increasing: "The story was going to happen. It really did not require any politician to do that, because like so many stories, we were building toward the crescendo: the Opening Ceremonies of the Sochi Olympics."

Brennan's comment also unveils a fundamental aspect of the coverage: that it was more for pre-Olympic priming than part of Olympic coverage itself. Both journalists believed that if something had happened to highlight the issue during the Games, then additional attention would have been paid; Whiteside offered that "Once in Sochi, I met with some gay rights advocates who had come over from the States to keep my pulse on the issue throughout the Olympics."

Both journalists indicated that journalistic norms of novelty, timeliness, celebrity, and controversy drove the coverage of Russia's controversial anti-gay legislation. For example, pre-Olympic coverage of stances from celebrity Olympians, the potential threat of a U.S. boycott, and President Obama's naming of three gay athletes to the delegation represented popular story angles that could pique audience interest. Other newsworthy events that helped drive the story included gold-medal figure skater Brian Boitano's announcement that he was gay, paired with the strategic timing of his announcement to support LGBTQ Olympic athletes and their allies.

Although threat of a potential U.S. boycott made for an interesting, dramatic, and therefore more newsworthy story for some media organizations, both journalists saw the possibility of such a decision as miniscule.

48

Based on lessons learned from prior Olympic boycotts, the story simply didn't have legs. As Brennan articulated: "I am not sure I ever got around to write about the boycott angle. People dismissed it so quickly. The boycott is the last thing you want to do. That was not going to happen."

Thus, the story was seen as a major issue before the Games, with both journalists ready to offer additional reporting, but only if ancillary events occurred, such as arrests or formal protests. Once the Games were about to commence, they noted that the anti-gay legislation received relatively less coverage than it could have received because a new topic was filling that void: the possibility of a terrorist attack. This, along with comparatively superfluous content about Sochi's substandard amenities, became primary because not only would a terrorist attack diminish all other stories within the Games, but also the people writing the stories were embedded in a location in which the potential attacks were rumored to occur. Even with an event as big as the Olympics, limited resources led to prioritizing potential terrorism over the anti-gay legislation. Not only was it not possible to have reporters specifically focused on the gay rights story, but Brennan also confirmed that there were other bigger reporting priorities: "It is how it should be: the terrorist threat is a bigger deal. If you are dealing with terrorism, that trumps almost anything."

Because the Sochi Olympics played out with little protest and no terrorist attack, reporters focused their limited time and resources on covering the medals, athletes, and sporting events instead of social policies and cultural tensions. Still, both Brennan and Whiteside claimed that the intense media gaze can cause Olympic fatigue, meaning that the lead up to the big show and the flurry of events throughout those 18 days get immediately forgotten by the next news cycle. Both considered the immediate shift of focus away from the anti-gay legislation and the issues surrounding it problematic. Whiteside argued that, "Once the Olympics ends, the world stops caring about the abuses taking place—and that appears to be the case." Brennan also noted how audience interest wanes when the Olympic flame goes out: "You go from an ember to a wildfire in a very short amount of time. And then often you cool back down to that ember status and move on." Nonetheless, Brennan claimed the story of gay rights and equal opportunity in sport deserves continued coverage. She said that covering the Olympics is challenging and fast-paced, requiring reporters to respond and then "quickly, we move on, while trying not to forget. This is one story we should not be moving on from."

All told, the interviews with longtime Olympic reporters lamented how coverage of critical social issues rise and fall at the whim of the news cycle. We now turn to an analysis of how the constraints of the newsmaking process affected coverage, or the ways in which the wildfire of media interest in Russia's anti-gay policies cooled to an ember once the Games began.

## Media-Based Implications and Beyond

Our analysis reveals two very distinctive aspects of the media framing equation which became apparent across the two different time frames of our study: before the Games and during the Games. As we describe in more detail below, political economic perspectives help explain how organizational constraints, professional norms, journalistic routines, and appeasing market audiences led to the differential treatment of Russian's anti-gay policies before the Games began and, alternately, during the 18-day Olympic showcase.

Before the Games, stories *emphasized* titillating and controversial themes related to Russia's legislation, debating whether the U.S. should push for reform in the Sochi Olympics, perhaps through boycotts, demonstrations, or the election of particular delegates. During the Games, however, *exclusion* became prevalent: the issue was largely dropped. The legislation no longer provided publicity value, and moreover, it became a bummer topic that would divert attention from the global spectacle of the Games. As NBC's Stephanie Gosk assured viewers during the Closing Ceremonies, "In the buildup, concerns about terrorism and criticism of Russia's anti-gay propaganda law dominated the headlines . . . in the end, the games went smoothly. The only real surprises took place right where they belong, on the podium" (Gosk, 2014).

Pairing our pre- and during-Olympic media analysis with reporter interviews, our findings indicate that the controversies surrounding the legislation were largely used initially for amplifying public interest in the Winter Olympics more than magnifying calls for reforming Russian policy or enhancing equality for LGBTQ citizens more broadly. The legislation became a context for a sport story much more than sport provided context for a legislative human rights story. Consistent with what the larger body of work in political economy has demonstrated, any controversy that might distract from or diminish the highly profitable sports coverage was relegated to smaller cable markets and off-peak broadcast hours. As Farhi (2014) wrote in his critique of NBC's coverage, "the network has largely pushed the controversial issues to the margins, usually out of prime time and into late-night hours, where the audience is smaller and the downer talk doesn't distract from the glossy main event."

Foundational tenets of political economy aid in explaining why such a juxtaposition took place in media coverage. If the Olympics represent the "biggest show on television" (Billings, 2008, p. 1), then any conflict surrounding the staging of these Games and the selection of host cities is wrought with potential damages to governmental and/or commercial interests. The legislation became a vehicle for discussing and publicizing the Olympics during the pre-Opening Ceremony period; the novelty and controversy fit the norms of professional news values and revved up audience interest. Interviews with *USA Today* journalists confirmed that this story needed to be told, but only as more time-sensitive stories permitted. As *USA Today*'s Erin Whiteside argued, "only the largest news organizations could have a reporter singularly focused on [the gay rights] issue. Due to limited resources, credentials, access, everyone else gets swept up in the whirlwind of covering an immense sporting event."

Initially a news hook used to drum up controversy and audience interest, Russia's contentious human rights violations were later dismissed as distracting "political stuff" once the Olympic torch was lit. "Politics," pundits and athletes alike insisted, had no place in sport once the Games began, and concerns about LGBTQ rights were forced back into the closet. Moreover, through problematic much-ado-about-nothing framing during game coverage, gay athletes and sports reporters became a surrogate voice for gay Russians, falsely reassuring American audiences that the situation on the ground wasn't all that bad for the country's gay, lesbian, transgender, and queer citizens. Perspectives from out athletes and commentators such as former Olympian Johnny Weir and NBC commentator Stephanie Gosk ignored the particular class and subject positions of these American spokespersons that were far more likely to be protected from verbal and physical abuses than are Russian citizens.

The *real* problem with mixing politics with sport, of course, is that Russia's oppressive legislation has a longer shelf-life than a single news cycle. Critical and influential events surrounding equal opportunity in sport occurred before and after the Sochi Games, yet received little public attention. As one example, in September of 2014, the International Olympic Committee informed future Olympic bidders that discrimination will be viewed as incompatible with the Olympic movement (Gibson, 2014), underscoring the notion that controversial discriminatory policies such as those in Sochi would not be tolerated in future host cities. However, this instruction—and virtually all other events surrounding the legislation—has largely been reduced to a footnote. Minor issues such as anchor Bob Costas' eye infection received more coverage than did the legislation, becoming a meme while the activists were largely stifled as the Olympic landscape unfolded.

As Kelly Whiteside noted, "Just like any big event, when the circus packs up and leaves town, the spotlight fades." The spotlight was on the Sochi legislation until threats of boycotts proved unfounded and talk of protests became unpalatable for an American public seeking saturated Olympic media entertainment. Then the focus diminished, even when the discrimination did not.

# References

Allen, K. (2013, August 18). You Can Play founder opposes Olympic boycott. *USA Today*. Retrieved October 30, 2015, from http://www.usatoday.com/story/sports/nhl/2013/08/18/patrick-burke-russian-olympics-anti-gay-laws/2669083/

Billings, A. C. (2008). *Olympic media: Inside the biggest show on television*. London, UK: Routledge.

Billings, A. C., Moscowitz, L. M., Rae, C., & Brown, N. (2015). The art of coming out: Traditional and social media frames surrounding the NBA's Jason Collins. *Journalism & Mass Communication Quarterly, 92*(1), 142–160.

Beam, R. A. (2008). The social characteristics of US journalists and their "best work". *Journalism Practice, 2*(1), 1–14.

Coddington, M. (2014). Defending judgment and context in "original reporting": Journalists' construction of newswork in a networked age. *Journalism, 15*(6): 678–695.

Costas, B. (Anchor). (2014, February 6). XXII Winter Olympics [Television broadcast]. In J. Bell (Executive Producer), *2014 Sochi Olympics*. New York, NY: National Broadcasting Co. Inc.

Costas, B. (Anchor). (2014, February 21). XXII Winter Olympics [Television broadcast]. In J. Bell (Executive Producer), *2014 Sochi Olympics*. New York, NY: National Broadcasting Co. Inc.

Farhi, P. (2014, Feb. 21). In coverage of Olympics, NBC has largely steered clear of controversy. *Washington Post*. Retrieved October 30, 2015, from https://www.washingtonpost.com/lifestyle/olympics/in-coverage-of-olympics-nbc-has-largely-steered-clear-of-controversy/2014/02/21/5e68a088-99aa-11e3-80ac-63a8ba7f7942_story.html

Gay, J. (2014, February 5). The winter Olympics (a special report)—the unsettled mood of an uneasy games: The 2014 Sochi Olympics are being widely worried about—but history says the competition will conquer all. *Wall Street Journal*, p. R10. Retrieved September 1, 2014, from http://search.proquest.com.

Gibson, O. (2014, September 25). Olympic anti-discrimination clause introduced after Sochi gay rights row. *The Guardian*. Retrieved September 15, 2014, from http://www.theguardian.com/sport/2014/sep/25/olympic-anti-discrimination-clause-sochi-gay-rights-row.

Gillespie, K. (2013, Aug. 16). Sochi: Canadian Olympians weigh in on Russia's anti-gay law. Retrieved October 30, 2015, from http://www.thestar.com/sports/amateur/2013/08/16/sochi_canadian_olympians_weigh_in_on_russias_antigay_law.html

Gitlin, T. (1980). *The whole world is watching: Mass media in the making and unmaking of the new left*. Berkeley, CA: University of California Press.

Goffman, E. (1974). *Frame analysis: An essay on the organization of experience*. New York, NY: Harper & Row.

Grekov, I. (2013, Aug. 8). Russia's anti-gay law spelled out in plain English. Policy.mic. Retrieved October 30, 2015, from http://mic.com/articles/58649/russia-s-anti-gay-law-spelled-out-in-plain-english.

Harris, R. (2014, Jan. 4). "Putin's Games" could still be compliment or curse. Associated Press. Retrieved October 30, 2015, from http://wintergames.ap.org/article/putins-games-could-still-be-compliment-or-curse.

Jenkins, S. (2014, February 23). A Sochi study in contradictions. *The Washington Post*, p. 01. Retrieved September 15, 2014, from http://www.lexisnexis.com/hottopics/lnacademic

Kothari, A. (2010). The framing of the Darfur conflict in the New York Times: 2003–2006. *Journalism Studies, 11*(2), 209–224.

Lewis, S. C., & Reese, S. D. (2009). What is the war on terror? Framing through the eyes of journalists. *Journalism & Mass Communication Quarterly, 86*(1), 85–102.

Maddow, R. (Host). (2014, February 7). Russia anti-gay law violates Olympic spirit. [Television broadcast]. In C. Gnazzo (Executive Producer), *The Rachel Maddow Show*. New York, NY: National Broadcasting Co. Inc.

McCombs, M. & Shaw, D. (1972). The agenda-setting function of mass media. *The Public Opinion Quarterly, 36*(2), 176–187.

Melvin, C. (Host). (2014, February 10). NFL prospect Michael Sam comes out of the closet [Television broadcast]. In S. Zilberstein (Executive Producer), *MSNBC Live*. New York, NY: National Broadcasting Co. Inc.

Melvin, C. (Host). (2014, February 15). U.S. Olympian Michael Eruzione discusses Russia's anti-LGBT laws [Television broadcast]. In S. Zilberstein (Executive Producer), *MSNBC Live*. New York, NY: National Broadcasting Co. Inc.

Mitchell, A. (Host). (2014, February 11). Moulton: "We haven't seen any problems at Sochi itself" [Television broadcast]. In S. De (Executive Producer), *Andrea Mitchell Reports*. New York, NY: National Broadcasting Co. Inc.

Nichols, J. M. (2014, February 4). Belle Brockhoff, lesbian Olympic snowboarder, speaks out about Sochi fears. *The Huffington Post*. Retrieved October 30, 2015, from http://www.huffingtonpost.com/2014/02/04/belle-brockhoff-lesbian-snowboarder_n_4723454.html.

Orwall, B., & Terlep, S. (2014, February 7). Russia antigay law puts leaders on the spot—some western leaders attending games stress their objections, commitment to human rights; others are staying away. *Wall Street Journal*, p. A10. Retrieved September 1, 2014, from http://search.proquest.com.

Rosen, K. (2013, August 13). U.S. athletes weigh in on Russia's gay rights issue. *USA Today*. Retrieved October 30, 2015, from http://www.usatoday.com/story/sports/olympics/2013/08/11/usa-track-athletes-react-anti-gay-law-russia/2640543/.

Scheufele, D. A. (2000). Agenda-setting, priming, and framing revisited: Another look at cognitive effects of political communication. *Mass Communication & Society, 3*(2–3), 297–316.

Steiner, L., & Bird, N. (2008). Reporters see indifference on genetically modified food. *Newspaper Research Journal, 29*(1), 63–76.

Socarides, R. (2014, February 10). Gay rights at Sochi, round one. *The New Yorker*. Retrieved September 15, 2014, from http://www.newyorker.com/business/currency/gay-rights-at-sochi-round-one.

Tenenboim-Weinblatt, K. (2014). Producing protest news: An inquiry into journalists' narratives. *The International Journal of Press/Politics, 19*(4), 410–429.

Wagner, A. (Host) (2014, February 18). Protests grow violent in Kiev [Television broadcast]. In D. Haller (Executive Producer), *NOW with Alex Wagner*. New York, NY: National Broadcasting Co. Inc.

Walters, S. (2014). *The tolerance trap: How God, genes, and good intentions are sabotaging gay equality*. New York, NY: NYU Press.

Walters, S. (2001). *All the rage: the story of gay visibility in America*. Chicago, IL: University of Chicago Press.

Weaver, D., Beam, R., Brownlee, B., Voakes, P., & Wilhoit, C. (2006). *The American journalist in the 21st Century: U.S. news people at the dawn of a new millennium*. Mahwah, NJ: Lawrence Erlbaum Associates.

Whiteside, K., (2013, December 18). Obama sends message with Sochi delegation; including gay athletes adds to heat on Russian anti-gay law. *USA Today*, p. 1C.

Williams, C. (2014, Feb. 6). Critics censure Russian rights record by snubbing Sochi Olympics. *Los Angeles Times*. Retrieved October 30, 2015, from http://www.latimes.com/world/worldnow/la-fg-wn-sochi-olympics-boycotts-protests-20140206-story.html.

Witt, A. (Host). (2014, February 8). Fast five headlines [Television broadcast]. In B. Barrett (Producer), *Weekends with Alex Witt*. New York, NY: National Broadcasting Co. Inc.

Witt, A. (Host). (2014, February 15). Billie Jean King being added to the U.S. delegation [Television broadcast]. In B. Barrett (Producer), *Weekends with Alex Witt*. New York, NY: National Broadcasting Co. Inc.

# 4

# UNIQUELY *GLEE*
## Transing Racialized Gender

*Gust A. Yep,*[1] *Sage E. Russo, Jace K. Allen,
and Nicholas T. Chivers*

> *[Transing is] playing in the uncertainty of withheld
> intelligibility.*
>
> —Petra Kuppers (2014, p. 612)

As media consumers and producers are increasingly exposed to diverse gender expressions, styles, identities, and embodiments through a multitude of images and messages both nationally and globally, gender itself has become an important topic of public discourse. For example, new media outlets have posed questions and positions regarding gender in relation to leadership, opportunities, harassment, and violence, among other issues, in the U.S. and abroad (Barnett, 2015; Halberstam, 2012; Horak, 2014; Wight, 2014). Likewise, traditional media outlets have featured coverage and discussion of gender in politics, relationships, and public spaces, and so on, and offered seemingly new gender images and expressions in their entertainment products (Booth, 2015; Capuzza, 2015; Cavalcante, 2013; Halberstam, 2012; Lester, 2015; Miller, 2015; Mocarski, Butler, Emmons, & Smallwood, 2013). Aptly called the "transgender turn," gender diversity has, in the process, become highly visible in the popular imagination (Stryker & Currah, 2014, p. 3). In this crowded landscape of mediated gender representations, how is gender diversity presented and characterized? To put it differently, how is gender diversity made intelligible? Using transing as a theoretical framework (Stryker, Currah, & Moore, 2008; Yep, 2013; Yep, Russo, & Allen, 2015) and focusing on Unique, a character featured in Fox's *Glee*, we examine how gender diversity is made intelligible in the popular prime time television series. We first offer a brief description of *Glee* and provide an overview of Unique's character, then introduce transing as our theoretical framework. Third, we discuss how gender diversity is made intelligible in the show through the process of transing, and conclude by exploring the implications of transing racialized gender.

## Unique in *Glee*

Featuring a group of high school misfits, outcasts, and so-called losers brought together by Spanish teacher Will Schuester (played by Matthew Morrison) at the fictional McKinley High School (MHS), Fox's *Glee* (2009–2015) is a comedic, musical drama set in Lima, Ohio. It revolves around the relationships, rivalries, and conflicts of the members of New Directions, the campus glee club, as they and Will interact with each other and with the school administration. Amidst the slapstick humor, witty banter, and musical performances, *Glee* pushes the boundaries of normativity in various ways by addressing topics such as homophobic bullying, teenage pregnancy, sexual infidelity, and trans identities. Winner of more than 60 awards, including Golden Globes, Emmy, and Screen Actors Guild awards, among many others (Awards, 2015), *Glee* was an immensely popular primetime show on U.S. network television.

Besides the abovementioned Will, a Spanish teacher who reinvigorates MHS's glee club, other central characters include Sue, played by the award winning actor Jane Lynch, who is constantly at odds with Will and the glee club, intent on either proving them inept with stinging one-liners or sabotaging their efforts with dramatic countermeasures; Kurt, played by Chris Colfer, who originally queered the group with his lack of hegemonic masculine tendencies, non-conforming sexuality, and soprano voice; Mercedes (Amber Riley), the soulful, proud Black woman, who is ready to lay some knowledge—including the teachings of Jesus Christ—on those needing it; Rachel (Lea Michele) the obnoxious and talented Jewish girl who dreams of nothing but singing on stage; Sam (Chord Overstreet), the decidedly absentminded (if not ditzy) and chiseled blonde heartthrob with a heart of gold; Artie (Kevin McHale), who often becomes the solid foundation everyone leans upon though he depends on others due to his inability to walk; Blaine (Darren Criss), who is Kurt's primary love interest and performs normative masculinity; Marley (Melissa Benoist), who has severe weight and social class insecurities; and Unique, (Alex Newell), a gender nonconforming Black student constantly navigating racialized gendered perceptions and normativities.

Wade "Unique" Adams is introduced in the third season.[2] Unique is a young, fat, seemingly middle class, Black American, who, at times, self identifies as a "proud Black woman" (4.16).[3] As do most of the others in New Directions, Unique dreams of becoming a star. Originally introduced as a member of Vocal Adrenaline, a rival glee club, and a fan of Kurt and Mercedes, Unique seeks out Kurt and Mercedes to tell them about being the target of disparaging and verbally abusive comments from the Vocal Adrenaline coach regarding Unique's body and size. Dressed in "men's" clothes (what we come to know as "Wade's" clothes), Unique confesses dreams of performing as her "true" self on stage to Kurt and Mercedes. Encouraged by Kurt and Mercedes to do so at the national show choir competition at the end of the third season, Unique is received with thundering applause. At the beginning of the fourth season, Unique transfers to MHS and joins New Directions, initiating many story arcs that revolve around Unique's struggles within and outside of the glee club, which continue through the fifth and final season of the show.[4]

## Transing: Our Theoretical Framework

Originally introduced by Stryker, Currah, and Moore (2008) as a theoretical approach and a critical practice, transing is a deconstructive tool to examine how gender is contingently assembled and reassembled with other attributes and structures of bodily being, such as race and body type. For example, how gender is made socially and culturally intelligible, at this moment in history, depends on racialized and bodily performances and expressions that are consistent with larger discourses (e.g., gender binary, Whiteness) and structures about the body (e.g., a racialized body as classifiably male or female within the current gender binary system) (Yep, 2013).

Transing communication, according to Yep and colleagues (2015), is based on four basic premises. First, gender is intersectional, that is, it is rendered meaningful through its simultaneous relationship with other vectors of social difference (e.g., race, body type). Second, gender is simultaneously a performative iteration (e.g., a repetitive set of stylized bodily acts) and an administrative structure (e.g., gender classification system in a culture); in other words, gender is both microscopic and macroscopic. Third, gender is multiple rather than dualistic, that is, there are more than simply two genders—male and female—in a culture; indeed, there are multiple, perhaps infinite, gender performances, expressions, and embodiments—a gender galaxy—in a given society. Finally, transing communication prioritizes the experiences and subjectivities of individuals in their own gendered bodies as they inhabit and enact identities and negotiate and navigate the social world (e.g., how people who do not fit into the gender binary system of a culture experience social life and live in society). In sum, transing recognizes the nuances and complexities of gender by simultaneously highlighting its intersectional, individual and structural, and multiple manifestations, and by recentering the subjectivities of the gendered bodies rather than the social imposition of gender categories on such persons in a given culture.

Using transing to examine a cultural text, such as *Glee*, we focus on how Unique is made culturally intelligible. According to Butler (1990), cultural intelligibility refers to the production of a normative framework establishing structures of apprehension and recognition of a subject as real and legitimate in a cultural domain. A normative framework is a lens through which people understand the social world via cultural norms and ideals. One such fundamental, omnipresent, pervasive, and hegemonic ideal in Western cultures is Butler's (1990) "heterosexual matrix" (p. 5), which is based on a set of idealized relations between sex, gender, and desire. It maintains that gender is understood to naturally follow from sex (conceived as a natural substance) and desire is understood to naturally follow gender (where maleness involves masculinity and masculinity is expressed through sexual desire for the "opposite" sex [i.e., a woman]; conversely, femaleness entails femininity and femininity is expressed through sexual desire for its "opposite" [i.e., a man]). As a result, intelligible genders are those that maintain the idealized relations between sex, gender, and desire. To maintain their coherence and continuity, gender is *regulated and required* to be a binary relation (i.e., male/female, masculine/feminine as distinct, independent, and oppositional). Butler elaborated, "the act of differentiating the two oppositional moments of the binary results in a consolidation of each term [man/woman, masculine/feminine], the respective internal coherence of sex, gender, and desire" (1990, p. 23).

Through cultural frameworks of apprehension—the process of "marking, registering, acknowledging without full cognition"—and recognition—the act of knowing individuals through social "categories, conventions, and norms" (Butler, 2009, p. 5), people who perform, express, or embody gender within the regulatory apparatus of the binary system become intelligible in society. Conversely, those who fall outside of the boundaries of the gender binary become unintelligible. Not viewed as culturally viable and legitimate subjects, the lives of unintelligible individuals are illegible, impossible, unreal, and not fully human (Butler, 1990, 1999, 2004, 2009). As such, Butler (2009) persuasively argued that their lives "are not quite—or, indeed, are never—recognized as lives" (p. 4). Thus, normativity is symbolically and materially violent, particularly for those who transgress its boundaries (Yep, 2003; Yep & Lescure, 2015). By examining cultural constructions of gender diversity, such as individuals who fall outside of the gender binary system, transing calls attention to such forms of "normative violence" (Butler, 1999, p. xxi). We now turn to transing Unique's racialized gender in Fox's *Glee*.

## Unique: Transing Racialized Gender

Transing, in many ways, highlights and interrogates the cultural frames of intelligibility, as elaborated by Butler, who wrote:

> To call the frame into question is to show that the frame never quite contained the scene it was meant to limn, that something was already outside, which made the very sense of the inside possible, recognizable. The frame never quite determined precisely what it is we see, think, recognize, and apprehend. Something exceeds the frame that troubles our sense of reality; in other words, something occurs that does not conform to our established understanding of things.
>
> (2009, p. 9)

Gender—more specifically, the gender binary—is, in this instance, "our established understanding of things." However, as previously discussed, gender is intersectional. McClintock astutely observed that gender "comes into being in social relation to other categories, if in uneven and contradictory ways" (1995, p. 9). Because such categories come into existence in and through their relationship to each other (Yep et al., 2015), gender and race, as one example, might be viewed as racialized gender; that is, they are, in McClintock's (1995) words, "articulated categories" (p. 5).

Using the notion of racialized gender and troubling the frame of cultural intelligibility of gender, we focus on representations of Unique in *Glee*. Based on our close reading of the show, four themes emerged through the process of transing. Such themes represent, in our view, mainstream cultural strategies to discipline and regulate gender. In particular, they appear to be ways to reify and secure the heterosexual matrix by reestablishing and reaffirming the coherence and continuity of the idealized relations between sex, gender, and desire (Butler, 1990). These themes are: (1) conflating genders and sexualities, (2) reifying boundaries, (3) maintaining unintelligibility, and (4) essentializing authenticity.

### *Conflating Genders and Sexualities*

This theme refers to the process of confusing, overlapping, and collapsing the above socially articulated categories. Although gender and sexuality are inextricably intertwined, they operate separately from one another, so conflating the two categories can have violent consequences. This conflation has come to be a common trope in social discourse in interpersonal, mediated, and institutional contexts (Yep et al., 2015).

The conflation of gender and sexuality occurs frequently in *Glee*. For example, in episode 4.05, gender identity and sexual identity are confused when Sue says to Unique, "I will not allow you to unleash a teenage maelstrom of gender-bent sexual confusion at this school." In this scenario, "gender-bent sexual" is used as a conjunctive adjective to describe Unique's gender identity as synonymous with sexual identity. The two articulated categories also overlap in episode 3.16, in which Kurt tries to discourage Unique from performing as a woman, saying that despite his own flamboyant style, even he wouldn't do that. Unique replies by saying, "that is because you identify as a man. I thought you of all people would understand," thus implying that Kurt's sexual identity would both directly affect his gender performance or identity and somehow give him special insight into Unique's gender identity. Perhaps most interestingly in this example, both sides overlap their identities with the other, assuming that their similar feelings of marginalization mean that they face the same oppressions. Further, the two categories are collapsed in episode 4.05 where Sue Sylvester defends her sensitivity to diversity regarding Unique's gender identity by stating, "You know, I'd think twice about calling someone a bigot who's had gay Cheerios, both male and female on her squad, and who resigned her post as principal in protest because this school wasn't doing enough to protect a gay student from being bullied." Assuming that Sue's track record (real or perceived) as an ally of lesbians and gays gives her special credence as an ally of the trans community is highly problematic considering that the trans community is already an invisible and highly marginalized category within the lesbian, gay, bisexual, transgender, and queer (LGBTQ) community (Spencer, 2015).

The conflation of gender and sexual identity in *Glee* is never more apparent than in episode 3.20. Unique has become a star for rival glee club Vocal Adrenaline, and Sue decides that the only way for New Directions to compete is to have their own "prop" performer, and demands that Kurt perform dressed as a woman:

Sue:    We have but one choice left to us: It's time to fight fire with the flaming flames of additional flamey gay fire. [Takes out a flapper dress to give to Kurt] Porcelain, you will wear this flapper dress and perform at Nationals as Porcelina. You already have the lady gait and the lady voice, and you'll have to start smoking, though, because this dress is a size two.

Kurt:   Okay, just because I'm gay does not mean I like to dress up like a woman.

Sue:    Oh, come on.

First, Sue's use of the word *additional* is critical here; it implies that there has already been some "flaming gay fire," presumably Unique's performance at the national competition. This is erroneous, because Unique's gender performance does not equate to homosexuality. However, because

Sue understands Unique to be gay, she turns to one of the gay men on her own squad to perform as a woman, essentially solidifying a bidirectional conflation of gender and sexual identity—transness is gayness and gayness is transness. Further, although Kurt explicitly denies the assumed inherent link between his sexual identity and his gender performance, Sue disregards his protest. This is especially salient because it is a direct rejection of the conflation of gender and sexuality from the voice of the marginalized identity, but is denied and unheard—that is, unintelligible—by the privileged identity.

Based on these scenes we maintain that the common conflation of gender and sexuality serves to discipline gender by reestablishing the idealized relations between sex, gender, and desire that are at the center of the heterosexual matrix (Butler, 1990). According to this matrix, Unique is expected to perform in masculine ways resulting directly from Unique's biological sex (i.e., as a "man"). Because Unique does not do so, the behavior violates the presumed coherence and continuity of gender following sex. In light of Unique's violation of expected masculine gender performance, Unique's gender is forcefully disciplined by equating it to non-conforming sexuality (i.e., homosexuality), one of the fundamental fears and powerful mechanisms of control of gender in heteropatriarchal culture. In such culture, to be fully human is to be heterosexual (Yep, 2003). By forcing Unique to be non-heterosexual based on violation of gender performance is to make Unique less than human. In addition, focusing exclusively on gender and sexuality and ignoring Unique's race reinscribes Whiteness. In other words, by not addressing Unique's racial specificity in these scenes, Whiteness is reinforced as an invisible marker of gender, sexuality, identity, and personhood (McLaren, 2000).

### Reifying Boundaries

The characters of *Glee* use particular policing practices to eliminate any flexibility beyond culturally constructed expectations of identity performance among and between intersections of gender, race, class, and sexuality, and many others. To explore how Unique's identities are bound and policed, we conceptualize reifying boundaries as the processes of substantiating, maintaining, and perpetuating socially constructed parameters of articulated categories of gender and race in a specific historical and cultural context.

The process of substantiating the parameters of identity is seen throughout the show. In episode 3.16, for example, Sue demands that Kurt and Mercedes encourage Wade to perform as Unique, to which Mercedes replies, "But Coach Sylvester, this is Ohio. I don't think that many people are gonna be down with that," indicating an awareness of the influence of geopolitical location on expectations of identity performance.

This signals an awareness that Unique's gender identity exists in a macroscopic as well as microscopic context—Unique is a subjective agent existing within social, political, and administrative structures—the recognition of which (without protest to their validity) substantiates the parameters of expected identity performances.

Unique participates in the maintenance of these articulated categories, specifically in episode 4.16 in which a fellow glee club member says, "Dude, back off," to which Unique retorts, "I am no dude. I am a *proud* Black woman." Here, Unique reifies the gender binary by rejecting one end ("no dude") and, by insinuated default, claiming the other end ("woman"). Further, by adding the adjectives "proud" and "Black" to her womanhood, Unique reinforces the socially constructed stereotype for her particular intersection of articulated categories (race and gender): the "strong Black woman," an archetype typically portrayed as self-reliant and sassy (Collins, 2004).

These constructed parameters of identity are perpetuated as Unique is repeatedly referred to using both gendered pronouns, separately or together, and by linking the use of these pronouns to the body. For example, in episode 3.20, Sue refers to Unique's performance with Vocal Adrenaline by saying, "Look at him slash her . . . Pretty as a picture with a booty that just won't quit," she effectively compartmentalizes Unique's gender identity while reducing Unique to a sexualized body—a rhetorical strategy typically associated with objectifying women, particularly women of color and the size of their buttocks (Collins, 2004).

These elements of reifying boundaries of articulated categories are brought to light clearly in episode 4.01 when multiple members of New Directions are sitting at a cafeteria table during lunch and Unique approaches to join them.

| | |
|---|---|
| Unique: | Unique offers her greetings and salutations. |
| Sam: | Wade, you can't wear that makeup and stuff in here. You have to understand how this stuff works. It's like *Game of Thrones*. |
| Artie: | Yeah, the peace between us and the-truly-popular-kids is weak . . . winter is coming. It's not gonna take much for us to get smacked down to the bottom again. |
| Blaine: | Maybe you should just save Unique for performances and be Wade the rest of the time, hm? |
| Unique: | All right . . . I'll go take off my face. [Sadly leaves the table] |

First, it is important to address the significance of Unique referring to the self in the third person, which occurs frequently throughout the series.

This practice creates an interesting contradiction of identity that reifies the boundaries between Unique's identities while simultaneously solidifying the gender binary. Unique consistently designates that her "truth" is to identify as a woman; she is Unique. However, the use of the third person—as if Unique were some other entity existing apart from Unique's body—perpetuates the idea that Wade and Unique are two separate people—one male and one female—planted firmly within and on either side of the gender binary. Not only does this add credence to the violent idea that transgender identity is a mental disorder (often referred to as Gender Identity Disorder [GID] or Gender Dysphoria [GD]), but it also works to eliminate the possibility of conceptualizing gender as a complex, fluid, and dynamic performance that can be situated betwixt and between, or even entirely outside of, the binary (Yep et al., 2015). In short, it occludes the discursive and material possibilities of gender as a galaxy.

In the very next lines of the cafeteria scene (episode 4.01), Sam and Artie exhibit policing strategies for maintaining boundaries. Given New Directions' relative success in national competition, the singers are experiencing some heretofore unknown peace in the social struggle that is high school. However, perhaps due to the precarious nature of the high school social structure, they see Unique's transcendence of gender identity boundaries as a threat to their current status, and work to reinforce them. Blaine's recommendation to save Unique for performances may be a well-intended compromise. But expecting Wade to present as a man throughout the day, and relegate Unique to a character on stage, isolates Unique's gender fluidity to the realm of entertainment or fiction and works to substantiate and maintain the lines around expected gender performances in the "real world." Unique succumbs to this gendered discipline by stating, "I'll go take off my face," which is a colloquialism for removing one's makeup, but also in this particular sense removing an identity, as if Unique is a mask that Wade wears.

As Unique at times challenges and at other times reinforces the boundaries surrounding racial, sexual, body, and especially gender identity, the students and faculty at MHS work to substantiate, maintain, and perpetuate these boundaries at almost any cost. The process of erecting and reinforcing the boundaries of these articulated categories serves, in part, to maintain the coherence and continuity of sex, gender, and desire (Butler, 1990). In addition, the processes of establishing boundaries of gender performance—to save "Unique for performances" and "be Wade the rest of the time"—suggest implicit rules of circulation for individuals who trouble the gender binary. This is, in Namaste's words, a "containment of gender transgression" in which the transgressor—Unique, in this case—is "framed as pure spectacle" devoid of subjectivity and personhood (2000, p. 11).

## Maintaining Unintelligibility

Social intelligibility refers to the ways that identities are acknowledged, apprehended, recognized, and validated through interpersonal and mediated interactions within larger social contexts. Dominant identities (e.g., White, heterosexual, and cisgender in U.S. American culture) are recognized and understood; they are validated through multiple channels of media and through interpersonal interactions in everyday life. Trans identities have often been decreed as socially unintelligible due to their defiance of the sex and gender systems that make social hierarchies easily palatable. Thus, maintaining unintelligibility is the process of perpetuating the invisibility, derealization, and erasure of certain marginalized identities (Butler, 2004).

The students and faculty at MHS are well versed in perpetuating the dominant systems through thoughtless enactment of social scripts which maintain current social hierarchies. Unique's gender identity is constantly confused and conflated with sexual identity and ultimately renders Unique invisible—and unintelligible—to the social eye. There seems to be no place where anyone understands Unique, so much so that in episode 4.01 Unique mentions being welcomed into the club with "open arms" even after ongoing misgendering (referring to Unique by the incorrect gender), containment (asking Unique to only perform as a woman on stage), and policing (not allowing Unique to audition for a woman's role in *Grease*). This implies that Unique (and other unintelligible identities) are unworthy or undeserving of having their identities recognized or validated; they should simply be content with being allowed in these spaces.

An attempt to gain visibly and access goes horribly wrong in episode 5.05, which explores Unique raising a concern of on-campus safety and requesting gender-neutral restrooms. Principal Sue thinks a purple porta-potty with yellow question marks installed in the middle of the choir room is a suitable solution. Both inconsiderate and impractical, the cartoonish porta-potty frames Unique's request and need for a gender-neutral restroom as ridiculous and unnecessary. Such hypervisibilty might seem contrary to perpetuating invisibility, but it ultimately contributes to the derealization—and hyperinvisibility—of Unique's identities and struggles by portraying gender diversity as trivial and frivolous. If Unique's struggles aren't considered valid or even real, then there is no reason for anyone, let alone a school administrator, to go out of her way to make a student troubling the gender binary feel more comfortable. In this case, derealization becomes the ultimate disciplinary tool to ensure that Unique's identity remains unintelligible.

The intersection of Blackness, gender, and sexual non-conformity has been a space of historical contention where subjects—such as Unique—are often overwhelmingly silenced and rendered invisible, unable to tell their own stories or participate in the creation of their own narratives (Crenshaw, 1992). In episode 4.01, Unique and Marley are chatting in the women's restroom when Sue comes out of a stall and assaults Unique with a string of racialized, body negative, transphobic slurs including, "Tina stomach-Turner," and "Urethra Franklin, you are a boy and you are fooling no one." Sue concludes by declaring, "I know full well that gender confusion is the liberal media's new darling."

A close reading of this scene suggests a number of ways in which Unique's racialized gender is made unintelligible. First, Sue's allusions to Tina Turner and Aretha Franklin are clearly racialized and cannot be ignored when examining the disgust and nauseating attributes she applies to Unique. The particular combination of Unique's fat, Black, gender non-conforming body is enough to make Sue physically ill, maintaining a stark Otherness that clearly thrusts Unique into unintelligible abjection (hooks, 1992). Further, Sue directly ascribes an unwanted identity (e.g., "boy") onto Unique with no regard for Unique's feelings on the subject, rendering Unique without any agency in self-definition in that moment, perpetuating forced silence and invisibility. Then Sue states, "you are fooling no one," fostering a common trope in transphobic narratives indicating that a non-conforming gender identity would only be enacted to entertain, trick, or play with the unsuspecting—ignoring the possibility that anyone would simply identify outside of the binary for themselves. Finally, Sue attempts to reduce Unique's identity to a sensationalized news story based on desire for high ratings and shock value by assuming that gender non-conformity is simply a story to be sold, while simultaneously delegitimizing Unique's identity by referring to "gender confusion."

The complex intricacies of Sue's snippy comments do more than just hurt Unique's feelings—they perpetuate the invisibility of narratives of gender diversity by removing (even if only temporarily) the agency for people to define themselves and tell their own stories, contributing to the derealization of trans identities and struggles, and preserving unintelligibility through social erasure (Butler, 1990, 2004). In so doing, unintelligibility maintains the coherence and continuity of sex and gender as social categories to congeal the gender binary system in the service of upholding the heterosexual matrix (Butler, 1990).

## Essentializing Authenticity

Discourses suggesting that there is some genuine, real, or authentic core to our identities rely on outdated and essentialist ideologies of articulated categories, assuming that there is some inherent, natural, and unchanging part of people's selves that influences or dictates their emerging identities. This narrative gives weight to arguments such as "born this way," privileging

65

hegemonic articulated categories that are normalized and naturalized into our social consciousness. In the process, it reinforces the popular cultural understanding of sex as a natural substance—rather than a social construction or a category that it is always already gendered—through which gender automatically follows (Butler, 1990). In order to understand how Unique's story contributes to these discourses, we define essentializing authenticity as the process of constructing, legitimizing, and validating the enduring realness of certain identities.

The cultural obsession with authenticity is constructed in two parts: there must be an identity that is culturally deemed authentic, and the identity must be performed in an authentic way. However, because social constructs are inherently unstable, these categories are fluid and ever-evolving, suggesting that identities and their performances are subject to shift and change depending on historical and political conditions. One's level of perceived authenticity is directly correlated to one's social intelligibility through cultural frameworks of apprehension and recognition as discussed above (Butler, 2009). The more hegemonic identity characteristics one has, the more socially intelligible one is. In turn, the more socially intelligible one is, the more visibility and validation the individual will receive.

So first, in order to be considered an authentic identity, Unique's needs and desires must be met and therefore legitimized through institutions and systems while simultaneously being validated through interpersonal interactions. In *Glee*, Unique's particular social location at the intersection of fat, Black, and gender non-conforming is a highly contested space where Unique's identities are often confused, policed, ignored, ridiculed, and ultimately rendered illegitimate, invisible, unreal, social unintelligible, and inauthentic.

In *Glee*, Unique's gender identity is only authenticated through anatomy and can only be explored within the confines of the gender binary with the ultimate purpose to reinforce the heterosexual matrix. Unique's anatomy is referenced multiple times in the series. For example, in episode 4.05, Sue declares that Unique is "smuggling more kielbasa under those gowns than a homesick Polish lady trying to sneak through customs." Sue is simultaneously reducing Unique's gender identity to genitalia, perpetuating gender boundaries by assuming gender is defined by and confined to the body. Further reducing Unique's identity, Sue calls upon on Black male stereotypes by referencing the size ("more kielbasa") of the genitalia (Collins, 2004). In the same episode, Will adamantly states that "Unique is definitely a guy" when Principal Figgens assumes Unique is a woman. Although Unique has used she/her pronouns and identifies as a "proud Black woman," when the question is posed about which characters Unique can play in the school musical, Will feels the need to designate the "truth." Thus, the legitimization of enduring realness occurs when gender is only considered valid when it is tied to a particular biological anatomy. Because Unique does not possess the anatomy that Sue and Will expect from a woman, Unique's identity is deemed as inauthentic, unreal, and illegitimate.

The second part of the construction of authenticity is the performance, or perhaps more accurately, the performativity—the everyday acts that serve to stabilize the highly precarious construct of gender (Butler, 1990). Performances of gender that are deemed authentic are those imitating the hegemonic performances that are celebrated in our current social structure. Further, intersectionally raced, sexualized, gendered, classed (and so on) bodies are expected to perform within their rigid stereotypical archetypes, while being concurrently compared to dominant hegemonic identities (i.e., White, U.S. American, cisgender, middle class, heterosexual, thin, able bodied).

Unique's gender performance is often referred to as something that should only happen on stage (episode 4.01), a joke or a stunt (episode 4.05), the "ultimate prop" (episode 3.20), trickery (episode 4.01), something "way outside of the box" (episode 4.05), and a multitude of other dehumanizing strategies that deauthenticate the assumed realness of Unique's performativity and identity. Unique's identity is constantly misunderstood, questioned, and policed, which ultimately leads to viewing Unique's identity performance as inauthentic or entirely disingenuous.

Assuming that there is a "true magical self" (episode 3.20) in everyone might sound uplifting and feel liberating, but it insinuates that the naturalization of socially articulated categories is intrinsic to human nature, assuming that although most people fall within the bounds of those categories, those who don't are not as valid, valuable, or worthy of rights, storylines, and love. This can be harmful to marginalized identities on institutional and interpersonal levels. Unique articulates this struggle perfectly in episode 4.08: "If I'm not being true to myself at least when I'm performing there won't be anything left inside of me to protect." The idea that there is a "true self" that needs to be performed maintains the arbitrary dichotomy between who we are and who others think we are (and desperately want us to be). Unique's allusion to the idea that there might not be anything left to protect after fighting the aforementioned tension demonstrates the immense impact that prolonged institutional and interpersonal invalidation can have on an individual (Yep, 2003).

## Entrenching the Heterosexual Matrix

Although *Glee* attempts to push the envelope regarding contemporary social issues, it does so in ways that actually reify the structures it seemingly questions. The characters in *Glee* are categorized as misfits or outcasts; as members of a marginalized community they seem to express great desire to fit into normative culture. In transing *Glee* and its representation of Unique, we have shown that it actually solidifies the very discourses and structures *Glee* problematizes. The situations and scenes in which Unique is the center only further entrench Butler's "heterosexual matrix" (1990, p. 5). In particular, this is done through conflating genders and sexualities where Unique's gender performance is repeatedly linked to sexuality instead of standing outside of the sexual system, reifying boundaries of the racialized gender and sexual systems instead of allowing for a fluidity outside of the expected norms, maintaining unintelligibility by erasing and derealizing Unique's identity performances, and essentializing authenticity by disallowing Unique's identity and rather ascribing one based solely on anatomy, and confining Unique's performance of "true" identity to the stage.

By highlighting how gender and race come into being in mutually constituting and uneven ways, the process of transing racialized gender calls attention to how such articulated categories are produced through Unique. A close reading of the show suggests that representations of Unique tend to highlight the spectacle of gender diversity through two distinct mechanisms of erasure of Unique's racial specificity. First, by conflating gender and sexuality (equating gayness and transness) through the spectacle of Unique's gender performance (focusing on Unique's flamboyant gender style on and off stage) while ignoring how gender is always already racialized (Unique as an African American person who performs gender non-normatively), race—more specifically, Unique's Blackness—is erased. Through this erasure, Whiteness—as a universal, omnipresent, and invisible force—reinserts itself to produce gender as an articulated category and a "[system] of intelligibility" (McLaren, 2000, p. 149). Second, by invoking racial stereotypes (Unique as potentially having a large penis based on cultural stereotypes of African American men) and racialized gender stereotypes (Unique is referred to as Aretha Franklin and Tina Turner) Unique's subjectivity and lived experiences as a young, fat, seemingly middle class, Black U.S. American are overlooked and disregarded. In this sense, Unique's racialized gender specificities are eradicated by Whiteness and racialized gender stereotypes.

In addition, transing racialized gender highlights the ways in which gender is disciplined and regulated in *Glee*. The themes we identified—conflating genders and sexualities, reifying boundaries, maintaining unintelligibility, and essentializing authenticity—are ultimately four powerful mainstream cultural strategies of disciplining gender diversity to protect the gender binary system. By sealing off gender borders, an internal cohesion and a deep separation between men/women and masculine/feminine are created to uphold the heterosexual matrix that normalizes and perpetuates patriarchy. Although visible in the show, gender diversity is symbolically eradicated, and gender non-conforming lives are deemed culturally unintelligible and unreal. They become spectacles for public entertainment and consumption without individual agency and subjectivity.

Transing racialized gender provides us with the analytical tools to identify and potentially challenge mainstream cultural strategies of disciplining and regulating gender in a society at a particular moment in history (Kuppers, 2014). By understanding how cultural unintelligibility is created and maintained we can contest and challenge such mechanisms, including the use of subversive tactics to denaturalize gender as a biological substance and to resignify gender as a set of repetitive bodily acts that have no original (Butler, 1990). But contesting cultural unintelligibility is not sufficient by itself (Butler, 1993; Yep & Lescure, 2015). We must change the terms of cultural intelligibility by creating alternative cultural codes of gender, that is, new and more inclusive frameworks of intelligibility (Butler, 1993). Although *Glee*'s Unique offers such great promise, our analysis, guided by transing racialized gender, points out how gender and race are ultimately disciplined and regulated to maintain White heteropatriarchical hegemony.

## Notes

1 Gust thanks Henry Lieu, a fellow traveler and a genius, who has expanded my worldview; Dr. Jessica Holliday, a true veterinarian, for taking good care of Pierre; and Yogi Enzo and Pierre Lucas, my "furry bodhisattvas," for their love, playfulness, and companionship.
2 Given that the English language consistently (re)produces the gender binary, we use "Unique" to refer to the character's gender—rather than "he" or "she"—in spite of Unique's occasional self identification as a "Black woman" and "Wade."
3 We use the first number for the season and the second for the episode of the show, such that 4.16 is an abbreviation for the sixteenth episode of the fourth season.
4 It is important to note that Unique is not the only character exemplifying gender diversity in *Glee*. Indeed, football coach Shannon Bieste transgresses the boundaries of femininity and masculinity in the first three seasons of the show and eventually comes out as a trans man in the last season. Although Bieste comes out as trans and his transition is handled with sensitivity, Unique is never identified—by self and others—as a trans person in the entire series.

## References

Awards. (n.d.). Retrieved February 1, 2015, from http://www.imdb.com/title/tt1327801/awards?ref_=tt_ql_4.
Barnett, J. T. (2015). Fleshy metamorphosis: Temporal pedagogies of transsexual counterpublics. In L. G. Spencer & J. C. Capuzza (Eds.), *Transgender communication studies: Histories, trends, and trajectories* (pp. 155–169). Lanham, MD: Lexington Books.

Booth, E. T. (2015). The provisional acknowledgment of identity claims in televised documentary. In L. G. Spencer & J. C. Capuzza (Eds.), *Transgender communication studies: Histories, trends, and trajectories* (pp. 111–126). Lanham, MD: Lexington Books.

Butler, J. (1990). *Gender trouble: Feminism and the subversion of identity*. New York, NY: Routledge.

Butler, J. (1993). *Bodies that matter: On the discursive limits of "sex."* New York, NY: Routledge.

Butler, J. (1999). *Gender trouble: Feminism and the subversion of identity* (10th anniversary ed.). London: Routledge.

Butler, J. (2004). *Precarious life: The powers of mourning and violence*. London: Verso.

Butler, J. (2009). *Frames of war: When is life grievable?* London: Verso.

Capuzza, J. C. (2015). What's in a name? Transgender identity, metareporting, and the misgendering of Chelsea Manning. In L. G. Spencer & J. C. Capuzza (Eds.), *Transgender communication studies: Histories, trends, and trajectories* (pp. 93–110). Lanham, MD: Lexington Books.

Cavalcante, A. (2013). Centering transgender identity via the textual periphery: *Transamerica* and the "double work" of paratexts. *Critical Studies in Media Communication, 30*(2), 85–101.

Collins, P. H. (2004). *Black sexual politics: African Americans, gender, and the new racism*. New York, NY: Routledge.

Crenshaw, K. W. (1992). Whose story is it anyway? Feminist and antiracist appropriations of Anita Hill. In T. Morrison (Ed.), *Race-ing justice, en-gendering power* (pp. 402–440). New York, NY: Pantheon Books.

Halberstam, J. J. (2012). *Gaga feminism: Sex, gender, and the end of normal*. Boston, MA: Beacon Press.

hooks, b. (1992). *Black Looks: Race and Representation*. Boston, MA: South End.

Horak, L. (2014). Trans on YouTube: Intimacy, visibility, temporality. *TSQ: Transgender Studies Quarterly, 1*(4), 572–585.

Kuppers, P. (2014). Trans-ing disability poetry at the confluence. *TSQ: Transgender Studies Quarterly, 1*(4), 605–613.

Lester, P. M. (2015). From abomination to indifference: A visual analysis of transgender stereotypes in the media. In L. G. Spencer & J. C. Capuzza (Eds.), *Transgender communication studies: Histories, trends, and trajectories* (pp. 143–154). Lanham, MD: Lexington Books.

McClintock, A. (1995). *Imperial leather: Race, gender and sexuality in the colonial contest*. New York, NY: Routledge.

McLaren, P. (2000). Unthinking whiteness: Rearticulating diasporic practice. In P. P. Trifonas (Ed.), *Revolutionary pedagogies: Cultural politics, instituting education, and the discourse of theory* (pp. 140–173). New York, NY: RoutledgeFalmer.

Miller, L. J. (2015). Becoming one of the girls/guys: Distancing transgender representations in popular film comedies. In L. G. Spencer & J. C. Capuzza (Eds.), *Transgender communication studies: Histories, trends, and trajectories* (pp. 127–142). Lanham, MD: Lexington Books.

Mocarski, R., Butler, S., Emmons, B., & Smallwood, R. (2013). "A different kind of man": Mediated transgendered subjectivity, Chaz Bono on *Dancing with the Stars. Journal of Communication Inquiry, 37*(3), 249–264.

Namaste, V. K. (2000). *Invisible lives: The erasure of transsexual and transgendered people*. Chicago: University of Chicago Press.

Spencer, L. G. (2015). Introduction: Centering transgender studies and gender identity in communication scholarship. In L. G. Spencer & J. C. Capuzza (Eds.), *Transgender communication studies: Histories, trends, and trajectories* (pp. ix–xxii). Lanham, MD: Lexington Books.

Stryker, S. & Currah, P. (2014). Introduction. *TSQ: Transgender Studies Quarterly, 1*(1–2), 1–18.

Stryker, S., Currah, P., & Moore, L. J. (2008). Introduction: Trans-, trans, or transgender? *WSQ: Women's Studies Quarterly, 36*(3–4), 11–22.

Wight, J. (2014). Saving Private Manning? On erasure and the queer in the *I am Bradley Manning* campaign. *QED: A Journal in GLBTQ Worldmaking, 1*(1), 118–129.

Yep, G. A. (2003). The violence of heteronormativity in communication studies: Notes on injury, healing, and queer world-making. In G. A. Yep, K. E. Lovaas, & J. P. Elia (Eds.), *Queer theory and communication: From disciplining queers to queering the discipline(s)* (pp. 11–59). Binghamton, NY: Harrington Park Press.

Yep, G. A. (2013). Queering/quaring/kauering/crippin'/transing "other bodies" in intercultural communication. *Journal of International and Intercultural Communication, 6*(2), 118–126.

Yep, G. A., & Lescure, R. (2015). The practice of normativities in everyday life. In D. B. Goltz & J. Zingsheim (Eds.), *Queer Praxis: Questions for LGBTQ Worldmaking* (pp. 93–106) New York, NY: Peter Lang.

Yep, G. A., Russo, S. E., & Allen, J. (2015). Pushing boundaries: Toward the development of a model for transing communication in (inter)cultural contexts. In L. G. Spencer & J. C. Capuzza (Eds.), *Transgender communication studies: Histories, trends, and trajectories* (pp. 69–89). Lanham, MD: Lexington Books.

5

# THE CHALLENGE OF WARRIOR WOMEN

## Gender, Race, and Militarism in Media

*Mary Douglas Vavrus*

"We kill for peace. We kill for each other."
Army Captain Anastasia Breslow
*Lioness*

Introducing herself and the women who are the subjects of *Women Serving in War*, the documentary she narrates, Minnesota National Guard Medevac pilot Jennifer Merrill tells viewers, "I'm just a chick who flies . . . but these ladies, they're the ones who laid the pathway for me . . . [They] went through a lot of grief and aggravation to allow us to follow in their footsteps" (Lamke & Halleen, 2014). In the United States, women such as these have had an official military presence since the establishment of the Women's Army Corps (WAC) in World War II (Meyer, 1996). With the end of conscription in 1973, the number of female service members has risen steadily; as of 2010, 14% of enlisted service members and 16% of commissioned officers were women (Patten & Parker, 2011, p. 4). Tanya Biank noted that as 11% of the fighting forces experiencing regular deployments to Iraq and Afghanistan, "today's generation of service-women [has] more war service than either their fathers or grandfathers" (2014, p. 5). Yet, in policy, law, and custom women are still Other to the norm of military masculinity (Enloe, 2000; Sjoberg, 2014).

Since September 11, 2001, U.S. media have addressed this otherness by producing a spate of non-fiction works about women in military service in Afghanistan and Iraq; an abbreviated list includes *The Lonely Soldier* (Benedict, 2009), *The Denver Post* series/digital newsbook "Betrayal in the Ranks" (Herdy & Moffeitt, 2004), and PBS's *Women in War* episode of the "Makers" series. Similar martial images and themes circulate through these texts to form what Stuart Hall has labeled a "regime of representation" (2001, p. 328)—in this case about women's experiences in military service. Crucial to understanding any such regime is examining how its constitutive representations produce what Foucault calls "truths" and link these to "specific effects of power" (1977, p. 14): that is, "'truth' is linked by a circular relation to systems of power which produce it and sustain it, and to effects of power which it induces and which redirect it." In this context, truths are relative, produced by discursive systems such as media, and may or may not be accurate or verifiable. However, it is not their accuracy or verifiability that makes them significant; instead, it is their use by powerful institutions such as the military and media that make truths seem to be true, regardless of their basis in actual fact.

This chapter thus explores, first, truths about women's military experience produced by the regime of representation that I term Warrior Women, and, second, these truths' circular relation to systems of power, particularly patriarchal power. To do so, I conduct a feminist analysis of six recently released, representative documentaries: *Lioness* (McLagan & Sommers, 2008), *Sisters in Arms* (Freeman, 2010), *Service: When Women Come Marching Home* (Rock & Stotter, 2012), *The Invisible War* (Dick & Ziering, 2012),[1] and two public television programs that aired in 2014, PBS's *Women in War* (Grady & Ewing, 2014—an episode in the *Makers* series) and Twin Cities Public Television's (TPT) program, *Women Serving in War* (Lamke & Halleen, 2014). Each of these documentaries has a companion web site and Facebook page, and several include more interactive digital platforms. I analyze all of this associated content to generate a full picture of this regime.

## Theorizing Warrior Women

A representational regime is composed of media constructions linked intertextually, accumulating "meanings across different texts, where one image refers to another, or has its meaning altered by being 'read' in the context of other images"; a regime, in other words, is "the whole repertoire of imagery and visual effects through which 'difference' is represented at any one historical moment" (Hall, 2001, p. 328). My analysis of the Warrior Women regime accounts for both words and images because in these documentaries' numerous talking head segments, words work together with imagery to construct women as warriors. Former CIA agent Valerie Plame provided an example of such intertextuality, citing a popular TV program in her arch observation about the CIA's early years: "it was a little bit like *Mad Men* with security clearances. The girls got the coffee" (Grady & Ewing, 2014). Hall (1997) noted that the representations a regime comprises are not simple reflections or re-presentations of the object(s) in a domain; rather, they discursively constitute the meanings of these objects, in part by persistently articulating—or connecting—specific meanings to an object or object domain and thus normalizing that meaning. These documentaries, for example, repeatedly articulate women to the military both to reveal the many roles women have held since World War II and to produce a regime of truth that normalizes women's presence in this historically masculine institution. In this way they amplify other post-World War II TV and cinematic treatments of military women as documented by Tasker (2011).

The Warrior Women regime is part of a proliferation of military-themed popular culture produced since September 11, 2001 (Stahl, 2010), and serves various purposes, two of which are germane to this chapter: It provides a site where gender, race, and military policy intersect—a site where viewers may negotiate what it means to be a service woman; and, second, it offers opportunities for military policy activism. In their images and words, these documentaries use discursive techniques of equalization and differentiation to humanize service women, and, in Butler's (2010) terms, make them both recognizable and grievable. Warrior Women thus positions service women as equals to service men—the martial subjects we have historically been conditioned to recognize and grieve as such. This regime's system of power produces truths by illuminating women's wartime labor, injuries, and deaths, and by indicting some aspects of the military's treatment of women while overlooking others. A system such as this is compelling and invites further examination because, as Butler has argued, representations of war act as trajectories of affect; thus they orient audiences to understand, sympathize with, and even empathize with their subjects. TV news coverage, for example, "positions citizens as visual consumers of a violent conflict that happens elsewhere, at least in the United States where geographical distance from our so-called enemies allows us to wage war without close domestic scrutiny of our actions" (Butler, 2010, p. xv). Although Butler develops these concepts mainly to understand how media representations construct victims of war as more or less grievable, her argument is applicable to the documentaries I review here because of their collective project to constitute women as victims of unjust and even dangerous military policies and practices.

For Butler, recognizability is not simply a realization that another human is within our field of perception, but full comprehension or apprehension of that human life's precariousness. Precariousness in this context "implies living socially, that is, the fact that one's life is always in some sense in the hands of the other . . . Reciprocally, it implies being impinged upon by the exposure and dependency of others, most of whom remain anonymous" (2010, p. 14). Precariousness, Butler asserted, is "coextensive with birth itself . . . which means that it matters whether or not this infant being survives, and that its survival is dependent on what we might call a social network of hands" (p. 14). Working in tandem with recognizability, grievability is a presupposition for recognizing that the loss of a person's life would matter, and presents itself even at celebrations of birth. But she added that,

> there can be no celebration without an implicit understanding that the life is grievable, that it would be grieved if it were lost, and that this future anterior is installed as the condition of its life . . . Without grievability, there is no life, or, rather, there is something living that is other than life . . . The apprehension of grievability precedes and makes possible the apprehension of pre-carious life.
>
> (p. 15)

This is the chief challenge the Warrior Women regime poses to media studies scholars working with feminist and critical race theories: it con-stitutes women as recognizable, grievable martial subjects by highlighting their interdependence, competence, and suffering while perpetuating and normalizing militarism.[2] In this chapter, I argue that through the discur-sive strategies of equalization (casting service women as equals to service men), and differentiation (illuminating gender differences to the exclusion of race), Warrior Women constructs the military as a post-racial sister-hood whose geo-political objectives and impacts on civilian populations go unexamined.

## Equalization: Women on Par with Men

As armed and uniformed Marine Staff Sergeant Juanita Towns walks down a dirt road in Afghanistan, her voiceover explains that she enjoys being out on patrol, just "like my brothers" (Grady & Ewing, 2014). Although it is unclear whether Towns means her siblings or military colleagues, her state-ment characterizes the goal of equalization: to show that the qualities of a good soldier can be found among women as well as men. All of these films include scenes of service women and men working together in appar-ent harmony, intercut with women explaining why they enlisted and then stayed in the military.[3] Wanting to serve their country and desiring military benefits top the list. CIA security analyst Gina Bennett summed up their sentiments when she asserted that, "women have been involved in war since the beginning of this nation, and we're still trying to get society to accept that women have the same calling to securing their nation as men. It is no different" (Grady & Ewing, 2014). Between their stated reasons for enlisting and images documenting their suffering—such as Sue Downes' agonizing recovery after her legs are blown off in an IED attack (Rock & Stotter, 2012)—these women become sympathetic, recognizable as warriors on par with the male soldiers long the proper martial subjects of our culture.

Like many men, service women enlisted to help with the war effort or from an ingrained sense of duty. Helen Miller, one of first female soldiers in the U.S. Army, enlisted with her friend at the beginning of World War II because, "we wanted to help get the war over with so that we could go on with our lives" (Lamke & Halleen, 2014). Lashonna Perry joined the Army in 2002 because she wanted to "help out" after the September 11th attacks (Rock & Stotter, 2012). Other women enlisted for familial reasons. Airman 1st Class Jessica Hinves's family taught her that, "it's every citizen's duty to join the military; if you can, you should" (Dick & Ziering, 2012). Alexis Courneen joined the Coast Guard to honor her veteran grandfathers and aunt: "of course that's what I wanted to do. Because there's nothing you can give back greater. There's no better sense of pride than [the military]" (Rock & Stotter, 2012). Embedded even in the derisive comments about female Army nurses made by one ABC news correspondent is recognition of their similarity to service men: "There's nothing like a dame, and the dames have finally come to the South Vietnamese war. This week about 38 pretty, young American Army nurses landed at Qui Nhon to help set up a huge, mobile field hospital. These girls are in good spirits, like most of the Americans in Vietnam" (Grady & Ewing, 2014).

Just as a desire to serve one's country is an equal opportunity motivator, so too are the material benefits that inspire women to enlist—especially after 1967 when President Johnson lifted the cap imposed by the Women's Armed Services Integration Act of 1948, which had limited the number of women to 2% of total enlistment. Johnson's move permitted women to be promoted to higher pay grades and ranks (WREI, 2013, p. 9), making the military a more attractive career option for women. By the end of conscription six years later, women were joining in much higher numbers (Grady & Ewing, 2014). Despite this trend, however, all branches of the military realized they needed to change recruitment tactics so that women would continue to enlist. "Young women," Christiane Amanpour observed, "were definitely part of the marketing plan" (Grady & Ewing, 2014). Recruiting ads in the 1970s used Second Wave feminist appeals including wage equity, work opportunities, and financial independence. One ad's voiceover, for example, claimed the Air Force as "a *now* place to be," with "exciting, glamorous" scientific and research jobs "open to a girl." An ad for the Navy featured African American women, jazzy background music, and a hip-sounding male voiceover explaining that women "make the same pay as a man doing the same job and get the same advantages as a man. It's opportunity, advancement, good pay, equality. The new Navy" (Grady & Ewing, 2014).

In Warrior Women documentaries, women voice their attraction to the military for reasons strikingly similar to those found in early ads: to be challenged by their work, afford college tuition or travel, and to acquire training for jobs such as helicopter pilot. These women confirmed that the marketing plan was indeed successful because all of them—even those suffering from PTSD—reported that they found military service to be beneficial. For example, Peggy Swanson of the World War II Army Air Corps said of her service experience that, "I think it made me a better person. It was a good experience. I don't regret any bit of it" (Lamke & Halleen, 2014). Former war correspondent Molly Moore pointed to women making the military a more populist organization: as women joined the military in increasing numbers, the military became a "microcosm of our society . . . You . . . look at the women who are breaking the glass ceiling and becoming CEOs, that's always going to be a very small percentage of women. But . . . women who are joining the military they're your neighbors, your family members, your friends next door" (Grady & Ewing, 2014). A key point made in all of these documentaries is that women take pride in their military service, a sentiment that helps to normalize women warriors by illustrating that in this way, too, women are indistinguishable from men.

Women's experiences around the front line during contemporary warfare illustrate both their similarity to and difference from service men. Along with other accounts (e.g., Benedict, 2009), these documentaries show that troops need not seek out combat because rapidly changing and multiple front lines bring the fight to them, often unexpectedly; this feature of modern warfare has made enforcing gender segregation of troops impossible. Women have been in and around combat since at least the 1989 invasion of Panama when the first woman officially led men into battle. For example, Air National Guard Major M. J. Hegar flew more than 100 search and rescue missions in Afghanistan, one in which her helicopter was shot down. Recounting how she shot back at "the enemy" while being rescued, Hegar boasted, "I have that warrior spirit. And it came out" (Grady & Ewing, 2014). Chairman of the Joint Chiefs of Staff General Martin E. Dempsey acknowledged that in Iraq and Afghanistan "there was no front line, there was no rear . . . This notion that you could somehow segment the environment" to separate women from men "just fell apart . . . it was an anachronism of history at that point" (Grady & Ewing, 2014). Although the combat exclusion's official demise came in 2013,[4] it was in place when these documentaries were produced, and confusion about its enforcement permeates the accounts of the service women featured in them.

*Lioness* (McLagan & Sommers, 2008) and *Sisters in Arms* (Freeman, 2010) focus much more on combat than do the other documentaries, and detail multiple problems women encounter when involved in fighting.

Canada opened its combat forces to women in 1989, so the soldiers appearing in *Sisters in Arms* were trained to fight; although they too experienced PTSD, their reminiscences lack the sense of betrayal U.S. women voiced after finding themselves in firefights, untrained in how best to fight back. The women featured in *Lioness* were part of the Army's Team Lioness, created in 2003 to foster a sense of cohesion among the female support soldiers accompanying male combat units on missions in Iraq. The film showcased activities that only they could perform, such as patting down Iraqi women to ensure they weren't smuggling weapons (McLagan & Sommer, 2008). *Lioness*'s scenes from Iraq show that being attached to combat units meant women were in the line of fire just as men were, yet they received neither training nor credit for enduring these conditions. The father of one Lioness even reported proudly (with tongue in cheek, one hopes) that his daughter was the best shot in her platoon not because she had been trained by the Army, but because she spent so much time "shooting all of them squirrels in Arkansas" (McLagan & Sommer, 2008). Non-Lioness female support teams also expressed dismay that they could not be rewarded for their combat-related contributions and sacrifices (some had limbs blown off, for example), and were even criticized for having a negative effect on *esprit de corps*. The latter accusation was countered by Joint Chiefs General Dempsey, however, who asserted that "not only were women competent, but they made us a better military" (Grady & Ewing, 2014).

All of these accounts serve to make women recognizable as warriors in terms Butler (2004) explained: "To ask for recognition . . . is precisely not to ask for recognition for what one already is. It is to solicit a becoming, to instigate a transformation, to petition the future always in relation to the Other" (p. 44). By making visible service women's competencies, suffering, and sacrifices, the Warrior Women regime enables their transformation to recognizability as it diminishes their status as Other to this martial realm.

## Differentiation: Women Changing Warfare

Warrior Women documentaries position military women as equal to their male counterparts; but as they establish parity, they also identify how gender difference plays out, both praising women for actions that only they can undertake and revealing gender-specific dangers of military service. Deploying difference to military advantage, women warriors work to, as Christiane Amanpour contended, "fundamentally redefine what war is and who our warriors are" (Grady & Ewing, 2014).

These documentaries typically make claims about women's positive impacts using essentialist terms, exemplified in CIA Analyst Gina Bennett's assertion that women are "patient, tenacious, and strategic in our perspective. Very long term in our focus" (Grady & Ewing, 2014). Featured in *Sisters in Arms*, Corporal Katie Hodges suggested that, "a woman maybe brings more patience to the job than a man. We have a different outlook on everything. I think it's fair to say that women are somewhat more emotional than men. I know I am. I think that's just the basic chemistry within us" (Freeman, 2010). Such comments about putative gender-specific traits construct them as beneficial overall, particularly in segments depicting activities only service *women* can do.

When the US invaded Afghanistan in 2001 and Iraq two years later, the Pentagon recognized the need for female troops to work with Muslim women, many of whom were not permitted to speak to or otherwise engage with men. Team Lioness was therefore created and dispatched to Iraq, while other female engagement teams were sent to Afghanistan. Lioness Ranie Ruthig remembered that most of their missions took place at night, when families were likely to be at home. Her voiceover narrates scenes of male soldiers securing an area after breaking down the doors of family homes, followed by Lionesses engaging women and children she described as "panic stricken" in order to gather intelligence. Rebecca Nava recounted giving "[Iraqi] kids candy, school supplies" in order to win their trust. Ruthig expressed regret about these tactics: "I felt like the Gestapo. All I could think of is what I'd do if they did this to me" (McLagan & Sommers, 2008). Anastasia Breslow read from her war diary a comment that if roles were reversed and she had been in the families whose homes were being invaded, she might plot against them too. Her entry ended with a weak reassurance: "We just have to have faith in the intel that these people are doing wrong" (McLagan & Sommers, 2014). In Afghanistan, female engagement teams worked to get from women intelligence about the location of Taliban forces and search for weapons women might be carrying under their robes. To accomplish these tasks, the female soldiers featured in *Women in War* tied on headscarves before donning helmets to patrol with the men; this gender signifier enabled what Marine Staff Sergeant Juanita Towns explained was "a lot of searching . . . We were looking for weapons, pistols, any kind of contraband they're not supposed to have" (Grady & Ewing, 2014). Scenes such as these from Iraq and Afghanistan show women warriors behaving as humanely toward women and children as their missions allowed, a suggestion that they make for a kinder, gentler combat force.

Women warriors also display compassion while recounting their military experiences. Army nurses Mary Beth Crowley and Donna Korf both expressed distress about having been in the midst of injury and death— especially of children—during the Vietnam War. Crowley remembered that, "I think what got me through it, was I used to cry in the shower. Almost every day." Korf, too, acknowledged crying about the many injured young people she encountered until, "one day you stop crying."

"You had to be strong," her interviewer affirmed; Korf replied: "Yes, and so did they . . . They took a lot of pain" (Lamke & Halleen, 2014). In 2002, Major General Heidi Brown led the only Army air defense force in Iraq. When one of her convoys was attacked, troops were taken prisoner while others were killed. Asked about the experience of losing soldiers under her command, a visibly distressed Brown replied that she felt "like a parent losing a child" (Grady & Ewing, 2014).

In addition to the mix of emotions they voice about about being involved in wartime brutality, women warriors openly express dismay and frustration at encountering gendered barriers to carrying out their duties. This is especially evident when they discuss combat, sexual harassment, and assault. In 2004, the Lionesses were involved in the deadly and destructive battle for Ramadi, a city in Iraq's largest province of Anbar. "If you control Anbar, you control Iraq," a male commander asserted (McLagan & Sommers, 2008). Despite being in firefights and sustaining injuries in Ramadi, the Lionesses received no credit for having been there—they were officially prohibited from fighting. In one poignant scene, the Lionesses gather for an informal reunion. After they greet each other and gush over Nava's infant, they settle into their seats to view *Shoot Out at Ramadi*, a History Channel documentary. When they discover their absence from the program's recounting of events, one observed that the film seemed to go out of its way to render them invisible. "That was *our* mission," another declared with disappointment (McLagan & Sommers, 2008).

The Lionesses' experiences and those of other women warriors in this regime illustrate how gender difference can exacerbate dangerous conditions when fighting breaks out. Voicing sentiments common to many of the women, Army nurse and Vietnam veteran Diane Carlson Evans observed that, "the combat zone [was] 360 degrees around you," and the only difference between the women and men "was we could be shot at, but we couldn't shoot back." Besides being perilous for women, this maintained a system in which women were "second class citizens," averred retired Brigadier General Pat Foote (Grady & Ewing, 2014).

Warrior Women documentaries all contain troubling accounts of male soldiers and military brass being hostile to women, but *Service* and *The Invisible War* focus most on stories about two other gendered hazards:[5] sexual assault and harassment. Sexual assault and harassment have long been problems in the military; although prior to 2012 several works documented the pervasiveness of military sexual assault, their authors were not able to draw Congressional attention to it. *The Invisible War* was different; its director and producer brought its exposé to the civilian public and the military in town-hall meetings to illuminate the twin problems of sexual assault and its subsequent (mis)treatment: women who reported their attacks were considered troublemakers, faced retaliation, and had little chance of seeing their perpetrator(s) punished, let alone prosecuted. Appearing in *Women in War*, Molly Moore affirmed *The Invisible War*'s narrative when she recounted her reporting on the numerous sexual assaults that occurred during the Navy's 1991 Tailhook convention. She noted wryly that women who had been attacked there faced many obstacles to getting their cases treated fairly because, "if there's one thing the military hates it's a trouble maker. And especially a female trouble maker" (Grady & Ewing, 2014). Warrior Women documentaries illustrate that simply being a woman is risky in a military that discourages sexual assault reporting yet maintains what one veteran called a "target rich environment" for sexual predators (Dick & Ziering, 2012). Former Marine 1st Lieutenant Ariana Klay's story in *The Invisible War* exemplifies this problem. Klay was stationed at Marine Barracks Washington (MBW), a prestigious assignment for which only the best Marines are recommended. When she arrived several of the male Marines declared to her that women at MBW were nothing more than "walking mattresses," there for the sole purpose of being "fucked." Soon thereafter, one of Klay's fellow officers raped her. Despite being told that she would be killed if she reported it, Klay did report the rape, only to see it covered up by other MBW officers. Then, like so many other service women who survive sexual assault, Klay attempted suicide—an experience she and her husband recall with palpable anguish (Dick & Ziering, 2012).

Both *The Invisible War* and *Service* reveal how common sexual abuse is for service women and how poorly the military both prevents and prosecutes it. These problems continue for many women once they are discharged and need the services of the Department of Veterans Affairs (VA). Although the VA's generally poor treatment of veterans experiencing PTSD and suicidal depression has recently come to light in news reports, *Lioness*, *Service*, and *The Invisible War* demonstrate how much worse its treatment of female veterans is, particularly those experiencing what the VA terms "military sexual trauma." From a dearth of professionals trained to treat sexual trauma to facilities that lack privacy for women using its services, the VA has proved dangerously ill equipped to treat women warriors, according to these documentaries.

Although the Warrior Women regime highlights numerous perils women face during and after military service, its exclusive focus on gender precludes an intersectional analysis that would consider how racial difference affects service women. Such inattention to race marks Warrior Women as postracial because despite featuring many women of color, none of them is asked whether she has experienced racism during her service, a time when race discrimination is common. According to Dempsey and Shapiro (2009), Hispanic and African American troops report "discrimination within their units and in the Army at large at much higher rates than common narratives of Army life would suggest" (p. 546).

Additionally, the only two veterans in these films who mention being homeless after returning from service are African American (Rock & Stotter, 2012). Their stories indicate that African American veterans face more difficulties returning home than do their white counterparts, but Warrior Women filmmakers fail to address this issue. Filmmakers sensitized to how race and gender intersect to produce differential relationships to institutional power and poverty might have pursued this as part of their project to improve the military for women; but absent such a discussion, Warrior Women "obfuscate[s] institutional racism" of the sort reported by Dempsey and Shapiro, and subtly "blames continuing racial inequalities on individuals who make poor choices for themselves and their families" (Squires, 2014, p. 6). A lack of engagement with racial oppression weakens Warrior Women's attempts to cast service women as recognizable subjects as it renders invisible a system of oppression that systematically degrades the lives of women of color.

## Spreadable Activism

Warrior Women's boundaries extend to the digital platforms associated with each documentary, and, for those that have been broadcast, to the comments sections of broadcasters' sites. These digital sites offer motivated viewers opportunities to engage in self-care and policy activism, thus making them spreadable. Spreadability here refers to means by which media texts may be changed and recirculated in their new form, exchanged as social currency, or used to spur activism. In a description apt for this chapter, Jenkins, Ford, and Green explained that, "the spreadability paradigm assumes that anything worth hearing will circulate through any and all available channels, potentially moving audiences from peripheral awareness to active engagement" (2013, p. 7). Active engagement is what the Warrior Women regime seeks; to achieve it, each documentary's web site includes links to content that models or enables activism: news stories about filmmakers meeting with legislators to advocate for military policy changes or interviews with the filmmakers, for example. Each website also includes a link to the film's Facebook page, where visitors can participate in conversations about the issues it raises; in some cases, websites include links to a related Twitter feed, You Tube channel, blog, or, as with *Service*, podcast.

*The Invisible War* has proved particularly spreadable, extending to town-hall meetings accompanying film screenings (some on or near military bases), PBS broadcasts, print media, the Web, Twitter, Facebook, and iTunes. Content on these sites is meant to impel public activism to remedy the military justice system's failure to prosecute perpetrators of sexual assault (Dick, 2013). For example, just prior to *The Invisible War*'s PBS broadcast in May, 2013, the Independent Lens blog posted an interview with Dick, who touts the film. Viewers have been "outraged and moved and compelled to want to take action and help," he claimed. Further,

> most of the people in the film have seen it—and they have been very, very pleased—they all have said the experience of participating in the film has significantly changed their lives for the better—it's been surprising [*sic*] therapeutic and empowering—they no longer feel invisible and discarded and ashamed. They feel validated and it's renewed their faith and trust in others.
>
> (Independent Lens, 2013)

In another interview, Dick and producer Amy Ziering directed viewers to the NotInvisible.org website, which urges visitors to "demand change" by signing a petition; to "host a screening . . . to spark conversation, awareness and change"; to donate to the Artemis Rising Invisible War Recovery Program; and to "join the conversation" protesting military sexual abuse on *The Invisible War* Twitter feed (Kim, 2012). Among the many resource organizations NotInvisible.org links to is RAINN (Rape, Abuse, & Incest National Network), which has partnered with the Department of Defense's Sexual Assault Prevention and Response Office (SAPRO) to host a hotline for military sexual assault survivors and design a mobile self care app: "DOD Safe Helpline." This app

> gives members of the military community access to resources and tools to help manage the short- and long-term effects of sexual assault. The app helps you create a plan that is right for you, from exercises that aid in reducing stress to tools to help you transition to civilian life. You can even store your customized plans and exercises so you can refer back to them at any time.
>
> (iTunes, n.d.)

Like that of *The Invisible War, Service*'s home page includes a short video trailer above a provocative diary entry: "Dear Diary, I left Afghanistan a year ago yesterday and I don't feel like having sex with my husband in Kansas tonight cuz he woke me up from a flashback where I saw Tim's arm lying in the sand." A description of the film follows, explaining that *Service* is "part of a much larger project. Through robust social media, SERVICE continues supporting women through open and closed Facebook groups where women can exchange information, find friendship and share solutions that have changed their lives" ("About the Documentary," n.d.). From this page visitors can connect with the Disabled American Veterans (DAV) organization, which assists injured veterans in their recoveries.

Warrior Women documentaries do not flinch from presenting difficult and painful consequences of women's military service, doing so to make women recognizable and grievable to military personnel and civilians alike. These affective renderings of service women's experiences that permeate Warrior Women offer viewers a space in which to engage with women warriors at a personal level—to grieve with them—then align themselves with projects meant to alleviate their suffering. The expressions of grief depicted throughout the Warrior Women regime exemplify what Butler (2004) contended: that grief

> furnishes a sense of political community of a complex order . . . by bringing to the fore the relational ties that have implications for theorizing fundamental dependency and ethical responsibility. If my fate is not originally or finally separable from yours, then the "we" is traversed by a relationality that we cannot easily argue against.
>
> (pp. 22–23)

These documentaries offer a sense of political community by first constructing a trajectory of affect along which viewers may align themselves, and then detailing concrete policy changes meant to help women warriors: eliminating combat exclusions, making the VA more responsive to women veterans, and moving sexual assault prosecutions outside of the military chain of command, and more. The Military Justice Improvement Act addresses the flawed assault prosecution system, and has been sponsored most visibly by New York Senator Kirsten Gillibrand (and blocked for a second time in the Senate in June, 2015); Gillibrand wrote the legislation after viewing *The Invisible War*, finding herself "gripped with anger and disgust and determination that I was going to do something about it" (Zremski, 2014). Given Gillibrand's and others' statements about the effectiveness of these documentaries, the claim that they have played a significant role in ameliorating some of the problems faced by warrior women is plausible.

## Challenging Warrior Women

Perhaps paradoxically, these documentaries' project of making post 9/11 women warriors grievable and recognizable poses challenges to media studies researchers interested in social justice. Warrior Women films construct military gender integration as a civil rights issue and celebrate women's participation in this struggle as a "sign of American modernity and democracy" (Tasker, 2011, p. 206). But Tasker cautioned that, "we should not romanticize or simply celebrate [military women]. It is clear that to a large extent a place appears for military women as and when their labor is required"; what's more, in "our current historical context of open-ended war and ongoing military interventions, that labor has been integral to American assertions of military authority" (p. 15). The subjects of Warrior Women work in the conflicted manner Tasker described: although they become recognizable and grievable combatting military patriarchy, their uncritical acceptance of the military's martial objectives serve to legitimate the violence on which military authority depends. And although Gray focused on racial difference, his point may be germane for Warrior Women as well:

> The connection between the promise of seeing more diversity in media and post-9/11 attacks on the United States links the regulatory role of race and difference with the discourse of homeland security and global terrorism. Domestically the discourse of racial diversity serves as an alibi for racializing and securing the "homeland" through increased surveillance, incarceration, and militarization in the name of national security.
>
> (Gray, 2013, p. 774)

In a similar way, Warrior Women works to diversify military-themed media by incorporating service women's experiences into them. However, the regime can also work as an "alibi" for normalizing and even intensifying militarism when its presence can be justified by kinder, gentler women warriors. Since 9/11, U.S. militarism such as that Warrior Women depicts has become commonplace—a situation I believe feminists should call out and interrupt whenever possible, if for no other reason than to challenge the violence and destruction accompanying it.

Feminists (and everyone else) should also be concerned about militarism, both because military service can have problematic consequences for women and because war devastates the populations subjected to it. According to Zarembo (2015), the rate of suicide among female veterans is about six times that of civilian women—a figure one epidemiologist called "staggering" and "obscenely high."[6] And then there is the death and injury toll incurred by war. Among Afghanis and Pakistanis, the death toll from the U.S. war in Afghanistan is about 149,000; another 162,000 people have been injured (Crawford, 2015). When Iraqi, U.S. military and private contractor deaths are factored in, the number of direct war deaths rises to 350,000. The economic cost of these wars is also remarkable: the US alone has already spent or obligated $4.4 trillion (Costs of War, 2014).

But these figures do not appear anywhere in Warrior Women, which renders war as if its human and material costs are borne almost entirely by the U.S. military. Although military service women endure an unimaginable amount of suffering in the performance of military duties, so too do the individuals living in lands the US has invaded. Militarism works against the goals of social justice that are part and parcel of feminist work by legitimating the notion that "we kill for peace," as Lioness Anastasia Breslow put it. If feminists are to challenge militarism, we might start by refusing to accept the dangerous truths the Warrior Women regime perpetuates, and instead cast peacekeepers and pacifists as heroic. In this way we can create our own mission—this one for the purpose of accomplishing representational regime change.

## Notes

1 Four of these documentaries were broadcast after being released in theaters and on DVD: *Lioness* appeared on PBS's Independent Lens in 2008; *Sisters in Arms* aired on BBC Radio 4 in 2013; *Service: When Women Came Marching Home* was broadcast on numerous local TV stations in 39 states; and *The Invisible War* appeared on PBS's Independent Lens in 2013.

2 Cynthia Enloe's definition of militarization guides my work:

> Militarization is a step-by-step process by which a person or a thing gradually comes to be controlled by the military or comes to depend for its well-being on militaristic ideas. The more militarization transforms an individual or a society, the more that individual or society comes to imagine military needs and militaristic presumptions to be not only valuable but also normal. Militarization, that is, involves cultural as well as institutional, ideological, and economic transformations.
> (2000, p. 3)

3 Warrior Women documentaries suggest that because U.S. service women enlisted voluntarily this is a sign they are committed to military life. Although service men who enlisted after the end of conscription did so voluntarily, that is not necessarily true prior to 1973 when many men were drafted—at times against their will.

4 In 2013 the Pentagon eliminated its combat exclusion policy for women, giving the branches of the military and the Special Operations Command three years in which to allow women to have access to about 250,000 jobs (Haring, 2014).

5 *The Invisible War* shows that service men are also victims of sexual assault; they, like women, experience negative effects of their attacks long after they occurred. Because they are the majority of military service members, more service men than women have been sexually assaulted, and they are less likely to report their attacks than are women (Dick & Ziering, 2012). But no matter the gender of the victims, sexual violence has its roots in patriarchal power. About male rape, Scarce wrote that rape is a "political weapon that is wielded by those who have more power over those who have less power" (2001, p. 234). In a rigidly hierarchical institution such as the military that has a history of enlisting sexual predators, rape has become an occupational hazard (Dick & Ziering, 2012). This has institution-wide consequences: as Joint Chief General Dempsey pointed out, sexual harassment erodes trust between soldiers, and trust is necessary for maintaining the military's effectiveness (Grady & Ewing, 2014).

6 Male veterans are also prone to suicide, especially those age 30 and younger; their rate of suicide is about three times higher than that of civilian men in the same age group (NBC, 2014).

# References

About the Documentary (n.d.) Service: When women come marching home. Retrieved June 1, 2015, from http://www.servicethefilm.com/index.php.

Benedict, H. (2009). *The lonely soldier: The private war of women serving in Iraq.* Boston, MA: Beacon Press.

Biank, T. (2014). *Undaunted: The real story of America's servicewomen in today's military.* New York, NY: New American Library.

Butler, J. (2004). *Precarious life: The powers of mourning and violence.* London, UK: Verso.

Butler, J. (2010). *Frames of war: When is life grievable?* London, UK: Verso.

Costs of War (2014, June). *Over 350,000 killed by violence, $4.4 trillion spend and obligated.* Retrieved June 9, 2015, from costsofwar.org.

Crawford, N. (2015, May 22). *War-related death, injury, and displacement in Afghanistan and Pakistan 2001–2014.* Brown University: Watson Institute for International Studies. Retrieved June 8, 2015, from http://watson.brown.edu/files/watson/imce/news/explore/2015/War%20Related%20Casualties%20Afghanistan%20and%20Pakistan%202001-2014%20FIN.pdf.

Dempsey, J. K. & Shapiro, R. Y. (2009). The Army's Hispanic future. *Armed Forces & Society, 35*(3), 526–561.

Dick, K. (Writer and Director) & Ziering, A. (Producer). (2012). *The Invisible War.* [Motion picture]. United States: Chain Camera Pictures.

Dick, K. (2013, June 3). Don't trust the Pentagon to end rape. *The New York Times.* Retrieved October 16, 2013, from http://www.nytimes.com/20113/06/04/opinion/don't-trust-the-pentagon-to-end-rape.html?nl=opinion&emc=edit_ty_20130604&_r=0.

Enloe, C. (2000). *Maneuvers: The international politics of militarizing women's lives.* Berkeley, CA: University of California Press.

Freeman, B. (Director, Writer, Producer). (2010). *Sisters in Arms.* [Motion picture]. United States: Women Make Movies.

Foucault, M. (1977). The political function of the intellectual. *Radical Philosophy, 17,* 12–14.

Grady, R. (Director and Producer) & Ewing, H. (Director and Producer) (2014, October 21). *Women in War.* Episode in *Makers: Women Who Make America.* Arlington, VA: Public Broadcasting Service.

Gray, H. (2013). Subject(ed) to recognition. *American Quarterly, 65*(4), 771–198.

Hall, S. (1997). The work of representation. In S. Hall (Ed.), *Representation: Cultural representations and signifying practices* (pp. 13–74). London, UK: Sage.

Hall, S. (2001). The spectacle of the "Other." In M. Wetherell, S. Taylor, & S. J. Yates (Eds.), *Discourse theory and practice: A reader* (pp. 324–343). London, UK: Sage.

Haring, E. (2014, January 19). Opinion: Combat integration: Not bad, not good enough. *Army Times.* Retrieved March 24, 2014, from http://www.armytimes.com/article/20140119/NEWS01/301190003/Opinion-Combat-integration-Not-bad-not-good-enough.

Herdy A. & Moffeitt, M. (2004). *Betrayal in the ranks.* [Digital newsbook]. Denver, CO: The Denver Post.

Independent Lens. (2013, May 9). *Invisible War Director Kirby Dick on the Healing Power of Film*. Retrieved November 3, 2013, from http://www.pbs. org/independentlens/blog/invisible-war-filmmaker-kirby-dick.

iTunes (n.d.) DoD Safe Helpline. Retrieved June 15, 2015, from https://itunes. apple.com/us/app/dod-safe-helpline/id536773115?mt=8.

Jenkins, H., Ford, S., & Green, J. (2013). *Spreadable media: Creating value and meaning in a networked culture*. New York, NY: NYU Press.

Kim, J. (2012, June 18). *ReThink interview: Kirby Dick and Amy Ziering on THE INVISIBLE WAR*. Retrieved November 1, 2013, from http://www.youtube. com/watch?v=mHcuF7w3CQc.

Lamke, S. & Halleen, S. (2014, November 9). *Women Serving in War*. St. Paul, MN: Twin Cities PBS.

McLagan, M. & Sommers, D. (Directors and Producers). (2008). *Lioness*. [Motion picture]. United States: Room 11 Productions.

Meyer, L. D. (1996). *Creating GI Jane: Sexuality and power in the Women's Army Corps during World War II*. New York, NY: Columbia University Press.

NBC News (2014, January 10). Young male vets have triple the suicide rate of other US men, study shows. Retrieved October 24, 2015, from http://usnews. nbcnews.com/_news/2014/01/10/22257614-young-male-vets-have-triple-the-suicide-risk-of-other-us-men-study-shows?lite.

Patten, E. & Parker, K. (2011, December 22). *Women in the U.S. military: Growing share, distinctive profile*. Pew Research Center: Social & Demographic Trends. Retrieved July 13, 2014, from http://www.pewsocialtrends.org/files/2011/12/ women-in-the-military.pdf.

Rock, M. & Stotter, P. L. (Directors). (2012). *Service: When women come marching home*. [Motion picture]. United States: Women Make Movies.

Scarce, M. (2001). *Male on male rape: The hidden toll of stigma and shame*. Cambridge, MA: Perseus Publishing.

Sjoberg, L. (2014). *Gender, war, and conflict*. Cambridge, UK: Polity Press.

Squires, C. R. (2014). *The post-racial mystique: Media & race in the twenty-first century*. New York, NY: New York University Press.

Stahl, R. (2010). *Militainment, Inc: War, media, and popular culture*. New York, NY: Routledge.

Tasker, Y. (2011). *Soldiers' stories: Military women in cinema and television since World War II*. Durham, NC: Duke University Press.

Women's Research and Education Institute (WREI). (2013). *Women in the military: Where they stand* (8th ed.) Washington, DC: Women's Research and Education Institute (WREI).

Zarembo, A. (2015, June 8). Suicide rate of female military veterans is called "staggering." *LA Times*. Retrieved June 8, 2015, from http://www.latimes.com/ nation/la-na-female-veteran-suicide-20150608-story.html#page=1.

Zremski, J. (2014, February 9). Gillibrand's stature in capital skyrockets. *The Buffalo News.com*. Retrieved November 1, 2014, from http://www.buffalonews. com/apps/pbcs.dll/article?avis=BN&date=20140209&category=CITYANDRE GION&lopenr=140208926&Ref=AR&profile=1026&template=printart.

6

# NURTURING NEW MEN AND POLISHING IMPERFECT FATHERS VIA HETERO- AND HOMOSOCIAL RELATIONSHIPS IN PIXAR FILMS

*Bruce W. Finklea*

Woody and Buzz. Mike and Sulley. Lightning McQueen and Mater. WALL-E and EVE. These pairs of Pixar characters are integral to the children's media landscape, and millions of viewers probably cannot imagine any of them without their counterparts. These relationships, which are crucial to character development, are the driving forces for each Pixar films' plot. Children's media are widely regarded as "teaching machines" (Giroux, 1999, p. 84) and are "potent agents of socialization" (Bryant & Bryant, 2003, p. 204). Therefore, it is important to examine how these mainstream cultural texts depict interpersonal relationships, gender, and their interplay.

## Evolution of the New Man

In 1980, Goldberg argued that society has long taught men they were "at their best when a task has to be completed, a problem solved, or an enemy battled" (p. 9), and that men are caught in an isolating and emotionally repressive cycle of trying to conform to an ideal version of masculinity. However, such attempts are futile because the ideal version of masculinity is in a constant state of flux (Harris, 1995), and are ultimately harmful to "*all* men because they lose access to stigmatized parts of themselves—tenderness, nurturance, the desire for connection, the skills of cooperation—that are helpful in personal situations and needed for the social good" (Rotundo, 1993, p. 291, emphasis in original).

Also during the 1980s, many researchers argued that males were socialized into being less skilled at creating and maintaining close personal relationships, which was known as the male deficit model (Wood, 2015). However, as understanding of gender's influence on relationships developed, researchers began to see that men do create and maintain close relationships, but in different ways than females. The alternate path model proposes that men use different means to nurture close friendships, primarily through shared activities, instrumental reciprocity (i.e., exchanging favors), covert expressions of intimacy (e.g., teasing each other, friendly competitions, playful punches or backslaps), and by compartmentalizing activities they share with different men (Wood, 2015).

Goldberg's (1980) call for a new type of male was eventually answered in the 1990s as a model of masculinity arose that showed males expressing wide range of emotion and more actively engaging with and valuing their families and friends. This version of masculinity is known as the New Man (see Barthel, 1992; Gillam & Wooden, 2008; Jeffords, 1994, 1995; MacKinnon, 2003; Malin, 2005). Rather than relying on external signifiers of strength, New Men are valued for internal strength and their "moral rather than muscle fiber" (Jeffords, 1994, p. 136). This form of masculinity was prominently seen in American culture and the media during the end of the twentith century and into the 2000s (see Malin, 2005).

The New Man model was highly visible at the time of the Million Man March and the rise of the faith-based Promise Keepers movement, both of which focused on helping men break away from older forms of masculinity and embrace a more emotionally expressive and relationship-centered form of manhood (Bartowski, 2000; Heath, 2003; Poling & Kirkley, 2000).

As shifts in the understanding of masculinities were happening in the real world, portrayals of men in the media were also changing. The shift to the New Man model of masculinity in mainstream media in the early 1990s allowed audiences to see men who were no longer confined to the alpha male roles often depicted in the media of previous decades. Notably, these New Men expressed more emotion and valued their relationships with others. Numerous films in the early 1990s (e.g., *Kindergarten Cop*, *Beauty and the Beast*, and *Toy Story*) and 2000s (e.g., *The Incredibles*, *WALL-E*) depict American culture's shift from older, traditional masculinities toward the acceptance of the New Man. According to Jeffords (1994), *Kindergarten Cop*, starring Arnold Schwarzenegger, showed audiences that beneath the layers of rock-hard muscle is a man's tender emotional core. Jeffords (1994) said movie heroes of the 1980s were so driven by societal demands for career success that their personal lives and emotional wellbeing were ignored, which Goldberg (1980) said was happening to men in the real world. The isolating model of masculinity showed "real men" as lonely, unhappy, and in emotional pain (Jeffords, 1994). Whereas male characters of the 1980s once found happiness in their skills as company men, in the 1990s, happiness came from their role as a family man.

According to Jeffords, Beast in Disney's *Beauty and the Beast* illustrated that "masculinity has been betrayed by its own cultural imagery: what men thought they were supposed to be—strong, protective, powerful, commanding—has backfired" to become a curse for men, and the only way to break it is for men "to be nurtured until their 'true' goodness arises" (1995, p. 171). Further, the audience is also "implicated in this curse of hyper-masculinity . . . No one can be free until men are released from the curse of living under the burdens of traditional masculinities" (p. 171).

Jeffords (1994, 1995) argued that the film blames Beast's troubled masculinity on the external factors of his upbringing and societal expectations. She equated Beast to a spoiled child who was not taught any manners. Belle teaches him how to behave properly, enabling him to shed his brutish behaviors and become a kinder, loving New Man. Meanwhile, pre-New Man models of masculinity are further rejected when Gaston—a muscular, domineering ladies' man and the film's main villain—fails to transform into a New Man and later dies during a fight with Beast. Trice and Holland concluded that *Beauty and the Beast* gives audiences unambiguous messages about masculinity, all of which are New Man traits: "Men should be kind, not selfish; they should be brave in defense of others, not gratuitously violent; and they should treat women with respect and as their intellectual equals, not as minions" (2001, p. 188).

Pixar's transformations of the iconic American cowboy in *Toy Story* and super hero in *The Incredibles* into New Men also illustrate the shift in mediated masculinities. Gillam and Wooden found male protagonists in *Toy Story*, *The Incredibles*, and *Cars* follow a similar "narrative trajectory" (2008, p. 3) as they become New Men. Each is or seeks to become the alpha male, but suffers emasculation. Each then bonds with another male character in a homosocial friendship while pursuing a feminized object or set of values, and eventually learns what it means to be a kinder, emotionally aware man.

These narrative patterns show audiences that New Men's strength is not purely physical, but rather, is derived from having a cohesive family unit (whether biological or not) and signified through cooperation, intelligence, and selflessness. Whereas Gillam and Wooden (2008) observed close homosocial relationships as instrumental in New Man transformations, Decker (2010) found that female characters can also serve as catalysts of change for male protagonists, similar to Jeffords' (1994, 1995) analysis of Belle's relationship with Beast. However, Decker noted these relationships are not always romantic (e.g., the child–caregiver dyad of Boo and Sully in *Monsters, Inc.* and platonic friendship between Marlin and Dory in *Finding Nemo*).

Later Pixar films, such as 2008's *WALL-E,* depict a male protagonist already functioning as a New Man (Bernard, 2011). The film reverses some gender stereotypes by showing the male-coded WALL-E as emotional, hopelessly romantic, and interested in holding hands, whereas female-coded EVE is seen as aggressive, unemotional, and focused on her job (Bernard, 2011). However, Long (2011) questioned WALL-E's acceptance as a New Man, noting his behavior is often viewed as childlike, which may prevent it from being interpreted as feminine.

## Pixar Males Become Better Friends and Family Men

This chapter extends prior research to determine whether the New Man narrative is evident in other Pixar films, and if so to compare the narrative trajectories of New Men in those other films to the films analyzed by Gillam and Wooden (2008). I also examine the Pixar films not included in Decker's (2010) analysis to determine whether females catalyze change in male characters, and if so how. I am additionally interested in comparing how lessons about masculinities differ in the narrative contexts of female-inspired change and male homosocial bonds. Finally, how are male protagonists depicted in the absence of a New Man narrative or transformation?

To answer these questions, I conducted a qualitative analysis of all 13 Pixar films released through June, 2012.[1] I approached each film as a separate case (Creswell, 2007; Stake, 2005; Yin, 2003); I identified key features in each case, followed by examining the cases for any common themes among them (Yin, 2003).

I viewed each film at least three times, completing a narrative analysis worksheet and making extensive descriptive notes for each film. I examined each film's male protagonist and the primary relationship he establishes during the film, whether homosocial (male–male) or heterosocial (male–female), and how those relationships affected the male characters. I looked for the development of New Man characteristics for the protagonist in each film, while also examining protagonists who do not undergo a New Man transformation. Throughout these Pixar films, each male character who changes into a New Man does so as a result of his interactions with other characters. No male character is depicted as catalyzing his own change. Therefore, similar to Gillam and Wooden (2008) and Decker's (2010) observations, a male's transformation is the result of a relationship with someone else.

### *Transformative Homosocial Narratives*

In their analysis, Gillam and Wooden (2008) identified three homosocial friendships resulting in protagonists' transformation into New Men in *Toy Story*, *The Incredibles*, and *Up*. My analysis of all Pixar films released through 2012 revealed similar narratives in *Up*, *Ratatouille*, and *Cars 2*. I found these additional homosocial bonds also aligned with the three key characteristics of Pixar's New Man narratives first identified by Gillam and Wooden: (1) male protagonists undergo some form of emasculation, (2) protagonists form a cooperative relationship with another male character in pursuit of a feminized object, and (3) these relationships transform the protagonist into a New Man who values bonds with friends and family.

## Threats of Emasculation

Protagonists in each of these narratives experiences some form of emasculation. *Up*'s Carl Fredricksen's masculine identity is threatened first by the loss of his wife, Ellie, and later by a judge ordering him to give up his isolated, independent lifestyle by moving into a retirement home. *Ratatouille*'s protagonists, Remy and Linguini, are also emasculated. The duo only achieves alpha status by working together, but when jealously drives them apart, Linguini puts Remy in the alley behind the kitchen, essentially reminding Remy of his place as a rat. Linguini is emasculated when he fails to inspire his kitchen staff to cook on the night of food critic Anton Ego's visit to the restaurant.

*Cars 2*'s Lightning McQueen struggles to balance his public and private lives after his initial New Man transformation in *Cars*. In public, McQueen still very much embodies an alpha male role. His racing career reiterates Old Man qualities such as dominance and physical superiority, but in private he is a New Man engaged in friendships and a romantic relationship. McQueen's dichotomous identity mirrors Jeffords's (1994) analysis of the Batman/Bruce Wayne character. She categorized Batman as the public face of masculinity displaying stereotypical Old Man qualities (e.g., toughness, strength, being a loner), while Bruce Wayne's private life is filled with emotion, mainly because of the lifelong grief stemming from the murder of his parents. *Cars 2* focuses on the conflict that arises for McQueen when his public and private lives collide on a global stage, and he struggles to commit to either portrayal of masculinity.

Initially, McQueen declines to race in the World Grand Prix because he wants to spend time with his friends and girlfriend in Radiator Springs, a decision reflecting how New Men value and invest time in relationships. However, fellow racecar Francesco Bernoulli, who is clearly jockeying for alpha male superiority, publicly criticizes McQueen for wanting to rest and spend time at home, presenting these choices as a sign of inferiority. Not wanting to be seen as either slow or weak, McQueen agrees to race. He soon faces another threat of emasculation from his best friend, Mater, whose hillbilly hijinks while traveling overseas embarrass McQueen and cost him a leg of the race. McQueen's struggle to preserve his public persona clashes with his New Man sensibilities, and he yells at Mater, saying that he does not want or need Mater's help. In McQueen's desperation to maintain his public image, he realigns with Old Man masculinity both by asserting overconfidence in his own abilities and by isolating himself from his closest friend. Despite McQueen's regression to a more independent, isolated, aggressive version of masculinity, he soon regrets his outburst and desires to fix his friendship with Mater.

## Bonds of Brotherhood Focus on the Feminine

As outlined by Gillam and Wooden (2008), protagonists in New Man narratives bond with another male in their pursuit of a female character or feminized object. None of these pairings is initially sought. In *Up*, Carl's interaction with Russell, who was under Carl's porch when the house began to fly, is coincidental. Remy and Linguini encounter each other out of happenstance in *Ratatouille*. In the first *Cars*, McQueen's initial interactions with Mater are not of his own choosing. (In fact, McQueen repeatedly tries speeding away to avoid interacting.) In the sequel, Sally must convince McQueen to take Mater with him for the race.

The bonds between these characters are sometimes depicted as literal and pragmatic. Carl and Russell are physically connected by a garden hose as they walk the floating house to the waterfall. Carl needs Russell's weight to keep the house from floating away. Linguini and Remy are only able to work together when the rat controls the human by pulling on his hair, as if he is a marionette. Although these characteristics of their bonds advance specific plot points, they also lay the groundwork for the emotional connections triggering New Man transformations.

Each of these narratives also focuses on the protagonists' feminized goals. Carl's focus is fulfilling Ellie's lifelong dream to move to South America. Linguini seeks romantic involvement with his fellow chef, Colette, and Remy wants to pursue his love of cooking. Meanwhile, McQueen's struggle between his New Man and Old Man personas is reflected in his desires. He wants relationships with Sally and Mater but also longs for the title of the fastest racecar in the world—and the latter can only be achieved at the expense of the former.

Another key aspect of the bonds in these films is that they must benefit both partners. Teamwork in Pixar films is viewed positively, unless it is for selfish reasons (Finklea, 2014), and these films clearly illustrate the pitfalls of teamwork for the sake of personal benefit. Carl uses Russell to move the house, but his singular focus on fulfilling Ellie's dream ends up driving Russell away. Linguini uses his apparent cooking skills to impress Colette, but this leads to resentment from Remy, resulting in the aforementioned emasculation. Lightning McQueen rejects teamwork with

Mater, which results in seriously damaging their friendship. Of course, all of these conflicts are resolved, and the partners learn how to live with each other in ways that are mutually beneficial.

### Finally Finding Family and Friends

*Up*, *Ratatouille*, and *Cars 2* end with the male protagonists developing deeper relationships with friends or family. Carl takes on the paternal role that Russell desperately seeks, and Russell eventually fills the void left by Carl and Ellie's infertility. However, Carl does not realize this until they complete his initial goal of landing the house at Paradise Falls, which is when Russell leaves on his own to try and rescue Kevin the bird. Only when Carl sits alone in the house does he realizes that moving the house brought him no closer to Ellie, freeing him to start a new adventure by helping Russell. This transition from devotion to Ellie to Russell marks a pivotal point in Carl's New Man transformation. He figuratively and literally lets go of the past and openly embraces his future. His newfound devotion to Russell is evidence that Carl has become emotionally connected to him.

Carl's friendship with Russell evolves into a deeper paternal connection. At the film's conclusion, Carl takes part in Russell's Wilderness Explorer ceremony with the other dads. The final scene shows the two at the ice cream parlor Russell used to visit with his father. Carl's transformation from a grumpy, isolated, elderly man into a kind, involved grandfatherly figure completes his New Man narrative.

*Ratatouille* concludes by showing that Linguini and Remy are successful when they work jobs at their new restaurant that are natural fits for their talents. Linguini is certainly not a chef, but he is a good waiter. Likewise, cooking is most satisfying for Remy when he is able to cook with his own paws, rather than having to hide beneath Linguini's toque. Both characters are happy and fully embrace who they are. Their transformations show true fulfillment and friendship can only happen once someone is free to completely express all facets of his or her personality, rather than repressing parts of oneself, as outlined by Rotundo (1993).

*Cars 2* also resolves the tension between Mater and McQueen, who apologizes and tells Mater that he will never push him away again. The two mend their friendship, and McQueen once again aligns himself with New Man masculinity. McQueen learns that maintaining his public hyper-masculine persona is not worth losing the personal relationships brought about through his initial New Man transformation.

### Transformative Heterosocial Narratives

New Man transformations are not catalyzed solely by friendships with male characters. Decker (2010) identified heterosocial pairings that result in becoming a New Man (e.g., Sulley and Boo in *Monsters, Inc.*, and Marlin and Dory in *Finding Nemo*). My analysis revealed a transformative heterosocial narrative (involving Francis the ladybug in *A Bug's Life*) not identified in Decker's study.

Similarly to Sulley in *Monsters, Inc.* and Carl in *Up*, Francis undergoes a transformation because of his interaction with children, in this case a Girl Scout-like troop of young female ants called the Blueberries. However, there is no child–caregiver relationship as in *Monsters, Inc.* or platonic friendship as observed in *Finding Nemo*. The Blueberries simply keep Francis company as he recovers, and his interactions are primarily limited to playing card games with them.

### "She's a guy!": Emasculation of the Feminine Male

As with many of Pixar's transformative narratives, Francis is first established as embodying several characteristics of Old Man masculinity, especially being overly aggressive. Francis is performing with a troupe of circus bugs when two flies in the audience mistake him for a female.

Fly One:  Hey, cutie! Wanna pollinate with a real bug? [Francis flies toward him.] Oh, come to papa!

Francis:  So, bein' a ladybug automatically makes me a girl? Is that it, flyboy? Huh?

Fly Two:  Yikes!

Fly One:  She's a guy!

In addition to having a gender-neutral name, Francis is also one of very few male characters with eyelashes, which is a characteristic primarily seen on animated female characters (see Decker, 2010; Wiersma, 2001). Francis, no doubt, acts in a hyper-masculine manner to compensate for the constant emasculation of being mistaken for a female. Francis is further emasculated when he is injured while rescuing Princess Dot. To make matters worse, he is taken to the ants' infirmary, where numerous characters assume he is female. Blueberry members call him "Miss Francis" and elect him as their "honorary den mother." A doctor also mistakes Francis for a female after seeing how the children flock to him, saying, "Oh, look. She's a natural mother."

### In Touch with His "Feminine Side"

Because Francis is not a main character, we do not get an in-depth look at the transformative process, but it is evident that through his interaction with the Blueberries, he changes into a New Man. The other circus bugs notice a difference in Francis later in the film, with one saying Francis

96

has "gotten in touch with his feminine side." Coding Francis's newfound softer masculinity as feminine mirrors Brydon's (2009) analysis of Marlin from *Finding Nemo* in which she concluded his emotionally expressive actions were indicators of being a mother, rather than a father. In addition to the toys in *Toy Story 3* making fun of Ken for being a "girl's toy," these mark the only instances in the narratives and in scholarship about Pixar where gender is viewed as a rigid, immutable concept.

Later, when the circus bugs leave Ant Island after defeating the grass-hoppers, the Blueberries gather around Francis, hugging him and crying. Francis fights back tears and says, "I'm not gonna cry." This is a major change from his characterization at the beginning of the film. Francis now displays vulnerability and talks about his affinity for the Blueberries. These character developments clearly signify Francis's transformation into a New Man.

### Comparing Transformative Homosocial and Heterosocial Narratives

Examining Pixar's narratives reveals that, as with the predominant use of male protagonists (Gillam & Wooden, 2008; Decker, 2010), trans-formative homosocial narratives greatly outnumber heterosocial ones. Homosocial New Man narratives were found in *Toy Story*, *The Incredibles*, *Cars*, *Ratatouille*, *Up*, and *Cars 2*, and heterosocial narratives were found in *A Bug's Life*, *Monsters, Inc.*, and *Finding Nemo*. Differences between the two narrative forms are apparent. Homosocial narratives show male characters learning a much wider variety of lessons (e.g., learning the value of teamwork, friendship, or family; how to express emotions; and how to be yourself) from their transformation into New Men. Meanwhile, het-erosocial narratives are primarily limited to helping males become better fathers or father figures. Thus, Pixar's heterosocial narratives, although empowering females with the ability to instigate change in male characters, are ultimately limited to family matters.

### Prepping for Paternity and Fixing Faulty Fathers

Both *Monsters, Inc.* and *A Bug's Life* show males (i.e., Sulley and Francis, respectively) coming in touch with paternal instincts that were unseen until their heterosocial interactions with children. Both males already have close friendships. Sulley and Mike Wazowski are best friends, and Francis has lots of friends in the circus troupe. However, neither initially exhibits paternal instincts. In *Finding Nemo*, Marlin learns how to become a bet-ter father through his interactions with Dory. Her fearless approach to life is the exact opposite of Marlin's overly cautious parenting style, but their friendship helps him adapt to Nemo's growing independence.

Although females are primarily limited to helping males transform into better family men, that type of transformative narrative is not catalyzed only by females. Mr. Incredible's adversarial homosocial relationship with Syndrome results in his becoming a better husband and father. Seeing how Buddy Pine grew up to become Syndrome shows Mr. Incredible the effects of a child lacking an involved male role model—the child, now an adult, still seeks the attention of his masculine idol. As a result, Mr. Incredible becomes more involved in his children's lives and a more attentive husband. Before his interaction with Syndrome, Mr. Incredible functions as a male torn between the old and new models of masculinity. Although he still embodies some stereotypical alpha male behaviors (e.g., not being emotionally expressive; being emotionally isolated from his family), he does show some characteristics of the New Man (e.g., his close friendship with Frozone, expressing compassion for a widow). Syndrome unwittingly teaches Mr. Incredible to overcome his emotional detachment from his family and to value the support (both emotional and physical) his family provides, which were the last hurdles to Mr. Incredible becoming a fully realized New Man. The most significant impact of Mr. Incredible's transformation is on his familial roles of father and husband, not on his public role as a super hero.

## Making Modern Males

Up, which presents the only homosocial transformative narrative featuring an adult and a child, illustrates a transformation grounded in the broader themes of New Man masculinity, not a focus on fatherhood. Although Carl does become a grandfatherly figure to Russell, Up's plot focuses on Carl's overall transformation into a New Man. At the end of the film, Carl is emotionally expressive, has learned the importance of teamwork, and values his relationship with Russell. He is no longer the isolated loner he had resigned himself to be. Carl's interaction with Russell helps heal the emotional wounds caused by Ellie's death and teaches him the value of opening oneself up to new relationships. This major shift aligns Carl's transformation more closely with becoming a New Man in general, rather than fixating on his role as a father figure, despite his ongoing involvement in Russell's life.

The remainder of Pixar's films with homosocial New Man narratives (i.e., Toy Story, The Incredibles, Cars, Ratatouille, Up, and Cars 2) also display a wider range of lessons learned by male protagonists. These lessons include expressing emotion, the value of teamwork and friendship, accepting one's own limitations, and not acting selfishly. Unlike the heterosocial narratives, these broader lessons focus on how males should relate to all people, not just their own family members. These lessons are also shown to help male characters attract the attention of potential female romantic partners.

Thus, homosocial narratives' lessons are overwhelmingly shown as essential for a male to become a desirable mate who is worthy of a romantic relationship, whereas the lessons in the heterosocial narratives fine tune these New Men into what could be termed "New Fathers."

## Male Protagonists Who Do Not Undergo Transformation

Some Pixar films do not feature transformative narratives for male protagonists. In *Toy Story 2* and *Toy Story 3*, Woody and Buzz continue to function as the New Men they became in the first film. *Brave*, the first Pixar film about a female protagonist, does not feature the transformation of a male protagonist. Thus, Flik from *A Bug's Life* and WALL-E are the only male protagonists not depicted in alpha male roles, nor do they undergo any type of transformative narrative. Instead, they become agents of change for other characters.

### Characteristics of the Non-Transformed Male

Flik and WALL-E's non-alpha male status does not mean they function as New Men. Unlike Bernard's (2011) evaluation of WALL-E, which concluded he already functions as a New Man, WALL-E and Flik do not initially exhibit the inherent dominance and authority of the New Man. Heath referred to the power still held by the New Man as "soft patriarchy" (2003, p. 436), in which men still enjoy the privilege of masculine power and are shown in positions of authority; however, any aggression or hyper-masculinity related to that authority appears tempered by the incorporation of what are stereotypically viewed as feminine qualities (e.g., emotional expression, high engagement with one's family) into portrayals of masculinities (Bartowski, 2000; Heath, 2003). Neither WALL-E nor Flik display this type of authority. Flik is subservient to the matriarchal rule of the colony, and WALL-E eagerly follows EVE's commands. Therefore, neither character initially operates as a New Man.

However, they do share some character traits with other Pixar protagonists, including those functioning as New Men. Both of these characters exhibit bravery, thus implying that bravery is a natural male characteristic (Finklea, 2014). Additionally, both characters express romantic desire toward females, which firmly places them in a heteronormative framework removing doubt about these non-alphas' sexuality (Finklea, 2014), which counters Long's (2011) assertion that WALL-E is construed as childlike to keep from being viewed as feminine.

Moreover, these characters already show a wide range of emotions, which is a trait not often expressed by Pixar protagonists until they experience emasculation. Flik expresses his feelings of inadequacy to Princess Dot when telling her that he wants to make a difference in the colony, and his romantic feelings toward Princess Atta are obvious. Meanwhile, WALL-E is perhaps the most emotionally expressive of all of Pixar's protagonists. He openly expresses fear, curiosity, romantic longing, happiness, concern for others, and many other emotions.

Another characteristic these characters share both with each other and with other male protagonists is their devotion to others. Flik repeatedly tries to improve living conditions for everyone in the colony. This is first seen when he is introduced trying to persuade colony officials to use his new harvesting machine. It is also reflected in his choice to voluntarily leave the safety of the island to search for bugs to help them fight the grasshoppers. Like Flik, WALL-E expresses a deep devotion toward others; however, it is primarily directed toward EVE.

Both Flik and WALL-E align with Goldberg's (1980) assertion that society often shows that men are at their best when they have a task to complete or a problem to solve. Flik wants to solve the problem of inefficient harvesting techniques and complete the task of protecting the colony from the grasshoppers, and WALL-E devotes himself to the task of compacting garbage, following and rescuing EVE, and eventually helping her complete her mission. At first glance, it seems ironic that these two non-transformed males so strongly embody this aspect of outdated ideas about masculinity, but even their commitment to problem solving and task completion shows their devotion and concern for others. They both work to better the lives of others, not themselves.

## Comparisons of Non-Transformative Narratives

WALL-E and Flik's characterizations as non-stereotypical males help drive their films' plots. This is done by positioning them as underdogs who are unhappy with traditional aspects of Old Man masculinity. For example, WALL-E strongly desires a relationship, which is reflected by his obsession with romantic sequences in *Hello, Dolly!* and his ongoing quest to hold EVE's hand. Unlike the images of men preferring to be alone, which are often associated with pre-New Man media (see Jeffords, 1994), WALL-E is not happy with his isolated existence and actively seeks out interaction with EVE. His longing for her companionship drives the majority of the film's plot. Similarly, Flik's desire to break with the traditions of the ant colony lead him to build his harvesting machine, challenge Hopper, and leave the island. The overwhelming odds against Flik's success clearly place him in an underdog role.

The audience is reminded of WALL-E and Flik's non-alpha status by depicting their subservience to females. EVE is clearly dominant, both in terms of personality and technology (Long, 2011), and Flik lives in a matriarchal ant colony ruled by a queen and two princesses. Yet, in both of these films, the male protagonists cause female characters to change, thus further reinforcing patriarchal power. This is most evident in *WALL-E*. EVE is shown as aggressive and uninterested in a romantic relationship with WALL-E for the majority of the film. Through EVE's interactions with WALL-E, however, her character changes, and she becomes caring and nurturing toward him (Bernard, 2011). Long (2011) interpreted this behavior as almost motherly. However, my reading of their relationship is that EVE's behavior was always more romantic than maternal. Despite these different opinions, changes in EVE can be directly attributed to WALL-E's influence. Pixar's depiction of EVE's transformation could send the message that her initial strong, unromantic personality is not acceptable for females (Finklea & Hardig, 2016).

Additionally, Flik is responsible for helping Princess Atta transition into power. The princess is unsure of herself, unable to make quick decisions, and scared of Hopper and his gang. Despite her royal status, she is uncomfortable in a position of power. It is Flik (the commoner) who exhibits bravery and the abilities to act decisively and take charge. Ultimately, because of Flik, Atta becomes more comfortable with her role as future queen.

*A Bug's Life* and *WALL-E* take two different approaches to the influence of males on female characters. Pixar depicts EVE's aggressive personality as in need of softening, and Princess Atta is shown as unsure of herself when in a position of authority. Although presenting these females in positions of power is to be commended, these examples of female power are undercut by the need for male guidance and influence. Giving these relatively powerless males some level of influence once again asserts hegemonic ideals about masculine authority into the narratives and establishes them as New Men. Pixar sends a message that females cannot have power without the help of a male, which further reinforces the stereotypes that males are the true leaders.

Flik and WALL-E provide important examples of how Pixar not only constructs masculinities, but also of how the influence of patriarchy limits the achievements of females by making them dependent upon the help and influence of males. Overall, Flik and WALL-E share many characteristics of the New Men seen in other films, but neither has the inherent dominance that New Men traditionally still exhibit until the final moments of each film. Moreover, because they do not have dominance or authority for the vast majority of their narratives, they neither suffer emasculation as do other male Pixar protagonists, nor are extensively influenced by females as Sulley and Marlin are. Therefore, their narrative trajectories differ from New Man narratives observed in other Pixar films.

## Promoting Family-Friendly Patriarchy

Analysis of Pixar's film collection reveals the company's heavy reliance on variations of the New Man model observed by Gillam and Wooden

(2008) and Decker (2010). Routinely, Pixar depicts males' homosocial narratives more prominently than heterosocial narratives, thus maintaining patriarchal and hegemonic control by continuing to restrict the presence and power of female characters.

Although the reasons for this type of storytelling are beyond the scope of this chapter, it is possible the homosocial narrative is deeply ingrained in Pixar's storytelling because it closely mirrors how the studio produces films. Pixar president Ed Catmull described the studio's peer-driven film-making process, saying, "There are really two leaders: the director and the producer. They form a strong partnership" (Catmull, 2008, p. 68). Pixar's predominantly male director-producer teams also seek out what could be conceptualized as a feminized object (i.e., the film goes through a cycle similar to pregnancy: conception, development, and delivery), just as outlined by Gillam and Wooden's (2008) New Man narratives.

Future analyses of these films may result in different conclusions, but the themes discussed in this chapter are prevalent. Hall (1980) said preferred readings of a text or discourse are ingrained with rules and standards of how a particular culture works. The company entices audiences to accept cultural standards presented on the silver screen as being natural and right. These messages clearly resonate with global audiences who continue to make each Pixar release a box office success. Although the prevalence of the New Man model is commendable, female characters have overwhelmingly been downplayed or ignored. Pixar's various narratives show audiences a variety of males capable of changing into New Men, a change that is always seen as a positive character development. These characters range in age, occupation, and marital status, but one thing they have in common is that none is capable of transformation without the influence of another character. This further distances these New Men from older models of masculinity that depicted males as having all the skills necessary to be self-sufficient (Wood, 2015).

Additionally, Pixar shows some male protagonists who do not transform, and, in fact, empowers them to become agents of change for females. Whereas male homosocial bonds result in a sweeping change into a New Man, female catalysts' involvement with fine-tuning males into better fathers or father figures confines their influence primarily to the domestic realm. Limiting females' influence to familial contexts mirrors findings that show women in the real world are expected to assume responsibility for domestic issues (Wood, 2015).

Lip service is paid to the notion of strong female characters. For example, many people celebrated Brave's Princess Merida's refusal to marry any of the suitors, and although she is given the power to choose, it is with the implicit understanding that she is merely delaying the inevitable. Eventually, she will conform to patriarchal expectations by marrying (Finklea, 2014; Finklea & Hardig, 2016). Females in positions of power and authority are depicted as needing a male's guidance and help to acclimate to a position of power or to soften an aggressive demeanor. As a result, Pixar consistently aligns its films with hegemonic frameworks that show males in positions of authority and influence, while largely subjugating females into secondary roles and showing them relying on males. Although mass audiences may think these female characters are shattering gender barriers, we see that these acts are clearly confined within the bounds of patriarchy, which ultimately is not challenged by these portrayals because of the way males—even as New Men—are still given power, authority, and the love of a woman.

## Note

1 The films analyzed are: *Toy Story* (1995), *A Bug's Life* (1998), *Toy Story 2* (1999), *Monsters, Inc.* (2001), *Finding Nemo* (2003), *The Incredibles* (2004), *Cars* (2006), *Ratatouille* (2007), *WALL-E* (2008), *Up* (2009), *Toy Story 3* (2010), *Cars 2* (2011), and *Brave* (2012). These films had a collective domestic box office haul of more than $3.26 billion with an average of $250 million per film, by October, 2015 (BoxOfficeMojo.com, 2015), which is evidence of their ongoing cultural appeal to mass audiences.

## References

Barthel, D. (1992). When men put on appearances: Advertising and the social construction of masculinity. In S. Craig (Ed.), *Men, masculinity, and the media* (pp. 137–153). Newbury Park, CA: Sage.

Bartowski, J. P. (2000). Breaking walls, raising fences: Masculinity, intimacy, and accountability among the Promise Keepers. *Sociology of Religion, 61*, 33–53.

Bernard, C. A. (2011). Performing gender, performing romance: Pixar's *WALL-E*. In R. C. Neighbors & S. Rankin (Eds.). *The galaxy is rated G: Essays on children's science fiction and television* (pp. 53–63). Jefferson, NC: McFarland.

Box Office Mojo. (April 2015) *Pixar*. Retrieved October 17, 2015, from http://www.boxofficemojo.com/franchises/chart/?id=pixar.htm.

Bryant, J. A., & Bryant, J. (2003). Effects of entertainment televisual media on children. In E. L. Palmer & B. M. Young (Eds.), *The faces of televisual media: Teaching, violence, selling to children* (2nd ed.) (pp. 195–217). Mahwah, NJ: Lawrence Erlbaum Associates.

Brydon, S. G. (2009). Men at the heart of mothering: Finding mother in *Finding Nemo. Journal of Gender Studies, 18*, 131–146.

Catmull, E. (2008). How Pixar fosters collective creativity. *Harvard Business Review, 86*(9), 64–72.

Creswell, J. W. (2007) *Qualitative inquiry & research design: Choosing among five approaches* (2nd ed.). Thousand Oaks, CA: Sage.

Decker, J. T. (2010). *The portrayal of gender in the feature-length films of Pixar animation studios: A content analysis* (Master's thesis). Auburn University, Auburn, Alabama. Retrieved October 17, 2015, from https://etd.auburn.edu/bitstream/handle/10415/2100/Jonathan%20Decker%20Thesis%20Final.pdf?sequence=2.

Finklea, B. W. (2014). *Examining masculinities in Pixar's feature films: What it means to be a boy, whether human, fish, car, or toy* (Doctoral Dissertation). Retrieved October 17, 2015, from http://acumen.lib.ua.edu/content/u0015/0000001/0001518/u0015_0000001_0001518.pdf.

Finklea, B. W., & Hardig, S. B. (2016). Seen but not heard: Exploring muted group theory in Pixar's *The Incredibles, WALL-E,* and *Brave.* In K. G. Roberts (Ed.), *Communication theory and millennial popular culture: Essays and applications* (pp. 119–127). New York, NY: Peter Lang.

Gillam, K., & Wooden, S. R. (2008). Post-princess models of gender: The new man in Disney/Pixar. *Journal of Popular Film and Television, 36,* 2–8.

Giroux, H. A. (1999). *The mouse that roared: Disney and the end of innocence.* Lanham, MD: Rowman & Littlefield.

Goldberg, H. (1980). *The new male.* New York, NY: Signet.

Hall, S. (2005). *Representation & the media.* [Video transcript]. Retrieved October 17, 2015, from the Media Education Foundation Web site: https://www.mediaed.org/assets/products/409/transcript_409.pdf.

Hall, S. (1980). Encoding/decoding. In S. Hall, D. Hobson, A. Love, & P. Willis (Eds.), *Culture, media, language* (pp. 128–138). London, UK: Hutchinson.

Harris, I. M. (1995). *Messages men hear: Constructing masculinities.* London, UK: Taylor & Francis.

Heath, M. (2003). Soft-boiled masculinity: Renegotiating gender and racial ideologies in the Promise Keepers movement. *Gender & Society, 17,* 423–444.

Jeffords, S. (1994). *Hard bodies: Hollywood masculinity in the Reagan era.* New Brunswick, NJ: Rutgers University Press.

Jeffords, S. (1995). The curse of masculinity: Disney's *Beauty and the Beast.* In E. Bell, L. Haas, & L. Sells (Eds.) *From mouse to mermaid: The politics of film, gender, and culture* (pp. 161–172). Bloomington: Indiana University Press.

Long, B. A.-M. (2011). *Creating gender in Disney/Pixar's* WALL-E (Honors thesis). Retrieved April 3, 2015, from http://dc.etsu.edu/honors/149/.

MacKinnon, K. (2003). *Representing men: Maleness and masculinity in the media.* London, UK: Arnold.

Malin, B. J. (2005). *American masculinity under Clinton: Popular media and the Nineties "crisis of masculinity."* New York, NY: Peter Lang.

Poling, J. N., & Kirkley, E. A. (2000). Phallic spirituality: Masculinities in Promise Keepers, the Million Man March, and sex panic. *Theology & Sexuality, 12,* 9–25.

Rotundo, E. A. (1993). *American manhood: Transformation in masculinity from the revolution to the modern era.* New York, NY: BasicBooks.

Stake, R. E. (2005). Qualitative case studies. In N. K. Denzin & Y. S. Lincoln (Eds.), *The Sage handbook of qualitative research* (3rd ed.) (pp. 443–466). Thousand Oaks, CA: Sage.

Trice, A. D., & Holland, S. A. (2001). *Heroes, antiheroes and dolts: Portrayals of masculinity in American popular films, 1921–1999.* Jefferson, NC: McFarland.

Wiersma, B. A. (2001). *The gendered world of Disney: A content analysis of gender themes in full-length animated Disney feature films.* (Doctoral dissertation). Retrieved from UMI. (UMI number: 99973222).

Wood, J. T. (2015). *Gendered lives: Communication, gender and culture* (11th ed.). Boston, MA: Wadsworth.

Yin, R. K. (2003). *Case study research: Design and method* (3rd ed.). Thousand Oaks, CA: Sage.

# 7

# THE BLIND GAZE OF THE ZOMBIE NORMALIZES THE LANDSCAPE

## Killing Off Inequalities When Walking Among the Undead

*Kim Baker*

Images of zombies roaming the remnants of society in search of a human meal may seem an unlikely landscape to detect inequalities that exist in our culture; yet, the television show *The Walking Dead* (*TWD*) does indeed provide the opportunity to analyze stereotypes and power relationships. The effects of media depictions interwoven into our newscasts, films, television shows, music, video games, and social media are key concerns to many media scholars. Experiences with media characters affect how we perceive the world and others (e.g., Strasburger, Wilson, & Jordan, 2009). Media depictions relay assumptions about race and gender and demonstrate continued power disparities. Mastro proposed that "mass media can serve as a powerful mechanism for re-shaping and re-defining social reality to redress current inequities," (2009, p. 337), but spotting examples thereof can be difficult. Shugart (2011) claimed that visibility in itself does not equate to accurate portrayals of disenfranchised groups; indeed, representations of marginalized groups may actually reinforce social stratification. Thus, our media experiences may both reflect and perpetuate cultural inequalities.

Based on McKerrow's (1989) principles guiding critical analyses, this chapter evaluates the first five seasons of *TWD* as a discourse of power (see Foucault, 1980). The *TWD* series represents a world in which societal structures and hegemony are exposed and old prejudices discarded. Those who cling to beliefs about racial and gender stereotypes become examples of how not to survive. Indeed, it is the sudden collapse of society and ensuing chaos that demonstrates how an egalitarian system emerges through necessity. In this chapter, after discussing the analytic approach and value of *TWD* as a cultural artifact, I review how *TWD* and its use of power symbols reflects society and propose how *TWD* characters (and we viewers in turn) eventually adopt a freed gaze among the blind gaze of the zombies—thus, recognizing and confronting stereotypical gender and racial roles.

## Dismantling Power in the World of *The Walking Dead*

McKerrow's (1989) principles for critical discourse serve as apt guidelines for highlighting the complexities of power in *TWD* obtained both through normative consent and physical coercion (see Therborn, 1980). In considering ideologies, an exploration of dominant power and the supporting web of rituals and rules legitimizing, maintaining, and normalizing social structures becomes important in uncovering the themes of discourse (McKerrow, 1989). In the quest to uncover dominance and present the means by which change may potentially be enacted, McKerrow offered eight principles to guide critical analyses. These provide a framework with which to analyze *TWD* as a Foucauldian discourse and consider how power in society is demonstrated and reinforced.

McKerrow's (1989) first principle is that understanding and evaluating are integral to the practice of critical analyses. *TWD* provides a rich text of varied storylines and complex characters, requiring multiple viewings to note the obvious and subtle ways in which ideologies are exposed. Second, McKerrow acknowledged the material power of discourse with agents able to modify discourse within existing ideologies. The abrupt downfall of society in *TWD* highlights initial belief systems and the characters' attempts to adapt for survival. Third, McKerrow stated that the transformative activity of critical rhetoric constitutes reasoning about beliefs rather than knowledge (i.e., doxastic as compared to epistemic). *TWD* characters demonstrate the struggle of discarding what they know to embrace changes for adapting to their new world. McKerrow also acknowledged the power of naming and advocated a nominalist rhetoric, as well as noting the difference between influence and causality. Throughout the seasons of *TWD*, symbolism is used to demonstrate what was and what is important; differences are often presented as influencing but not necessarily causing characters' actions. McKerrow also stressed that understanding and evaluating that which is not included in symbolic acts are as important as recognizing what is present. Finally, he argued that interpretations should recognize the possibility of polysemic interpretations, and that criticism can be considered performance. Combined, the framework guides my interpretations of power, gender, and race in *TWD*.

Foucault (1977/1980) discussed the individual as restrained both physically and mentally within the confines of governmental control and social structures. Incorporating Bentham's (1791) ideas of a panopticon (i.e., an idealized prison designed to situate prisoners around a central monitoring tower), Foucault (1977) explained the process of power for an increasingly modernized society. Power is obtained through the central tower because of the belief that we are consistently being watched regardless of whether a seer is present; also, people are cogs in power machinery, both trapped within and playing an integral part in its continued existence. Unlike prior societies in which power may have been obtained through physical dominance and harsh punishments, Foucault (1977) described modern societies as maintaining power through a bureaucracy of rules and an increased reliance on others to provide basic needs (e.g., growing food, building shelter). In such societies, symbols reinforce power and promote obedience (Foucault, 1980). Foucault (1977) sought to understand how symbols demonstrate technological changes and differentiate a society from past cultures. Informed by McKerrow's (1989) principles and Foucault's (1980) work regarding power, I critically analyze *TWD* to spotlight power structures and how these are challenged and may eventually change.

As Hassler-Forest (2011) discussed, the zombie genre provides an excellent means to analyze the destruction of a patriarchal society and the subsequent evolution of social constructions. Although Hassler-Forest's (2011) analysis of *The Walking Dead* comic series revealed continued heteronormativity and a perpetuation of the White hero myth, the first five seasons of *TWD* present more complex character development. Further, as is typical of most screen adaptions, *TWD* deviates from the original text when the zombie world is lifted from the pages of the graphic novel.

As McKerrow (1989) and Hart and Daughton (2005) have suggested, a critical text should demonstrate both the status quo of power structures and resistance to dominating rule. In an analysis of British imperialism, for example, Johnson (2003) argued that dominance and ideology, and the ways in which each is challenged, serve as critical components for deconstructing a text. *TWD* represents an appropriate text to use for a critical analysis—society collapses abruptly, survivors begin to realize life as before will not return, and the ensuing chaos sets the stage for power structures to change. The machinery of modernization discussed by Foucault (1977) has failed, physically releasing the human cogs. Yet attaining mental freedom is a challenge. Survivors first attempt to repair what has been lost then try to adjust to a lack of government. Growing awareness that power structures have collapsed becomes increasingly obvious in a world where death by zombie is among the greatest threats. The zombie gaze, blind to humans as anything other than a food source, forces survivors also to see others for who they now are. Prejudicial perspectives are negated as the other becomes one who either hinders or helps survival. As the show progresses, those unable or unwilling to adapt to an "-ism free" society are often banished, turned into one of the zombie masses, or literally deconstructed into a meal. In its first five seasons, characters have navigated a landscape in which society abruptly changes after the dead rise to feed upon the living. Although the premise is simple and familiar, the attempts of survivors to accept and adjust to a world in which traditional structures have disappeared provide a richly complex text to explore the destabilization of power and challenges to heteronormativity.

Although the complexity of *TWD* alone elevates the show to one worthy of study, its popularity points to the potential effects on a large segment of society. The series has increased in popularity since its record-breaking opener for a new cable series, has gained more followers each season, and is a top-ranked On Demand show (Kondolojy, 2014). On Nielson social media chatter rankings, *TWD* is unrivaled with numbers thrice those of other shows. It has spawned a follow-up show *The Talking Dead* and a spin-off *Fear the Dead*, with the latter also breaking records as the top-ranked pilot for a cable series (Kondolojy, 2015). Live events, theme park rides, tours of filming sites, and memorabilia sales also indicate the show's passionate following.

Viewer engagement taking the form of online comments and live events (in which people often dress as favorite characters) suggests that gender and race do not appear to be deciding factors for character popularity or liking. Viewer comments reflect attitudes based on what the characters do rather than how they appear, and generally reflect interest in how they will help others survive. Fan photos at events reflect a range of race, age, and gender with responses to characters typically based on character behaviors. Fan favorites include a rural White guy (i.e., redneck: Daryl); a powerful Black female whose choice of weapon is a sword (Michonne); a tough yet physically unimposing White female who was formerly an abused wife (Carol); an Asian male (Glenn), and the soft-spoken, yet physically imposing Black male (Tyreese), who dies in season four.

## Deconstructing Symbolism in *The Walking Dead*

Foucault (1982) discussed resistance to power as a means to develop a new form of power through the process of individuals confronting their own identities, and to question how they are influenced by others and thus confined within societal beliefs and a system of cultural controls (e.g., norms, roles, rules). Individuals are subjects who must first recognize that they are subjects within a system of restraints they have participated in establishing before they can resist that power. Yet Foucault (1979) does not credit individuals or particular entities with possessing or controlling power; rather, power is produced within society and permeates through-out rather than emerging from a centralized source. Foucault (1977) questions how power comes to be rather than questioning who has power (e.g., Bourdieu, 1994). Dominant institutionalized structures demonstrate power; yet more subtle forms of power related to panoptic surveillance also normalize behavior. Analyses of power, therefore, should engage in micro-level inspections to reveal instances and tactics of power and discipline, including how signs and symbols represent beliefs of knowl-edge (Foucault, 1979). Baudrillard (1994) said this process of uncovering power exposes political and religious simulacra which, along with media images, seduce us into normalizing behavior. Baudrillard (1974) also sug-gested that when power disappears, eventually all that remains is a type of simulated power and nostalgia for power. *TWD* is an appropriate text to demonstrate both the initial power and the attempts to reestablish insti-tutionalized structures and symbolic power. In *TWD*, these simulations ultimately fail when the objects of power and their meanings disappear. An analysis of symbols in *TWD* demonstrates the ensuing types of power and the chaos emerging from the collapse of patriarchal rule. Artifacts of the recent past reference old power and are irrelevant in a new world under the rule of a zombie gaze.

## Zombies Form: Society Falls

The pilot episode of *TWD*, "Days Gone By," opens with an iconic Western figure of a badge-adorned, White male sporting guns, a cowboy hat, boots, and a swagger. Yet barely a minute passes before that mythical hero is deconstructed and blown away. Rick takes out his gun, not to protect but to put two bullets between the eyes of a pajama-clad little girl indifferent to these symbols of power. The teddy-bear-toting zombie reaches up with outstretched arms to Rick and to the audience, seeking not a savior but a meal. The storyline then shifts a few days back in time to Rick awaken-ing in the hospital after being shot while on duty as a sheriff's deputy in a Southern town. The dead flowers by the bed and a complete lack of activ-ity lead him to realize things are not normal. Rick stumbles through town trying to comprehend the lack of order and people. Through his eyes we witness the destruction of the modern power elements of society, or what Marx and Engels (1848) termed superstructure, and the halt of any pro-duction of normal culture. No longer does a military checkpoint and tank represent the security of an elected government. They are relics, fading signs of the past, hunks of worthless metal. The bourgeoisie against whom workers should unite has fallen. But, so, too, has the proletariat. The machine of creating has stopped. The masses finally have the power. Only now, they are literally mindless zombies with the ceaseless goal of eating humans. The superstructures have changed, as have the symbolic meanings of the objects produced under that superstructure. These objects—now littering the landscape—belong to a past culture and hold little connection with what they once symbolized. They have little relevance in the new world; an abandoned cell phone is less useful than the rock lying beside it. The abandonment of symbols which once exemplified differences between the haves and have nots demonstrates the disappearance of some of the subtle forms of power Foucault (1979) discussed.

## Power Failures

Within the first hour of Rick's awakening, he (and we) are transported into a dystopian society. Rick struggles throughout the first four seasons, negotiating his former role of protector and his new role as survivor. From the first episode in which he is forced to kill the zombie girl, to season four in which he takes savage pleasure in mutilating a man attempting to rape his son, to season five in which he seems unable to trust any stranger, Rick struggles with holding onto former norms while surviving in a world with few rules. When Rick first realizes what the world has become, he reverts to what he knows: structure and order. Although the power structure that created society no longer exists, he still places himself into a familiar patriarchal role. At first, it seems as if this will allow former rules, roles, and norms to continue among his fellow survivors; however, the continued threat of the blind gaze from a mob of bodies seeking to feast begins to transform Rick and the others into seeing the world according to a new binary: survivor or zombie. Before finally shedding old beliefs completely, though, characters try to recreate a new order within the old to escape the gaze of the zombie. These attempts include reestablishing customs of the past. In doing so, they expose the past as a false world in which symbols had replaced reality.

## Simulacra Exposed

Baudrillard (1994) described simulacra in postmodern society as a representation so closely copying reality that the falseness cannot be discerned. This process of simulating creates signs and objects whose meanings are determined from how members of society produce and consume these imitations. Baudrillard (1994) discussed simulating as the process of believing in false realities. Although space constraints limit an in-depth explanation, a simplistic example provides context. A cheap copy of an expensive brand both represents the original and simultaneously has its own presence. At first glance, the copy simulates the original fairly accurately; however, if you analyze both closely, you begin to see the differences. The longer you look, the more you may see the copy for what it really is—and the original more clearly by comparison. The characters of

*TWD* struggle to rebuild the original by creating these simulated worlds; however, just as a cheap handbag quickly falls apart, so too do these imitation worlds. These imitations, meant to provide comfort by reestablishing former structures, instead show how symbols hold power through self-imposed beliefs in their power. For viewers, these attempts to simulate are easily detected. The original culture characters attempt to recreate is also exposed for its socially constructed simulacra for viewers, and, eventually through the seasons, for the characters. Stereotypical beliefs and practices of old in *TWD* are exposed through the characters' attempts to mimic the past until they escape the confinements of old beliefs and practices by literally and figuratively burning them down.

### Zombies Rise to Power: Survivors Flee Toward the Past

*TWD* characters create numerous simulated spaces in which normalcy is attempted. Some of the best examples are the farmhouse, the prison, Woodbury, Terminus, and the Alexandria Safe-Zone. In season one, Rick reunites with his wife and son, and they and other survivors eventually find others at a farm. The place mimics the past, complete with food, fresh water, meals, and blessings, but this simulated world does not last. It is exposed as one in which a group of walkers (former loved ones) is kept by the farm owners who hope for a cure. Just as in the larger world, the farmhouse becomes overrun by walkers. It burns, and the survivors flee, eventually arriving at a prison. They rid the prison of zombies and barricade themselves against the outside world. Again, survivors begin simulating their lost culture, with gardening and school time. And, again, the larger world presses in with walkers lining the fences in an unending gaze. During school time, kids learn how to kill for protection. Occasional forays outside the prison remind viewers and characters that the created space is a pseudo world. Meanwhile, another group led by a former political leader has created a different simulated world also incorporating bygone symbols. In Woodbury, the Governor barricades an entire town appearing as any pre-walker community, complete with shops, homes, electricity, and flags flying. The residents believe they are there willingly; however, the Governor rules through social consent by power structures both overt (e.g., weapons), and hidden (e.g., charismatic rhetoric that silences dissent). Eventually, these two simulated worlds collide, resulting in the destruction of both the prison and Woodbury. Images of walkers amidst torn American flags and trampled gardens remind viewers that the larger world is the real one and that those with the real power now—the zombies—just caused the humans to scatter.

Scenes such as these represent what Barthes (1967/1972) discussed as a sign-system representing a society's ideology and reflecting the hyperreality of simulated words. Baudrillard (1994) explained hyperreality as the

111

products of postmodern societies in which a simulation has become more real than the original (e.g., Disneyworld, video games). In *TWD*, these simulated worlds are destroyed, and, in doing so, the hyperreality of the former postmodern society and its obsession with imitation are exposed. Each attempt to mimic the past becomes more distorted and problematic. In season four, survivors reunite at Terminus after being forced to scatter from battle. They enter warily, demonstrating that they (and we) should be suspicious of simulated spaces, and rightly so. Symbols and activities of the former world such as picnic tables, BBQ grills, gardens, and smiling greeters hide cannibalistic activities in the back. The survivors are imprisoned and stripped of all possessions in the season four finale, but in the process are freed from the last restraints of the beliefs of the former world. Season five begins with Terminus burning, taking with it any remnants of old power structures. Survivors are reunited within the world of walkers and realize that the power structures of the old world have disappeared and cannot be recreated. When they eventually discover the Alexandria Safe-Zone, a place resembling all the rituals and ideologies of the old world, they no longer view the walls and order as secure, but dangerous—more dangerous than the zombie-filled real world. By now, they have become freed from the dominant power of old and no longer seek the security hyperreality creations feature. Freed from prior power restraints, an egalitarian society emerges.

## Exposing Ideologies to Gain a Freed Gaze

Season five of *TWD* ends with characters having very different moral codes than when their journeys began. It is here that we as viewers can also reflect on how the patriarchal and hegemonic powers that once ruled are an oddity. Brummett (1984) described ideology as the ways in which a system of artifacts maintains power over people even when the culture that created such no longer exists. For the main characters of *TWD* in season five, the old ideology is gone. In the first season Rick's motto and rule was "You kill; you die." By season five, Rick disowns his once-prized symbols: his badge and role as protector. He points his gun without hesitation with a new motto: "Kill or die." With the dismantling of power, sexist and racist structures also collapse. Those holding stereotypical beliefs of the former world are now the oddities in the new world.

### *Zombies Gaze Blindly: Survivors See More Clearly*

In an analysis of the role of females in apocalyptic films of the 1990s, Deutsch (2000) proposed that blockbuster hits such as *Armageddon* use females as props with little value except to juxtapose their weaknesses against the strengths of men to enhance the latter. Similarly, Furia and

Bielby (2009) studied the representations of females in military films since World War II, arguing that the socially constructed definition of gender as a binary is sustained through the predominantly masculine portrayals of soldiers. In contrast, *TWD* provides a cast of complex characters that belie stereotypes. Although *TWD* is not a military film, the show does have elements of constant war against the army of the undead, as well as other people. Yet male and female characters are equally represented, and gender differences are neutralized over the seasons. The apocalyptic setting, in which both males and females are equally likely to wield swords or hold babies, erases traditional gender roles out of necessity. A group is strongest against threats when individuals drop counterproductive labels and act from their strengths. Rick's group evolves into a strong family unit capable of defending itself against challenges. The complexity of multiple storylines limits exploration of all representations here; yet, individual changes and relationships among main characters demonstrate these transformations through both discarding the concept of gender and redefining roles based on individual strengths deemed most beneficial for the survival of the group.

### Gender Erased

In an analysis of the film *Boys Don't Cry*, Cooper (2002) proposed that heteronormativity is challenged when gender is questioned. Cooper (2002) showed the ultimate effects of prejudicial reactions when beliefs are challenged (trans man Brandon Teena was murdered), and, in doing so, provided a way to consider how *TWD* also confronts heteronormativity. Yet, with *TWD*, not only are gender norms exposed, but old perspectives also become considered as abnormal. The main characters demonstrate complex personalities that belie molds. Michonne is a sword-toting physical threat who can both protect the group and mentor Rick's teenage son, Carl. Physically imposing Tyreese prefers rocking an infant to fighting, and avoids killing. The ways in which characters contribute are rarely questioned unless in the context of how their actions either help or hurt the group's chances to survive.

When traditional gender views resurface, their illogicalness becomes apparent. For example, in season five, two female newcomers who are physically and mentally tough initially follow the orders of two male companions, Abraham and Eugene. As a former soldier, Abraham clings to rules and order to avoid reliving his inability to prevent the rapes and eventual deaths of his wife and sons. Only a mission to escort Eugene to a site with a possible cure removes a gun from Abraham's suicidal hand. Yet, when Eugene admits he lied about the mission, Abraham reverts to the power he knows best: physical strength. He beats Eugene and threatens the others. In contrast to the other two females, Maggie, an original member of the group, unhesitatingly returns equal force, and Abraham sinks to the ground, broken. He is no longer the tough leader. His patriarchal ways are thwarted, and Eugene is physically weakened. The females lead the group to safety, and, in doing so, realize their prior submissive roles were, in part, self-imposed.

Although *TWD* offers other examples similarly discarding gender labels, the relationship between Carol and Daryl most clearly shows how *TWD* challenges stereotypical representations of gender.

## Roles Challenged

Carol best represents the shift from a patriarchal to an egalitarian female role. She also demonstrates one way in which the television series differs from the comic series. In the comic series, Carol commits suicide, perpetuating the notion of the weak female. In the television series, she not only rejects suicide but arguably becomes the strongest character, although this is a transition accomplished, in part, by her relationship with Daryl.

At first, Carol is submissive and rarely speaks. When her husband physically assaults her, Carol is saved when Shane, a domineering male group member, beats him. In contrast, Daryl at first appears to enact stereotypical aloof masculinity; he is a muscular country boy in a leather vest packing a crossbow atop a chopper with an indifferent attitude and a convict older brother calling the shots. Carol and Daryl are the characters most unlikely to become friends. Yet, Carol soon hacks at the dead body of her abusive husband in a fit of rage, and begins transforming herself physically, starting with cutting her hair. When her daughter Sophia is missing, Daryl—the unlikeliest of heroes—searches in earnest day after day. In one scene, with Carol alone and crying, Daryl brings her a flower. But this is no prequel to a stereotypical love-making or comfort session; Daryl stands in the doorway and relays a tale in which the Cherokee rose represents the tears of mothers who lost children on The Trail of Tears, adding that he believes the one he brings blooms for her little girl. He leaves, and, in doing so, removes the threat of reducing characters to binary gender representations.

Any doubts that these deviations from patriarchal authority are just momentary lapses go up in flames when the search for Sophia ends. The little girl, now a walker, emerges from a burning barn. Daryl cannot man up and kill her; Rick must. Daryl uses his physical strength to restrain Carol but is also grieving. Carol and Daryl experience additional struggles, and eventually their relationship is important, not their gender. In a powerful scene, Daryl sees a bloody trail and believes walkers have gotten Carol. He breaks down alone in a deserted cell block, pounding the concrete in anguish, then begins a suicide mission to hunt the responsible walkers. He discovers Carol barely alive, having successfully saved herself. The typical portrayal of a man swooping in for a helpless woman is shown; only it is Daryl, not Carol, who is saved as he scoops her up. Although carried in his arms, Carol seems the stronger of the two. She had fought to survive whereas Daryl had not been strong enough to want to live upon facing the thought of her death.

Through the seasons, Carol becomes the toughest character as the men struggle mentally. The patriarchal power at one point threatens to reappear when Carol kills two fellow members whose contagious illnesses threaten the group's survival. Rick banishes her—seemingly, for daring to enact the masculine role of leader. Yet this is not simply a role reversal. Carol does break down when alone but quickly resolves to survive. Ensuing episodes temporarily frame Carol as the White male hero. She kills two girls out of necessity while a male traveler stands aside holding a baby, unable to do the deed. Then, as the banished outsider, she returns to save the others by cloaking herself with the smells of the undead and walking among them to torch Terminus. In saving the group and being accepted again, she seems to save herself from spiraling into despair. In doing so, gender roles are obliterated.

When Carol and Daryl are later alone and take refuge in a battered women's shelter where Carol had once stayed, they hear the moans of zombies and spot the silhouette of a mother and child against a frosted glass door. Carol hesitates but starts forward to do what needs to be done. When Daryl lays a hand on her shoulder to indicate that he will do it, this is not the act of a male hero protecting the little lady. It is of a friend who knows Carol is perfectly capable but can let someone else shoulder the burden. Strapped with guns and resolve, Carol watches from a window as Daryl takes the time to show respect by burning the corpses. Echoing the sentiment of laying ashes to old roles, the two discuss how their old selves have also been burned away. We see that they don't have to prove anything about who they are other than survivors, because, in this world, no other label matters.

## Sex Unrestrained

As power and gender roles are deconstructed, sexual restraints are also discarded. *TWD* demonstrates the change of sexual norms both through the ways in which sexual acts are shown and in new forms of punishment for sexual deviance. Survival necessitates being in a group. Sex between adults is no longer an activity behind closed doors. In *TWD*, sexual acts are rarely relied upon for dramatic effect, and, when included, are presented with little fanfare. In one scene at an abandoned store, Maggie and Glenn embrace while Rosita and Abraham engage in intercourse only a few aisles away. In this world, sex and sexual preferences just are. When a female character reveals she is a lesbian, the other characters barely give a shrug, accepting her and her potential partner as just two more survivors. Two male characters are shown embracing and kissing, just as any two people would when relieved to find the other survived a threat. This new attitude toward sex as a natural part of living, with the choice of partner as one's own business, is made even more noticeable when considering how sexual deviance is now defined.

## Deviance Redefined

As power structures of old are discarded, the ways in which characters judge the actions of others are reduced to considering what has to be done to survive and how to accomplish those acts with minimal harm to others. Although main characters may kill to survive, they do not typically harm for enjoyment. Deviance has been redefined as acts that purposely or unnecessarily harm another. Sexual deviants in particular are not tolerated.

Abusers are exiled or die. Carol's abusive husband not only dies but is also chopped to pieces. Shane, Rick's former best friend, left Rick for dead then manipulated Rick's wife to take him as a partner. Carl later puts a bullet between the man's eyes as Shane begins to turn into a walker. The Governor forces Maggie to strip and touches her, and Michonne later kills him. As power structures and social order crumble over the seasons, retribution for acts of sexual brutality and deviancy are swift and unquestioned. In the fourth season, a flashback reveals that Terminus had been a safe haven until a group of men took advantage of the kindness of the residents and enslaved the men and women for sexual pleasure. The original Terminus group, however, eventually became free and literally made a meal of the rapists. Later in the season, Beth, an innocent teenager, is manhandled and threatened with rape in a disturbing scene in which she is forced to suck on a lollipop. Yet she lures the would-be rapist into a room, smashes him with the jar of lollipops, and leaves him to be eaten by one of his rape victims who had just committed suicide and turned into a walker.

*TWD* once again provides a contrast to other horror shows. In a content analysis of slasher films, Welsh (2010) showed that females engaging in sex acts often pay the price for their indiscretions with a gory end to their life. In *TWD*, sexual acts between consenting adults are normal and natural, whereas exercising control over another is deviant.

In considering the ways in which attitudes shifted in *TWD*, Foucault's (1990) extensive discussions of sexuality provide insight. Foucault (1990) argued that society attempts to repress discussions of sex, and that sex is a socially constructed means of control over our lives by those allowed to speak about it and to determine its importance and meaning for others. Yet societal debates of sex, equal marriage rights, and sexuality lose meaning in *TWD*, where no legal structures exist and few social constructs prevail. Survival negates discussion and requires action. Morality becomes what survivors say it has become. Just as Rick eventually touts, "Kill or die," only one sexual rule exists: Harm another and suffer.

Rick, the first character we meet, demonstrates the obliteration of old stereotypes and rules through his transformation from law enforcer to judge and punisher. Rick, Michonne, and Carl are taken hostage by a group of men Rick had allowed to live when he still believed in the old system of justice. Held at gunpoint and forced to watch as his son was about to be raped, Rick pays homage to the undead as the ones in power when he bites his captor's neck to strip away an artery. Reaching the would-be rapist, Rick shows no mercy, staring directly into the man's face while eviscerating him. Michonne wields her sword to slash the others who had been waiting to engage in the vile act. They have shed all connections to prior rules. The new standard is to kill those who deserve to die. Family has been redefined as those who help you survive and others are considered those against you. Daryl eventually rejects his homophobic and racist brother for his new family, and by season five the survivors no longer label themselves or others according to race, age, sexual orientation, or gender. They now think of themselves and the relationship with others in ways former rules cannot define.

## Zombies Devolve: Survivors Evolve

Although the collapse of power structures and erasure of gender roles are the most noticeable ways in which *TWD* represents an egalitarian society, racial stereotypes are also discarded. This is most clearly evident in the shifts toward the new definition of family, in the portrayal of Black masculinity, and the deconstruction of walkers.

### Family Ties

From season one, *TWD* challenges power structures and gender roles; racial prejudices are discarded more slowly. Only in season four do racial divisions decisively diverge from oft-typical Black and White groupings. Michonne and Carl demonstrate the shift from stereotypical viewpoints to one in which judgments are based on being trusted to help one survive. Rick, at first, does not trust the aloof Michonne and even considers using her as a pawn to negotiate an exchange for one of their people held captive by the Governor. Carl, however, considers her as family after she saves him. When attempting to retrieve the only photograph remaining of his mom after she dies, Carl becomes trapped. Michonne cuts a path through walkers to reach him, and, rather than scold him for risking their lives, spots the photograph and merely nods. The relationship is later threatened when the group is forced to scatter from the prison. Michonne finds Carl and Rick's trail but turns the other way, reverting to her prior self-exile made complete with customized walkers walking alongside her, limbless, jawless, and chained. They are tools to allow her to walk among the dead. When a Black female zombie eerily similar in appearance ambles along beside her, Michonne rejects a realization of the reversal to her old self. She hacks the look-alike walker and looks for Carl and Rick. She finds them needing her help, and, in embracing, they redefine family. The acceptance of others regardless of the ways in which prior norms may have labeled a person is reinforced.

In the opening episode of season four, Bob, a Black male, joins the group. His relationships with others at first seem to fall along racial lines and he interacts mainly with two other Black members. Non-Black members are suspicious of Bob, but most newcomers are initially distrusted. Yet, when Daryl leads a run to get medical supplies with Bob, Tyreese, and Sasha, the bond of family demonstrates race is irrelevant. Overrun by walkers, the group flees, clinging to packs with medicines for a dying group member. Bob, however, went after something different. When liquor bottles tumble out of Bob's pack as Daryl protects him, it is not race that matters but loyalty to the group. Daryl never hesitates in turning his back to the other two when he slams the bottle into Bob's chest and threatens him. When Bob redeems himself in later episodes, he is accepted by everyone, including Daryl.

Early *TWD* episodes show racially segregated groups; yet the show does not rely on superficial stereotypes. When Rick leaves the hospital weak and confused, a Black father and son care for him. The two are a strong family, and Morgan struggles with needing to kill his walker wife who wanders the streets outside their home. The two men reminisce about how alike their families were. Rick eventually leaves to find his wife and son but gives Morgan a radio to stay in touch. Although Rick tries every morning to reach Morgan, they lose touch. Eventually Morgan's son dies and he journeys to find Rick. The bond of family, once again, negates racial stereotypes.

## Black Masculinity Deconstructed

Although *TWD* has Latino, Asian, Black, and White characters, race is rarely mentioned, and the characters demonstrate complex personalities that belie labels. Even when an episode could fall into stereotypical representations, it does not. For example, when Rick's group first enters the prison, they find prisoners unaware of what has occurred outside the walls. Instead of the most muscular Black man being shown as the bad guy, it is the non-Black man that is the most threatening. The Black man and the smallest White guy fight on Rick's behalf, claiming afterward that it was the right thing to do. Scenarios such as these and the character

118

Tyreese demonstrate most effectively the challenges to stereotypical Black masculinity.

In an analysis of Black male identities in *Tales from the Hood*, Fulmer (2002) noted that typical character portrayals represent extremes: either passive or aggressive, asexual sidekicks or oversexed players, impoverished or obscenely rich. Fulmer argued that in folklore tales in the horror genre, the plots of *Tales from the Hood* often reconfigure characters to provide morality tales that challenge hegemonic influences. In doing so, the typical White male character is in part merely replaced by the Black male according to the standard power structure rather than creating a new space for the Black male identity (Fulmer, 2002). Yet, in *TWD*, Tyreese defines his own identity and is accepted by others. He has no skill with a firearm and takes no offense when a female attempts to show him. He will kill to protect his group but otherwise avoids it, and is most comfortable taking care of children. When ridiculed by a captive Terminus member and told he will die with an infant in tow, Tyreese pays little attention and comforts the child. In essence, Tyreese is as other *TWD* characters, complex and seeking to define individually and as a group what morality means in a new world. Race and gender no longer matter in an apocalyptic world. Even the force of the undead reflects this indifference, both in its sightless gaze and in the loss of human form.

### Humans Revived Among the Undead

In an analysis of two popular zombie texts in South African culture, Murray (2013) proposed that the use of zombies provides a gaze at the human form devoid of sexuality. Similarly, *TWD* shows a mass of walkers reflecting a world of newly formed perspectives. They are decaying, not only losing their sexual forms but also their identifying characteristics of race and ethnicity. Additionally, they represent the phases of change. In the first seasons, the undead are recognizable with intact features showing their previous gender and race. Symbolic remnants of the old world—hair bows, uniforms, jewelry—remind us they were human and were once labeled based on appearances. Over time, as the living negotiate their identities and discard useless labels, zombies also shed connections with their former lives. Some disintegrate when trapped in water, some are burned by chemical bombs, some lose body parts to injuries, and all are slowly deteriorating from a lack of food. Their forms are becoming "-less": featureless, genderless, and pale imitations of their past selves. Likewise, the living have shed their possessions along with their prior ideologies, but have evolved to embrace a new perspective. Uniforms, badges, expensive clothes, and other symbols of power have long since been discarded, along with notions of stereotypes. Society has collapsed, yet a new way of living and seeing others emerges from the ashes.

*TWD* demonstrates an apocalyptic world in which characters and society devolve and evolve when the status quo of power collapses and hegemony is challenged. The survivors navigate a changed landscape under the gaze of the undead and, in doing so, create a new moral code and adopt new perspectives. In essence, they do not join the zombie in becoming blind to others but see others more clearly when released from old world structures. Thus, we as viewers see and experience the characters adopting their own gaze: a freed gaze.

## References

Barthes, R. (1967). *Elements of semiology*. New York, NY: Hill and Wang.

Barthes, R. (1972). *Mythologies*. New York, NY: Hill and Wang.

Baudrillard, J. (1994). *Simulacra and simulation*. Ann Arbor, MI: University of Michigan Press.

Bentham, J. (1791). *Panopticon or the inspection house*. Whitefish, MT: Kessinger Publishing.

Bourdieu, P. (1994). *Language and symbolic power*. Oxford, UK: Polity.

Brummett, B. (1984). Rhetorical theory as heuristic and moral: A pedagogical justification. *Communication Education, 33*(2), 97–107.

Cooper, B. (2002). *Boys Don't Cry* and female masculinity: Reclaiming a life and dismantling the politics of normative heterosexuality. *Critical Studies in Media Communication, 19*(1), 44–63.

Deutsch, J. I. (2000). Gender representations: As the world ends: Traditional gender roles in apocalyptic science-fiction films of the late 1990s. In E. H. Olesky, E. Ostrowska, & M. Stevenson (Eds.), *Gender in film and the media: East–west dialogues* (pp. 39–45). Frankfurt and New York, NY: Peter Lang.

Foucault, M. (1977). *Discipline and punish: The birth of the prison*. New York, NY: Pantheon Books.

Foucault, M. (1980). *Power/knowledge*. New York, NY: Pantheon Books.

Foucault, M. (1982). The subject and power. In H. Dreyfus & P. Rabinow (Eds.), *Michel Foucault: Beyond structuralism and hermeneutics* (pp. 208–226). Chicago, IL: The University of Chicago Press.

Foucault, M. (1990). *The history of sexuality: The use of pleasure* (Vol. 2). New York, NY: Random House LLC.

Fulmer, J. (2002). "Men Ain't All": A reworking of masculinity in *Tales from the Hood*, or, *Grandma Meets the Zombie*. *Journal of American Folklore, 115*, 422–442.

Furia, S. R., & Bielby, D. D. (2009). Bombshells on film: Women, military films, and hegemonic gender ideologies. *Popular Communication, 7*(4), 208–224.

Hart, R. P., & Daughton, S. (2005). *Modern rhetorical criticism* (3rd ed.). Boston, MA: Pearson.

Hassler-Forest, D. (2011). Cowboys and zombies: Destabilizing patriarchal discourse in *The Walking Dead*. *Studies in Comics, 2*(2), 339–355.

Johnson, R. (2003). *British imperialism*. New York, NY: Palgrave Macmillan.

Kondolojy, A. (2014). Cable top 25: *The Walking Dead* tops cable viewership for the week ending November 16, 2014. *General Sentiment*. Retrieved October 11, 2015, from http://tvbythenumbers.zap2it.com/ 2014/11/18/cable-top-25-the-walking-dead-tops-cable-viewership-for-the-week-ending-november-16-2014/329123/.

Kondolojy, A. (2015). *Fear the Walking Dead* becomes most-watched series premiere in cable history with 10.1 million viewers. Retrieved October 11, 2015, from http://tvbythenumbers.zap2it.com/2015/08/24/fear-the-walking-dead-becomes-most-watched-series-premiere-in-cable-history-with-10-1-million-viewers/452459/.

Marx, K., & Engels, F. (1848). Manifesto of the Communist Party. In *Marx/Engels selected works (Vol. 1)*, tr. Samuel Moore in cooperation with F. Engels, 1888. Retrieved October 11, 2015, from https://www.marxists.org/archive/marx/works/1848/communist-manifesto/index.htm.

Mastro, D. (2009). Effects of racial and ethnic stereotyping. In J. Bryant & M. B. Oliver (Eds.), *Media effects: Advances in theory and research* (pp. 325–341). New York, NY: Routledge.

McKerrow, R. E. (1989). Critical rhetoric: Theory and praxis. *Communication Monographs, 56,* 91–111.

Murray, J. (2013). A zombie apocalypse: Opening representational spaces for alternative constructions of gender and sexuality. *Journal of Literary Studies, 29*(4), 1–19.

Shugart, H. A. (2011). Consuming passions: "Educating Desire" in *Brokeback Mountain. Critical Studies in Media Communication, 28*(3), 173–192.

Strasburger, V. C., Wilson, B. J., & Jordan, A. B. (2009). *Children, adolescents, and the media.* Thousand Oaks, CA: Sage Publications.

Therborn, G. (1980). *The ideology of power and the power of ideology.* London: Verso.

Welsh, A. (2010). On the perils of living dangerously in the slasher horror film: Gender differences in the association between sexual activity and survival. *Sex Roles, 62*(11/12), 762–773.

# Part II

# CONTEXT
## Audiences, Effects, Reception

# 8

# MANIPULATING RACE AND GENDER IN MEDIA EFFECTS RESEARCH

## A Methodological Review Using the Media FIT Taxonomy

*Charisse L'Pree Corsbie-Massay*

Mass media play an intricate role in individual development, activation, and perpetuation of stereotypes regarding race and gender. Media content is both the outcome and source of widespread societal differences, making the investigation of race and gender in media a complicated task. Many researchers deploy empirical research to study this relationship, manipulating race and gender in a controlled environment and measuring subsequent effects including interpersonal and intrapersonal attitudes, support for social policy, and behaviors. Studies draw on methodologies established by earlier scholars, but no comprehensive review of these strategies has been conducted. The current chapter addresses the question: How do we know what we know about the effects of race and gender in media?

In 1948, social scientist Sidney Wax sent letters requesting accommodations at Toronto hotels; whereas letters from Mr. Lockwood received a reply and a reservation offer from 90% of the hotels, letters from Mr. Greenberg (a patron with an ostensibly Jewish surname) received a reply from 52% and a reservation offer from less than 40% (Allport, 1954). In the decades since, studies have demonstrated that White names such as Emily and Greg are deemed more employable than Black names such as Lakisha and Jamal (Bertrand & Mullainathan, 2004), professors are less likely to respond to emails from students with female or non-White (e.g., Black, Hispanic, Chinese, Indian) names (Milkman, Akinola, & Chugh, 2014), and that grammar, as an indicator of class, can affect responses to housing requests (Ahmed & Hammarstedt, 2008; Hanson & Hawley, 2011).

This research is rapidly expanding, and extends beyond academia; even Hollywood producers create content based on these research strategies to further affect public discourse. The TV show *What Would You Do* captured public reactions to different young people trying to cut a bike chain: a White man, a Black man, and a White woman. Whereas most passersby ignored the young White man, several confronted the young Black man and one even called 911; more shockingly, some men offered to help the young White woman cut the bike chain ("Bicycle Thief"; S3E3, 2010). Bloggers have also picked up these methods and their social experiments occasionally go viral: José Zamora received more responses to his résumé when he went by "Joe" (Zamora, 2014) and women bloggers have observed a sizable drop in online insults and rape threats when using a male profile picture (Golden, 2014; Millard, 2015). By integrating research, statistics, and social experiments, this renaissance in public discourse demonstrates trends to improve general understanding of race and gender issues.

Several researchers have extended this methodology to investigate whether such discrimination manifests after exposure to mass mediated messages. After presenting a novel taxonomy that integrates media format, industry, and technology (the Media FIT Taxonomy), I use the taxonomy to describe the methodological trends in experimental studies designed to test the effects of race and gender in media. This chapter is not a summary of race and gender trends in media content, nor is it a systematic review of the effects of race and gender in media. This review will not define race and gender; instead, it will reveal how social scientists have defined race and gender in research and how these implicit definitions affect our overall understanding of race and gender.

## Defining, Categorizing, and Investigating Media Research Methods

Media is simultaneously the method by which information is transmitted from a source to a receiver and the transmitted message. It is the format in which the message is encoded (e.g., text, video) and the platform in which it is distributed (e.g., newspapers, television). It is interpersonal and mass communication, as well as broadcast and interactive content. It is both an industry and the content of the message itself. Taking this one step further, mass media or publicly available media is information from a single source to many (potentially anonymous) receivers, and includes legacy and broadcast outlets such as newspapers, radio, and television, and interactive content such as social media and video games. To understand how race and gender affect viewers, we must unpack how researchers manipulate these constructs across dimensions and what effects are being measured. Cognitive processes may differ when race and gender are deployed through text, images, or video; measurement and impact differs between media industries such as journalism, advertising, and entertainment; and research questions are often deployed at specific intersections (e.g., print advertising, broadcast news) thus impeding researchers from achieving a robust overall understanding of race and gender.

The Media FIT Taxonomy allows for the comparison of methodologies across three dimensions to highlight the trends and gaps in the literature: (1) *format*, or the transmission presentation of content, including nonvisual audio, static text or images, synchronized video, and interactive media; (2) *industry*, or the genre and business conventions of content, including journalism, advertising, entertainment, and Peer-to-Peer (P2P) e-commerce; and (3) *technology*, or how content reaches the consumer, including analog (i.e., media that record and reproduce information in a continuous manner; e.g., records, printed word), electronic (i.e., media that record and reproduce information with the assistance of electricity but without computer code; e.g., broadcast radio and television), and digital (i.e., media that record and reproduce information via binary code; e.g., websites, video games). A visualization of these three dimensions is available in Figure 8.1, which presents industry specific examples within each cell. For example, media including newspapers, magazines, and print ads are static text or images distributed via analog technology, whereas television content is synchronized video distributed via electronic technology. The Media FIT Taxonomy ensures that media format, industry, and technology are explicitly addressed when reviewing experimental research investigating the effects of race and gender in media.

Although not a formal meta-analysis, the current chapter deploys meta-analysis methodologies to assess and compare the research investigating race and gender in media (Rosenthal, 1991). Searches were conducted across multiple databases including PsycINFO, PubMed, and Google Scholar, using key terms including "race," "gender," "media," and "experiment," resulting in a primary set of studies; a set of secondary and tertiary studies was generated by reviewing the reference sections of the primary studies to discover studies that may not have appeared in original searches. Studies were drawn from a wide variety of disciplines, including psychology and media studies, as well as business, computer science, and industry journals. Eligible studies featured an experimental design where race or gender was compared across at least two different conditions (e.g., Black and White, male and female), and materials conformed to a specific media industry designed to share content publicly to potentially anonymous viewers, resulting in a final $N = 83$ studies. Exploratory surveys or content analyses demonstrating racial and gender differences in media use, credibility, or interest were not eligible; studies of publically available social media were eligible, but investigations of interpersonal communication (e.g., emails) were not.

| FORMAT | | | | | |
|---|---|---|---|---|---|
| | | Non-Visual Audio | Static Text | Static Images | Synchronized Video | Interactive Media |
| **TECHNOLOGY** | **Analog** | J: | J: Newspapers | J: Newspapers | J: Newsreel | J: Letters to Editor |
| | | A: | A: Print Copy | A: Print Images | A: Trailers | A: Clipping Coupons |
| | | E: Recorded Sound | E: Books, Magazines | E: Comics, Magazines | E: Movies | E: Choose Your Own Adventure |
| | **Electronic** | J: Radio News | J: | J: | J: TV News | J: Call-In Radio |
| | | A: Radio Commercials | A: Electronic Billboards | A: Electronic Billboards | A: TV Commercials | A: |
| | | E: Radio Programming | E: Promo Content for Video Products | E: Promo Content for Video Products | E: TV Programming | E: Funniest Home Videos |
| | **Digital** | J: Podcasts | J: Online Articles, Blogs, Social Media | J: Online Articles, Blogs, Social Media | J: Online Streaming | J: Virtual Reality |
| | | A: Streaming Ads | A: Banner Ads | A: Banner Ads | A: Pre-roll Ads | A: Advergames; Interactive Ads |
| | | E: Recorded Sound | E: Blogs | E: Viral Memes | E: User-Generated Content (UGC) | E: Video Games |
| | | P2P: Personal Digital Assistants | P2P: Auction Sites | P2P: Auction Sites | P2P: Auction Sites | P2P: Auction Sites |
| J: Journalism | | | A: Advertising | | E: Entertainment | P2P: Peer 2 Peer |
| **INDUSTRY** | | | | | | |

*Figure 8.1* Media FIT Taxonomy.

*Note:* Grayed cells indicate that no studies in this review have addressed the effect of race or gender in that particular intersection of format, technology, and industry.

Eligible studies were categorized using the Media FIT Taxonomy, and findings are presented according to the five format categories.

In the following sections, each category and subcategory is defined. I describe *how* race and gender are activated and manipulated within each category, and identify gaps in the literature that inhibit an overall understanding of these concepts. It is important to note that not all studies purporting to study digital technology are categorized as "interactive media"; instead, studies are classified according to their actual manipulations, so studies manipulating non-interactive formats and displayed using digital technology (e.g., static text or images via blogs, broadcast video via computer display) are categorized and discussed alongside studies with similar manipulation strategies deploying earlier technology.

### Category 1: Audio (n = 7; 8.4% of total studies)

Audio includes any information or messages passed exclusively through an auditory stream; non-visual audio can be distributed via analog formats (e.g., records), electronically (e.g., radio journalism), or digitally (e.g., non-playing characters in video games). Despite the importance of gender and race via spoken word, only one-twelfth of all reviewed studies manipulated audio, and all but one of these compared male and female voices.

Although gender is one of the most salient social cues in human speech and activates stereotypes associated with gender (Lee, Nass, & Brave, 2000), much of this research was ineligible for the present review because it did not incorporate media industry conventions. For example, a large body of exploratory research investigates gendered vocal differences in speech communication research (e.g., pitch, timbre, linguistic style; Klatt & Klatt, 1990; Pernet & Belin, 2012; Simpson, 2009; Xu et al., 2013). Effects of gendered voices have been addressed in the psychology literature (DeCasper & Spence, 1986; Puts, 2005) and in user interfaces (Nass & Brave, 2005); these studies investigate the format of voice using different technologies, but do not conform to an industry standard, and thus are not included in this review.

Studies manipulating voices in radio advertising featured voiceover actors, either professional or amateur, to test the effects of spokesperson gender on perceived product qualities. Men and women record the same ad copy, often sampled from commercials with which the participant is not familiar. Some studies also feature multiple actors within each gender and aggregated gender conditions to mitigate individual effects (Martin-Santana et al., 2014; Whipple & McMannon, 2002). Despite the advent and popularity of digital voice technology, only two reviewed studies compared synthesized gendered voices using digital distribution technologies. Lee, Liao, and Ryu (2007) investigated synthesized male and female voices in educational interactive interfaces, and Mullenix, Stern, Wilson, and Dyson (2003) investigated the effects of male and female synthesized voices using persuasive messages. Both studies found that traditional gender stereotypes were applied to synthesized voices.

Most of the studies in this category focus on gender. The few investigating objective vocal differences between races yield conflicting results (Purnell, Idsardi, & Baugh, 1999; Walton & Orlikoff, 1994; Xue & Fucci, 2000; Xue, Hao, & Mayo, 2006). Although the racialized deployment of animated voices in industry content has been noted (Lugo-Lugo & Bloodsworth-Lugo, 2008), only one study investigated effects of race in audio by manipulating the name of a spokesperson to compare Anglo (i.e., Mary Tucker, Charles Martin) and Hispanic (Maria Trevino, Carlos Martinez) names (Deshpandé & Stayman, 1994).

## Category 2: Text (n = 20; 24.1% of total studies)

Text refers to static, or non-interactive, words and images. Although commonly referred to as print when distributed via analog platforms (e.g., newspapers, magazines), this media category is a pillar of digital technology. We spend 22% of our online time on social networking sites,

20% of our online time reading content, 20% of our online time conducting searches, and 19% of our online time fielding emails ("How people spend their online time," 2012), and each of these activities is dominated by information presented via static text or images, thus demonstrating this category's importance even in a mediated society.

More than half the reviewed studies manipulated race or gender using non-interactive text or images deployed across industry formats, including news articles, blog posts, and P2P communications including e-commerce. Studies were evenly distributed between those testing race and those testing gender in this category, but only two investigated the intersection of race and gender. Of studies in this category, 75% deployed journalism industry conventions and 15% deployed P2P industry conventions; only one study deployed entertainment and one study deployed advertising industry conventions. Two primary methodologies of manipulating text were identified: names and linguistic style.

### Manipulating Names (n = 14, 70% of text studies, 16.9% of total studies)

Names connote information about an individual, including race and gender, as well as socioeconomic status, religion (Carpusor & Loges, 2006), and nationality (Ahmed & Hammarstedt, 2008). This simple and effective strategy, originally deployed by Wax (1948) some 70 years ago, is a mainstay of the featured research. However, almost all of the studies in this subcategory investigated gender effects on perceived source credibility in journalism and blogs. Only a handful manipulated racialized names, most often in P2P e-commerce.

Researchers begin with real world samples of target artifacts (e.g., news articles, blog posts) to maintain credibility and realism; after standardizing for format, length, and voice, researchers change the source's name to reflect the target social category. In studies that manipulate gender, names were considered male-gendered (e.g., Patrick), female-gendered (Patricia), or gender neutral (Pat). Interestingly, most of the names used to explicitly investigate gender effects would be considered White (Patricia vs. Patrick), thereby implicitly reinforcing Whiteness-as-normal (Devos & Banaji, 2005). In fact, only Nunley, Owens, and Howard (2011) manipulated racialized names, revealing an impact on prices in eBay auctions among sellers with low ratings.

### Manipulating Other Linguistic Indicators (n = 6, 30% of text studies, 7.2% of total studies)

Similar to names, linguistic indicators such as grammar and speech patterns connote information by activating stereotypical knowledge of the participant; however, this category also included studies that featured explicit group labeling, thus indicating race and gender without deploying stereotypes. Studies in this category explored race, gender, and the intersection thereof, most often using journalism or P2P industry conventions.

Despite the value in explicit labeling, this methodology was deployed in only a handful of studies: one study manipulated pronouns by asking participants to read a job description featuring either gender inclusive or gender exclusive language (Stout & Dasgupta, 2011), and two studies deployed explicit labeling to activate social categories (e.g., "The Essence of America" vs. "The Essence of Black America," Appiah, 2004; NBA vs. WNBA, Cundiff 2013). However, instead of testing effects based on the race and gender of the individuals *presented* in media content, these studies investigated effects of media targeting, or the degree to which participants were interested in the group or product after being exposed to a spokesperson who was either a member of their in-group or not.

Several studies deployed other linguistic strategies that implicitly activate associations of gender and race. Lee (2007) manipulated comments between partners in a computer mediated trivia game to indicate gender: comments from a female partner included emoticons, tag questions, and apologies (e.g., "Sorry, no clue—any ideas?"), whereas male comments were more direct, referenced quantity, and featured elliptical sentences (e.g., "either a or b, 50% confident) (p. 200). Alhabash et al. (2014) manipulated profiles on a dating website using stereotypes to imply race without a picture; the Black profile featured a lower education level, lower paying job, and fewer languages spoken. Although not explicitly manipulating race, Besbris, Faber, Rich, and Sharkey (2015) found that items on the e-commerce site eBay received fewer bids if the seller was from a disadvantaged neighborhood, and that this stigma was greater for sellers from disadvantaged Black neighborhoods. These strategies reveal that gender and race can be manipulated by deploying cognitive associations to activate different groups, and assume that participants are aware of stereotypes and cultural trends.

### Category 3: Images (n = 32; 38.6% of total studies)

In an attempt to separate stereotypes from phenotypes, or physical differences (e.g., body shape, skin tone), the majority of studies manipulated race and gender by replacing actors or digitally adjusting physical features in still images. Many of the studies in this category investigated advertising (59.4%) and journalism (25%) industry conventions; the remaining studies investigated entertainment and P2P communications.

As with the manipulation of names, researchers begin with real world samples of original content and change the featured image(s), but the strategies differed by industry. Studies that investigate traditional print journalism (Knobloch-Westerwick, Appiah, & Alter, 2008), entertainment (Mastro, Behm-Morawitz, Kopacz, 2008; Weaver, 2011), and social media (Spence, Lachlan, Westerman, & Spates, 2013) swapped headshots of authors or images of story subjects, drawing images from a wide variety of sources. Advertising studies were more likely to generate novel ads for the purposes of research (Appiah, 2001a, 2001b, 2009; Wang & Arpan, 2008). Replicating the format of traditional print ads, researchers manipulated images with limited copy to encourage a focus on visual content. Almost all advertising studies described confirming the realism of their materials with professional agencies, a pilot testing strategy unique to studies addressing advertising-related research questions.

Several studies investigating race deployed multiple strategies to avoid individual-related, single exposure effects. Some featured multiple iterations within each condition to increase generalizability (Dixon, 2007; Appiah, 2001a, 2001b, 2002, 2004, 2009). Several studies also digitally "painted" (Gilliam, Iyengar, Simon, & Wright, 1996, p 15) faces to manipulate race via skin tone while holding other facial features constant (Gilliam & Iyengar, 2000; Dixon & Maddox, 2005; Dixon, 2006, 2007). Going a step further, Ayres, Banaji, and Jolls (2011) and Doleac and Stein (2013) manipulated race using hand models with different skin tones; although this eliminates the confounding nature of facial features, it still assumes that dark skin indicates Blackness; neither study mentions that darker skin might indicate Latino, Middle Eastern, or other non-White ethnic groups.

### Category 4: Video (n = 19, 22.9% of total studies)

Video is defined as moving visual images distributed via analog (e.g., film), electronic (e.g., television, videotape), or digital (e.g., online video, pre-roll ads) distribution formats; although sound is not required, none of the studies reported using silent video. Despite the prevalence of video content in our current media environment, less than a quarter of the reviewed studies manipulated video, and almost all in this category (84.2%) investigated race. The majority of studies (63.2%) in this category deployed journalism or politicized entertainment industry conventions (Dixon, Schell, Giles, & Drogos, 2005; Goff, Eberhardt, Williams, & Jackson, 2008; Oliver, 1996), and the remainder (36.8%) deployed advertising industry conventions.

Beginning with original news clips to maintain realism and credibility, several researchers edited still images into preexisting footage to indicate suspect race (Dixon 2006, 2007; Dixon & Azocar, 2007; Gilliam & Iyengar, 2000; Gilliam, Iyengar, Simon, & Wright, 1996; Oliver, 1999); this simple strategy demonstrated significant effects in studies that embed a 3–10 second manipulation in a 15–30 minute video. Many researchers used stock images and mug shots, or "digitally painted" versions of the same face. Some researchers edited sections of content to manipulate race; these strategies ranged from replacing footage (e.g., a White or Black male suspect being led away in handcuffs; Peffley, Shields, & Williams, 1996) to editing multiple political ads that feature different racial imagery (e.g., neutral images, race comparison, undeserving Blacks; Valentino, Hutchings, & White, 2002). These methods eliminate audio editing, and replicate static images strategies. All of the studies manipulating racial content in video addressed journalism-related questions regarding suspect race and perceived guilt, punishment, and social policy attitudes.

Almost half of the studies deploying video stimuli produced entirely new footage; these were diverse in their research questions and production complexity. Some researchers hired actors to manipulate spokesperson gender in Public Service Announcements or PSAs (Perse, Nathanson, & McLeod, 1996), journalist (Miller & Kurpius, 2010) or interviewee race (Gilliam, Iyengar, Simon, & Wright, 1996) in news stories, and employee race on a company website (Walker et al., 2009). In each of these studies, stimuli across conditions were matched in their script and structure, differing only in the gender or race of the featured actor. Other studies deployed animated or virtual agents, bypassing the need for actors and avoiding the single exposure confounds described in text and images. To manipulate gender in advertising, Pierce (2001) created three animated characters (female gender, male gender, and gender neutral) based on traditional gender stereotypes (e.g., high heels and red lips vs. tie and mustache) and recorded male and female voice actors for a 30-second commercial. To manipulate race in PSAs, O'Mally and Worrell (2004) created avatars in Flash with different skin tones. No studies investigated the effects of racialized animated characters despite their prevalence in popular children's media (Lugo-Lugo & Bloodsworth-Lugo, 2009).

Recent work also demonstrates a strategy for creating a media kit that can be deployed for a variety of research questions using the same raw footage across multiple studies. Corsbie-Massay and Read (unpublished) recorded more than a dozen actors delivering every line in a two-minute script. Actors were pilot tested to confirm perceived age, gender, and race, and represented several different ethnic and gender groups, including race- and gender-ambiguous. The researchers then created seven different videos manipulating racial and gender exclusion to empirically test demographic composition.

### Category 5: Interactive Media (n = 8, 9.6% of total studies)

Although individuals can interact with all of the aforementioned media categories, interactive media *require* user engagement to consume and experience the entire message; users have individual control over the message presentation, the media experience, and even the narrative. If video defined twentieth-century mass media, interactivity and digital technologies define twenty-first-century media. Some aforementioned studies deployed digital platforms (e.g., blogs, social networking sites, online commerce) and allowed participants to freely read or engage with the stimulus content at their leisure, but studies categorized as interactive required specific participant engagement as part of the manipulation above and beyond outcome measures. Of the interactive studies, 75% manipulated race, 25% manipulated gender, and all but two deployed entertainment industry conventions.

Two primary strategies emerged in interactive media manipulation: participants either played video games available for commercial use or engaged in virtual worlds using avatars designed by the researchers. Anderson and Murphy (2003) and Eastin (2006) compared the effects of playing a male or a female character in popular video games among young women, but researchers were forced to rely on prefabricated characters and physical features. Since then, character customization has become more widespread, allowing researchers to design experimental characters. These options are not available in console video games, but are popular in virtual worlds, and allow greater control over confounds such as avatar characteristics and the immersive environment. Groom, Baileson, and Nass (2009) developed racialized avatars by mapping the faces of real men and women onto avatar frames, thus manipulating both skin tone and facial features. Peck, Seinfeld, Aglioti, and Slater (2013) re-skinned female avatars with purple skin to unpack effects of race as compared to color. No reviewed study similarly compared gendered avatars.

### Cross Category Manipulations (n = 10; 12.0% of total studies)

Several studies deployed more than one of the aforementioned strategies to activate race and gender. Some cross category strategies manipulated several categories within text and images including names and faces (Ansdager, 2003; White & Ansdager, 1991), linguistic strategies and images (Appiah, 2004), and linguistic strategies and names (Hanson & Hawley, 2011). Some studies manipulated race and gender across multiple categories: Pierce (2001) and Dixon (2006, 2007) manipulated audio and static images in video stimuli, and several researchers manipulated static images and text in digital platforms such as social media to emulate the experience of interactive media. Interestingly, no studies manipulated text in video, despite the prevalence of static text in popular media (e.g., titles of organizations at the bottom of a news interview). Furthermore, only Walker et al. (2009) investigated media format as a moderating variable, and found that racial differences were attenuated when participants watched actors delivering testimonials via video as compared to when participants read the testimonial script and saw profile pictures via static text or images.

Cross category studies often assume that manipulating race and gender through multiple strategies will increase the salience of the manipulation and provide a heightened response to these constructs; however, cross category manipulations may activate stereotypes instead of categories and exhibit a multiplicative effect. Yang et al. (2014) created a Black avatar by manipulating images (i.e., skin tone), stereotypical indicators via hairstyle (i.e., cornrows vs. "short, conservative haircut"), and linguistic strategies via speech patterns and grammar (i.e., "stereotypical inner city dialect," p. 699); participants controlled this stereotypical avatar while playing a violent video game, further activating the stereotype of Black men as violent. This confounded manipulation may exaggerate outcomes by activating more than just race.

# Trends in Research Methods

Addressing how researchers manipulate race and gender via media formats and distribution technology is only part of the puzzle of unpacking the effects of race and gender in media. As described earlier, industry format, or genre conventions associated with different areas of the media industry, can influence our understanding of race and gender, and reveal implicit trends in research questions and discourse.

## *Patterns in Industry Conventions*

Eligible studies were contextualized within an industry format, including journalism, advertising, entertainment, and P2P communication such as e-commerce and social media; industry conventions informed content, context, and outcome variables.

### *Advertising/Public Relations (n = 35; 42.2% of total studies)*

The largest number of studies reviewed deployed advertising and public relations industry conventions, and of those, a larger percentage manipulated race (77.1%) than gender (22.9%): 60% used static text or images to investigate race, 20% used video, usually to investigate race, and 14.3% used non-visual audio to investigate gender. Only two advertising/PR studies deployed interactive strategies to investigate race. The emphasis on print media to assess the effects of race and gender in advertising limits the generalizability of these findings to other media, including video advertisements and interactive online content. Although some studies have begun to investigate the effect of racialized and gendered avatars in online advertising and e-commerce, these are limited.

*Journalism (n = 32; 38.6% of total studies)*

Studies deploying content and context associated with the journalism industry accounted for another large segment of the research. Investigations of race (43.8%) and gender (50.0%) were evenly distributed within journalism-related research, with two studies exploring the intersection of race and gender. Despite this seemingly well-distributed area of research, several patterns emerged. There was a bifurcation in the research into the effects of race and gender in journalism; whereas many studies investigating gender focused on source credibility using both names and images of potential journalists, most studies investigating race focused on attitudes toward criminals using images. Only three studies manipulated race to assess source credibility in sports reporting (Mastro, Seate, Blecha, & Gallegos, 2012), social media sharing (Spence, Lachlan, & Spates, 2013), and interviewee race in news packages (Miller & Kurpius, 2010), with conflicting results. Further, no studies investigated race and gender of the victim or victims' advocates. This gap in the empirical research contraposes the extensive critical commentary about social phenomena such as the "Missing White Woman Syndrome" (Liebler, 2010) and White washing, which demonstrate biases in stories considered newsworthy, but researchers have not yet examined how race and gender affect viewers' response to the plight of different groups.

The majority of journalism studies were categorized as text or images (62.5%), with the remainder categorized as video. Rapid changes in the information landscape require updated studies to understand how these processes apply to new modes of communication that may render different effects. It is not sufficient to generalize 30-year-old findings using print journalism to a new digital interactive environment, where stories, sources, and suspects differ with every mouse click. Furthermore, citizen journalists and bloggers are changing the industry, resulting in a greater diversity of expertise and broader definitions of journalist, and the effects of race and gender may be moderated by venue formality (Flanagin & Metzger, 2003; Armstrong & McAdams, 2009; Baiocci, 2010). Although it may appear that many of the questions regarding race and gender in journalism have been answered, new platforms require new studies.

*Entertainment (n = 10; 12.0% of total studies)*

Few studies deployed entertainment-related research questions, or media designed solely for leisure activity. Of these, eight manipulated race in traditional media (80%), two manipulated gender in video games (20%), and none investigated intersectionality.

The representation of race and gender in entertainment media is well studied by critical scholars, but this research interest has not been replicated in experimental effects studies. The majority of entertainment studies were categorized as interactive media (60%), which included video games and virtual worlds, and only two studies deployed video to test the effect of suspect race in police-based reality programming. This bias may be due to the diversity of content and expectations of quality regarding entertainment programming; manipulating or constructing believable novel entertainment stimuli can be complicated for individuals not trained in media production. However, both Mastro, Behm-Morawitz, & Kopacz (2008) and Weaver (2011) work around this by utilizing mock storyboards and IMDB.com webpages respectively to mimic real television shows and movies to investigate how racialized casts and storylines affect audiences' interest, without creating video content. The strategy of investigating entertainment media through platforms other than video offers great promise as researchers consider racial and gender biases in entertainment.

## Peer-to-Peer (P2P) Communications (n = 6; 7.2% of total studies)

The emerging industry of P2P communications was featured in a small percentage of studies, which manipulated race and gender in platforms specifically designed to connect individuals, bypassing traditional media outlets and turning any individual into a message source. Reviewed studies including social networking sites and popular e-commerce websites such as eBay and Craigslist were categorized as text or images because they manipulated race and gender via static text and static images. All but one manipulated race.

Despite its relatively recent emergence in the media landscape, online commerce is a fast growing media industry and research in this area was some of the most diverse and innovative. Digital field studies allow for larger samples than could ever be deployed in a lab setting, which permits more permutations; names were manipulated to make salient different racial and gender combinations. The most impressive methodology featured ten conditions in a 2 (Gender: Male, Female) x 5 (Race: White, Black, Latino, Chinese, Indian) design (Milkman, Akinola, & Chugh, 2014). Digital technology also facilitates multiple manipulations of race and gender (e.g., skin tone of hands, labeling and other linguistic strategies in social networking sites, interactive voice assistants).

## Patterns in Research Methodology

Several research trends emerged across the reviewed studies, including issues that have been problematic in media effects research for some time; 80.8% of studies deployed a single exposure methodology, and 89.0% of the studies were conducted in a laboratory setting. However, other issues such as pretesting stimuli, conducting manipulation checks, and population biases also limit the generalizability of findings for a global understanding of the cognitive processes regarding race and gender in media.

Only 43.0% of studies described piloting the experimental stimuli and 30.8% conducted manipulation checks; instead, researchers often deployed what they deemed obvious manipulations of race and gender, generating names and characteristics without citation or research. Although some studies deployed birth records from 1974 of Black and White boys and girls (Bertrand & Mullainathan, 2004), no study since has sought birth records, despite sampling participants born ten to fifteen years later. In addition, no study has investigated other implications of names as moderators; "Tyrell" or "Keshia" may denote Blackness, but other associated differences in perceived education or socioeconomic status may moderate overall effects. Future studies should investigate the social stigma of certain names with respect to race, gender, and other social categories.

Studies providing detailed demographics reported an average of 64.8% White and 61.9% female participants; furthermore, the vast majority (92.7%) of studies were conducted in the United States, thus dominating the academic understanding with American models of gender and race. This sampling bias provides a very specific understanding of the effects of race and gender in media that cannot be generalized to a global population, or even a diverse population within the United States. Although this trend has been repeated across behavioral sciences (Henrich, Heine, & Norenzayan, 2010), more diverse samples are required.

Furthermore, the lack of intersectional awareness described in research design was also evident in the reporting of participant demographics and the subsequent interpretation of findings; two-thirds of the studies reported participant gender and half the studies reported participant race, but more interestingly, half of the studies investigating race did not include the gender composition of their sample and half the studies investigated gender did not include the racial composition of their sample. These omissions inhibit researchers' ability to investigate or acknowledge different effects between groups; how would "Patrick" and "Patricia" affect non-White audiences?

Studies also emphasized traditional binaries; the majority of studies investigating race compared Blackness and Whiteness, and all of the studies investigating gender compared femaleness and maleness. Only a handful of studies compared racial groups outside of the Black/White binary or included a gender-neutral condition. Although these binaries have dominated the discussion for decades, other traditionally marginalized groups (e.g., Latino, multiracial, trans) are being addressed in public discourse and researchers should empirically investigate the splintering of these constructs. The comparison of Black and White or male and female is an important starting point in understanding the mechanisms of race and gender, but it is not generalizable to an increasingly diverse community.

By combining different methods (e.g., images, names, labeling) and formats, researchers can investigate a wide range of marginalized groups and intersectional identities.

## So What Are Race and Gender?

I have avoided defining race and gender here, in order to investigate methodological implementations of these constructs. The studies featured in this review, and organized by using the Media FIT Taxonomy, define race and gender according to names, skin tone, and stereotypical features such as speech patterns, which rely on the spreading activation of norms and stereotypes in order to activate the social constructs of "race" or "gender." Therefore, the question remains: Are we testing the effects of race and gender or racial and gender stereotypes? Although researchers try to separate the phenotype from the stereotype, these supposed exemplary physical indicators (e.g., dark skin, breasts) vary, and can even denote other unintended groups (e.g., dark skin can indicate South Asian ethnic groups, not all women have breasts); although some studies investigate the spectrum of these phenotypes, the vast majority of studies are still deploying exemplary binaries to test inherently nebulous categories that vary from culture to culture and person to person.

Despite these confounds, the methods described in this chapter can be deployed in any community and any culture. It is my hope that future researchers will extend this research to create better understanding of the effects of race and gender in media especially with respect to marginalized and intersectional communities. We engage with mediated indicators of race and gender every day, and it is therefore essential that we understand how these seemingly small differences affect our understanding of our world and ourselves, and that we go beyond traditional binaries: What happens when we refer to "Bruce" as "she"?

## References

Ahmed, A. M., & Hammarstedt, M. (2008). Discrimination in the rental housing market: A field experiment on the Internet. *Journal of Urban Economics, 64*, 362–672.

Alhabash, S., Hales, K., Baek, J., & Oh, H. J. (2014). Effects of race, visual anonymity, and social category salience on online dating outcomes. *Computers in Human Behavior, 35*, 22–32.

Allport, G. W. (1954). *The nature of prejudice.* New York, NY: Perseus Books.

Anderson, C. A., & Murphy, C. R. (2003). Violent video games and aggressive behavior in young women. *Aggressive Behavior, 29*, 423–429.

Ansdager, J. (2003). Racial and regional differences in readers' evaluations of the credibility of political columnists by race and sex. *Journalism & Mass Communication Quarterly, 80*, 57–72.

Appiah, O. (2001a). Black, White, Hispanic, and Asian American adolescents' responses to culturally embedded ads. *Howard Journal of Communication, 12,* 29–48.

Appiah, O. (2001b). Ethnic identification on adolescents' evaluations of advertisements. *Journal of Advertising Research, 41,* 1–16.

Appiah, O. (2004). Effects of ethnic identification on web browsers' attitudes toward and navigational patterns on race-targeted sites. *Communication Research, 3,* 312–337.

Appiah, O. (2009). Reaching the model minority: Ethnic differences in responding to culturally embedded targeted- and non-targeted advertisements. *Current Issues and Research in Advertising, 31,* 27–41.

Armstrong, C. L., & McAdams, M. J. (2009). Blogs of information: How gender cues and individual motivations influence perceptions of credibility. *Journal of Computer Mediated Communication, 14,* 435–456.

Ayres, I. Banaji, M. R., & Jolis, C. (2011). *Race effects on eBay.* Retrieved October 30, 2015, from http://papers.ssrn.com/sol3/papers.cfm?abstract_id=1934432.

Bertrand, M., & Mullainathan, S. (2004). Are Emily and Greg more employable than Lakisha and Jamal? A field experiment on labor market discrimination. *The National Bureau of Economic Research.* Retrieved October 30, 2015, from http://www.nber.org/papers/w9873.

Besbris, M., Faber, J. W., Rich, P., & Sharkey, P. (2015). Effect of neighborhood stigma on economic transactions. *Proceedings of the National Academy of Sciences, 112,* 4994–4998.

Carpusor, A. G., & Loges, W. E. (2006). Rental discrimination and ethnicity in names. *Journal of Applied Social Psychology, 36,* 934–952.

Cundiff, J. L. (2013, January). *Communicating non-normative status through asymmetrical gender marking: Implications and consequences.* In E. Thomas & J. Cundiff (Chairs), Challenging the White male default: An analysis of social identity norms in contemporary society. Symposium conducted at the annual conference of the Society for Personality and Social Psychology, New Orleans, LA.

DeCasper, A. J., & Spence, M. J. (1986). Prenatal material speech influences newborns' perception of speech sounds. *Infant Behavior and Development, 9,* 133–150.

Deshpandé, R., & Stayman, D. M. (1994). A tale of two cities: Distinctiveness theory and advertising effectiveness. *Journal of Marketing Research, 31,* 57–64.

Devos, T., & Banaji, M. R. (2005). American = White? *Journal of Personality and Social Psychology, 88,* 447–466.

Dixon, T. L. (2006). Schemas as average conceptions: Skin tone, television news exposure and culpability judgments. *Journalism & Mass Communication Quarterly, 83,* 131–149.

Dixon , T. L. (2007). Black criminals and White officers: The effects of racially misrepresenting law breakers and law defenders on television news. *Media Psychology, 10,* 270–291.

Dixon, T. L., & Azocar, C. L. (2007). Priming crime and activating Blackness: Understanding the psychological impact of the overrepresentation of Blacks as lawbreakers on television news. *Journal of Communication, 57,* 229–253.

Dixon, T. L., & Maddox, K. B. (2005). Skin tone, crime news, and social reality judgments: Priming the stereotype of the dark and dangerous Black criminal. *Journal of Applied Social Psychology, 35,* 1,555–1,570.

Dixon, T. L., Schell, T. L., Giles, H., & Drogos, K.L. (2005). The influence of race in police–civilian interactions: A content analysis of videotaped interactions taken during cincinnati police traffic stops. *Journal of Communication, 58,* 530–549.

Doleac, J. L., & Stein, L. C. D. (2013). The visible hand: Race and online market outcomes. *The Economic Journal, 123,* F439–F492.

Eastin, M. S. (2006). Video game violence and the female game player: Self- and opponent gender effects on presence and aggressive thoughts. *Human Communication Research, 32,* 351–372.

Flanagin, A. J., & Metzger, M. J. (2003). The perceived credibility of personal web page information as influenced by the sex of the source. *Computers in Human Behavior, 19,* 683–701.

Gilliam, F. D., Iyengar, S., Simon, A., & Wright, O. (1996). Crime in Black and White: The violent, scary world of local news. *The International Journal of Press/Politics, 1,* 6–23.

Gilliam, F. D., & Iyengar, S. (2000). Prime suspects: The influence of local television news on the viewing public. *American Journal of Political Science, 44,* 560–573.

Goff, P. A., Eberhardt, J. L., Williams, M. J., & Jackson, M. C. (2008). Not yet human: Implicit knowledge, historical dehumanization, and contemporary consequences. *Journal of Personality and Social Psychology, 94,* 292–306.

Goldberg, P. (1968). Are women prejudiced against women?. *Society, 5,* 28–30.

Golden, J. N. (2014). Why I'm masquerading as a White bearded hipster guy on Twitter (despite being a Black woman). *xojane.* Retrieved October 30, 2015, from: http://www.xojane.com/issues/why-im-masquerading-as-a-bearded-white-hipster-guy-on-twitter.

Groom, V., Bailenson, J. N., & Nass, C. (2009). The influence of racial embodiment on racial bias in immersive virtual environments. *Social Influence, 4,* 231–248.

Hanson, A., & Hawley, Z. (2011) Do landlords discriminate in the rental housing market? Evidence from an internet field experiment in US cities. *Journal of Urban Economics, 80,* 99–117.

Henrich, J., Heine, S. J., & Norenzayan, A. (2010). The weirdest people in the world? *Behavioral and Brain Sciences, 33,* 61–83.

How people spend their online time. (2012). [Infographic]. Retrieved October 30, 2015, from http://www.go-gulf.com/blog/online-time/.

Klatt, D. H., & Klatt, L. C. (1990). Analysis, synthesis, and perception of voice quality variations among female and male talkers. *The Journal of the Acoustical Society of America, 87,* 820–857.

Knobloch-Westerwick, S., Appiah, O., & Alter, S. (2008). News selection patterns as a function of race: The discerning minority and the indiscriminating majority. *Media Psychology, 11,* 400–417.

Lee, E. (2007). Wired for gender: Experientiality and gender-stereotyping in computer-mediated communication. *Media Psychology, 10,* 182–210.

Lee, K. M., Liao, K., & Ryu, S. (2007). Children's responses to computer-synthesized speech in educational media; Gender consistency and gender similarity effects. *Human Communication Research, 33,* 310–329.

Lee, E., Nass, C., & Brave, S. (2000). Can computer-generated speech have gender?: An experimental test of gender stereotype. Proceedings from *CHI EA '00: Extended Abstracts on Human Factors in Computing Systems*, New York: ACM, 289–290.

Liebler, C.M. (2010). Me(di)a Culpa?: The "Missing White Woman Syndrome" and media self-critique. *Communication, Culture & Critique, 3*, 549–565.

Lugo-Lugo, C. R., & Bloodsworth-Lugo, M. K. (2009). "Look out new world, here we come"?: Race, racialization and sexuality in four children's animated films by Disney, Pixar, and DreamWorks. *Cultural Studies <=> Critical Methodologies, 9*, 166–178.

Martin-Santana, J. D., Muela-Molina, C., Reinares-Lara, E., & Rodriguez-Guerra, M. (2014). Effectiveness of radio spokesperson's gender, vocal pitch and accent and the use of music in radio advertising. *Business Research Quarterly, 18*, 143–160.

Mastro, D. E., Behm-Morawitz, E., & Kopacz, M. A. (2008). Exposure to television portrayals of Latinos: The implications of aversive racism and social identity theory. *Human Communication Research, 34*, 1–27.

Mastro, D., Seate, A. A., Blecha, E., & Gallegos, M. (2012). The wide world of sports reporting: The influence of gender- and race-based expectations on evaluations of sports reporters. *Journalism & Mass Communication Quarterly, 89*, 458–474.

Milkman, K. L., Akinola, M., & Chugh, D. (2014). What happens before? A field experiment exploring how pay and representation differentially shape bias on the pathway into organizations. *Journal of Applied Psychology*. Advance online publication.

Millard, A. B. (2015, March 25). It happened to me: I posed as a man on Twitter and nobody called me fat or threatened to rape me for once. *xojane*. Retrieved October 30, 2015, from http://www.xojane.com/it-happened-to-me/i-was-a-man-on-twitter.

Nass, C., & Scott, B. (2005). *Wired for speech: How voice activates and advances the human-computer relationship*. Cambridge, MA: The MIT Press.

O'Mally, A. K., & Worrell, T. R. (2004). Statistics or stories, Black or White? Examining influences of African American organ donation. *Howard Journal of Communications, 25*, 98–114.

Oliver, M. B. (1999). Caucasian viewers' memory of Black and White criminal suspects in the news. *Journal of Communication, 49*, 46–60.

Peck, T. C., Seinfeld, S., Aglioti, S. M., & Slater, M. (2013). Putting yourself in the skin of a Black avatar reduces implicit racial bias. *Consciousness and Cognition, 22*, 779–787.

Peffley, M., Shields, T., & Williams, B. (1996). The intersection of race and crime in television news stories: An experimental study. *Political Communication, 13*, 309–327.

Pernet, C. R., & Belin, P. (2012). The role of pitch and timbre in voice gender categorization. *Frontiers in Psychology, 3*, 1–11.

Perse, E. M., Nathanson, A. I., & McLeod, D. M. (1996). Effects of spokesperson sex, public service announcement appeal, and involvement on evaluations of safe-sex PSAs. *Health Communication, 8*, 171–189.

Pierce, K. (2001). What if the Energizer bunny were female? Importance of gender in perceptions of advertising spokes-character effectiveness. *Sex Roles, 45*, 845–858.

Puts, D. A. (2005). Mating context and menstrual phase affect women's preferences for male voice pitch. *Evolution & Human Behavior, 26*, 388–397.

Rosenthal, R. (1991). *Meta-analytic procedures for social research*. Newbury Park, CA: Sage.

Simpson. A. P. (2009). Phonetic differences between male and female speech. *Language and Linguistics Compass, 3*, 621–640.

Spence, P. R., Lachlan, K. A., Westerman, D., & Spates, S. A. (2013). Where the gates matter less: Ethnicity and perceived source credibility in social media health messages. *Howard Journal of Communications, 24*, 1–16.

Stout, J. G., & Dasgupta, N. (2011). When he doesn't mean you: Gender-exclusive language as ostracism. *Personality and Social Psychology Bulletin, 36*, 757–769.

Valentino, N. A., Hutchings, V. L., & White, I. K. (2002). Cues that matter: How political ads prime racial attitudes during campaigns. *American Political Science Review, 96*, 75–90.

Walker, H. J., Field, H. S., Giles, W. F., Armenakis, A. A., & Bernerth, J. B. (2009). Displaying employee testimonials on recruitment websites: Effects of communication media, employee race, and job seeker race on organizational attraction and information credibility. *Journal of Applied Psychology, 94*, 1354–1364.

Walton, J. H., & Orlikoff, R. F. (1994). Speaker race identification from acoustic cues in the vocal signal. *Journal of Speech Language and Hearing Research, 37*, 738–745.

Wang, X., & Arpan, L. M. (2008). Effects of race and ethnic identity on audience evaluation of HIV public service announcements. *The Howard Journal of Communications, 19*, 44–63.

Weaver, A. J. (2011). The role of actors' race in White audiences' selective exposure to movies. *Journal of Communication, 61*, 369–385.

Whipple, T. W., & McMannon, M. K. (2002). Implications of using male and female voices in commercials: An exploratory study. *Journal of Advertising, 31*, 79–91.

White, H. A., & Ansdager, J. L. (1991). Gender and credibility of newspaper columnists. *Journalism Quarterly, 68*, 709–718.

Xu, Y., Lee, A., Wu, W., Liu, X., & Birkholz, P. (2013). Human vocal attractiveness as signaled by body size projection. *PLoS ONE, 8*(4), 1–9.

Xue, S. A., & Fucci, D. (2000). Effects of race and sex on acoustic features of voice analysis. *Perpetual and Motor Skills, 91*, 951–958.

Xue, S. A., Hao, G. J. P. & Mayo, R. (2006). Volumetric measurements of vocal tracts for male speakers from different races. *Clinical Linguistics & Phonetics, 20*, 691–702.

Yang, G. S., Gibson, B., Lueke, A. K., Huesmann, R., & Bushman, B. J. (2014). Effects of avatar race in violent video games on racial attitudes and aggression. *Social Psychological and Personality Science, 5*, 698–704.

Zamora, J. (2014, August 30). *José vs. Joe: Who gets a job* [Video File]. Retrieved October 30, 2015, from https://www.youtube.com/watch?v=PR7SG2C7IVU.

# 9

# PORTRAYALS OF LATINOS IN THE MEDIA AND THE EFFECTS OF EXPOSURE ON LATINO AND NON-LATINO AUDIENCES

*Dana Mastro and Alexander Sink*

In his 2014 satirical film *Fugly!*, Colombian-American actor John Leguizamo played a struggling Latino comedian/actor who, in response to his girlfriend's question regarding whether he got the part of "the rapist or the mugger," counters with: "I got the drug dealer!" (Reyes, 2014). This on-screen exchange satirizes the well-documented and longstanding tendency to confine Latinos to a limited set of stereotypical roles in mass media. When asked about this issue in interviews, Leguizamo commented that Latino actors today experience greater opportunities than they have in the past; however he stressed that, "This industry still has some issues with us that should be gone by now" (Reyes, 2014).

Certainly, evidence from content analyses documenting representations of Latinos in media over the decades offers support for such claims (see Mastro, 2009 for review). In fact, despite headlines in the popular press proclaiming that "TV is More Diverse than Ever" (Kang, 2015), all evidence indicates that Latinos have been largely excluded from these advances (Associated Press, 2015; Negrón-Muntaner et al., 2014). Importantly, studies testing the implications of exposure to Latinos' portrayals on both Latino and non-Latino audiences demonstrate that media depictions can influence a wide array of cognitive, attitudinal, and behavioral outcomes in a manner consistent with the media message. To help illuminate this issue, we synthesize the existing social scientific research on Latinos in the media, focusing on quantitative examinations of the portrayal of Latinos across the media landscape, in order to then discuss the effects of exposure to such content on both Latino and non-Latino audiences.

## Portrayal of Latinos on Television

Although the manner in which Latinos are presented in (and thoughtfully integrated into) mass media offerings is a primary contributor to the effects of exposure (Entman, 1994), the sheer number of depictions is additionally meaningful because it informs perceptions about the group's strength, cohesiveness, and standing in society (Harwood & Roy, 2005). Television has long been criticized for failing to offer an array of favorable Latino characters (Mastro & Greenberg, 2000). Indeed, Latinos have historically experienced both underrepresentation and misrepresentation in this medium.

Latinos have faced decades of underrepresentation on television, on both absolute and comparative bases. When the number of Latinos on TV is measured against Census data, a clear trend of underrepresentation emerges (Mastro & Behm-Morawitz, 2005; Mastro & Sink, in press). The 1950s is the only decade in which Latinos appeared on television at a rate consistent with their proportion in the actual population (Mastro & Behm-Morawitz, 2005). During this period, 3% of all TV characters were Latinos, as seen in popular programs such as *The Cisco Kid* and *I Love Lucy*. Perhaps when considering that only 2.4% of the population was Latino at this time, the fact that Latinos were proportionally depicted on television seems less remarkable. It must also be noted that the majority of these characters were portrayed by White actors (e.g., El Toro in *The Adventures of Kit Carson*).

The number of Latinos on primetime television declined throughout the 1960s and 70s, despite a steady increase in the U.S. population. In the 1980s, Latinos constituted just 1% of television characters (Gerbner & Signorielli, 1979; Greenberg & Baptista-Fernandez, 1980), yet comprised approximately 8% of the country's population. The 1990s saw only slight increases in the number of Latinos on television, with analyses estimating Latinos made up between 1.1% and 1.6% of primetime television characters (Mastro & Behm-Morawitz, 2005). In U.S. society, however, the Latino population had continued to increase, with approximately 11% of the U.S. population identifying as Latino during this decade (Mastro & Behm-Morawitz, 2005).

The premieres of three situation comedies with predominantly Latino casts (e.g., *The George Lopez Show*) in the early 2000s seemed to signal major improvements for the number of Latinos on primetime (Mastro & Behm-Morawitz, 2005). However, only incremental changes in quantity were seen; estimates showed Latinos comprised between just 3.8% and 6.5% of the TV population (Children Now, 2004; Mastro & Behm-Morawitz, 2005). Although an increase from previous decades, this was far below Latinos' proportion of the U.S. population at the time. The most recent analyses of Latinos on primetime television (the Fall

2013 season) indicate Latinos' portrayals are still abysmally low when compared to Census data. Despite the fact that the real-world Latino population in the U.S. has risen to roughly 16%, Latino characters comprised less than 3% of the primetime population (Mastro & Sink, in press). Encouragingly, the 2014–2015 television season saw the premieres of two shows with predominantly Latino casts on major networks (*Cristela* and *Jane the Virgin*). Yet the promise of this programming was short-lived, as only *Jane the Virgin* was renewed for the 2015–2016 season.

The gross underrepresentation of Latinos on television might be less troubling if these infrequent depictions provided a more auspicious set of media models. Unfortunately, research indicates that this is not the case. Historically, Latinos have been confined to a limited pool of stereotypic and often negative archetypes on television (Greenberg & Baptista-Fernandez, 2005), some of which have persisted for decades (Mastro & Behm-Morawitz, 2005). In addition, Latinos rarely serve as central narrative figures, but are generally in secondary or nonrecurring roles (Mastro & Behm-Morawitz, 2005). One of the earliest themes in the portrayal of Latinos on television was as the object of ridicule (Mastro & Greenberg, 2000), including inarticulate sidekicks such as Pancho on *The Cisco Kid* (1950–56) and dimwitted foils such as Sergeant Garcia on *Zorro* (1957–1959) (Berg, 2004). This characterization is designed to provide comic relief. With a lazy disposition, thick accent, lack of intelligence, and inferior status, such figures are easy targets for derision (Mastro & Greenberg, 2000). This stereotype has persisted, with modern examples including the romantically-challenged Fez on Fox's syndicated *That 70's Show* (1998–2006) and arguably even George from ABC's *The George Lopez Show* (2002–2007), alongside numerous other characters from short-lived primetime series (e.g., *Greetings from Tucson*, 2002–2003).

Of course, Latinos are not exclusively portrayed as unintelligent and bumbling, with broken English; however, many other early and ongoing characterizations also rely on negative stereotypes. For example, another prominent characterization is that of the criminal. This archetype is typified as young, aggressive and male with an unkempt appearance and a dishonest nature (Berg, 1990). Such characters were common in early adventure shows such as *Zorro*, and remain a staple in primetime. In contrast, the presentation of Latinos as law enforcers has emerged as a counterpoint to this criminal character. In this role, Latinos are represented as well-groomed, honest, articulate, and respected authority figures (Mastro & Behm-Morawitz, 2005). Yet these two opposing images often go hand in hand, frequently in the same program. The co-occurrence of Latino criminals and Latino law enforcers is prevalent on contemporary TV, including in NBC's *Law and Order: Special Victims Unit* (1999–). This long-running crime drama has, for several seasons, featured an attractive, composed, and accomplished Latino detective who often clashed with Latino thugs. Although it is encouraging to see Latinos as respected authority figures, the persistent pairing of these two types of roles is troubling, and likely contributes to the finding that Latinos on primetime engage in the most conversations about crime and violence when compared to other racial/ethnic groups (Mastro & Behm-Morawitz, 2005), thereby further linking Latinos to criminal behavior.

Although the characterizations discussed thus far have focused on males, Latinas appear in equally constrained ways on television. They are less likely to be featured in the context of crime than males are; instead, Latinas are often presented as objects of the sexual desire and fantasy of their White costars. These exotic and seductive women are marked not only by their sensuality, but also by a hot-temper, heavy accent, and sexual aggressiveness (Berg, 1990). The wildly popular character Gloria from ABC's *Modern Family* (2009–) has been widely criticized for reinforcing this narrow stereotype (Valdez, 2013). Research indicates that males on TV are at times also sexualized on television (Berg, 1990), with Latino exotic lovers frequenting daytime soap operas and primetime reality programming (e.g., *The Bachelor*'s Juan Pablo).

The small number of recent content analyses examining Latinos on TV offers conflicting evidence about the persistence of these stereotypes. On the one hand, Mastro and Behm-Morawitz (2005) found that Latino characters' incomes and intelligence were comparable to their White and Black counterparts. On the other hand, Latino characters are commonly over-represented as accented and inarticulate (Mastro & Sink, in press). It seems reasonable to suggest that portrayals of Latinos on television are inequitable in terms of both quantity and quality, and have shown little improvement over the last 60 years.

## Portrayal of Latinos in Film

Many of the stereotypes perpetuated on television were derived from early film depictions (see Wilson, Gutiérrez, & Chao, 2013, for review). Unfortunately, quantitative content analyses of race/ethnicity in film are less common than in television, possibly owing to challenges in unitization in film. Sampling difficulties may also play into this absence. More than 500 films are released in the United States alone each year (MPAA, 2014). Due to a general lack of quantitative studies, our empirical knowledge of the number of Latinos in film is limited. However, a recent analysis of top grossing films across 11 countries found that Latino characters made up just 1.6% of the total population in these movies (Smith, Choueiti, & Pieper, 2014), which provides some evidence for underrepresentation when compared with real-world demographics.

The lack of quantitative content analyses of film also constrains our ability to provide generalizable information about the quality of these images. It is possible, however, to connect film stereotypes with television stereotypes by examining influential characters throughout cinematic history. The notion of the Latino criminal can be traced back to some of the earliest greaser films of the early 1900s, wherein Mexican men were presented as pillaging bandits (Berg, 1990). In the decades to follow, portrayals of criminality decreased, with Latinos next presented as well-dressed, hot tempered objects of desire. First popularized by Italian actor Rudolph Valentino in films such as *The Kissing Bandit* (1948), the Latin lover archetype quickly became a staple in popular film (Trevino, 1984). Sexualized depictions of Latinas also became prevalent, and remain common today. For both genders, these characters are often one-dimensional figures whose only defining feature is sexual. Early films also popularized images of Mexican men as weak, sleepy, peasants or peons, particularly in the spaghetti western films of the 1960s (Trevino, 1984). Compared with the greaser who, although diabolical, was often a worthy adversary for the cowboy heroes, the peasant's ignorance was often a tool used to provide comic relief, with his weaknesses contrasting the strength and wits of the White heroes. This character directly parallels the buffoon-like character presented on TV.

Despite the persistence of these stereotypes, Latino actors and filmmakers have achieved considerable fame and esteem in Hollywood. Indeed, superstars such as Jennifer Lopez and Gael Garcia Bernal are wildly popular among audiences and widely sought after in the industry. Yet, these successes do not appear to have signaled a new era in the quality of Latino portrayals in film.

## Portrayal of Latinos in Video Games

Scholars have devoted considerable attention to the relationship between video game use and outcomes such as aggression (see Anderson & Bushman, 2001 for review) and gender-related attitudes (Dill & Thill, 2007). However, social scientific examinations of representations of race and ethnicity in this medium are fairly uncommon. Because video games offer unique, interactive affordances not present in television and film, representations of race/ethnicity in this context especially warrant further examination. Players assume a much more active role in this medium, controlling and driving the events that unfold on screen. As Everett and Watkins argued, "players are not only watching race; they are also performing and, as a result, (re)producing socially prescribed and technologically mediated notions of race" (2008, p. 149). Understanding the state of these mediated notions of race/ethnicity, then, is of considerable interest.

To the best of our knowledge, as of this writing (October 2015) only two quantitative content analyses of race/ethnicity in video games exist, both of which report the existence of strikingly few Latino characters.

In their examination of the top-selling game titles for the seven major consoles, Knowlee and colleagues (2001) found that more than 50% of player-controlled characters were White males, with Latino characters totaling just 2% of the video game population. Data from the 2000 Census showed Latinos comprised 12.5% of the U.S. population at that time, marking a considerable disparity between character and real-world populations. All of the Latino characters found in this content were male figures in sports video games (the majority of which were baseball simulators). Williams, Martins, Consalvo, and Ivory (2009) found comparable results in their analysis of 150 top-selling games. Of the 4,966 human characters, a mere 2.71% were Latino, whereas the majority (80.05%) was White. Latinos were not primary characters in any game. The authors contended that unlike television, which has at times shown modest gains for Latinos, video games have continued largely to ignore Latinos through non-inclusion or by presenting them in secondary roles. In sum, both studies show a systematic underrepresentation of Latinos in this medium.

Although video games have been criticized for hosting "extreme and blatant racial tropes" (Leonard, 2006, p. 83), little empirical evidence exists to support this assertion. Some scholars (e.g., Everett & Watkins, 2008) have argued that the urban/street sub-genre of gaming— (e.g., *Grand Theft Auto* series and *True Crime: Streets of LA*), which typically features gang-related narratives wherein violent or illegal acts are essential to progressing through the game's narrative—promotes criminalized and sexualized depictions of Latinos. In these games, Black and Latino characters are said to appear more frequently. However, lacking empirical assessments of this content, the quality of Latino characterizations in video games is largely unknown. What has been documented is that only 2% of hero characters are Latino (Knowlee et al., 2001). Additionally, 83% of Latino characters exhibit physical harm and pain after being injured (compared with 43% of White characters), despite appearing most frequently in sports-related games. Unfortunately, nothing beyond the broad conclusion that Latinos are overrepresented as athletes and underrepresented as heroes, can be determined.

## Implication of Exposure to Media Images of Latinos

Given the often unfavorable nature of media depictions of Latinos, the impetus for much of the research investigating the effects of exposure has been concerned with the potentially harmful consequences for interethnic relations in society. Accordingly, the bulk of the research in this area has concentrated on the implications of consuming such content on non-Latino audiences (Whites, in particular). However, a significant body of research has studied the implications of consuming such content on Latino audiences. Each subset will be discussed in turn.

## Implications of Exposure on Non-Latino Audiences

Fairly consistently, research demonstrates that both short- and long-term exposure to Latino portrayals can influence the development and structure of cognitions regarding Latinos, race/ethnicity-based policy preferences, and a wide array of interethnic emotions, judgments, and behaviors (see Mastro, 2009, for review).

### Influence on Cognitions and Attitudes

Media images have long been theorized to contribute to the construction and maintenance of racial and ethnic stereotypes (e.g., Gerbner, 1998; Mackie, Hamilton, Susskind, & Rosselli, 1996). This research argues that through the implicit and explicit racial/ethnic messages offered in mass media content, audiences develop a media-formulated understanding of racial/ethnic groups and race-related issues. Specifically, through short- and long-term use of mass media, consumers associate specific attributes—including behaviors, qualities, values, attitudes, demographics, status-based positions, physical locations, and the like—with different groups.

Although limited, empirical tests of this association indicate that exposure to media depictions of Latinos contributes to the construction of real-world stereotypes about Latinos in a number of domains. Indeed, a survey by Mastro, Behm-Morawitz, and Oritz (2007) revealed that increases in television consumption enhanced the influence of exposure to TV representations of Latinos, especially when viewers had less closeness in their real-life contact with Latinos. The more television White viewers consumed, the more their evaluations of Latinos in society reflected the TV characterizations (in terms of common stereotypical portrayals as criminal, unintelligent, and lazy), indicating a greater reliance on televised images when forming social judgments.

Additional support for this association can be gleaned from work by Tukachinsky, Mastro, and Yarchi (2015), who used multi-level modeling to examine the influence of television depictions of Latinos over two decades (1987 to 2009) on contemporaneous national-level attitudes about Latinos among Whites, when controlling for sex, age, education, and political orientation. Their findings revealed that images of highly professional Latino characters significantly contributed to positive attitudes toward Latinos in society. On the other hand, the portrayal of hyper-sexual Latino characters was associated with negative attitudes toward Latinos. It should be noted that neither depictions of good Latino characters nor liked Latino characters had a significant effect on Whites' attitudes toward Latinos, which may suggest that more specific aspects of these favorable characterizations need to be isolated to identify any potential prosocial effects stemming exposure. This interpretation is particularly plausible when considering the existing research addressed in our consideration of prosocial outcomes below. Alternatively, the overall small number of Latino depictions found on primetime TV over these decades may have contributed to the limited findings. Still, the results underscore the fact that the manner in which diverse groups are portrayed in the media is critical.

## Influence on Intergroup Dynamics

The stereotype-related outcomes outlined in the previous section are, fundamentally, a function of intergroup processes. Yet, theories of intergroup relations have only infrequently been applied to tests of this relationship. The limited body of research has applied assumptions rooted in social identity theory (Tajfel & Turner, 1986) and self-categorization theory (Turner, 1982, 1985) to flesh out processes and effects relevant to this context of how the media may impact stereotyping. Empirical tests of these models' tenets have provided fairly consistent support. For Whites, exposure to stereotypical media representations of Latinos seems to promote intergroup comparisons which advantage Whites and serve White identity needs, particularly among those who are highly identified with their racial ingroup (Mastro, 2003). That is, for White audience members whose self-concept is strongly tied to their race, exposure to negative Latino stereotypes provides an opportunity for downward intergroup comparisons, which support their self-concept. Equally consequentially, research indicates that when exposure to media depictions of Latinos prompts unfavorable stereotyping of Latinos in U.S. society, support for race-related policies (e.g., affirmative action) decreases (Mastro & Kopacz, 2006).

In addition, when the contextual features of media depictions of Latinos minimize the potential to appear racist, intergroup bias is increased (Mastro, Behm-Morawitz, & Kopacz, 2008). Put differently, biased responses to stereotypical media depictions of Latinos (especially among White viewers who are highly identified with their race) are enhanced when the content offers sufficient ambiguity for the reaction to be deemed unrelated to ethnicity/race. Consistent with social identity-based frameworks, this ability to advantage one's ingroup through beneficial comparisons with a mediated outgroup seems to aid in esteem maintenance (although these findings were not robust).

## Language in Media-Related Intergroup Processes

Theory and empirical tests of the role of language in communicating stereotypes reveals that subtle and seemingly unconscious biases in linguistic messages can maintain and perpetuate stereotypes (Maass, Salvi, Arcuri, & Semin, 1989; Wigboldus, Semin, & Spears, 2000). In particular, the degree of linguistic abstraction used to describe people or events has been argued to serve as an implicit marker of intergroup bias, thereby perpetuating stereotypes. According to the linguistic category model (LCM: Semin & Fiedler, 1988), people can describe behavior using four classes of words that vary in their level of abstraction (from concrete to abstract). Work testing LCM shows that people exhibit linguistic intergroup bias (LIB: Maass et al., 1989) when evaluating and describing the behaviors of ingroup and outgroup members. Specifically, desirable ingroup behaviors and undesirable outgroup behaviors are described using abstract language, implying dispositional attributions. Alternatively, undesirable ingroup behaviors and desirable outgroup behaviors are described with more concrete language, implying situational attributions (Fiedler, Bluemke, Friese, & Hoffmann, 2003; Maass et al., 1989). As a result, stereotypes can be transmitted and sustained, without overt demonstrations of discrimination or prejudice (Carpenter & Radhakrishnan, 2002; Maass et al., 1989). Such linguistic intergroup bias has been found in a wide array of media fare including international coverage of sports and war (Maass, Corvino, & Arcuri, 1994) and print news coverage of immigration in the US (Mastro & Dragojevic, 2014). Experimental tests investigating the effects of consuming such messages have supported notions rooted in LIB. Generally speaking, this work reveals that under certain conditions, when news coverage abstractly addresses outgroup members, exposure promotes unfavorable evaluations of the group in society (Mastro, Tukachinsky, Behm-Morawitz, & Blecha, 2014). In particular, the use of abstract language in print news reports on immigration (involving U.S.–Mexico Border Patrol support) has been found to promote broad-based stereotyping about U.S. Latinos. Yet when the same topic is covered in a concrete fashion, such judgments do not emerge. Consistent with LIB, then, these findings suggest that the specific features of the language used to describe racial/ethnic ingroup and outgroup members in the media is consequential in that it may transmit and maintain stereotypes and promote undesirable intergroup dynamics in society.

### Emotions and Intergroup Processes

Atwell Seate and Mastro (2015b) experimentally examined the effect of viewing threatening immigration news coverage on group-level emotions. Using an intergroup emotions theory (IET) approach, their findings indicated that exposure to intergroup threat (i.e., Mexican immigration to the U.S.) on TV news prompted group-level contempt emotions among White viewers which predicted active and passive harming behaviors, measured in terms of policy preferences and information sharing actions on the topic of immigration. Consistent with existing research, these effects were moderated by the degree of identification with the

White ingroup. More specifically, although viewing news depictions of immigration threat did not directly influence active or passive harming behaviors, the results indicated that exposure affected behaviors indirectly through contempt, increasingly so as ingroup identification rose. In particular, exposure to immigration threat in the news provoked greater contempt as identification with the (White) ingroup increased. In turn, contempt prompted both active (i.e., signing a petition in support of English-only laws) and passive (i.e., sharing immigration-related news stories) harming behaviors.

Yet, despite the disconcerting nature of the findings reported to this point, it is important to note that research additionally demonstrates that exposure to auspicious characterizations of Latinos can reduce bias and encourage more sympathetic intergroup positions.

## Prosocial Outcomes

Consistent with existing research assessing the potential for positive media messages about Blacks to prompt more favorable race-related judgments and behaviors among White viewers (e.g., Bodenhausen Schwarz, Bless, & Wanke, 1995; Power, Murphy, & Coover, 1996; Ramasubramanian, 2001), Mastro and Tukachinsky's (2011) work underscores the constructive influence of respectable media depictions of Latinos on intergroup dynamics. Their research revealed that although favorable portrayals can encourage prosocial outcomes, not all positive depictions are equivalent. Based on a series of experiments that varied the presentation of positive Latino media models, their results revealed that exposure to portrayals that both supported shared norms about valued features Latinos and were not seen as atypical or outliers generated the most favorable results in White audiences. Certainly auspicious depictions are always more desirable than disparaging ones, but when it comes to promoting positive changes in consumers, it seems that the most effective portrayals are those which exemplify naturally existing, widely understood positive features of the group.

## Implications of Exposure on Latino Audiences

The majority of work addressing the implications of exposure to media depictions of Latinos has focused on outcomes such as stereotyping, prejudice, and discrimination among White audiences. Yet Latinos are also affected by exposure to media messages about their group. Only a handful of studies, however, have taken a quantitative approach to addressing this relationship. This work revealed that the quality of media depictions of Latinos contributes to perceptions of self, group, societal intergroup dynamics, and identity management.

## Perceptions of Self, Group, and Intergroup Dynamics

Given the results from content analyses discussed above (revealing that media depictions of Latinos, across decades and forms, are often tied to negative stereotypes), it is unsurprising that exposure to a variety of media genres has been found to negatively influence Latino adolescents' and adults' self-esteem (Rivadeneyra, Ward, & Gordon, 2007; Schmader, Block, & Lickel, 2015). For example, Schmader, Block, and Lickel's (2015) experimental examination of the effects of exposure to unfavorable film depictions of Mexican Americans on Mexican American viewers found that demeaning and objectifying content can be particularly damaging to self-esteem and implicit group attitudes, even when the content is deemed entertaining. Their research further demonstrated that exposure can have additional negative emotional consequences, including evoking shame and anger, and illustrated that specific facets of group identity can miti-gate (e.g., group pride) or intensify (e.g., group importance) undesirable emotional and identity-based responses to stereotypic media depictions of one's group. In the same vein, survey research by Rivadeneyra, Ward, and Gordon (2007) suggested that exposure to mass media offerings (includ-ing television, movies, music and magazines) negatively influences Latino adolescents' self-esteem along a number of dimensions including social and appearance self-esteem. This association was particularly pronounced among those high in ethnic identification and those who actively engaged with the content. On the other hand, in their cross-sectional survey of 117 Latino elementary school children, Subervi-Velez and Necochea (1990) found no association between English or Spanish-language television use and self-concept.

Recent efforts have also been directed at understanding the influence of media use on perceptions about one's group in society. Experimental tests examining the effects of watching negative stereotypical TV news depictions of Latinos revealed that exposure affects Mexican American viewers' perceptions of their own ingroup's entitativity; that is, the extent to which group members perceive their group as an organized, effective, coherent unit (Atwell Seate & Mastro, 2015a). Along the same lines, findings based on survey data indicated that among Mexican Americans, exposure to English language media in the US (as opposed to Spanish language U.S. media) contributes to perceptions of prejudice and discrimination against Mexican Americans in U.S. society (Ortiz & Behm-Morawitz, 2015). Ortiz and Behm-Morawitz found that among Mexican American adults, viewing English-language television was associated with increased perceptions of prejudice and discrimination against Mexican Americans in U.S. society. Additionally, Spanish and English language television exposure interacted such that at low levels of Spanish-language television use, English-language TV consumption was unrelated to perceptions of prejudice. However, at moderate and high levels of Spanish-language television viewing, consumption of English-language TV was linked with greater perceptions of prejudice against Latinos in the US.

Although favorable mediated characterizations of Latinos are relatively scarce, admirable models do exist, particularly in domains of pop culture such as music and sports. One might expect that exposure to such figures may support positive aspects of identity and conceptualizations of self and group for Latino audiences. Empirical evidence tentatively supports this position. In an experiment investigating the impact of viewing a well-liked Latina pop-star (vs. a comparable White pop-star) on Latinas' self-concept, McKinley, Mastro, and Warber (2014) found that exposure increased self-esteem, via the ability to engage in group comparisons that positively differentiate the Latino ingroup from the relevant (White) outgroup. More specifically, exposure to the popular Latina musician generated ingroup favoring responses in terms of both ingroup musical ability and rhythmic ability. In turn, these intergroup comparisons favoring Latinos on musical ability promoted appearance esteem, whereas ingroup favoring responses for rhythmic ability enhanced social self-esteem. Although consistent with theories of social identity (Tajfel & Turner, 1986), these results should be considered cautiously given the narrow media domain and the small sample of 62 female college students.

## Identity Management

Because media use is often an active process, researchers have also begun to examine whether and how patterns of selection and avoidance affect audiences. The limited work in this area demonstrates that Latino audiences are likely to thoughtfully and creatively use media to manage group identity needs (Abrams & Giles, 2009). In other words, although many of the reasons that audience members select or reject media content are tied specifically to individual needs (e.g., enjoyment, diversion), group-level factors such as ethnic identity also contribute to media usage patterns and preferences (e.g., Harwood, 1999a, 1999b). Empirical evidence suggests that audiences both consciously and unconsciously select and avoid media content to sustain ethnic group identity and support perceptions of group vitality (Abrams, Eveland, & Giles, 2003; Abrams & Giles, 2007, 2009). Yet, given the offerings commonly found across the media landscape, some audiences (White males in particular) are more easily able to satisfy their identity needs through mass media fare than others are. Members of non-White groups must strategically negotiate media offerings to reinforce group identity (Harwood & Roy, 2005), and, even if thoughtful and careful media selections are made, exposure may still harm group identity and perceptions of group vitality.

To illustrate, viewing stereotypical television depictions of Latinos appears to prompt racial/ethnic comparisons among White viewers, which serves to sustain group identity (Mastro, 2003; Mastro, Behm-Morawitz, & Kopacz, 2008). Thus, exposure to unfavorable characterizations of Latinos in the media (including longstanding themes associated with criminality, lack of education, and roles in service-positions) provides Whites an opportunity to make intergroup comparisons that advantage their ingroup, and consequently boost their self-concept. For Latinos, however, exposure to such inauspicious characterizations of their group presents a challenge in maintaining group identity needs, as evidenced by research (noted above) revealing the damaging effects of such portrayals on Latinos' views about their group's entitativity and perceptions about discrimination against Latinos in society (Atwell Seate & Mastro, 2015a; Ortiz & Behm-Morawitz, 2015). Work by Abram and Giles (2009) lends insights into how media selection processes operate in this environment. Their survey-based investigation of Latinos' use of media to meet group identity needs indicated that ethnic identification meaningfully predicts media selection and avoidance to gratify aspects of group identity, such as pride in one's ethnic group. Additionally, both media selection and avoidance significantly predicted perceptions of Latino group vitality. This study suggested that media use and avoidance can play an important role in how groups perceive themselves and manage aspects of their self and group concept.

## Final Reflections on Current and Future Research

Taken together, the quantitative research addressing Latinos and the media provides insights into: (1) how media messages about Latinos can promote more harmonious intergroup outcomes, (2) the features of media messages that may damage intergroup relationships, (3) the implications for self among both Latino and non-Latino audience members, and (4) the attributes of audience members that moderate these relationships. Based on these findings, it is clear that both the quantity and quality of media messages are critical in these relationships. This is not to say, however, that media effects occur in a vacuum—a variety of attributes of audience members can amplify or alleviate outcomes associated with exposure. Further research elucidating these relationships is critical because it has the potential to open the door to enhancing the positive effects of exposure to constructive images, diminishing the negative outcomes associated with consuming unfavorable characterizations, and changing stereotypes altogether. Given strong evidence of ongoing and even increasing levels of segregation in U.S. society (Logan & Stults, 2011), the significance of media messages in interethnic relationships cannot be denied. Indeed, it is fair to say that media offer an important context to positively influence intergroup dynamics given the motivation on the behalf of media producers, consumers, and researchers to encouraging such ends.

# References

Abrams, J., Eveland, W., & Giles, H. (2003). The effects of television on group vitality: Can television empower nondominant groups? In P. Kalbfleisch (Ed.), *Communication yearbook 27* (pp. 193–219). Mahwah, NJ: Erlbaum.

Abrams, J., & Giles, H. (2007). Ethnic identity gratifications selection and avoidance by African Americans: A group vitality and social identity perspective. *Media Psychology, 9,* 115–134.

Abrams, J., & Giles, H. (2009). Hispanic television activity: Is it related to vitality perceptions? *Communication Research Reports, 26,* 247–252.

Associated Press (2015, January 20). TV networks make unequal progress toward on-screen diversity. *The Washington Times.* Retrieved October 25, 2015, from http://www.washingtontimes.com/news/2015/jan/20/tv-networks-make-unequal-progress-toward-on-screen/?page=all.

Atwell Seate, A. & Mastro, D. (2015a). The effect of media exposure on perceptions of group entitativity: A preliminary investigation. *Communication Research Reports, 32,* 29–34.

Atwell Seate, A. & Mastro, D. (2015b). Exposure to immigration in the news: The impact of group-level emotions on intergroup behavior. *Communication Research.* Advance online publication.

Anderson, C. A., & Bushman, B. J. (2001). Effects of violent video games on aggressive behavior, aggressive cognition, aggressive affect, physiological arousal, and prosocial behavior: A meta-analytic review of the scientific literature. *Psychological Science, 12*(5), 353–359.

Berg, C. R. (1990). Stereotyping in films in general and of the Hispanic in particular. *Howard Journal of Communications, 2*(3), 286–300.

Berg, C. R. (2004). A crash course on Hollywood's Latino imagery. In T. Schatz (Ed.), *Hollywood: Cultural dimensions: ideology, identity and cultural industry studies* (pp. 211–226). London, UK: Routledge.

Bodenhausen, G., Schwarz, N., Bless, H., & Wanke, M. (1995). Effects of atypical exemplars on racial beliefs: Enlightened racism or generalized appraisals? *Journal of Experimental Social Psychology, 31,* 48–63.

Carpenter, S. & Radhakrishnan, P. (2002). The relation between allocentrism and perceptions of in-groups. *Personality and Social Psychology Bulletin, 28,* 1528–1537.

Children Now (2004). *Fall colors 2003–2004: Prime time diversity report.* Retrieved October 26, 2015, from http://www.bus.iastate.edu/emullen/mgmt472/Prime%20time%20diversity%20report.pdf.

Dill, K. E., & Thill, K. P. (2007). Video game characters and the socialization of gender roles: Young people's perceptions mirror sexist media depictions. *Sex Roles, 57*(11–12), 851–864.

Entman, R. (1994). Representation and reality in the portrayal of Blacks on network television news. *Journalism Quarterly, 71,* 509–520.

Everett, A., & Watkins, S. C. (2008). The power of play: The portrayal and performance of race in video games. In Katie Salen (Ed.), *The ecology of games: Connecting youth, games, and learning* (pp. 141–164). Cambridge, MA: MIT Press.

Fiedler, K., Bluemke, M., Friese, M., & Hoffmann, W. (2003). On the different uses of linguistic abstractness: From LIB to LEB and beyond. *European Journal of Social Psychology, 33,* 441–453.

Gerbner, G. (1998). Cultivation analysis: An overview. *Mass Communication and Society, 1,* 175–194.

Gerbner, G., & Signorielli, N. (1979). *Women and minorities in television drama, 1969–1978.* Philadelphia: University of Pennsylvania, The Annenberg School of Communications.

Greenberg, B. S., & Baptista-Fernandez, P. (1980). Hispanic-Americans: The new minority on television. In B. Greenberg (Ed.) *Life on television: Content analysis of U.S. TV drama* (pp. 3–12). Norwood, NJ: Ablex.

Guzmán, B. (2001). *The Hispanic population: Census 2000 brief.* Retrieved October 26, 2015, from http://www.census.gov/prod/2001pubs/c2kbr01-3.pdf.

Harwood, J. (1999a). Age identification, social identity gratifications, and television viewing. *Journal of Broadcasting & Electronic Media, 43,* 123–136.

Harwood, J. (1999b). Age identity and television viewing preferences. *Communication Reports, 12,* 85–90.

Harwood, J., & Roy, A. (2005). Social identity theory and mass communication research. In J. Harwood & H. Giles (Eds.), *Intergroup Communication* (pp. 189–211). New York, NY: Peter Lang.

Kang, C. (2015, January 29). With shows like 'Empire,' 'Black-ish' and 'Cristela,' TV is more diverse than ever. *The Washington Post.* Retrieved October 25, 2015, from http://www.washingtonpost.com/business/economy/with-shows-like-empire-black-ish-and-cristela-tv-is-more-diverse-than-ever/2015/01/29/0ac38f82-a576-11e4-a2b2-776095f393b2_story.html.

Knowlee, K. H., Henderson, J., Glaubke, C. R., Miller, P., Parker, M. A., & Espejo, E. (2001). *Fair play? Violence, gender and race in video games.* Oakland, CA: Children Now.

Leonard, D. J. (2006). Not a hater, just keepin' it real: The importance of race-and gender-based game studies. *Games and Culture, 1,* 83–88.

Logan, J. & Stults, B. (2011). *The persistence of segregation in the 21st century metropolis: New findings from the 2010 Census.* Census Brief prepared for Project US2010. Retrieved October 25, 2015, from http://www.russellsage.org/sites/all/files/US2010/US2010_Logan_20110324.pdf.

Maass, A., Corvino, G., & Arcuri, L. (1994). Linguistic intergroup bias and the mass media. *Revue de Psychologie Sociale, 1,* 31–43.

Maass, A., Salvi, D., Arcuri, L., & Semin, G. (1989). Language use in intergroup contexts: The linguistic intergroup bias. *Journal of Personality and Social Psychology, 57*(6), 981–993.

Mackie, D., Hamilton, D., Susskind, J., & Rosselli, F. (1996). Social psychological foundations of stereotype formation. In C. Macrae, C. Stangor, & M. Hewstone (Eds.), *Stereotypes and stereotyping* (pp. 41–78). London, UK: Guilford Press.

Mastro, D. (2003). A social identity approach to understanding the impact of television messages. *Communication Monographs, 70,* 98–113.

Mastro, D. (2009). Racial/ethnic stereotyping in the media. In R. L. Nabi and M.B. Oliver (Eds.) *The SAGE handbook of media processes and effects* (pp. 377–392). Thousand Oaks, CA: Sage.

Mastro, D. (2015). Why the media's role in issues of race and ethnicity should be in the spotlight. *Journal of Social Issues, 71*, 1–16

Mastro, D. E., & Behm-Morawitz, E. (2005). Latino representation on primetime television. *Journalism & Mass Communication Quarterly, 82*(1), 110–130.

Mastro, D., Behm-Morawitz, E., & Kopacz, M. (2008). Exposure to TV portrayals of Latinos: The implications of aversive racism and social identity theory. *Human Communication Research, 34*, 1–27.

Mastro, D., & Dragojevic, M. (2014, May). *Evidence of linguistic intergroup bias in U.S. print news coverage of immigration.* Paper presented at the International Communication Association annual conference, Seattle WA.

Mastro, D. E., & Greenberg, B. S. (2000). The portrayal of racial minorities on prime time television. *Journal of Broadcasting & Electronic Media, 44*(4), 690–703.

Mastro, D. & Kopacz, M. (2006). Media representations of race, prototypicality, and policy reasoning: An application of self-categorization theory. *Journal of Broadcasting & Electronic Media, 50*, 305–322.

Mastro, D., & Sink, A. (in press). Phenotypicality bias on television? A quantitative content analysis of primetime TV. In M. Cepeda & D. Casillas (Eds.), *The Routledge companion to Latina/o media.* New York, NY: Routledge.

Mastro, D., Tukachinsky, R., Behm-Morawitz, E., & Blecha, E. (2014). News coverage of immigration: The influence of exposure to linguistic bias in the news on consumer's racial/ethnic cognitions. *Communication Quarterly, 62*, 135–154

McKinley, C., Mastro, D., & Warber, K. (2014). Social identity theory as a framework for understanding the effects of exposure to positive media images of self and other on intergroup outcomes. *International Journal of Communication, 8*, 1049–1068.

MPAA (2014). *Theatrical market statistics*, 2014. Retrieved October 26, 2015, from http://www.mpaa.org/wp-content/uploads/2015/03/MPAA-Theatrical-Market-Statistics-2014.pdf.

Negrón-Muntaner, F., Abbas, C., Figueroa, L., & Robson, S. 2014. *The Latino media gap: A report on the state of Latinos in U.S. media.* Report from the Center for the Study of Ethnicity and Race at Columbia University, the Hispanic Foundation for the Arts, and the National Association of Latino Independent Producers. Retrieved October 25, 2015, from http://www.columbia.edu/cu/cser/downloads/Latino_Media_Gap_Report.pdf

Oritz, M., & Behm-Morawitz, L. (2015), Latinos' perceptions of intergroup relations in the U.S.: The cultivation of group-based attitudes and beliefs from English and Spanish-language television. *Journal of Social Issues, 75*(1), 90–105.

Power, J., Murphy, S., & Coover, G. (1996). Priming prejudice: How stereotypes and counter-stereotypes influence attribution of responsibility and credibility among ingroups and outgroups. *Human Communication Research, 23*, 36–58.

Ramasubramanian, S. (2007). Media-based strategies to reduce racial stereotypes activated by news stories. *Journalism & Mass Communication Quarterly, 84*, 249–264.

Reyes, P. (2014, November 7). John Leguizamo's 'Fugly': A funny take on a Latino actor's life. Retrieved October 25, 2015, from http://www.nbcnews.com/news/latino/john-leguizamos-fugly-funny-take-latino-actors-life-n242606.

Rivadeneyra, R., Ward, L. M., & Gordon, M. (2007). Distorted reflections: Media exposure and Latino adolescents' conception of self. *Media Psychology, 9*, 261–290.

Schmader, T., Block, K. & Lickel, B. (2015). Social identity threat in response to stereotypic film portrayals: Effects on self-conscious emotion and implicit ingroup attitudes. *Journal of Social Issues, 75*(1), 73–89.

Semin, G. & Fiedler, K. (1988). The cognitive functions of linguistic categories in describing persons: Social functions and language. *Journal of Personality and Social Psychology, 54*, 558–568.

Smith, S. L., Choueiti, M., & Pieper, K. (2014) *Gender bias without borders: An investigation of female characters across 11 countries.* Retrieved October 26, 2015, from http://annenberg.usc.edu/pages/~/media/MDSCI/gender-bias-without-borders-full-report.ashx.

Subervi-Velez, F. & Necochea, J. (1990). Television viewing and self-concept among Hispanic American children—A pilot study. *The Howard Journal of Communication, 2*, 315–329.

Tajfel, H., & Turner, J. C. (1986). The social identity theory of intergroup behaviour. In S. Worchel & W. G. Austin (Eds.), *Psychology of intergroup relations* (pp. 7–24). Chicago, IL: Nelson.

Tukachinsky, R., Mastro, D., & Yarchi, M. (2015). Documenting portrayals of race/ethnicity on primetime television over a 20-year span and their association with national–level racial/ethnic attitudes. *Journal of Social Issues, 71*(1), 17–38.

Turner, J. (1982). Towards a cognitive redefinition of the social group. In H. Tajfel (Ed.), *Social identity and intergroup relations* (pp. 15–40). Cambridge, UK: Cambridge University Press.

Turner, J. *(1985).* Social categorization and the self-concept: A social cognitive theory of group behavior. In E. J. Lawler (Ed.), *Advances in group processes: Theory and research* (Vol. 2, pp. 77–122). Greenwich, CT: JAI.

Trevino, J. S. (1985). Latino portrayals in film and television. *Jump Cut, 30*, 14–16.

Valdez, M. (2013, October 1). Is Sofia Vergara's 'Modern Family' character a stereotype? Actress defends Latina Gloria to critics. Retrieved October 25, 2015, from http://www.latintimes.com/sofia-vergara-modern-family-character-stereotype-actress-defends-latina-gloria-critics-131623.

Wigboldus, D. H. J., Semin, G. R., & Spears, R. (2000). How do we communicate stereotypes? Linguistic bases and inferential consequences. *Journal of Personality and Social Psychology, 28*(12), 5–18.

Williams, D., Martins, N., Consalvo, M., & Ivory, J. D. (2009). The virtual census: Representations of gender, race and age in video games. *New Media & Society, 11*(5), 815–834.

Wilson, C. C., Gutiérrez, F., & Chao, L. M. (2013). "Bamboozling" stereotypes through the 20th century. In C. C. Wilson, F. Gutiérrez, and L. M. Chao (Eds.), *Racism, sexism, and the media: The rise of class communication in multicultural America* (pp. 68–102). Thousand Oaks, CA: Sage.

# 10

# UNDERSTANDING HOW THE INTERNET AND SOCIAL MEDIA ACCELERATE RACIAL STEREOTYPING AND SOCIAL DIVISION

## The Socially Mediated Stereotyping Model

*Travis L. Dixon*

Over the last two decades, communication scholars have provided mounting evidence for two key observations. First, the news media present a distorted representation of the world regarding crime and race (Dixon & Linz, 2000a; Dixon & Williams, 2015; Entman, 1992; Romer, Jamieson, & de Coteau, 1998; Sorenson, Manz, & Berk, 1998). Second, consumption of these distorted images can reinforce stereotypical notions of various racial groups, especially African Americans (Dixon, 2006a, 2008a; Oliver & Fonash, 2002; Oliver, Jackson, Moses, & Dangerfield, 2004). However, the overwhelming majority of this research has studied the content and effects of traditional media such as television and newspapers. Little work has systematically examined the extent to which the Internet and social media may also reinforce racial prejudice.

The current chapter calls for scholars to focus attention on the changing distribution system of news, and proposes a model to help guide our thinking about the effects of stereotypical content in socially mediated contexts. I review the key content studies and what they have contributed to this area. Then, I discuss the effects of these distorted news portrayals. I discuss how the Internet has changed the nature of news consumption and why this has significant practical and theoretical implications. I also present some data suggesting that Internet news consumption, especially via social media, might propagate stereotypical thinking. I then review

the historical theoretical approaches to studying the impact of news stereotypes and propose a theoretical synthesis. Following this synthesis, I
present the Socially Mediated Stereotyping Model (SMSM) that better
equips researchers to assess the effects of stereotyping in a digital media
context.

## The Rise of the Black Perpetrator and the White Hero or Victim

A significant amount of research in the 1990s and early 2000s assessed
news, race, and crime on local TV news (Dixon & Linz, 2000a, 2000b;
Entman, 1992, 1994; Gilliam & Iyengar, 1998, 2000; Gilliam, Iyengar,
Simon, & Wright, 1996; Romer et al., 1998; Sorenson et al., 1998). My
research team examined this topic from a number of angles (Dixon &
Azocar, 2006; Dixon & Linz, 2000a, 2000b). We focused on local television news in Los Angeles and employed intergroup comparisons (two
racial groups compared on an attribute/role). We utilized inter-role comparisons whereby a single racial group (e.g., Blacks) is compared across
two attributes (e.g., criminal versus officer). Finally, we undertook inter-
reality comparisons, in which we contrasted the racial distributions of
various roles on television news (e.g., perpetrators) to the racial distribution contained in official reports (e.g., arrest records).

The intergroup comparisons revealed that both Blacks and Latinos
were more likely than Whites to appear as perpetrators. The inter-role
comparisons showed that Blacks and Latinos were more likely to appear
as suspects when compared to officers, but that the opposite was true
of Whites. Finally, our inter-reality comparisons found that Blacks were
overrepresented as perpetrators, Whites were overrepresented as victims
and officers, and Latinos were underrepresented across all crime roles
(Dixon & Azocar, 2006; Dixon & Linz, 2000a, 2000b).

During the 1980s and 90s our results consistently suggested that news
portrayals distorted social reality, especially regarding Blacks. Certain
contextual aspects of race and crime portrayals made these distortions
worse, whereas others made them better. For instance, local news shows
appeared to reinforce the notion of Black and Brown defendants being
particularly scary and incorrigible as evidenced by racialized prejudicial
pretrial depictions (Dixon & Linz, 2002). Prejudicial information—news
about a crime defendant that might bias a jury against the suspect—was
twice as likely to appear in a local TV news story involving a White
victim and Black defendant. Prejudicial pre-trial information was three
times more likely to appear in a story with a Latino defendant and a
White victim.

This last finding was one of the first times that we saw Latinos emerging in a more stereotypical depiction when compared to Blacks; we have

replicated this pattern in other types of news programs. For example, our analysis of crime news, terrorism, and undocumented immigration on network and cable newscasts (e.g., ABC news, CNN) found that Blacks were underrepresented as perpetrators and victims when making inter-reality comparisons with crime reports (Dixon & Williams, 2015).

However, when we focused on immigration and terrorism, the pattern changed. Suspects identified as immigrants in these news stories were grossly overrepresented as having Latino heritage. Moreover, Latinos were significantly more likely to appear as undocumented immigrants in the news than would be expected based on official data. We also found that Muslims were significantly overrepresented as terrorists on news programs when compared with FBI statistics on U.S. terrorism (Dixon & Williams, 2015).

Meanwhile, Whites portrayed in crime stories continue to be over-represented in sympathetic roles such as victim or officer (Dixon, 2015; Dixon, Azocar, & Casas, 2003; Romer et al., 1998). The consistent White victimization findings and the 1990s Black perpetration findings served as the justification for a series of effects studies conducted over the first decade of the 2000s. Given that content analyses demonstrate the association of people of color with criminality and Whites with victimization and law enforcement, watching television news might have two specific psychological effects. First, it may create a cognitive association between mental conceptions of Blacks and perpetration. Second, it might reinforce a schema of Whites as occupying the role of officers and victims.

## The Effects of Traditional News Exposure on Seeing Black Perpetrators and White Officers

Over the course of the first 10 years of the new millennium, many of us turned to the question of what effects such biased portrayals may have on news consumers (Dixon, 2006a, 2006b, 2007, 2008c; Dixon & Azocar, 2007; Oliver & Fonash, 2002; Oliver et al., 2004). Cultivation and social cognition theories shaped many of these investigations (Gerbner, Gross, Morgan, & Signorielli, 2002; Shrum, 2009).

### Experimental Evidence for Stereotype Reinforcement

The most difficult challenge for media effects scholars is teasing out the relationship between cause and effect: are racist stereotypes more accessible because we live in a racist culture or because people repeatedly watch racist news programming? Which factor causes which result? To address these concerns, my colleagues and I conducted a series of experiments designed to understand the impact of repeated exposure to stereotypical news coverage on stereotype activation and use.

We hypothesized that frequently viewing newscasts overrepresenting Black criminality would develop and reinforce a cognitive association between Black men and lawbreaking. Thus, we measured whether and how watching biased news coverage of Black criminals contributed to the chronic activation of the Black criminal stereotype. In addition, we tested whether viewing such content increased the accessibility of the stereotype when viewers subsequently made relevant policy judgments. We did this by exposing participants to a news program featuring large ratios of Black to White suspects, large ratios of White to Black suspects, all race-unidentified suspects, or all non-crime stories. We also asked participants about how much news they watched on a daily basis.

We found that heavy news viewers were more likely than light news viewers to believe, when exposed to large ratios of Black rather than White suspects, that the world is a dangerous place and to experience emotional discomfort when witnessing such images (Dixon, 2006a; Dixon & Azocar, 2007). Heavy news viewers were also more likely than light viewers to assume, when exposed to either a majority of Black rather than White criminals or race-unidentified criminals, that a subsequent race-unidentified perpetrator was culpable for his offense (Dixon, 2006b; Dixon & Maddox, 2005). Further, we found that race-unidentified suspects are assumed to be African American and that race-unidentified officers are assumed to be White, especially among heavy news viewers (Dixon, 2007).

These studies suggest that heavy news viewing perpetuates fear of Black perpetrators and a willingness to assume that Black suspects are guilty. Moreover, the research suggests that because chronically biased news coverage activates racialized stereotypes, participants found the images more accessible and used this to explain the stories we showed to them. A number of other experimental studies have replicated and extended all of these findings (Gilliam & Iyengar, 1998, 2000; Gilliam et al., 1996; Johnson, Adams, Hall, & Ashburn, 1997; Oliver, 1999; Oliver & Fonash, 2002; Peffley, Shields, & Williams, 1996).

It is important that some of our experiments involved the assessment of and/or exposure to news images of race-unidentified suspects. We thought that soliciting reactions to race-unidentified suspects might be an effective way to demonstrate whether news programs reinforced cognitive links between Blacks and criminality. Would viewers, even when shown a suspect of nondescript status, tend to assume that the offender was a Black man? The answer was yes. People misremembered race-unidentified suspects as Black suspects. They also became equally punitive when exposed to Black and race-unidentified suspects, and their support for the Black community declined after exposure to race-unidentified suspects. Apparently, the cognitive association between Blacks and criminality is so strong that simply thinking about crime conjures images of African

Americans. When exposed to a majority of White suspects, none of these effects was observed.

### Survey Research and Stereotype Reinforcement

Experimental studies provide the strongest evidence that a causal agent (watching TV news) produces a particular outcome (stereotyping of Blacks) (Babbie, 2012; Wimmer & Dominick, 2005). However, they generally lack external validity, meaning that we are unsure of the extent to which we might observe the same effect in the real world with actual stimuli. Survey research tends to have stronger external validity than experiments do, and researchers have often used surveys to address questions about the effect of news on stereotypical conceptions of crime and race.

For example, I have used surveys to assess whether television news reinforced already firmly lodged stereotype biases (Dixon, 2008a, 2008b), and found that even after controlling for prior racial attitudes, attention and exposure to crime news was positively correlated with a general concern about crime. In other words, the more crime news you watch, the more afraid of crime you become. In addition, crime news exposure was positively associated with the culpability ratings of Black and race-unidentified criminals, but not with White criminals: the more crime news you watch, the more likely you are to believe that Black suspects are guilty. Finally, and most telling, respondents with heavier exposure to local news content over-representing Black men as criminals had a stronger perception that all African Americans are violent.

This reaction was found even among respondents who condemned explicit racism, meaning that independent of one's prior racial attitudes, seeing Black men depicted as criminals in the news is positively connected with negative racial thoughts about all African Americans. Even people who are consciously sympathetic to Blacks can unconsciously stereotype Black men if they watch extensive amounts of TV news portraying Black male criminality.

## Digital Media, News, and Stereotyping

Based on the literature, therefore, we know three things about traditional television news: news content has historically reproduced stereotypes of African Americans; experiments demonstrate a causal relationship between television news exposure and stereotypical thinking about African Americans; and these effects occur both within and beyond the laboratory setting and thus can be observed with survey tools. However, the bulk of this prior work focused on traditional broadcast television news; today increasing numbers of Americans turn to the Internet and digital media for news (Pew Research Center, 2013). How is race depicted in these new outlets? Are the effects on stereotyping more pronounced or less problematic? Our team has done some limited work in this area and found that stereotypes continue to be perpetuated on the Internet (Josey, Hurley, Hefner, & Dixon, 2009), and that Internet news sources are linked with racist ideas (Melican & Dixon, 2008).

We must intensify our investigations of digital media because the news and information landscape has changed. Americans no longer rely on traditional news sources for prepackaged information, but today repackage, bundle, and transmit their own filtered forms of information to one another. Users cobble together news from various sources including websites, newsfeeds, and YouTube videos. What are the effects on stereotyping within this context? Do self-reinforcing search behaviors and closed social networks reify racial prejudice?

Social media and user-created aggregation of Internet information sources provide an interesting point of study for those of us interested in race, media use and social justice. Due to the "one to many" format of traditional news, the professional editorial function determined the content to which an audience member was exposed. However, news stories now appear on one's social media feed based on the selection of friends or sources. In addition, the algorithms of social media continue to send digital users content aligning with their prior online behaviors. Psychological theories of selective exposure and social identity theory suggest that the probability of conversations justifying racism and stereotyping is magnified under conditions where receivers self-select reinforcing stories. Below I overview some data that might help illustrate this point, and then I offer a theoretical synthesis, followed by an outline of the Socially Mediated Stereotyping Model (SMSM) that may help us move forward in this new context.

## Internet News Studies of Race and Crime Stereotyping: New Findings, New Frontier

Internet-distributed news might be especially potent in shaping racial conceptions because the Internet offers an unprecedented ability to choose certain kinds of content over others. Users can shape their media diets to confirm the worst stereotypes about outgroup members. We may have observed this when we examined Internet news consumption patterns and reported user trust of online news sources (Melican & Dixon, 2008). Some Internet-only news sources (having no mainstream counterpart) reflect extreme partisan views (e.g., Drudge Report), whereas others present Internet content aligned with traditional media (e.g., CNN.com or ABCnews.com). We found participants who sought out Internet-only web news reported more racism than did those who consumed more mainstream content. Further, respondents having strong trust in Internet-only sites with extreme views also expressed more racial hostility compared to those who sought out mainstream messages online.

However, the above assumes that online-only Internet news might be more biased than traditional news, even when traditional outlets repost their content online. Our studies of news content reveal that this may not be the case; for example, we found that the websites of online-only news outlets and news outlets having traditional media counterparts both stereotyped African Americans as poor, Muslims as terrorists, and Latinos as undocumented immigrants (Josey et al., 2009). I became curious to test directly whether Internet news consumption overall, and not specific online sources, might reinforce racial stereotypes.

## Web News Consumption

Above I reported on a pair of surveys I conducted that assessed the relationship between traditional news consumption and stereotypical beliefs regarding Blacks (Dixon, 2008). These surveys also asked about respondents' Internet news consumption, and here I report on a secondary analysis of the data as an initial test of whether web news contributes to racial stereotyping. I asked 500 Los Angeles based respondents a series of questions regarding their consumption of newspapers, local television news, network television news, and web news. I controlled for a number of factors including age, gender, education, income, racism, race, and overall television viewing. To test stereotype activation, I used a dependent measure similar to one I have utilized before: predicting the culpability/incorrigibility of a hypothetical race-unidentified suspect. I then submitted the entire series of variables to a hierarchical multiple regression analysis. Table 10.1 indicates that Internet news consumption ($\beta = .19$) positively predicts culpability judgments for the hypothetical suspect. This replicates what I have found in the past with traditional news, but extends it to online news.

## Social Media Effects

Another compelling avenue for study involves Internet news distributed by social media. In many ways online news operates much like traditional news in that journalists post content for mass distribution. However, social media users can repost online news or citizen journalist pieces, blog, comment, and more. Many people use social media for activist purposes and to raise awareness of issues. My 2008 surveys did not assess the impact of social media, the effects of which—because social media offer users an opportunity to actively engage in producing and sharing news about social issues with their friends—may differ from those of traditional or online news (Pew Research Center, 2013, 2014).

167

*Table 10.1* SRS Urban Sample: Web News Use Predicts Incorrigibility of Unidentified Suspects

| Variable | $\beta$ |
| --- | --- |
| Age | .20* |
| Females (Reference Males) | .03 |
| Education | .10 |
| Conservatism | −.07 |
| Income | .01 |
| Racism | .22* |
| Blacks (Reference Whites) | −.42* |
| Latinos (Reference Whites) | .12 |
| Others (Reference Whites) | −.17 |
| Overall Television Viewing | .08 |
| Newspaper Exposure | −.01 |
| % People of Color in Neighborhood | .14 |
| Crime Rate (Crimes per Thousand) | .01 |
| Local TV News Consumption | .04 |
| Network TV News Consumption | −.18 |
| Internet (Web) News Consumption | .19* |

*Note:* Final Model: $F(16, 127) = 2.62$, $p < .001$, $R^2 = .25$; *$p < .05$. **$p < .01$, ***$p < .001$

I tested this notion with a small sample of 40 left-leaning activist graduate students at a small southern college. I included similar controls as in my earlier studies: age, gender, education, conservatism, income, racism, and race, and attempted to predict the belief in Black violence (a measure I have used in several studies) with the following variables: attention to crime news, news trust, newspaper exposure, online news use, social media consumption, and blogging about social issues. The results are displayed in Table 10.2. Surprisingly, I found that social media consumption ($\beta = .54$) was the only predictor that was very strongly associated with this stereotypical belief in Black violence. However, I neglected to directly ask the respondents whether they used social media for counter-stereotypical activism.

*Table 10.2* Convenience Progressive School Sample: Social Media Use Predicts Black Violence Stereotype

| Variable | $\beta$ |
| --- | --- |
| Age | −.08 |
| Females (Reference Males) | −.30 |
| Education | .21 |
| Conservatism | .06 |
| Income | .09 |

| | |
|---|---|
| Racism | .23 |
| White Respondents (Reference Others) | .24 |
| Attention to Crime News | .22 |
| Newstrust | −.44 |
| Newspaper Exposure | −.44 |
| Internet (Web) News Consumption | .18 |
| Social Media Consumption | .54** |
| Blogging about Social Issues | −.29 |

*Note:* Final Model: $F(12, 20) = 2.42$, $p < .05$, $R^2 = .35$; *p < .05. **p < .01, ***p < .001

## Theoretical Challenges of Digital Media

The above-mentioned studies suggest a need for a programmatic investigation of socially mediated news and racial stereotyping. Racial stereotypes seem to persist in online news outlets and to influence race and crime judgments. However, much more research is needed to investigate the potential content and effects of social media. Moreover, prior theoretical models might need fine-tuning to better guide this new era of investigation. I believe we will be well served by a synthesis of four mass communication theories: cultivation/accessibility, agenda setting, social identity, and selective exposure. After a brief consideration of these theories, I present a model integrating the most relevant components of each—the Socially Mediated Stereotyping Model (SMSM).

### *Cultivation and Accessibility's Declining Relevance?*

Cultivation is one of the most oft-cited and heuristically valuable theories in media effects research (Gerbner et al., 2002; Shrum, 2009). Fundamentally, it suggests that our perceptions of social reality are shaped by our media consumption such that the more we consume television the more our view of the social world reflects the television world. Psychologists, political scientists, and communication scholars have utilized notions emanating from social cognition to drill down on processes explaining the cultivation effect (Dixon, 2000, 2001; Potter, 1991; Price & Tewksbury, 1997; Scheufele & Tewksbury, 2007; Shrum, 2009).

Two key constructs to emerge from this theorizing include *chronic activation* and *chronic accessibility*. Chronic activation denotes how consistent exposure to stereotypical images triggers chains of associations in the brain. Chronic accessibility denotes how, after years of chronic activation, viewers learn to draw upon stereotypes to explain their world, thus generating meaning through the use of stereotypes (Fiske & Taylor, 1991; Kunda, 1999).

However, as Metzger (2009) noted, cultivation as originally formulated might not fully apply to spaces on the Internet. The original notion assumed that the same formulaic messages pervaded all of media due to the one to many composition of traditional media outlets (Gerbner et al., 2002; McQuail, 1997). However, today users can create their own content which competes with Internet content produced by traditional media sources (Melican & Dixon, 2008). With the Internet, citizens can use both kinds of content to create unique mediated spaces designed specifically around their interests. Social media users can inhabit self-contained media worlds in ways that simply did not exist prior to online news distribution. Therefore, although cultivation and accessibility might continue to play a role, it may be a diminished role. Instead, we must consider the specific media diets of users, and for what purposes users approach their consumption.

## The Role of Agenda Setting

Instead of cultivation effects we might consider how social media and Internet news set the agendas of individual users (Metzger, 2009). Agenda setting suggests that the media do not tell us what to think, but rather what to think about (McCombs & Reynolds, 2002): repeated media messages make us think certain issues are more important than others, and we consider these highlighted issues when making judgments about relevant policies and issues (Price & Tewksbury, 1997; Scheufele & Tewksbury, 2007).

This theory has powerful implications for online news distribution and effects. Even though people inhabit individual media worlds online, issues may begin to trend within their network. As a result, major issues continue to be debated and discussed even within one's tailor-made social media realm. People in the network might share posts which represent either traditional mediated content or alternative media content, some of which may be extreme and inflammatory. The sharing might create discussion, but this discussion might be very much linked to the personal identities of those participating in the debate.

## Social Identity Theory

Scholars have used social identity theory (SIT) to predict media stereotyping effects, and this theory might have even more relevance in the digital media environment. As originally constructed, this theory posits self-construct protection comes at the expense of perceptual distortions of outgroup members (Tajfel & Turner, 2004). In other words, we feel better about ourselves by negatively judging and evaluating outgroup members. Mastro and her colleagues have applied this theory to numerous investigations of traditional entertainment media consumption and race/ethnicity (Mastro, 2004; Mastro, Behm-Morawitz, & Kopacz, 2008), finding that

Whites process mediated images of Latinos in stereotypically meaningful ways in order to boost their own self-concepts.

This theoretical perspective offers extremely useful insight regarding online distribution of news and information. Obviously, people might process Internet-distributed news in ways that promote outgroup stereotyping, which may explain how and why people seek and share information that others view as inflammatory. Digital media offer an opportunity for social exchange that SIT does not fully address. As articulated, SIT describes a connection between one's ingroup identity and outgroup psychological processing, but does not focus on exchanges between ingroup members.

### Selective Exposure and Social Utility

The rise of digital media has in some ways encouraged a return to classic conceptualizations of media effects, including selective exposure, which posits that we choose consumption based on our own attitudes and predispositions (Knobloch-Westerwick, 2012; Vidmar & Rokeach, 1974).

Selective exposure plays an integral part in our interactions with digital media. Our consumption of web news often starts with a search engine or a habitual click on bookmarked (i.e., already filtered) sources. Knobloch-Westerick and her colleagues have worked on this phenomenon for some time and have concluded that social utility is the driving force behind selective exposure (Knobloch-Westerwick, 2012): people make decisions about media consumption based on their potential future social interactions. This suggests that beyond social identity, one must consider how social media create social utility. Selective exposure remains pivotal in the new media context; along with cultivation and social identity theory, it may have great explanatory power regarding stereotyping in the digital era.

## The Socially Mediated Stereotyping Model (SMSM)

Given the changes in the delivery and content potential of digital media, we must re-conceptualize our theoretical approach to understand the effects of socially mediated news. I propose that we consider the Socially Mediated Stereotyping Model (SMSM) that applies and extends prior theory to Internet news consumption. The SMSM contends that the default digital media consumer is susceptible to unconscious bias reinforcement through the process of mediated accessibility. This bias strengthens when users seek stereotype confirmation and lessens when users focus on counter-stereotypical social activism. I argue strongly for a consideration of individual differences in the exploration of the psychological effects of social media consumption (Oliver, 2002). Below I present two propositions of the SMSM and three media groups that it predicts. Following this I propose a series of studies to test the underlying principles of the SMSM.

## SMSM Propositions

Proposition 1 of the SMSM states: Dominant themes proliferating on social media make racial stereotypes more accessible but are shaped by agenda setting and media diets. Social media users are susceptible to dominant themes presented in digital media newsfeeds as predicted by both cultivation and agenda setting. These themes have been shown thus far to largely conform to the problematic stereotypical depictions inhabiting traditional news outlets (Josey et al., 2009). However, this susceptibility is moderated by media choice and by the interplay of new and traditional media agenda setting.

Although traditional media has historically set the agenda, social media users can influence the traditional media agenda by disseminating alternative content; with enough attention those stories can become prominent or trend—in popular terms, they can go viral. Some of these viral postings get picked up by traditional media news outlets, which may supplement the original posting with additional commentary or journalistic investigation. Such alternate content may or may not be controversial or inflammatory, but it does represent a sea change in that it is user-generated. When it is racially inflammatory, it may go a long way to increasing the accessibility of racial stereotypes for social media consumers.

However, users can also reinforce traditional media's influence on the agenda by reposting stories from traditional news outlets. The agenda propagating one's news feed and hence one's media diet matters because certain agenda items (e.g., immigration reform) may be more rife with racial stereotypes than others (e.g., tornadoes hit Midwest). Therefore the particulars of an individual's media diet play a large part in what is activated during his or her engagement with digital media. Moreover, the user's news feed might derive from a combination of other users, traditional media corollaries, independent media corollaries, or the user herself. The more one's news feed contains problematic racialized stereotypes, the more a user's social media use will increase the accessibility of stereotypes and subsequent unconscious bias.

However, although the SMSM suggests that the themes present in social media might lead to stereotype activation, the social aspects inherent in social media also must also be considered. This is explored in the second proposition of the SMSM.

Proposition 2 of the SMSM states: Social utility will moderate the effects of social media on stereotyping via selective exposure. The significant SIT work suggesting that we seek to feel better about ourselves through the derogation of others should be enhanced by focused attention to the properties of social media. If this proposition is correct, users should seek, post, and discuss content with others in an ingroup community that makes them feel better about themselves while stereotyping outgroup members. The process of using social media content to uphold the values of the ingroup while derogating the outgroup should occur especially with ingroup members heralding from socially marginalized groups such as White supremacists. Moreover, the social utility function of selective exposure and social media use should also motivate specific posts and discussions designed to promote and stabilize ingroup membership at the expense of outgroup members. In this case, social media content serves the social utility function of ingroup valuation. These postings will likely include heavily editorialized and often-untrue news postings that rely on outgroup stereotypes. Therefore, as members of these ingroups use social media, they should also display increased stereotype endorsement over time.

However, for ingroup members who see their identity as closely tied to the removal of racial stereotypes in society, the opposite should occur. They should use social media to share posts, online news, and other content that counters racial stereotypes. The process of selective exposure would have them either resist or severely critique racist and stereotypic content. This would also percolate through social utility as these ingroup members seek to sustain an identity as anti-racist activists. Therefore, we should see less stereotyping over time from people with this view.

### SMSM-Predicted Social Media Groups

#### Unconscious Bias Group

This group resembles traditional media consumers, and will generally not pay much attention to the news content of their feeds, instead engaging the social network on mostly non-controversial topics. This group may also include lurkers who read and post few things. Because these people will most likely ingest a media diet dominated by the most popular and trending stories, they are likely to receive stereotypical information. As a result, the accessibility processes outlined in Proposition 1 will reinforce the unconscious stereotypical bias of this group.

#### Stereotype Confirmer Group

Members of this group will perceive their identity as being under assault, and will largely blame outgroup members. They will highlight news clippings, blog posts, and videos that confirm the negative stereotypes of outgroup members. Users in this group will demonstrate a penchant for rumor, innuendo, and the spreading of inaccurate information, particularly about outgroup members. As articulated in the second proposition of the SMSM, they will use this information to maintain solidarity with other ingroup members, and will demonstrate greater stereotyping than seen in the unconscious bias group.

### Anti-Stereotype Activist Group

Members of this group will see their role as utilizing digital media tools to break down stereotypes. They will seek to debate mainstream discourse regarding racial stereotypes. Their newsfeed will be populated by content that critiques traditional news media stereotypes, undertakes critical analyses of news events, and encourages other social media users to engage politically for social change. This group will demonstrate fewer stereotypes than both the unconscious bias and stereotype confirmer groups. As predicted by Proposition 2 of the SMSM, they will generate social utility from online interactions with other anti-stereotyping activists interested in resisting the power of stereotypes.

## Investigating the Utility of the Social Media Stereotyping Model

The SMSM could be a useful starting point to examine stereotyping effects in the new media environment. However, we must first test the model's validity. Validation tests should employ a survey of social media users' attitudes and activism combined with an observation of social media use; a systematic content analysis of social media user sharing behavior, content and sources; and an experiment assessing content frames and the development of racialized attitudes and activist behavior.

A diverse group of participants could take part in a survey that could be administered to measure respondents' racial attitudes, political attitudes, media exposure, social activism, and cross-racial contact. Participants could then be asked to allow researchers to follow their news feeds for a year. The combination of these two methods would allow us to assess whether the three groups predicted by the SMSM manifest in the real world. A content analysis investigating the source and content of shared posts regarding race and crime could be informative on multiple levels. Besides the manifest content (the messages and their sources), we could also discover some catalysts of social justice and policing discussions. To what extent do social activists and stereotype confirmers (including inflammatory extremists) set the agenda? Can stereotype confirmers resist and subvert the social activists' messaging and vice versa?

Controlled experiments allow us to understand the potential causal impact of social media messages. For example, a study could assess implicit bias and support for outgroup members after exposure to social media news reports of criminality varied by race of the perpetrator and of the officer. This would help us examine more closely the existence and structure of the unconscious bias group.

In summary, traditional media stereotyping research has suggested that the messages spread from one or a few sources to many receivers have led to the chronic activation of stereotypes, which then makes the stereotypes more accessible when making judgments. The new media environment challenges that conceptualization of effects, and no single theoretical perspective can be deployed to explain the digital world we now occupy.

The SMSM incorporates multiple theoretical perspectives. It proposes that exposure to social media still makes racial stereotypes more accessible, but this process is mediated by users' specific social media diets. It also proposes that social utility and selective exposure drive the effects of social media. As a result, social media consumption will lead to stereotype use at both an implicit (unconscious bias group) and explicit (stereotype confirmer group) level. However, it is also possible that the tools available to activists might allow them to counter the stereotypes that continue to proliferate in society. Researchers who wish to make an impact in the new media arena must be prepared to assess these multiple possibilities when conducting their research. The SMSM presents a useful path for moving forward that goes beyond the limitations of prior theoretical notions and old contexts.

## References

Babbie, E. (2012). *The practice of social research* (13th ed.). Boston, MA: Cengage Learning.

Dixon, T. L. (2000). A social cognitive approach to studying racial stereotyping in the mass media. *African American Research Perspectives, 6*(1), 60–68.

Dixon, T. L. (2001). Social cognition and racial stereotyping in television: Consequences for transculturalism. In M. Asante, V. Milhouse & P. Nwosu (Eds.), *Transcultural realities* (pp. 215–224). Thousand Oaks, CA: Sage.

Dixon, T. L. (2006a). Psychological reactions to crime news portrayals of Black criminals: Understanding the moderating roles of prior news viewing and stereotype endorsement. *Communication Monographs, 73*, 162–187.

Dixon, T. L. (2006b). Schemas as average conceptions: Skin tone, television news exposure, and culpability judgments. *Journalism & Mass Communication Quarterly, 83*, 131–149.

Dixon, T. L. (2007). Black criminals and White officers: The effects of racially misrepresenting law breakers and law defenders on television news. *Media Psychology, 10*, 270–291.

Dixon, T. L. (2008a). Crime news and racialized beliefs: Understanding the relationship between local news viewing and perceptions of African Americans and crime. *Journal of Communication, 58*, 106–125.

Dixon, T. L. (2008b). Network news and racial beliefs: Exploring the connection between national television news exposure and stereotypical perceptions of African Americans. *Journal of Communication, 58*, 321–337.

Dixon, T. L. (2008c). Who is the victim here?: The psychological effects of overrepresenting White victims and Black perpetrators on television news. *Journalism: Theory, Practice, & Criticism, 9*, 582–605.

Dixon, T. L. (2015). Good guys are still always in White?: Positive change and continued misrepresentation of race and crime on local television news. *Communication Research*. Retrieved April 5, 2015, 2015, from http://crx. sagepub.com/cgi/reprint/0093650215579223v1.pdf?ijkey=TAHgEbkbqt9ncF z&keytype=finite.

Dixon, T. L., & Azocar, C. (2006). The representation of juvenile offenders by race on Los Angeles area television news. *Howard Journal of Communications, 17*, 143–161.

Dixon, T. L., & Azocar, C. (2007). Priming crime and activating blackness: Understanding the psychological impact of the overrepresentation of African Americans as lawbreakers on television news. *Journal of Communication, 57*, 229–253.

Dixon, T. L., Azocar, C., & Casas, M. (2003). The portrayal of race and crime on television network news. *Journal of Broadcasting & Electronic Media, 47*, 495–520.

Dixon, T. L., & Linz, D. G. (2000a). Overrepresentation and underrepresentation of African Americans and Latinos as lawbreakers on television news. *Journal of Communication, 50*(2), 131–154.

Dixon, T. L., & Linz, D. G. (2000b). Race and the misrepresentation of victimization on local television news. *Communication Research, 27*, 547–573.

Dixon, T. L., & Linz, D. G. (2002). Television news, prejudicial pretrial publicity, and the depiction of race. *Journal of Broadcasting & Electronic Media, 46*, 112–136.

Dixon, T. L., & Maddox, K. B. (2005). Skin tone, crime news, and social reality judgments: Priming the stereotype of the dark and dangerous black criminal. *Journal of Applied Social Psychology, 38*, 1555–1570.

Dixon, T. L., & Williams, C. L. (2015). The changing misrepresentation of race and crime on network and cable news. *Journal of Communication, 65*, 24–39.

Entman, R. (1992). Blacks in the news: Television, modern racism, and cultural change. *Journalism Quarterly, 69*, 341–361.

Entman, R. (1994). Representation and reality in the portrayal of Blacks on network television news. *Journalism Quarterly, 71*, 509–520.

Fiske, S. T., & Taylor, S. E. (1991). *Social cognition* (2nd ed.). New York, NY: McGraw-Hill.

Gerbner, G., Gross, L., Morgan, M., & Signorielli, N. (2002). Growing up with television: Cultivation processes. In J. Bryant & D. Zillmann (Eds.), *Media effects: Advances in theory and research* (2nd ed.) (pp. 43–67). Hillsdale, NJ: Lawrence Erlbaum Associates.

Gilliam, F. D., & Iyengar, S. (1998). The superpredator script. *Nieman Reports, 52*(4), 45–46.

Gilliam, F. D., & Iyengar, S. (2000). Prime suspects: The influence of local television news on the viewing public. *American Journal of Political Science, 44*, 560–573.

176

Gilliam, F. D., Iyengar, S., Simon, A., & Wright, O. (1996). Crime in Black and White: The violent, scary world of local news. *Harvard International Journal of Press/Politics, 1*(3), 6–23.

Johnson, J. D., Adams, M. S., Hall, W., & Ashburn, L. (1997). Race, media and violence: Differential racial effects of exposure to violent news stories. *Basic & Applied Social Psychology, 19*, 81–90.

Josey, C. L., Hurley, R. J., Hefner, V., & Dixon, T. L. (2009). The portrayal of race online: A content analysis of the portrayal of racial stereotypes in a new media environment. In R. A. Lind (Ed.), *Race/gender/media: Considering diversity across audiences, content, and producers* (2nd ed.) (pp. 135–142). Boston, MA: Pearson.

Knobloch-Westerwick, S. (2012). Selective exposure and reinforcement of attitudes and partisanship before a presidential election. *Journal of Communication, 62*(4), 628–642.

Kunda, Z. (1999). *Social cognition: Making sense of people.* Cambridge, MA: The MIT Press.

Mastro, D. (2004). A social identity approach to understanding the impact of television messages. *Communication Monographs, 70*, 98–113.

Mastro, D., Behm-Morawitz, E., & Kopacz, M. A. (2008). Exposure to television portrayals of Latinos: The implications of aversive racism and social identity theory. *Human Communication Research, 34*, 1–27.

McCombs, M., & Reynolds, A. (2002). News influence on our pictures of the world. In J. Bryant & D. Zillmann (Eds.), *Media effects: Advances in theory and research* (2nd ed.) (pp. 1–18). Mahwah, NJ: Lawrence Erlbaum Associates.

McQuail, D. (1997). *Audience analysis.* Thousand Oaks, CA: Sage.

Melican, D. B., & Dixon, T. L. (2008). News on the net: Credibility, selective exposure, and racial prejudice. *Communication Research, 35*, 151–168.

Metzger, M. J. (2009). Media effects in the era of Internet communication. In R. Nabi & M. B. Oliver (Eds.), *The Sage handbook of media processes and effects* (pp. 561–576). Thousand Oaks, CA: Sage.

Oliver, M. B. (1999). Caucasian viewers' memory of Black and White criminal suspects in the news. *Journal of Communication, 49*(3), 46–60.

Oliver, M. B. (2002). Individual differences in media effects. In J. Bryant & D. Zillmann (Eds.), *Media effects: Advances in theory and research* (2nd ed.) (pp. 507–524). Mahwah, NJ: Lawrence Erlbaum Associates.

Oliver, M. B., & Fonash, D. (2002). Race and crime in the news: Whites' identification and misidentification of violent and nonviolent criminal suspects. *Media Psychology, 4*, 137–156.

Oliver, M. B., Jackson, R. L., Moses, N. N., & Dangerfield, C. L. (2004). The face of crime: Viewers' memory of race-related facial features of individuals pictured in the news. *Journal of Communication, 54*, 88–104.

Peffley, M., Shields, T., & Williams, B. (1996). The intersection of race and crime in television news stories: An experimental study. *Political Communication, 13*, 309–327.

Pew Research Center. (2013). *In changing news landscape, even television is vulnerable: Trends in news consumption—1991–2012.* Retrieved November 21, 2013, from http://www.people-press.org/2012/09/27/in-changing-news-landscape-even-television-is-vulnerable/.

177

Pew Research Center. (2014). *Stark racial divisions in reactions to Ferguson police shooting.* Retrieved August 18, 2014, from http://www.people-press.org/2014/08/18/stark-racial-divisions-in-reactions-to-ferguson-police-shooting/.

Potter, W. J. (1991). Examining cultivation from a psychological perspective: Component subprocesses. *Communication Research, 18,* 77–102.

Price, V., & Tewksbury, D. (1997). News values and public opinion: A theoretical account of media priming and framing. In G. A. Barnett & F. J. Boster (Eds.), *Progress in the communication sciences* (pp. 173–212). New York, NY: Ablex.

Romer, D., Jamieson, K. H., & de Coteau, N. J. (1998). The treatment of persons of color in local television news: Ethnic blame discourse or realistic group conflict? *Communication Research, 25,* 268–305.

Scheufele, D. A., & Tewksbury, D. (2007). Framing, agenda setting, and priming: The evolution of three media effects models. *Journal of Communication, 57,* 9–20.

Shrum, L. J. (2009). Media consumption and perceptions of social reality: Effects and underlying processes. In J. Bryant & M. B. Oliver (Eds.), *Media effects: Advances in theory and research* (3rd ed.) (pp. 50–73). New York, NY: Routledge.

Sorenson, S. B., Manz, J. G., & Berk, R. A. (1998). News media coverage and the epidemiology of homicide. *American Journal of Public Health, 88,* 1510–1514.

Tajfel, H., & Turner, J. C. (2004). The social identity theory of intergroup behavior. In J. T. Jost & J. Sidanius (Eds.), *Key readings in social psychology* (pp. 276–293). New York, NY: Psychology Press.

Vidmar, N., & Rokeach, M. (1974). Archie Bunker's bigotry: A study in selective perception and exposure. *Journal of Communication, 24,* 36–47.

Wimmer, R. D., & Dominick, J. R. (2005). *Mass media research: An introduction* (8th ed.). Belmont, CA: Wadsworth.

# 11

# OUR COUNTRY, OUR LANGUAGE, OUR SERVER

## Xenophobic and Racist Discourse in *League of Legends*

*Robert Alan Brookey and Charles Ecenbarger*

On June 4, 2013, Riot Games opened Latin American servers for its popular online game *League of Legends* (*LoL*). Riot claimed that these new servers would provide improved connections for South American players, reducing lag and enhancing game play. What Riot Games did not highlight was that for several months *LoL* players had been posting complaints online about Spanish-using players on North American servers. The complaints varied, with some claiming that the Spanish-using players had poor game skills, were rude and disrespectful, and harassed English-using players. Some claimed that they were unable to communicate with Spanish-using players, and subsequently would lose matches when teamed with these players. Many of these complaints appeared in online forum threads with titles such as "South American server needed," "Make a separate server for Hispanics" and "Mexicans need their own server." The purpose of these threads was to convince Riot Games to create separate servers for Spanish-using players, and make North American servers for English-using players only. Posts to these threads often argued that Spanish-using players should not even be on North American servers, and that their presence, if not illegal, was at best improper.

If these arguments sound familiar, they should, because they are similar to those contained in the discourse surrounding illegal immigration. As Ono and Sloop (2002) observed in their analysis of the media coverage of California's Proposition 187, Latinos are not only specifically linked to illegal immigration, but also characterized as ill behaved and disrespectful of U.S. law, and therefore both criminal and immoral. In other words, the immigration discourse asserts a division between law-abiding citizens and scofflaws and miscreants. Kilty and Haymes (2000) reminded us that racist attitudes toward Latinos are not just manifest in immigration law, but in policies regarding language and education. Laws and resolutions define English as the official language in many states, and efforts to defund and eliminate bi-lingual education reveal how language operates as a marker of national identity. In other words, the immigration discourse asserts an expectation that English should be spoken in the US, and those who use another language (Spanish for example), do not respect where they are and hence do not belong.

The fact that similar arguments are present in complaints about cyberspace is noteworthy. After all, the boundaries of cyberspace lack the geo-political implications of national borders. Or do they? Cyberspace has often been presented as a social context unburdened by the physical and political boundaries of the material world; online video games have been offered as places to unlock human potential, solve social problems, and facilitate greater understanding (McGonigal, 2011). The controversy surrounding *LoL*, however, demonstrates that offline conflicts are not always resolved online, but instead may be reproduced. *LoL* provides a valuable opportunity to examine issues of race and national identity as they manifest in cyberspace, because it is one of the most popular online games with 27 million people playing on any given day (Tassi, 2014).

*LoL* is a Massive Online Battle Arena (MOBA), a genre designed to heighten competition among players while simultaneously requiring collaboration and cooperation. MOBAs do not employ a grand narrative to contain and advance game play; instead players are automatically assigned to teams to compete in matches that last an average of 25–45 minutes, and after which any experience and accrued items are not retained. Rather than playing with thousands of others, MOBA players only engage with nine others in each match. The competitiveness of a MOBA, coupled with the necessity of player cooperation in teams, can lead to conflicts among players, and these conflicts have spilled out into online forums. The complaints about Spanish-using *LoL* players on North American servers represent a case in point, and this chapter offers a critical analysis of those complaints.

Although the complaints leveled against Spanish-using players in *LoL* can be characterized as racist, in that they attempt to segregate these players, we also believe this discourse also reveals a xenophobia, a fear of the threat posed by these players motivated by issues of competition. We begin with a discussion of the research on race and video games, and we argue that research should also consider the concept of xenophobia, particularly when considering the competitive aspects of video games in general, and *LoL* specifically. We then provide an analysis of the *LoL* discourses in which we identify how the arguments contained in these online forums are not just racist, but also xenophobic.

## Video Games and Racism

The literature examining and defining racism is extensive, but several theorists help us understand the concept in relation to the context of *LoL*. For example, Harris defines racists as people who believe in "stable racial categories of superior and inferior kinds from birth," racist situations as "racially motivated predicaments of segregation, discrimination, and exclusion," and racist ideas as "the criteria for deciding, prima facia, personal character virtues, group membership, right and privileges" (1999, p. 17). The *LoL* discourse certainly can be defined as a racist situation given that it attempts to exclude Spanish-using players, but as others have argued, gaming communities can be exclusive by nature (Egenfeldt-Nielsen, Smith, & Tosca, 2008). Therefore, it is important to recognize the differences in the way racism operates in a virtual space such as an online video game.

As Nakamura (2002) has argued, race in cyberspace is not an analog for the representation of race in traditional media, nor does it reproduce real time racial experiences to the degree it does not engage corporeal bodies. Instead, Nakamura used the term cybertypes to refer to racial stereotypes in the context of cyberspace: "Cybertypes are the images of race that arise when the fears, anxieties, and desires of privileged Western users . . . are scripted into a textual/graphical environment that is in constant flux and revision" (2002, p. 6). Online video games are textual/ graphical environments in which players interact through avatars reflecting race in ways that need not correspond to real world categories. Players choose their avatar's race from categories including elves and dwarves as well as humans. Therefore, players in an online game cannot assume the race of other players because the physical aspects of race are hidden behind the avatar, but this does not dissuade players from making racial assumptions.

For example, Monson (2012) found racial essentialism encoded into almost every facet of the online game *World of Warcraft* (*WoW*), and argued the game replicates racial stereotypes in much the same way as they are manifest in society. Additionally, Packer (2014) analyzed the behavior and interactions of millions of *WoW* players, and noticed players generate their own narratives that can depart from the intended narrative of the game design, and that these player generated narratives often reflect existing racial stereotypes. In addition, the representation of characters in video games often reproduces a norm of the White male as a

181

central narrative figure. Williams et al. (2009) found that White males are overrepresented as characters in games when compared to the actual U.S. population, with a corresponding underrepresentation of women, Latinos, and Native Americans. Waddell et al. (2014) discovered that the characters in Massively Multiplayer Online Role-Playing Games (MMORPGs) are disproportionally White and male, and Brock's (2011) critical analysis of *Resident Evil 5* found that Whiteness is a centralized concept in both game design and online discussions of the game.

The literature reveals a recursive relationship between game play and attitudes about race, one that pivots on a subject position marked by Whiteness, and, as Nakamura (2002) noted, a sense of Western privilege. In other words, game play centers on a White racial identity and a sense of social and geographic place. As Brock (2011) has observed, White racial privilege and entitlement also extend into online discussions, and as we will show, this same privilege and entitlement can be found in online *LoL* forums and in the arguments for segregation and exclusion revolving around who does, and does not, belong on North American servers.

On this point it is important to note that racism functions as an ideology, providing a distorted view of human relations (Miles & Brown, 2003). Despite the fact that video game play crosses most racial lines (Shaw, 2012), White players can view non-White races as what is so often called the "other," who may pose a threat and whose very presence in the game may be suspect. If the gamer subject is indeed marked by a White, Western identity, then it is useful to extend the analysis of race and racism by engaging game play from the perspective of xenophobia. We believe this perspective is valuable because it connects race to one of the most important aspects of video game play: competition.

## Xenophobia and Competition

In their analysis of African politics, Fouchard and Segatti defined xenophobia as "discourses and practices that are discriminatory to foreign nationals" (2015, p. 2). Xenophobia emerges when a nation, or more importantly when citizens who identify with a nation, feel threatened by external groups, and believe that foreigners are undermining or eroding their national identity, an identity which is often coded in racial terms. Indeed, when Miles and Brown discussed the ideological function of racism, they argued "racism and nationalism arose together, are often articulated together, and have an influence on each other" (2003, p. 9). Johnson (2010) argued that European politicians have used xenophobia and racism as a mobilizing force in their rhetoric to close off Europe from the threat posed by foreign countries and peoples. Fouchard and Segeatti (2015), however, also pointed out that national identities prompting xenophobia, although often real, can be based on imagined communities.

In that same respect, Wimmer (1997) has argued that xenophobic discourse is sometimes not linked to actual competition between two groups, but the perception of competition: "xenophobia and racism [appeal] to the pact of solidarity into which the ethnicized bureaucracy and a national community have entered and which at times of intensified social conflict seems fragile, especially from the viewpoint of those threatened by loss of their social standing" (1997, p. 32).

This understanding of xenophobia is valuable to our analysis of the *LoL* discourse for three reasons. First, xenophobia is a discourse articulated by national identity either real or imagined, and in the case of the controversy surrounding *LoL*, national identity is both real and imagined. In other words, the comments are based on arguments that take the real world geographic location (or assignment) of a server as signifying real world geo-political space: North American servers signify North America. However, the actual game space, where the competition takes place, is a virtual space with no real world location, therefore any national identity associated with the game server, is indeed, imagined. Second, as in other manifestations of xenophobia the supposed foreign players encroaching on North American servers are perceived as a threat because they undermine the game play of English-using players, and they participate in disrespectful and insulting behavior (trolling). Finally, the threat motivating xenophobic discourse can revolve around a sense of competition, and given that competition is an important aspect of video games generally, and *LoL* specifically, we should consider the relationship between xenophobia and competition.

Competition is a hallmark of video games, which often pit players against each other. Success and failure is directly and immediately registered as game rank. Much of the literature on competition and video games focuses on the competitive aspects of electronic sports (eSports) including professional, semi-professional, and amateur video gaming competition. For example, Witkowski (2012) observed that *Counter-Strike* gaming teams playing pro/am tournaments take on a seriousness and embodied discipline similar to other professional sports. Taylor (2012) has studied the practice of eSports cultures extensively, and although she did not engage in an extended analysis of race, she did observe that race and ethnicity can be problematic, because although eSports team rosters may be identified with geographic regions, team membership crosses national and racial lines. Despite this diversity, Taylor noted that the culture of eSports in North American is still dominated by White males.

Yet, as Witkowski observed, competition and cooperation are often interlaced in video game play: "Competition . . . means 'to strive together'; as implied, this requires other people or things such as environments, time, previous performances, or records to strive with or to quest again in order to compete" (2014, p. 161). Although *LoL* has pro/am tournaments and an eSports culture, most players do not participate in these competitive venues. Still, the characteristics of competition that Witkowski outlined apply. In *LoL* a player is required to sign into a client, called the *LoL Launcher*, which allows the player to enter a matchmaking system that randomly places the player onto a team with four other players. Players are often teamed with individuals they have never met or played with before, and cooperation and communication between players on a team in *LoL* is needed in order to compete successfully. Therein lies the way by which xenophobia is both motivated and manifest. *LoL* allows for in-game chat so that teams can coordinate and strategize, and sometimes English-using players are teamed with Spanish-using players. Indeed, the complaints raised in the forums mentioned above often claimed that the lack of communication resulted in defeat, and the call for separate Spanish language servers was an issue of competition and collaboration and not race.

## Critical Rhetoric and Discursive Formations

The purpose of our analysis is to identify the arguments that have emerged in the forums and threads justifying the need for Spanish language *LoL* servers. Our analysis is a rhetorical criticism of these forums, and is informed by McKerrow's (1989) theoretical work on critical rhetoric, which argues that rhetorical analysis should take up issues of politics and power through an examination of discursive fragments. Specifically, McKerrow wanted to move rhetorical analysis away from the traditions of public address that focused on significant speeches and discrete texts. Drawing on the work of Foucault, McKerrow argued that power relations are often manifest in multiple discourses across a variety of sources, rather than just a speaker addressing an audience. Although Foucault was not theorizing rhetoric specifically, his concept of "discursive formation" clearly contributes to this critical rhetoric approach: "Whenever one can describe, between a number of statements, such a system of dispersion, whenever, between objects, types of statement, concepts of thematic choices, one can define a regularity (an order, correlations, positions and functionings, transformations) . . . we are dealing with a discursive formation" (1972, p. 38). Foucault argued that critical analysis should trace ideas across a variety of texts, and it is this diffuse approach to textual analysis that McKerrow offers in his theory of critical rhetoric.

Adding to McKerrow's work Ono and Sloop (1995) call for an analysis of "vernacular discourse," or the "discourse operating within local communities rather than speeches preserved in history textbooks" (1995, p. 20). They argued that oppressed groups often do not have access to public channels of communication, and therefore any analysis of domination and freedom should consider the discourse emerging from oppressed communities, which can include independent media produced by and for these communities as well as the everyday speech occuring in these communities. Ono and Sloop's analysis of immigration rhetoric mentioned above is an excellent example of the examination of vernacular discourse, and it is an approach ripe for the type of discourse we have chosen to analyze in this chapter.

With the advent of Web 2.0, the production of discourse has become more dispersed and fragmented, and online discussion forums and chatrooms have become important venues for the type of vernacular discourse described by Ono and Sloop. Although these online outlets provided platforms for oppressed groups who previously had limited access to public channels of communication, these platforms are also open to those who may have limited power but do not align themselves with the oppressed. Indeed, online platforms are sometimes used to further the project of oppression as Brookey and Cannon (2009) found in their analysis of the sexist and heterosexist discourse in the virtual world *Second Life*. The *LoL* discourse reflects the type of everyday speech that Ono and Sloop describe, yet many of the posts reaffirm racist and xenophobic ideas of domination. Thus the critique of domination that McKerrow described should extend to everyday discourse, even that which attempts to reassert domination. In addition, and as our analysis will reveal, these forums are not monolithic, and many posts challenge the racist and xenophobic arguments. Therefore the *LoL* discourse reflects a debate in which domination is both asserted and challenged.

The texts for this analysis were chosen to illustrate the core of the debate and the wide range of Web sites in which the debate appeared. The largest discussion appeared on the official *League of Legends* web forums and spun off onto social networking sites, Wikis, and online petitions. We chose texts based on the amount of activity on the thread and the website on which it was presented. Smaller, less engaged discussions were not selected but often echoed the discussions on larger, more popular threads and forums. Since the South American *LoL* server went on line, the topic of Spanish-using players has not been at the forefront of *LoL* discussions.

The specific texts we consider for this analysis are three freely accessible Web forums and an online petition. The *League of Legends* game forum generated two threads we included in our analysis. The *League of Legends* wiki, which acts both as a web forum and a community hub for *League of Legends* players, provided one thread. The Raptr gaming tool, allowing players to post comments, leave status updates, follow friends, and so forth, yielded one thread. Finally, we studied an online petition posted on Change.org, created by a *LoL* player asking Riot Games to remove South Americans from North American servers.

The forums chosen for our analysis illustrate the discourse surrounding non-English-using players in *League of Legends*.[1] Our purpose is not to generalize about the players of *LoL*, nor to draw conclusions about the effects of the game. Instead, we focus on the arguments contained in this discourse, and the claims they make about Spanish-using players. Our purpose is to explore whether xenophobia as a critical construct adds to our understanding of video game culture generally, and how racism is manifest in gaming and virtual environments. All quotes are taken verbatim, errors and all; when singular pronouns are required we have purposefully violated the standards of gender-neutral language, acknowledging that gamer identity is decidedly gendered masculine (Waddell et al., 2014). Finally, we have included the dates of the posts so that they can be located in the threads, and we have aligned our criticism to the temporal order of these posts within the threads, thereby showing how the arguments emerged.

## "Ok, now this may sound extremely racist, but . . ."

We locate the beginning of this discourse with a thread started on the *League of Legends* Wiki Forums on January 14, 2013 entitled "South American server needed." The post read:

> Ok, now this may sound extremely racist, but I'm tired of South Americans in games with their buddies that their only goal is to troll people. Not only is there an extreme language barrier, making it tough to communicate with them during games (except for those of us who know Spanish, myself included). Not only does this result in a vast majority of games to result in defeat, but they will then proceed to troll you. Not only is it irritating, it provides a poor gaming environment. Along with all of those, I feel that there is a huge difference in skill levels between North American gamers to South American gamers. Over the past week, I have lost more games that I care to admit, the main reason being that it would be a buddy and I (support and adc) and then the other 2 or three would be hispanic players set on trolling.

This post clearly articulates the concern about competition. This poster believes his ability to compete is undermined by the presence of Spanish-speaking players on his team, and that these players are more interested in disruptive behavior (trolling) than cooperative game play. The poster also assumes that because these players speak Spanish, they are from South America, and rather boldly claims that South American players are categorically inferior to players from North America. Finally, as indicated by the title of the post, the poster believes that South Americans should have their own servers, thereby suggesting that these players should not be on North American servers. Even the author of this post

186

acknowledges these arguments are "extremely racist," and we would add they are based on broad stereotypical generalizations and reflect the definitions of both racist situations and ideas offered by Harris (1999). The post is motivated by the intent to discriminate, segregate, and exclude, and underlying that motivation is the belief that what are perceived to be foreign players are imposing on the rights and privileges of English-using, North American players.

In some cases, which we will discuss below, this post was challenged and its claims questioned. Most contributors, however, supported and repeated these claims. Specifically, on January 15, 2013 another player posted:

> I could not agree with you more. Im Argentinian, and the only reason that i play the North American server is: language. There is a Brazilian server, but i can't play it. You may ask why? It's the same reason that made you make this post. I don't speak portuguese , and i don't intend to, just to play in that server. I do handle english rather well (lucky me), but others don't. I would love to se a South American server for various reasons: I hate the spanish talking in na [North American] server. I mean, if it's an english server, you should know to speak english . . . You're right about trolling, i've seen more Mexican / Chilean trolls than US trolls.

This post supports all the claims of the original post, with this player identifying as being from South America, and thereby trying to provide some justification for the claims. In other words, this post indirectly suggests that the problem with Spanish-using players is so severe, and their behavior is so detrimental to game play, that even bilingual players want them off North American servers. This particular poster seems to want to signify the difference between good immigrants who adopt English and proper behavior, and bad immigrants who do not.

The thread containing these posts was relatively brief, and was finished in 11 days. Another thread entitled "Mexicans need their own server" was started on the *League of Legends* forum on March 31, 2013, and continued until January 8, 2014. The thread began with this post: "I tend to play four-five games a day where I get a person who speaks Spanish on my team, and every single one of those games, we end up losing because they can't understand me, or anyone else on the team. Please make a server for mexico, or maybe a filter for english speaking people only." The fact that Mexico is on the North American continent is pointed out later in the thread, yet this error reveals a xenophobic logic equating English-using players with North America, and North America with the U.S., a logic also found in immigration discourse. Working under this logic any players speaking Spanish are assumed to be located outside North America (specifically, the United States), and therefore should be playing on another server. Again, this is all anchored in an anxiety over competitive play and skills.

Because of its longevity, this thread became a prominent forum for complaints about Spanish-using players. It is important to keep in mind that players interact in this game using avatars that often do not carry physical racial characteristics that would mark a player as White or Latino. Therefore language becomes the racial and national identity marker, as it did in the immigration debate mentioned earlier. Although the discussion within this thread focuses on the use of language, some of the posters argue that their complaints are not racist. For example, one player asked:

> how is this racist? we havent said anything against mexicans or spanish people except those that deserved it. we just want to segregate english speakers and non english speakers because isnt that what riot has already done with the other countries and servers?

On April 2, 2013 another player weighed in:

> Of course I completely agree with the whole spanish speakers need to get out, seriously ruining the game. It's not to be racist or anything, but when you are playing a game with primarily english speaking players and you can't communicate with your team because you can only speak spanish, is a severe disadvantage, especially in a team-based game.

Although this post minimally acknowledges that other languages are spoken in North America, on May 13, 2013, in the same thread, another post draws the territorial lines of the English language around the game itself:

> First off, I'm a polyglot, I can speak 4–5 languages, Eng, Fr, Canto, DE, RUS. I can kind of comprehend Spanish to an extent, but when I play a game I'm here to play a game, not spend time learning a language, especially a game that was made in ENGLISH, in an ENGLISH predominant country, for EVERYONE to enjoy as per THEIR discretion . . . So if you're going to come on "English-Speaking Soil" (Metaphorically, as soil doesn't exist in cyber-space) you'd better have the ability to speak English or Get the f*ck out . . . This is by no means a racist joust, you need to understand whose house you stand in, before you think you can start shouting out rules.

This post suggests that *LoL* is primarily an English game originating in an English speaking country. Language marks the server territory of the game (the soil) and players who do not use English should stay out. Of course, the metaphor becomes mixed when the game server becomes a house, but the point remains the same: players who do not use English have no right to be on North American servers. In addition, in an environment in which the real world visual signifiers are hidden behind avatars, language in *LoL* has become the signifier for race and national identity. Consequently, and despite claims to the contrary, the fact that this discourse focuses on language in no way mitigates the racist intent of the posts to segregate and exclude.

Posts such as these are reflected in a similar thread on the *League of Legends* forums, created on April 18, 2013, and entitled "Make a separate server for Hispanics." This thread is relatively short, and begins with this post: "Most Hispanics are really, really, really bad at League . . . It's time to end the frustration of people jibbering in Spanish and playing terribad champs like Rengar and feeding like a boss." In this post, the issue of competition is also related to Spanish-using players, and reveals how their supposed lack of game skills spoils the game for the supposed superior English-using players. Other posts in this thread express similar sentiments, with one calling for the segregation of Hispanics in the game, and another that demands "no greencard no NA server!"

A short-lived (one day) thread appeared on Raptr with the title "Mexicans have officially ruined NA servers." The original post on March 2, 2013 read: "There's a reason they are the biggest minority in the world, and the fact that they have zero intelligence and are never successful with anything other than making beans, and now they've invaded the NA servers as well as the NA continent." This thread contained many posts challenging the original post and characterizing it as racist, leading the original poster to make even more blatantly racist statements, including "I bet you've never seen a successful Mexican in person other than the owner of a local restaurant"; and "The minority scum is in every single match now. There is no avoiding them."

In addition to these threads, a petition was started on March 31, 2012 on Change.org entitled: "Remove South Americans from the North American *League of Legends* server." Only 162 people supported the petition, and it took a year for it to generate 100 signatures. Still, on June 4, 2013, Riot Games opened up Latin American servers, and allowed players to switch to those servers at no cost. Usually, players would need to create a new *LoL* account to switch servers, because players are often required to choose a server and location when they sign up for the game and create an account, although Riot Games has begun allowing players to purchase server transfers to different regions. Strangely, although the original intention of these threads was fulfilled, some players continued to post negative comments about Spanish-using players. The *League of Legends* forums thread continued for six months after Riot opened the new servers, and although there were calls to close the thread, negative comments about Spanish-using players kept it going.

Although negative comments were the driving force behind these threads, many threads contained posts by players who challenged some of the stereotypical and racist generalizations. For example, the original "Mexicans need their own server" post was quickly challenged:

> You've got a strong assumption that Mexican = No hablo inglés. The majority of folks I know of Mexican descent were either born state-side or speak English. The likelihood is that they speak English and understand what you're saying, they just don't care. If my American accent weren't so damn obvious, I'd claim No hablo inglés any time I didn't want to answer something . . . I see a bigger problem with bad English speakers who whine and complain about someone doing poorly when they do just as bad if not worse. If you look at the post and how its played out as a whole, you're basically seeing people's bias and racial bigotry, just shy of racial slurs.

Further on down the thread, on May 13, 2013, another player made this post:

> Why do you feel entitled that folks speak English? If I consider how many years of English I had to take alone, then take into account how many grammar mistakes I see regularly, it becomes pretty clear that English is not an easy language. Spanish is actually a lot easier to learn when its all said and done, their rules actually make sense. Plenty of folk don't know when to use your or you're.

In addition to identifying the bigotry, these posts also highlight the irony of improper English usage by the posters complaining about others' failure to use English. In addition, the first post also suggest that problems with cooperation and competition may be the fault of players who harbor negative feelings about Spanish players. This sentiment is also reflected in a post made to the Raptr forum on March 3, 2013:

> I don't know how many Hispanic players you had to queue with to make a stupid statement like that. People who steal roles and auto-lock is like 80% of the League community in general lol. It seems to me that you had one bad game because they took the role you wanted, you lost, and you're making excuses. Yeah, I understand that there are those days you get bad teammates, but rank reflects how well you can carry your team (even if they're bad) not just how good you are. That is why you're suppose to

learn every role so when that happens you're comfortable with the role you end up with . . . You should be more sportsman-like even if things don't go your way, and if you act like that then you're just as bad as them.

This is an interesting post because it equates bigotry and racism with poor sportsmanship. The poster points out how good players are able to accommodate a variety of gaming circumstances, including finding ways of cooperating with players who do not speak English. In other words, players who cannot successfully play with non-English-using players are themselves poor players.

In the discourse we analyzed, the racist views were obvious and related to a larger argument revealing xenophobic concerns. Although language is presented as a barrier to collaboration and competition, it also operates as a marker for race and national identity. Spanish-using players are considered a foreign threat, and should be moved off North American servers. English-using players have demarcated the North American servers as English-using zones, thus demonstrating the belief that players who do not speak English do not belong there, and their mere presence signifies improper game behavior.

In contrast, other players have countered this xenophobia and racism by pointing out that good competition requires cooperation regardless of the circumstances. Although the arguments contained in this discourse may need no rebuttal, we included the counter-comments in our analysis because they bring these xenophobic arguments into sharp relief. They also demonstrate that not all players in *LoL* share these concerns or hold these views about Spanish-using players. Finally, and perhaps most importantly, they reveal that the threats about competition, collaboration, and social standing are perhaps, as Wimmer (1997) suggested, just xenophobic perceptions.

## Game Over?

Although racism in video games and video game culture is a worthy subject of study, we hope that we have demonstrated that the study of racism could be augmented by a consideration of xenophobia. Gaming culture and gamer identity are marked by both racial and national forms of identity, and some gamers are threatened by those they perceive to be different. The *LoL* discourse we analyzed reveals arguments that speak to the sense of a foreign threat, manifested in language and assumed to be from over the border, whether that border is defined geographically or digitally. The need for cooperation and teamwork in *LoL* has led to a belief that Spanish-using players are problematic due to their unwillingness or inability to communicate with English-using players. This has engendered racist and xenophobic discourse that has gone as far as calling for (and ultimately achieving) segregated servers.

Through analysis of multiple discursive fragments we have found that, indeed, power relations in this debate emerge in multiple discourses across a variety of sources as Foucault and McKerrow have suggested. By examining a variety of sources such as the *League of Legends* Web forum, the gaming social network Raptr, an informative *LoL* Wikipedia, and an online petition website, a discursive formation begins to take shape. Different outlets show that there was uniformity among the arguments being made for removing Spanish-using players from North American servers, so much so that eventually, Riot did open up servers for players from South America. Unapologetically, and perhaps without explicit understanding of what was being suggested, players calling for a Spanish-using server managed to recreate the xenophobic and racist atmosphere found in the American political debate involving immigration, for no other reason than that English-using North American players were losing *LoL* matches.

It would seem that the discourse calling for the removal of Spanish-using players from North American servers has calmed down since the Spanish language servers were introduced. However, racism and xenophobia are still a rampant problem that Riot is attempting to address. In fact, on July 21, 2014, Riot announced that players who exhibit racist behavior would be banned from the game (Orland, 2014), and followed through with that threat on September 17, 2014, when one of the most accomplished players in *LoL*'s professional tournaments, Dennis "Svenskeren" Johnsen, was suspended from three World Championship Event matches and fined $2,500 for making racist comments during a game. This may seem a light fine, but it was a highly visible ruling that underscored Riot's position. Furthermore, Riot has also implemented an automated system within the game that punishes players for using excessive hate speech during a match. According to the game's lead social system designer, Jeffrey Lin, players can receive warnings or be permanently banned based on the type of hate speech (Beres, 2015). Although we see this as a positive move on the part of Riot, it seems problematic that Riot defines different levels of hate speech, and we certainly do not imagine that it has solved the problem of racism in online games, or *LoL* for that matter.

The fact that comments continued to be posted about Spanish-using players months after the new *LoL* servers were opened suggests that racist attitudes were not appeased, or perhaps some players still felt threatened. As we have argued, looking at this discourse from a perspective of xenophobia provides a new dimension to our understanding of racism in video games. We do not presume to have found a solution, but in the spirit of social transformation championed by McKerrow (1989), we hope we have shed more light on the problem. If anything, the xenophobic threads woven throughout the discourse we analyzed illustrate that the Internet is not the cyberutopia some have dreamed it to be.

## Note

1 Our Office of Research Integrity (IRB) determined that this research did not require internal review.

## References

Beres, D. (2015, May 25). *"League Of Legends" introduces automated system to battle abusive language*. Retrieved April 1, 2015, from http://www.huffingtonpost.com/2015/05/25/league-of-legends-harassment_n_7436158.html

Brock, A. (2011). "When keeping it real goes wrong": *Resident Evil 5*, racial representation, and gamers. *Games and Culture, 6*(5), 429–452.

Brookey, R., & Cannon, K. (2009). Sex lives in Second Life. *Critical Studies in Media Communication, 26*(2), 145–164.

Egenfeldt-Nielsen, S., Smith, J. H., & Tosca, S. P. (2008). *Understanding video games*. New York, NY: Routledge.

Foucault, M. (1972). *The archaeology of knowledge and discourse on language*. New York, NY: Pantheon.

Fouchard, L. & Segatti, A. (2015). Introduction of xenophobia and citizenship: The everyday politics of exclusion and inclusion in Africa. *Africa, 85*, 2–12.

Harris, L. (1999). *Racism*. Amherst, NY: Humanity Books.

Johnson, L. (2010). The integration of the European Union and the changing cultural space of Europe: Xenophobia and webs of significance. *International Journal For The Semiotics Of Law—Revue internationale de Sémiotique juridique, 25*(2), 211–224.

Kilty, K. & Haymes M. (2000). Racism, nativism, and exclusion: Public policy, immigration, and the Latino experience in the United States. *Journal of Poverty, 4*(1/2), 1–25.

McGonigal, J. (2011). *Reality is broken: Why games make us better and how they can change the world*. New York, NY: Penguin Books.

McKerrow, R. (1989). Critical rhetoric: Theory and praxis. *Communication Monographs, 56*(2), 91–111.

Maiberg, E. (2014, January 27). *League of Legends revenues for 2013 total $624 million [UPDATE]*. Retrieved April 1, 2015, from http://www.gamespot.com/articles/league-of-legends-revenues-for-2013-total-624-million-update/1100-6417224/.

Miles, R. & Brown, M. (2003). *Racism*. New York, NY: Routledge.

Monson, M. (2012). Race-based fantasy realm essentialism in the *World of Warcraft*. *Games and Culture, 7*(1), 48–71.

Nakamura, L. (2002). *Cybertypes: Race, ethnicity, and identity on the internet*. New York, NY: Routledge.

Ono, K. & Sloop, J. (1995). The critique of vernacular discourse. *Communication Monographs, 62*, 19–46.

Ono, K. & Sloop, J. (2002). *Shifting borders: Rhetoric, immigration, and California's proposition 187*. Philadelphia, PA: Temple University Press.

Orland, K. (2014, July 22). Riot starts getting tough on toxic LoL players with "instant" bans. *Ars Technica*. Retrieved June 14, 2016, from http://arstechnica. com/gaming/2014/07/riot-starts-getting-tough-on-toxic-players-with-instant-bans/.

Packer, J. (2014). What makes an Orc? Racial cosmos and emergent narrative in *World of Warcraft*. *Games and Culture, 9*(2), 83–101.

Shaw, A. (2012). Do you identify as a gamer? Gender, race, sexuality, and gamer identity. *New Media & Society, 14*(1), 28–44.

Tassi, P. (2014, January 27). *Riot's "League of Legends" Reveals Astonishing 27 Million Daily Players, 67 Million Monthly*. Retrieved April 1, 2015, from http://www.forbes.com/sites/insertcoin/2014/01/27/riots-league-of-legends-reveals-astonishing-27-million-daily-players-67-million-monthly/.

Taylor, T. L. (2012). *Raising the stakes: E-sports and the professionalization of computer gaming*. Cambridge, MA: The MIT Press.

Waddell, T., Ivory, J., Conde, R., Long, C., & McDonnell, R. (2014). White man's virtual world: A systematic content analysis of gender and race in massively multiplayer online games. *Journal For Virtual Worlds Research, 7*(2), 1–13.

Williams, D., Martins, N., Consalvo, M., & Ivory, J. (2009). The virtual census: Representations of gender, race and age in video games. *New Media and Society, 11*(5), 815–834.

Wimmer, A. (1997). Explaining xenophobia and racism: A critical review of current research approaches. *Ethnic and Racial Studies, 20*(1), 17–41.

Witkowski, E. (2012). On the digital playing field: How we "do sport" with networked computer games. *Games and Culture, 7*(5), 349–374.

Witkowski, E. (2014). Competition and cooperation. In Be. Perron & M. J. P. Wolf (Eds.), *The Routledge companion to video game studies* (pp. 158–165). New York, NY: Routledge.

# 12

# #IFTHEYGUNNEDMEDOWN

## Postmodern Media Criticism in a Post-Racial World

*Christopher P. Campbell*

After the 2014 fatal shooting of Michael Brown, an unarmed 18-year-old African American man, by a White police officer in Ferguson, Missouri, some news organizations included in their immediate coverage a photo of Brown taken from his Facebook page. In a now iconic image, Brown stands in a Nike tank top, unsmiling, and flashing a peace sign (misidentified by some news organizations as a gang sign). Later, less incendiary photos from Brown's Facebook page surfaced. Within a few days of Brown's death, the hashtag #IfTheyGunnedMeDown appeared on social media. Young African Americans posted two photos of themselves, representing positive and potentially negative images, questioning which photo would be used by the media if they were shot by police. These posts reflected an insight into the notion of media representation that likely escapes most audience members who regularly view news coverage of Black men. These young African Americans perceptively and concisely identified the problems inherent in dominant media representations of Black men as pathological criminals, a persistent representation that affects both racial attitudes and public policy decisions.

Stuart Hall, whose work on race and representation influenced a generation of critical media scholars, had died only a few months before the Ferguson shooting. He would have quickly recognized the meaning of these postings. His work challenged the "preferred reading" of media texts; he described the cultural power of analyzing those meanings as the "politics of signification" (1980, p. 138). In this chapter, I will describe the work of Hall and others who have examined race and media through the lens of representation to show how media texts generate powerful meanings about African Americans and other people of color. Second,

I will argue that the #IfTheyGunnedMeDown posts are consistent with a body of work in media studies that has largely failed to effect change in media representations of people of color. Finally, I will ask whether social media or other pop culture texts have the potential to shift the discussion to an audience beyond the academy.

## Media Representation and Race

Hall used the term *representation* to describe the complex ways in which the mass media both present images and re-present images that have multiple meanings, especially about race and ethnicity. For Hall, the analysis of media representations is key to unlocking the power of the dominant meanings—meanings that indirectly serve the interests of the wealthiest and most powerful members of a society. His notion of representation is transformational and

> a way of constantly wanting new kinds of knowledges to be produced in the world, new kinds of subjectivities to be explored and new dimensions of meaning which have not been foreclosed by the systems of power which are in operations.
>
> (Jhally, 1997)

As John Fiske explained, "The definition of culture as a constant site of struggle between those with and those without power underpins the most interesting current work in cultural studies" (1992, p. 292). He called Hall's seminal essay, *Encoding/Decoding*, a "turning point" in cultural studies, because it "introduces the idea that television programs do not have a single meaning but are relatively open texts, capable of being read in different ways by different people and suggests that "there is a necessary correlation between people's social situations and the meanings that they may generate from a television program" (p. 292).

Hall (1980) described decoding media texts through two levels of analysis. Simply put, the first level is the denotative or preferred reading—that which was intended by the producer—and the connotative (negotiated and/or oppositional) readings of the same message. What Hall would describe as a negotiated reading of media texts allows for analysis beyond the meaning intended by their producers. According to Hall, such readings require a recognition of the dominant ideology at work and how that ideology is "shot through with contradictions" (1980, p. 137). Hall wrote, "Negotiated codes operate through what we might call particular or situated logics: and these logics are sustained by their differential and unequal relation to the discourses and logics of power" (p. 137). In this way, the denotative, commonsense meanings of the stories can only be understood within the context provided by connotative, interpretive readings.

196

Hall ultimately described oppositional readings of media messages in which audiences resist the preferred meaning and recognize deeper, problematic meanings. As Hall said, "One of the most significant political moments . . . is the point when events which are normally signified and decoded in a negotiated way begin to be given an oppositional reading. Here the 'politics of signification'—the struggle in discourse—is joined" (p. 138). Fiske and Hartley described this highest level of analysis of media messages as that which recognizes the "mythology" or "ideology" that hides in the coding of media messages: "This, the third order of signification, reflects the broad principles by which a culture organizes and interprets the reality with which it has to cope" (1978, p. 46).

Other cultural studies scholars have advanced similar notions about representation in interpreting media texts. Louis Althusser (1971), for instance, described the concepts of hailing and interpellation to explain how media messages coax audiences into specific understandings that serve the interests of the message producers. As Fiske noted, "These terms derive from the idea that any language, whether it be verbal, visual, tactile or whatever, is part of social relations and that in communicating with someone we are reproducing social relationships" (1992, p. 289). Likewise, Antonio Gramsci (1971) used the concept of *hegemony*—the subtle, unseen political, social and economic ideology that reflects the interests of the wealthy and powerful—to describe the way in which media representations function.

Like Althusser and Gramsci, Roland Barthes was concerned with the subtle functioning of hegemony. In his seminal work *Mythologies* (1957/1972), Barthes described his efforts to examine French society through the prism of cultural myths:

> The starting point of these reflections was usually a feeling of impatience at the sight of the "naturalness" with which newspapers, art and common sense constantly dress up a reality which, even though it is the one we live in, is undoubtedly determined by history . . . I hate seeing Nature and History confused at every turn, and I wanted to track down, in the decorative display of *what-goes-without-saying*, the ideological abuse which, in my view, is hidden there.
>
> (p. 11, emphasis in original)

Barthes was concerned with how artifacts of popular culture—advertising, photojournalism, studio wrestling, and others—reflected a kind of groupthink that doesn't allow for more complicated interpretations of events. Similarly, Clifford Geertz argued that "as a frame for thought, common sense is as totalizing as any other . . . It pretends to reach past illusion to truth, to, as we say, things as they are" (1983. p. 84).

Cultural studies scholars have frequently addressed the notion of representation in news coverage, which routinely reflects mythical common

197

sense about the events of the day. Fiske and Hartley (1978) identified "myth chains" as one of the ways in which journalistic storytelling embeds ideological understandings, and they argued that "news reporting and fiction use similar signs because they naturally refer to the same myths in our culture" (p. 65). Himmelstein (1984) identified the "myth of the puritan ethic" (p. 205) in news coverage that routinely extolled the values of hard work and middle-class life while implicitly questioning the values of the underclass. Richard Campbell (1991a, 1991b), in describing the myth-making capacity of journalism, suggested that the notion of "balance" was itself a "code word for . . . middle American values." He continued, "These values are encoded into mainstream journalism—how it selects the news, where it places its beat reporters, who and how it promotes, how it critically reports and thereby naively supports government positions" (1991a, p. 75).

Sociologist Herman Gray (1986, 1991, 1995) has examined racial representations in both prime time television programs and journalism and identified the "twin representations" of African Americans in fictional and nonfictional television (1986, p. 304), contrasting the upper middle-class life portrayed on *The Cosby Show* with underclass Black life portrayed in a contemporaneous PBS documentary, *The Vanishing Family: Crisis in Black America*. Gray argued that race as it was portrayed on fictional television was consistent with The American Dream, and appealed "to the utopian desire in blacks and whites for racial oneness and equality while displacing the persistent reality of racism and racial inequality or the kinds of social struggles and cooperation required to eliminate them" (1986, p. 302). Gray argued that the underclass Black life on nonfictional TV, on the other hand, failed to "identify complex social forces like racism, social organization, economic dislocation, unemployment, the changing economy, or the welfare state" in explaining the crisis in the urban underclass (p. 300).

Gray concluded that

> the assumptions and framework that structure these representations often displace representations that would enable viewers to see that many individuals trapped in the under class have the very same qualities (of hard work and sacrifices as seen on *Cosby*) but lack the options and opportunities to realize them.
>
> (p. 303)

My own work on race and news expands on Gray's examination of the twin representations of African Americans (as well as Hispanic and *other* Americans); in describing my approach in *Race, Myth and the News*, I wrote, "The danger of the commonsense claim to truth is in its exclusion of those who live outside the familiar world it represents" (1995, p. 18). My first study (Campbell, 1995) found that the racial mythology embedded in broadcasts across the United States represented "a hegemonic consensus about race and class that sustains myths about life outside of white, 'mainstream' America" (p. 132).

I identified three persistent myths in representations of race in American journalism (Campbell, 1995; Campbell et al., 2012). In the "myth of marginality," people of color (who are ignored) are less significant and are marginalized in news coverage (1995). In the hundreds of newscasts I viewed, I observed the general invisibility of people of color in the news, including news in cities with large minority populations. Additionally, I cited other studies (including Entman, 1990, 1992 and Gist 1990) providing evidence of the underrepresentation and stereotypical portrayal of minorities in all forms of daily news coverage.

Second, I identified a "myth of difference" in local TV newscasts in which people of color are routinely represented differently than White people. Television news reinforced historical stereotypes about people of color, both "positive" stereotypes of successful African American athletes and entertainers and negative stereotypes (especially of African American and Hispanic men) as violent criminals. I closely analyzed several stories that reflected a pattern of subtle racial biases in the newsroom and argued that well-intended journalists (and audience members) "are likely unaware of the biases and stereotypical thinking that are deeply rooted in the cognitive and cultural processes in a society that is dominated by white, middle-class perceptions" (p. 82).

Finally, in my analysis of local television news coverage of Martin Luther King, Jr. Day, I identified a "myth of assimilation," in which people of color, especially African Americans, are shown to have overcome racism and become fully assimilated into the American mainstream, where equality has been achieved. This is now referred to as post-racialism. Stories about the King holiday were dominated by a theme of racial harmony, despite the evidence of lingering racial hostility in many of the cities adopting that theme. I wasn't surprised by this; as I wrote:

> The social and professional processes that dictate how news is covered are based on an implicit common sense, a common sense that may have more to do with stereotyped notions about the world than with a true understanding of it. Most Americans would like to believe that their country is a tolerant and fair one, that discrimination does not exist, that equal opportunity is there for all. But what we would like to believe and what actually exists are clearly at odds.
>
> (1995, p. 111)

I was concerned about news organizations creating a mythical world in which racial harmony is the norm while continuing to bombard audiences with stories about people of color suspected of violent crimes.

In reflecting on the work of Gray (1986, 1991) and Jhally and Lewis (1992), I noted: "If our society is the just and fair one that was portrayed on King Day, the constant barrage of menacing images of minorities that more commonly appear on local TV news will undoubtedly fuel racist attitudes" (p. 111). When revisiting representations of race on local television news in 2012 (Campbell, LeDuff and Brown), we found few changes to the myths I had identified in 1995; indeed, the mythic representations of race in journalism in the age of the Barack Obama presidency seemed even more problematic.

Certainly, the gap between Black and White opportunity in the United States has not closed during the Obama era, and the 2007 recession had a more dire impact on Black America than on the population at large. According to the Economic Policy Institute (2014), the African American community suffered a "dramatic increase in unemployment and a staggering loss of income" during the recession (p. 1). The institute found that the median Black household's income fell 10.1%, compared to 5.4% for White households. A few other numbers similarly reflect the disparities: Twenty-six percent of Black American families live in poverty; 11% of White families live in poverty (U.S. Census Bureau, 2014). About 32% of White Americans have college degrees; fewer than 19% of African Americans have graduated from college (JBHE.com, 2013). Black unemployment is over 11%. White unemployment is 5.4% (Rosen, 2014). Joblessness among Black teenagers is nearly 38%; 17% of White teenagers are jobless (PBS Newshour, 2014). African Americans are jailed at a rate of six times the rate of Whites (Drake, 2013). African Americans are arrested at a rate 10 times higher than people who are not Black (Heath, 2014). The notion of post-racialism—the belief that America has overcome its racist legacy—seems preposterous in the face of such statistics, although it continues to reflect the attitude of more than half of White Americans, who hold "explicit anti-Black attitudes" (Edsall, 2013, p. 1). Remarkably, most Whites believe there is more anti-White than anti-Black discrimination, which they believe has been "all but eliminated" (Fletcher, 2015). Although research by media scholars has for decades pointed out the penchant for media institutions to provide gross misrepresentations of African Americans and other minority populations, there has not been a significant change in those misrepresentations in the primary (sometimes called "mainstream," a term now loaded with conflicting political connotations) media systems in the U.S.

## Race, Media, and Postmodernism

My interest here is in whether the social media posts following Michael Brown's shooting reflect a new postmodern media criticism, moving the critique of problematic racial representations into the realm of popular culture, where it is then addressed by traditional news organizations. Certainly, this would not be the first time that pop culture has illuminated racial attitudes in the United States. As early as the 1960s, comedian Richard Pryor pushed the envelope by challenging racial inequities during his hilarious but incendiary performances. As Pryor biographer Scott Saul noted, "He's talking about the gap between how [Blacks and Whites] travel through the world and perceive it. And people are starting to have a conversation through him, this very conversation about racial injustice in America" (on *Fresh Air*, 2014). Satirical television programs in the 1970s and 1980s—e.g., NBC's *Saturday Night Live* and Fox's *In Living Color*—also ventured into race in a way that mainstream media had not.

*Rolling Stone* media critic Jon Katz presciently argued in 1992 that young Americans were looking to places other than traditional organizations for news and information. He contended that popular music, non-news television and the film industry informed America's youth far more than newspapers or TV newscasts did:

> Straight news—the Old News—is pooped, confused and broke . . .
>
> In the place of Old News, something dramatic is evolving, a new culture of information, a hybrid New News—dazzling, adolescent, irresponsible, fearless, frightening and powerful. The New News is a heady concoction, part Hollywood film and TV movie, part pop music and pop art, mixed with popular culture and celebrity magazines, tabloid telecasts, cable and home video.
>
> Increasingly, the New News is seizing the functions of mainstream journalism, sparking conversations and setting the country's social and political agenda.
>
> (Katz, 1992, p. 33)

As far as the "New News" and its role in the media discussion about race, Katz argued that film director Spike Lee was "far ahead of his mainstream competitors on racial issues. So is [rapper] Ice Cube" (p. 35). Although Katz's article significantly pre-dated the advent of social media and did not use the term postmodernism, this new means of information dissemination reflects a kind of postmodern "New News" on steroids, with young people flocking to social media sites to share news and opinions about relevant events, including events related to race. Young African Americans especially are flocking to Twitter, at a significantly higher rate than young Whites (Smith, 2014).

But first a word about postmodernism, a slippery concept at best, and one that tends to defy definition as it applies to media studies. For instance, *Television Quarterly* once headlined an article, "'We Know It When We See It': Postmodernism and Television" (Campbell & Freed, 1993). The authors described "PoMo" as "newfangled attitudes about oldfangled ideas" (p. 75) and cautioned about approaching media criticism with a postmodern filter: even "trying to define and categorize PoMo style is a decidedly logical, rational and modern critical practice—the very essence of what postmodernism wants to resist at all turns" (p. 76).

Collins (1992) similarly argued that postmodernism has been employed in divergent, contradictory ways, and listed six different applications of the term:

> (1) a distinctive style; (2) a movement that emerged in the sixties, seventies, or eighties, depending on the medium in question; (3) a condition or milieu that typifies an entire set of socioeconomic factors; (4) a specific mode of philosophical inquiry that throws into question the givens of philosophical discourse; (5) a very particular type of "politics"; and (6) an emergent form of cultural analysis shaped by all of the above.
>
> (p. 327)

More recent discussions include the notion of post-postmodernism, called automodernity by Robert Samuels (2010), which posits that new media herald a new cultural and technological period that empowers individual media users in a way that traditional media have not. Baya's analysis of automodernity noted that this period "transcends the initial postmodern diagnosis and requires new perspectives upon understanding audiences" (2013, p. 157). He argued that with digital communication and the "omnipresence" of media messages, audiences spend increasing amounts of time both receiving and producing media content. As Baya observed, "The average 'digital youth' user simultaneously operates his laptop for working, socializing on instant chat or on networks such as Facebook, participating in online games, giving feedback on blogs and engaging in several other types of electronic conversations—multitasking and mixing work with leisure, private with public space" (p. 157).

## #IfTheyGunnedMeDown

Acknowledging the ephemeral nature of the concept of postmodernism, I proceed with an analysis that, in a simple sense, argues that postmodern elements of contemporary media defy and challenge traditional media in a way that is worthy of analysis, especially when it comes to representations of race. Perhaps more significantly, I'll argue that the impact of the social media critique becomes more profound as it generates coverage by traditional media outlets and reaches larger (and older) audiences. That was particularly true of the social media posts following Michael Brown's shooting, an event that—along with other high-profile killings of Black men by White police officers—launched a series of protests across the United States that continued into 2015. Within six weeks of the shooting, the phrase #IfTheyGunnedMeDown was used on Twitter more than 168,000 times (Vega, 2014), prompting *The New York Times* to comment, "The speed with which the shooting of Mr. Brown has resonated on social media has helped propel and transform a local shooting into a national cause" (Vega, 2014).

The power of Black Twitter, a collective of African American Twitter users who function as a kind of "media response team" (Vega, 2014), is a function of the fact that young African Americans use Twitter at a rate much higher than Whites (Pew Research Center 2014). Generally, the news coverage of the Michael Brown shooting was consistent with the kind of stereotypical coverage vilified by cultural studies scholars; Brown was just another Black criminal, and White officials provided a commonsense explanation of the shooting. But in its coverage of the hashtag campaign, *The New York Times* addressed issues of media representations that typically go uncovered. The *Times* interviewed a 32-year-old blogger who said news photographs in stories that involved African American men often "removed context from a situation" (Vega, 2014). The newspaper also reported on another young Black man who had posted his own #IfTheyGunnedMeDown photos and noted that Black victims are "portrayed as if they deserved it, cop versus robbers, good guys versus black guys" (Vega, 2014). A 19-year-old student told the *Times* that the Black social media movement deserved to be taken seriously: "Hashtag activism is activism . . . We might be tweeting from a couch, but we're also getting up and doing the work that needs to be done" (Vega, 2014).

The #IfTheyGunnedMeDown campaign quickly reached hundreds of thousands of social media users, and a much larger audience as coverage of the campaign exploded. Many major national news organization—including *The New York Times*, *USA Today*, *The Washington Post*, *The Christian Science Monitor*, *The Los Angeles Times*, *Time* magazine, and NPR—featured extensive coverage of the campaign, including multiple examples of the #IfTheyGunnedMeDown postings. *Washington Post* reporter Soraya Nadia McDonald suggested that the campaign questioned

> if it's possible for people, especially young black men, to live their lives online without worry that an innocent photo of them gettin' gully at a party will somehow become appropriate as evidence of black thuggery . . . The hashtag asks if black teens have the same right as others to make mistakes—to do dumb things and post then post about it on Facebook or clown around with their friends—without becoming branded in perpetuity.
>
> (2014)

In its coverage, National Public Radio sought out young people who had tweeted #IfTheyGunnedMeDown photos:

> There's that ambiguous "they" in the hashtag, and we asked the tweeters who, in their minds, it referred to. Generally they said it referred to those with power and authority—in particular the police and the media. "But it could have been directed to anyone who is small-minded enough to fear a young black person automatically if it's nighttime, if he's wearing a hoodie, if his music is too loud, or if he's reaching for his wallet," said Brianna Chevonne. "It can apply to anyone of any race who is ignorant enough to be fearful of young black people to the point they would take their lives."
>
> (NPR Staff, 2014)

The hashtag campaign was also covered in Europe. The BBC ended its story this way: "The hashtag has proved wildly popular and been used more than 100,000 times in the last 24 hours. '#IfTheyGunnedMeDown Tweets should be required reading in every journalism class in America,' said one commentator" (BBC Trending, 2014).

Six months after Michael Brown's death, the hashtag had been used on social media sites more than two million times. It had inspired a mural at the Center for Civil and Human Rights in Atlanta and at least two songs, extending its impact outside of traditional media. Other hashtag campaigns that surfaced amid the Ferguson protests also merited national coverage. CNN, ABC, *The Washington Post*, *USA Today*, the BBC, and other major news organizations reported on 300,000-plus posts with the hashtag #CrimingWhileWhite, which told the stories of young White people who recognized their privileged treatment from police that would have been unlikely had they been Black. The posts described things such as "When I was 22 I pushed a cop when I was drunk at a bar. I was told to go home and sleep it off" and "Pulled over in high school. Black friend searched & asked if he has dope—Cop tells me I must be lost & to get home" (Williams, 2014). Although generally intended as an important acknowledgement of White privilege, some African Americans took offense. As one wrote, "#WhitePrivilege is being able to use a hashtag to admit to committing crimes and being applauded for bravery" (Williams, 2014).

Similarly, when riots broke out at a pumpkin festival in Keene, New Hampshire two months after the Michael Brown shooting, the hashtag #pumpkinfest was used to highlight the differences in the news coverage (and the treatment by police) of the White rioters. One post, labeled "Your media guide to the difference between #Ferguson and #pumpkinfest," included photos from each event, with the Ferguson protestors labeled "thugs, animals, destroying their community" and the Keene rioters "rowdy, mischief, booze filled revelers" (Kleeman, 2014). But the #pumpkinfest campaign received less news coverage, thereby limiting its impact.

The substantial coverage of the #IfTheyGunnedMeDown campaign by traditional news organizations is a sign that those organizations recognize the significance of hashtag activism. Perhaps those organizations may begin to address journalistic conventions that continue to marginalize Black and Brown men, and will consider alternative approaches to cover violent crime. As the #IfTheyGunnedMeDown activists have succinctly observed, journalism has failed the poor communities in which violence and police violence thrive. Crimes in those communities are generally covered as singular events without history, without context. Coverage of the roots of that behavior—failed economic policies, disastrous public education, substance abuse, racism—is not part of the journalistic routine and gets only sporadic attention. Is it possible that journalism will acknowledge this weakness and more effectively provide coverage that helps explain the crises in America's poorest communities? Probably not. As I pessimistically observed 20 years ago,

> America's racial myths—rooted in the nescience of hundreds of years of White supremacy—endure despite the best intentions of the news media. It may well be that the very nature of those media—and of the society in which they exist—may not allow them to function in a manner that will contribute to more accurate portrayals of life outside of the mainstream. That would require newsroom process and social forces to be systematically questioned and altered.
>
> (Campbell, 1995, pp. 135–136)

## Race and Postmodern Media

So the real hope for the media's ability to address police violence and other forms of contemporary racism may not be in traditional journalism but in the postmodern efforts of hashtag activists and other forms of non-news media, what Katz (1992) described as the New News. Postmodern media addressing race in a more complicated way than traditional journalism include websites such as Buzzfeed (see "If Black people said the stuff White people say"), films such as 2014's *Dear White People* (based on a social media site examining the "micro-aggressions" of contemporary racism), and cable television programs such as the Comedy Channel's *The Daily Show* (with its "Senior Black Correspondent") and *The Nightly Show with Larry Wilmore* (once *The Daily Show*'s Senior Black Correspondent). Prime time network television in 2015—e.g., *Blackish* and *Fresh Off the Boat*—has shown an inclination to address race in new ways. Even the popular ABC drama *Scandal*, which through-out its run had adopted a post-racial stance in which the African American star's race was rarely addressed, aired an episode in March of 2015 in which the Ferguson episode was fictionally recreated a few blocks from the White House. On HBO's *Last Week Tonight with John Oliver* the week after the Michael Brown shooting, the satirist delivered a stinging 15 minute diatribe ridiculing the racist police response, the militarization of police forces in Ferguson and elsewhere and, indirectly, the traditional news media's "neutral" approach to the events in which White authority figures are cited to provide "balance" to a story in which the racist behav-ior of those authorities was otherwise ignored.

And postmodern media are gaining a significant foothold in American culture. When *The Daily Show*'s longtime host and executive producer John Stewart announced his exit from the program in February of 2015, *The New York Times* observed the role the satirist played in contem-porary culture: "For a segment of the audience that had lost its faith in broadcast and print news outlets or never regarded them as sacrosanct in the first place, Mr. Stewart emerged a figure as trusted as Walter Cronkite or Edward R. Murrow" (Itzkoff, 2015). Such a comparison might draw guffaws from traditionalists, but it is indicative of the poten-tial of postmodern media to serve the role that journalists once performed in a democratic society, which includes explaining how race and racism function, notions that traditional journalism has generally been inept at addressing. Even President Barack Obama, in an interview with *Rolling Stone*, acknowledged Stewart's impact:

> I don't watch a lot of TV news . . . I like *The Daily Show*, so sometimes if I'm home late at night, I'll catch snippets of that. I think Jon Stewart's brilliant. It's amazing to me the degree to which he's able to cut through a bunch of the nonsense—for young people in particular, where I think he ends up having more credibility than a lot of more conventional news programs do.
> (Wenner, 2012)

There are no simple answers to questions about the impact postmod-ern media might have on journalism, racial attitudes, and public policy. Several questions seem particularly significant: Will the problematic news representations of African Americans and other people of color have less impact in a world in which the audiences for traditional journalism are drying up and young people are exposed to less stereotypical news cover-age and more complicated discussions of race in non-news media? Will journalists reconsider newsroom conventions that focus on *crimes* instead of *crime*? That is, will news organizations consider new approaches to the coverage of the root causes—the economic, social and educational disparities that disproportionately affect African American and Latino communities—of the stories about violent crime that they tell on a daily basis? Will the efforts of hashtag activists and other voices from postmodern media have an impact on public policy?

Within six months of the Michael Brown controversy in Ferguson, several other stories about police brutality against people of color gained national coverage. In Cleveland, a 12-year-old African American boy was shot and killed by police who mistook the pellet gun he was playing with for a real weapon. In New York, Eric Garner, a Black man, died after a police officer used a chokehold to subdue him after he was arrested for selling loose cigarettes at a store in Staten Island; Garner's last words, "I can't breathe," became a rallying cry for protestors. A Hispanic man armed only with rocks was repeatedly shot by police officers in Pasco, Washington, and a South Asian man was hospitalized after being slammed to the ground by a police officer in Madison, Alabama. Protest marches and social media campaigns of varying impact followed all of these incidents. Activists called for investigations, indictments, and changes in police procedures.

If nothing else, the attention paid by traditional media with large audiences to the social media campaigns and protests was significant, and the public debate seems to have expanded. The #IfTheyGunnedMeDown campaign was preceded by the Occupy Wall Street movement, which also utilized social media to accentuate the economic disparities between the vast majority of Americans and the wealthiest, known as the "1 percent." The Occupy protests worked to raise awareness about income inequality, which became a focus of widely publicized political debate in the ensuing months. But the likelihood of significant changes to American-style capitalism seem remote, and the police brutality protests, despite pithy catch phrases useful on social media and in street protests—Hands Up, Don't Shoot; I Can't Breathe; Black Lives Matter—may be equally ineffective at bringing about long-term changes to public policy and flawed journalistic coverage of the issues.

The Ferguson protests did have some tangible impacts. In February 2015, the *St. Louis Post Dispatch* published an extraordinary, 14-part multimedia project titled "Ferguson" that examined the shooting, the protests, the investigation, policing, civil rights, the courts, religion, education, the economy, and solutions. This is precisely the kind of journalism that is all too rare in the US, the kind that might help explain racism and the factors contributing to the animosity between police and minority communities. In terms of public policy, at the height of the Ferguson protests, President Obama requested $75 million in federal funding to arm local police forces with body cameras, although the efficacy of that approach was questioned, especially because videotape from cell phones that caught police misconduct in other high-profile cases didn't have much of an impact (Friedman, 2014). In March 2015, a Justice Department civil rights investigation concluded that the Ferguson police department was racially biased and "routinely" violated the constitutional rights of the city's Black citizens (Horwitz, 2015), and led to the resignation of Ferguson's city manager and police chief.

But some observers questioned the real impact of the #IfTheyGunned-MeDown campaign and the related protests. The son of Malcolm X, Ilyasah Shabazz, opined in *The New York Times* that his father would have been "heartened by the youth-led movement taking place across the nation, and abroad, in response to institutional brutality." He continued:

> In a sense, his ability to boil down hard truths into strong statements and catchy phrases presaged our era of hashtag activism.
>
> But he would be the first to say that slogans aren't action. They amount to nothing but a complaint filed against a system that does not care. In his speeches, he did not simply cry "Inequality!"—he demanded justice, and he laid out the steps necessary to achieve it.
>
> (2014)

Media mogul Oprah Winfrey and activist Al Sharpton also weighed in on the movement's lack of focus and identifiable leadership. While promoting her film *Selma*, which captured a pivotal moment in the civil rights protests of the 1960s, Winfrey commented, "I think that what can be gleaned from our film . . . is to really take note of the strategic intention required when you want real change" (Somashekhar, 2015).

Cultural critic Michael Eric Dyson questioned President Obama's reaction to the Ferguson protests, noting the first African American president's continued role as the media's exemplar of post-racial America. Rather than vilifying the horrid, racially motivated behavior of White police officers, according to Dyson, the president was, "vague, halting and sincerely noncommittal" (2015). Dyson, an African American who has written widely about the role of race in popular culture, continued,

> Instead, [President Obama] lauded the racial progress that he said he had witnessed "in my own life," substituting his life for ours, and signaled again how his story of advancement was ours, suggesting, sadly, that the sum of our political fortunes in his presidency may be lesser than the parts of our persistent suffering.

Post-racialism in the media lives on when America's Black president serves as a constant, powerful contrast to the realities of racism. The young African Americans who posted their photos under the #IfTheyGunnedMeDown hashtag may have contributed to an awakening of those realities, but the long-term impact of that campaign and the other anti-racism protests that surfaced in 2014 remains to be seen. As the media critic/public intellectual Noam Chomsky observed of the Occupy Wall Street movement, "The Occupy tactic was a remarkably successful tactic . . . It just lighted a fire all over the place. People were just waiting for something to light the spark. And it was extremely successful, but it's a tactic, and tactics are not strategies. A tactic has a half-life; it has diminishing returns" (2013).

Ultimately, the Ferguson protests and related social media campaigns will likely not trigger dramatic shifts in American public policy or in traditional media approaches. Local TV news audiences will continue to be bombarded with murder-of-the-day coverage of poor Black and Hispanic communities, and journalists will largely continue to ignore the context for the horrible realities of life in America's most impoverished communities. Sadly, the good news may be that audiences for traditional journalism are rapidly shrinking, and future generations of social media-savvy audiences will rely more heavily on media that have the potential to provide representations of people and communities of color that refute the mythical notions that have dominated news coverage for decades.

# References

Althuser, L. (1971). *Lenin and philosophy and other essays* (Ben Brewster, trans.). London, UK: Monthly Review Press.

Barthes, R. (1972). *Mythologies* (Jonathan Cape Ltd., trans.). New York, NY: Hill & Wang. (Original work published 1957.)

Baya, A. (2012). Post-postmodernism: Automodernity and its relevance to understanding contemporary media audiences. *Procedia—Social and Behavioral Sciences*, 71, 154–159.

BBC Trending. (2014, August 11). The two faces of Michael Brown. BBC. Retrieved October 24, 2015, from http://www.bbc.com/news/blogs-trending-28742301.

Campbell, C. (1995). *Race, myth and the news*. Thousand Oaks, CA: Sage.

Campbell, C., LeDuff, K. & Brown, R. (2012). "Yes we did"?: Race, myth and the news revisited, In C. Campbell, K. LeDuff, C. Jenkins & R. Brown (Eds.) *Race and news: Critical perspectives* (pp. 3–21). New York, NY: Routledge.

Campbell, R. (1991a). *60 Minutes and the news: A mythology for middle America*. Urbana, IL: University of Illinois Press.

Campbell, R. (1991b). Word vs. image: Elitism, popularity and TV news. *Television Quarterly*, 24(1), 73–81.

Campbell, R. and Freed, R. (1993). "We know it when we see it": Postmodernism and television. *Television Quarterly*, 26(2), 75–87.

Chomsky, N. (2013). *The more solidarity spreads, the more you can do: Reflections on class war, rebellion and solidarity* (Interview by Free Speech Radio News). Retrieved October 24, 2015, from http://chomsky.info/interviews/2013----.htm

Collins, J. (1992). Postmodernism and television. In R. C. Allen (Ed.) *Channels of discourse, reassembled*, Chapel Hill, NC: University of North Carolina Press, 327–353.

Drake, B. (2013). Incaceration gap widens between whites and blacks. Pew Research Center. Retrieved October 24, 2015, from http://www.pewresearch. org/fact-tank/2013/09/06/incarceration-gap-between-whites-and-blacks-widens/.

Dyson, M. E. (2014, November 29). Where do we go after Ferguson? *The New York Times*. Retrieved October 24, 2015, from http://www.nytimes. com/2014/11/30/opinion/sunday/where-do-we-go-after-ferguson.html?_r=0.

Economic Policy Institute. (2014). The state of working America. Retrieved October 24, 2015, from http://www.stateofworkingamerica.org/fact-sheets/ african-americans/.

Edsall, T.B. (2013). The persistence of racial resentment. *nytimes.com*. Retrieved October 24, 2015, from http://opinionator.blogs.nytimes.com/2013/02/06/ the-persistence-of-racial-resentment/.

Entman, R. M. (1990). Modern racism and the images of blacks in local television news. *Critical Studies in Mass Communication, 7*(4), 332–345.

Entman, R. M. (1992). Blacks in the news: Television, modern racism and cultural Change. *Journalism Quarterly, 69*(2), pp. 341–361.

Fiske J. & Hartley J. (1978). *Reading television*. London, UK: Methuen.

Fiske, J. (1992). British cultural studies and television. In R. C. Allen (Ed.). *Channels of discourse, reassembled*. (pp. 287–326). Chapel Hill, NC: University of North Carolina Press.

Fletcher, M. A. (2014, October 8). Whites think discrimination against whites is a bigger problem than bias against blacks. *Washington Post*. Retrieved October 24, 2015, from http://www.washingtonpost.com/blogs/wonkblog/wp/2014/ 10/08/white-people-think-racial-discrimination-in-america-is-basically-over/.

*Fresh Air* (radio show). (2014, December 11). Richard Pryor, a comedic pioneer who was "always whittling on dynamite". National Public Radio. Retrieved October 24, 2015, from http://www.npr.org/2014/12/11/369641000/richard- pryor-a-comedy-pioneer-who-was-always-whittling-on-dynamite.

Friedman, U. (2014, December 3). Do police body cameras actually work? *The Atlantic*. Retrieved October 24, 2015, from http://www.theatlantic.com/ international/archive/2014/12/do-police-body-cameras-work-ferguson/383323/.

Geertz, C. (1983). *Local knowledge: Further essays in interpretive anthropology*. New York, NY: Basic Books.

Giste, M. E. (1990). Minorities in media imagery. *Newspaper Research Journal, 11*(3), 52–63.

Gramsci, I. (1971). *Selections from the prison notebooks* (Quentin Hoare and Geoffrey Nowell-Smith, eds. and trans.). New York, NY: International Publishers.

Gray, H. (1986). Television and the new black man: Black male images in prime-time situation comedy. *Media, Culture & Society, 8*, 223–242.

Gray, H. (1991). Television, black Americans, and the American dream. In R. K. Avery & D. Eason (Eds.). *Critical perspectives on media and society* (pp. 294–305). New York, NY: Guilford.

Gray, H. (1995 ). *Watching race: Television and the struggle for blackness*. Minneapolis, MN: University of Minnesota Press.

Hall, S. (1980). Encoding/decoding. In S. Hall, D. Hobson, A. Lowe, & P. Wills (Eds.). *Culture, media, language* (pp. 128–138). London, UK: Hutchinson.

Heath, B. (2014, Nov. 19). Blacks arrested up to 10 times more, *USA Today*, 1, 4.

Himmelstein, H. (1984). *TV, myth and the American mind*. New York, NY: Praeger.

Horwitz, S. (2015, March 3). Ferguson police routinely violate blacks' rights, federal review finds. *The Washington Post*. Retrieved October 24, 2015, from http://www.washingtonpost.com/world/national-security/justice-dept-review-finds-pattern-of-racial-bias-among-ferguson-police/2015/03/03/27535390-c1c7-11e4-9271-610273846239_story.html.

Itzkoff, D. (2015, Feb. 10). Jon Stewart will leave 'The Daily Show" on a career high note. *The New York Times*. Retrieved October 24, 2015, from http://www.nytimes.com/2015/02/11/arts/television/jon-stewart-leaving-daily-show.html?_r=0.

JBHE.com. (2013). Good news! More than 5 million African Americans now hold college degrees. *The Journal of Blacks in Higher Education*. Retrieved October 24, 2015, from http://www.jbhe.com/2013/02/good-news-more-than-5-million-african-americans-now-hold-college-degrees/.

Jhally, S. (Producer). (1997). *Stuart Hall: Representation & the media* (video). Northampton, MA: Media Education Foundation.

Jhally, S., & Lewis, J. (1992). *Enlightened racism:* The Cosby Show, *audiences, and the myth of the American Dream*. Boulder, CO: Westview.

Katz, J. (1992, March 5). Rock, rap and movies bring you the news. *Rolling Stone*, 33–35, 40, 78.

Kleeman, S. (2014, October 19). One perfect tweet calls out the hypocrisy of how the media talks about black violence. *News.Mic*. Retrieved October 24, 2015, from http://mic.com/articles/101766/one-perfect-tweet-calls-out-the-hypocrisy-of-how-the-media-talks-about-black-violence.

McDonald, S. N. (2014, August 11). After Michael Brown's killing, #IfTheyGunnedMeDown shows how selfies shape history. *The Washington Post*. Retrieved October 24, 2015, from http://www.washingtonpost.com/news/morning-mix/wp/2014/08/11/after-michael-browns-killing-iftheygunnedmedown-shows-how-selfies-shape-history/.

NPR Staff (2014, August 16). *Behind a twitter campaign, a multitude of stories*. National Public Radio. Retrieved October 24, 2015, from http://www.npr.org/blogs/codeswitch/2014/08/16/340669034/behind-a-twitter-campaign-a-multitude-of-stories.

PBS Newshour (2014). Unemployment rates are higher for young people, minorities. *PBS Newshour*. Retrieved October 24, 2015, from http://www.pbs.org/newshour/bb/unemployment-rates-higher-young-people-minorities/.

Pew Research Center (2014). *African Americans and technology use: Detailed demographic tables*. Pew Research Internet Project. Retrieved October 24, 2015, from http://www.pewinternet.org/2014/01/06/detailed-demographic-tables/.

Rosen, R. (2014). Why is the black unemployment rate so high?. *The Atlantic*. Retrieved October 24, 2015, from http://www.theatlantic.com/business/archive/2014/06/why-is-the-black-unemployment-rate-so-high/372667/.

Samuels, R. (2010). *New media, cultural studies, and critical theory after postmodernism: Automodernity from Zizek to Laciau*. New York, NY: Palgrave Macmillan.

Shabazz, I. (2015, February 20). What would Malcolm X think? *The Washington Post*. Retrieved October 24, 2015, from http://www.nytimes.com/2015/02/21/opinion/ilyasah-shabazz-what-would-malcolm-x-think.html?_r=0.

Smith, A. (2014, January 6). *African Americans and technology use*. Pew Research Internet Project. Retrieved October 24, 2015, from http://www.pewinternet.org/2014/01/06/african-americans-and-technology-use/.

Somashekhar, S. (2015, January 2). Protestors slam Oprah over comments they lack leadership. *The Washington Post*. Retrieved October 24, 2015, from http://www.washingtonpost.com/news/post-nation/wp/2015/01/02/protesters-slam-oprah-over-comments-that-they-lack-leadership/.

U.S. Census Bureau. (2013). *Poverty rates for selected detailed and Hispanic groups by state and place: 2007–2011*. Retrieved October 24, 2015, from http://www.census.gov/prod/2013pubs/acsbr11-17.pdf.

Vega, T. (2014, August 12). Shooting spurs hashtag effort on stereotypes. *New York Times*. Retrieved October 24, 2015, from http://www.nytimes.com/2014/08/13/us/if-they-gunned-me-down-protest-on-twitter.html?_r=0.

Wenner, J. (2012, April 25). Ready for the fight: *Rolling Stone* interview with Barack Obama. *Rolling Stone*. Retrieved October 24, 2015, from http://www.rollingstone.com/politics/news/ready-for-the-fight-rolling-stone-interview-with-barack-obama-20120425#ixzz3RvHV82ID.

Williams, L. C. (2014, December 4). #CrimingWhileWhite is the only thing you need to read to understand white privilege. *thinkprogress.org*. Retrieved October 24, 2015, from http://thinkprogress.org/justice/2014/12/04/3599492/criming-while-white/.

# 13

# THE DEMOCRATIC POTENTIAL OF FEMINIST TWITTER

*Linda Steiner and Stine Eckert*

Feminist activists have always used available media technologies to disseminate feminist news and to promote and celebrate feminist causes. Feminists have often developed new ways of organizing and structuring the production of feminist communication first in print, then broadcasting and cable (especially public, educational, and governmental) channels. Given this history, as well as a general tendency to celebrate new media technologies, the sense that social media are powerful engines for contemporary feminism is unsurprising. Recent feminist efforts to exploit blogging and Twitter have experienced uneven success. Online campaigns organized by feminists have led to both policy formation and personal transformation, from convincing Facebook to ban pro-rape content to using Twitter to push Ani DiFranco to cancel a songwriting workshop because it was scheduled at a former plantation which at the time operated as a museum that sanitized slavery. Appreciating how young feminist bloggers embraced pop culture, television critic Emily Nussbaum (2011) enthusiastically described how the blogosphere blurred the lines between confession, call to arms, and stand-up routine: "this new looseness of form in turn emboldened readers to join in, to take risks in the safety of the shared spotlight." Moreover, she said, if women could share stories, they "could be allies instead of rivals."

Feminist activists Courtney Martin and Vanessa Valenti agreed. Their 2013 #FemFuture report argued that feminist blogs, online organizing (including petitions), and social media campaigns have transformed how advocacy and action function. The #FemFuture report also warned that a critical lack of infrastructure, support, and financing was causing frustration and burnout among bloggers and online activists. Martin and Valenti complained that online feminism was disconnected from larger organizational and movement efforts. As detailed below, they recommended creating radical intersectional relationships bridging feminist activists, organizers, foundations, students, teachers, academics, philanthropists, and online feminists.

Martin and Valenti predicted and explicitly welcomed dissent to their approach. Nonetheless, as *The Nation* staffer Michelle Goldberg (2014) wrote in "Feminism's Toxic Twitter Wars," they were "floored" by the vitriolic "wave of coruscating anger and contempt"—akin to "a Maoist hazing"—that greeted their "earnest and studiously politically correct report." Goldberg claimed: "Yet even as online feminism has proved itself a real force for change, many of the most avid digital feminists will tell you that it's become toxic" and that "the slashing righteousness of other feminists" leaves some women feeling emotionally savaged. She quoted an activist who participated in the #FemFuture event, then the editor of *Feministing.com*, saying that she believed in the empowering potential of online feminism but felt scared, "backed into a corner." The writer worried that online feminism "is becoming dysfunctional, even unhealthy."

Goldberg's essay provoked another round of debate, if not vitriol. Two days later, *Slate* (Grose, 2014) described Goldberg's piece as landing "like an earthquake, with tremors still rippling throughout the Internet." Goldberg's claim that Black women expect White feminists to berate themselves for minor racial transgressions, thus creating an environment of perpetual psychodrama, was especially provocative. Some people accused Goldberg of racism given this approach to racial conflict within feminism. Nina Bahadur (2014), deputy editor of the *HuffPost Women*, agreed that vitriol was problematic; nonetheless, she complained that Goldberg had misrepresented the divide as a narrative about how non-White feminists "bully" White feminists.

## The Concept of Fluid Public Clusters

This study considers the activist and democratic potential of social media, especially Twitter. That is, we ask: How and how effectively can feminists and feminist organizations use Twitter to disseminate feminist analyses, raise key issues, and highlight major problems, and thereby convince people to take these seriously and to respond to the issues/problems? We define feminist Twitter as conversations and critiques on Twitter that discuss, support, and activate social justice, including gender equality, and that aim to undo unfair oppressions of all kinds.

We first summarize Martin and Valenti's report; after all, to the extent that their analysis is incorrect, their solutions may also miss the mark. Then we provide historical background and a review of scholarship about feminism and race. Given the racial dimensions of and around the #FemFuture report, we then briefly compare Black (feminist) and feminist

Twitter (i.e., that eschews a racial identity).[1] The two Twitter spaces face analogous challenges and have similar visions. In a *Slate* essay titled "Black Twitter's not just a group—it's a movement," Kwame Opam (2013) positioned Black Twitter as turning on a shared mission and activist purpose, and focusing on issues important to the Black community. He criticized the media's un-nuanced representation of Black Twitter merely as "What Black people say and do on Twitter." Opam added that Black Twitter addresses concerns affecting everyone, or at least "all people willing to engage effectively with the issues the movement's thinkers are tackling" and "all groups who are marginalized because of race, gender, or class." Notably, African Americans are disproportionately involved in tweeting, and trending topics often reflect African American culture, memes, and topics. Overall, 73% of African American Internet users—and 96% of those aged 18–29—use some social networking site, and 22% of online Blacks use Twitter, compared with 16% of online Whites (Smith, 2014).

After discussing some specific narratives of and through feminist Twitter, we analyze online posts responding to two essays about feminism and race on Twitter: Goldberg's (2014) "Feminism's Toxic Twitter Wars" in *The Nation* (which yielded 881 responses between publication in January and May, when the comment threat was closed), and Bahadur's (2014) "Why the Problem of Online Toxicity Is Not the Same Thing as White Feminists vs. Non-White Feminists" in the *Huffington Post* (which drew 38 comments between publication January and March, when the comment threat was closed). Following Stuart Hall's (1975) approach to textual analysis, we remained open to emerging arguments, explanations and solutions that commenters addressed to make sense of what became called the feminist Twitter wars.

We apply the concept of fluid public clusters (Eckert, 2014). Building on the plurality and hierarchies of public spheres (Fraser, 1990; Squires, 2002), the concept of fluid public clusters online highlights the emergence of relatively messy (especially compared to the notion of a single public sphere) constellations of people with shared interests (Eckert, 2014). Network scholars treat clusters as subgroups within a network whose nodes are more connected to one another than to those outside the subgroup (Himelboim, Smith, & Shneiderman 2013). Some alternative terms for these clusters are disparaging, including Gitlin's (1998) "sphericules." Eckert, however, acknowledged that the landscape of social media changes over time, sometimes quickly. Moreover, social media spaces and participants are also dynamic. This theory understands publicness as reflecting the two conditions that Gitlin (1998) described as necessary for deliberation: having spaces with a similar degree of equivalent access, and interactions directed toward others and society (i.e., not working in or toward isolation). We conclude by further incorporating the theory of intersectionality, based on Kimberlé Crenshaw's (1989) insight that "intersectional experience is greater than the sum of racism and sexism" (p. 141).

## The #FemFuture Report

Online feminism offers an alternative space suffused with feminist values that can influence and counter the sexism, racism, and homophobia of popular culture and news media. Therefore, without denying the healthy differences, multiplicity, and diversity within feminism, Martin and Valenti called for new stronger connections, including between grassroots advocacy and service organizations, educational institutions, coalitions, unions, legacy media, policy makers, politicians, and entrepreneurs. Consistent with their earlier work (Beetham & Valenti, 2007), much of the #FemFuture discussion of online activism emphasized blogs and YouTube. It highlighted how online storytelling and relationship building via blogs enable young women to feel part of a community, and to participate in and influence larger public conversations.

Increasingly, feminist hashtags are being recognized for success in promoting progressive causes around the world, although these social media campaigns have also drawn harsh criticisms. Issues of *Feminist Media Studies* published in 2014 and 2015 (14:6, 15:1, and 15:2) carried dozens of brief essays acknowledging how feminist hashtags drew attention to violence against women (of all colors), among other causes, but also were vulnerable to a liberal/White salvation narrative, essentially reinforcing a kind of epistemic violence against women. Martin and Valenti themselves noted instances when Twitter hashtags drew impassioned attention to women's problems around the world. For example, Janet Mock advocated for trans women, especially trans women of color, by using the Twitter hashtag #girlslikeus; the National Black Justice Coalition used #blacktransproud to promote racial justice and trans equality. Several anecdotes recalled how feminists strategically used Twitter for publicity. For instance, already a contributor to *Feministing* and *TheGrio*, Zerlina Maxwell's tweets led to gigs for several magazines and newspapers, including *Essence* and the *Washington Post*, CNN.com, *Fox & Friends*, as well as other media outlets. Maxwell said, "Twitter shrinks the world and makes everyone accessible" (quoted in Martin & Valenti, 2013).

But Martin and Valenti also noted significant problems. They bemoaned what they called the "band-aid" business structure of most feminist enterprises, whose random fundraising drives, crowd-funding and subscriptions never earned significant sums, leaving feminist spaces under-resourced and overwhelmed. Men bloggers, they said, typically spent far more energy than did women on ramping up revenue generation to make their work sustainable. For feminists, blogging was the third shift (after other activist work and a paying job). They warned, "An unfunded online feminist movement isn't merely a threat to the livelihood of these hard-working activists, but a threat to the larger feminist movement itself." Without more support, they argued, the online feminist movement risked a high burnout rate, further privileging the privileged and amplifying the voices of activists—including anti-feminists—who could afford to work for free. Moreover, online feminists rarely leverage friendships emerging from the online feminist world, and lack the time, support, and skills necessary to reach across borders and work strategically for shared long-term gains.

#FemFuture listed several solutions, including strategic planning and coalition building to connect institutional and online feminism and to sustain collaborations between the two sectors. Nonprofit organizations have the space, resources, and womanpower that online feminists crave, and online feminists often deploy the communications innovations that non-profit organizations need. They called on feminists to use online tools to barter and share resources, skills, objects, and intelligence, and to develop innovative technology, promote business literacies, and, especially, create financially sustainable structures. Non-profit foundations could develop funding specifically for online feminism; meanwhile, for-profit venture capitalists could invest in revenue-generating tools that would benefit feminism.

## Responses to #FemFuture in U.S. News Media

Martin and Valenti conceded feminism's "complicated history" and feminists' continuing need to struggle against racism, homophobia, classism, and oppressions. Their point was that the Internet allowed for greater accountability and learning, helping to push mainstream feminism to be less monolithic. Nonetheless, according to Goldberg (2014), the online activists and feminist writers whose daylong conversation was the basis of the report were "savaged as a cabal of white opportunists," although nine of the 21 attendees were women of color. People also complained the meeting excluded those outside New York (Martin and Valenti said they had no travel budget) as well as indigenous women, mothers, and veterans, whose concerns were not explicitly addressed. Goldberg said that the controversy left a lasting taint.

Goldberg particularly mocked critiques by Mikki Kendall, a Black feminist Army veteran who had created the hashtag #SolidarityIs ForWhiteWomen. Kendall's tweets had asked where #FemFuture movements provided space for people without Internet access, and compared #FemFuture to a racist Southern suffragist who endorsed lynching. #SolidarityIsForWhiteWomen immediately trended worldwide; women of color expressed frustration at the condescension, erasure, and racism they have experienced at the hands of feminism, which demanded that they silence and suppress their particular needs to protect solidarity (i.e., White prerogative). To Kendall (whose blog *hoodfeminism* is notably subtitled "Life at the Intersection"), feminist elites were merely reasserting their privilege.

Goldberg quoted feminists saying Black women feel disempowered and at the mercy of White authority, so Black women want to feel that they have credibility and authority. Meanwhile Anna Holmes, who is Black, called White feminists' competition to prove their commitment to intersectionality "gross," "dishonest," and "patronizing." Indeed, Holmes, who founded the blog *Jezebel* but left after three years, told Goldberg she would never start a women's Web site today: "[The women's blogosphere] feels like a much more insular, protective, brittle environment than it did before. It's really depressing."

To Bahadur (2014), online toxicity is not necessarily racial, or a matter of "minorities vs. the privileged." She agreed that online conversations often contain vitriol and personal attacks absent in offline conversations, and go beyond the schisms in feminism. No wonder, then, that she anticipated—and feared—that her response to Goldberg would draw "criticism that I'm not feminist enough, or Woman-Of-Color-enough, or educated enough on what I'm writing about." On one hand, Bahadur said, critiquing, correcting, and asking for inclusion in response to someone else's work is not always toxic, and may be constructive. She rejected the claim that the issue was middle-class White women against all the groups they oppress. Moreover, if a woman disagrees with an article she reads online, why shouldn't she say so? On the other hand, if supposed allies in struggle tear to shreds every piece about feminism or women of color, fewer people will write about those topics, thus depriving us of important voices and valid viewpoints.

Ultimately Bahadur called on people to remember that another human is behind each post—someone who could be hurt by a nasty response—and to support other feminists, even if we disagree with them. Moreover, Bahadur linked to a new post by Kendall (2013) reminding feminists that allies work together for more than one cause. Kendall gave straightforward rules for White women who wanted to be helpful: listen actively but silently; do not speak for women of color (unless you see someone being bullied); and do not try to defend yourself.

## Different Perspectives, but With Respect: Reader Comments

Bahadur's essay drew relatively civil discourse among people with different opinions. With Bahadur occasionally chiming in, the majority of commenters supported her plea for listening to women's different voices. Commenters certainly agreed that online toxicity was a problem, which they sometimes attributed to the inability of all kinds of feminists to handle criticism, and sometimes to a toxic in-group/out-group mentality. Pauline, for example, said: "I'm tired of women eviscerating each other on the Internet . . . . I'm all for respectful debate, but the message too often gets lost in vitriol." Michelle said that, having participated in those toxic conversations, she no longer called herself a feminist. She added, "Because they fight each other, backbite each other so bad, they'll never come together!!! Nothing will ever be accomplished."[2] A former student who expressed bitterness about the entire feminist enterprise asserted:

> I've come to absolutely despise "feminist" discourse on the Internet. If it's not complaining about something really petty and/ or personal (but ultimately politically and academically worth- less . . . no matter how hard they try to stretch it), then it's wordy, worthless dreck regurgitated from the bowels of academia and applied pointlessly to some meaningless aspect of pop culture.

Commenters suggested, among other solutions, politeness, listening, focusing on what people have in common, and acknowledging people's efforts to make sense of conversation. Goldberg put race at the forefront of the debate, as was reflected in comments on her article. Commenters to Bahadur, however, focused on online toxicity among feminists. Precisely because historically women have been silenced, Jennifer said she always tries "to read the words of other women with love . . . . And even if I vehemently disagree, I try to phrase my responses respectfully and politely."

The 881 comments to Goldberg's essay offered a variety of assessments, explanations and solutions for the disputes. About half of commenters agreed with Goldberg that Kendall and like-minded bloggers must be "called out." For instance, juli1 commented:

> Yes, we need to communicate, but attacking people is not com- municating. It's like marriage or any other relationship, you need to "fight fair" and show the same respect for the other person, the same regard that you want for yourself. Treating potential allies like enemies accomplishes nothing.

Expressing appreciation for *The Nation* article, K.A. said that, despite their long history as activists and supporters of feminist organizations, she and her wife find themselves less and less able to relate to feminists online: "It has become quite toxic, and seems to be worse and worse over maybe just the past 3–5 years."

The other half vehemently criticized Goldberg's portrayal of women of color as "trouble makers." For instance, Cosmo accused Goldberg of missing how people were discussing intersectionality:

Of course the dialogue is going to be loud and she is bound to hear things she is not pleased with. But I don't care and we won't keep quiet; we have been trying to be heard for so long and some like the author of this piece still refuse to listen because the thing we say hurts her feelings. And seriously the way she portrays Mikki Kendall is disgusting. Total fail.

Similarly condemning *The Nation* for "such a hateful piece," ATRWibben said Twitter was not to blame for exposing how some feminists resist critiques. Indeed, ATRWibben added, *The Nation* should not give a platform to a feminism that ignores those far from the centers of power and who can teach us about the operation of power.

Commenters added that the aggression is symptomatic of marginalization, and undermines respectful discourse. Several dismissed the issues that Goldberg raised as unimportant. Will was one of many saying feminism has more significant problems to tackle:

Feminism is every First World Problem rolled up into one convenient package and then handed to upper-class white Western women so that they can pretend that they're victims of global Capitalist oppression instead of the perpetrators and engine of it. Who exactly do you think put that iPhone together for you, Missy?

Few commenters blamed technology per se for the toxicity. But several did distinguish feminists on Twitter/online from feminists "on the ground" in the "real" world who work for social justice. Several commenters pointed out that Black and White women on Twitter belong to an elite that can afford to tweet (to get book deals and make a career from commenting). Some argued that these class divisions are more prominent than divisions by gender or race. The conversations switched back and forth over the gender-race-class nexus, demonstrating the intersectionality of social justice issues. Nonetheless, a self-described non-White male troll attacked and insulted women and feminists on *The Nation* site; vitriol and slurs often derail online discourse, but this problem has been especially vicious when leveled against feminists, women of color and feminist women of color.

## Historical Background, Racial Divisions, and Online Incivility

Feminism, as with other progressive movements, has always experienced infighting, divisions, and divisiveness. Conflict, including over ideological purity, was already a feature of first wave feminism. Moreover, a consistent tension for feminists has hinged on media representations, access, and visibility. Suffragists needed their own news outlets to serve the broadest feminist community possible, so they could find sister advocates outside the local area to develop their identities as new women and to help promote the cause (Steiner, 1992). Nonetheless, suffragists consistently argued over principles and strategy; competing suffrage papers offered opposing versions of how to be a "new woman" and how to justify women's enfranchisement. As the provocative editor of *The Revolution*, to take one prominent example, Elizabeth Cady Stanton enjoyed criticizing suffrage leaders, including suffrage editors. That said, the editors created and sustained a kind of national suffrage community, albeit one that was almost entirely White. Meanwhile, very few non-suffragists subscribed to or even read these journals, much less wrote letters to the editors. So the content, including the letters, expressed, promoted, and celebrated the emerging views of the suffrage community, with rare and only highly respectful expression of dissent.

Feminism's second wave saw the emergence of much more highly segmented media; periodicals targeted ecofeminists, celibate women, prostitutes, Marxists, and women of specific religions and professional groups. As before, however, non-converts rarely read even the outlets most interested in reaching and serving a broad audience—such as *Ms.* magazine, with its newsstand distribution. Buying or subscribing to feminist media involved some cost and some intent and so rarely reached unsympathetic eyes. Extreme or hostile letters were unlikely, although a few were published; writing the editor required an investment of time and effort without knowing whether the letter would be published. That said, second wave feminist groups and media outlets were not averse to denouncing one another, addressing divisive issues, or publicizing dissent. In a 1976 *Ms.* article "Trashing: The Dark Side of Sisterhood," for example, Jo Freeman condemned what she called the social disease infecting the women's movement. The famous and widely repeated quote from radical feminist Ti-Grace Atkinson made a similar point: "Sisterhood is powerful. It kills. Mostly sisters."

This highly abbreviated history is intended to highlight significant differences as well as continuities with contemporary feminisms. First, the Internet, blogs, and Twitter allow relatively easy, immediate, and constant access to a variety of perspectives and opinions. These platforms enable a community to communicate quickly not only with members but also outsiders, and to mobilize support as well as literal presence, say, for a riot, march, or rally. Moreover, social media and online sites with little or no moderation widely democratize responses and information. This means that loyal-but-critical feminists can respond to essays and articles, and to one another, but so can bored outsiders who come upon feminist sites through casual browsing, as well as determined trolls.

Dissent and divisiveness continue to characterize feminism. A trans-sexual student of online social dynamics (Cross, 2014a) recently observed: "The often aimless, unchecked anger striking both within and without [feminism has] created a climate of toxicity and fear that not only under-mine our highest ideals, but also corrode the comforts of community for the very people who most need it." Katherine Cross said she did not pub-lish or respond to critical posts and articles she had received, partly in fear of being attacked by bigots, but more importantly from fear that her own community would condemn her "for being insufficiently radical, too nuanced or too forgiving, or for . . . an innocently ignorant mistake . . . . I fear the moment I get tarred as a 'collaborator,' 'apologist' for privilege, or a 'sell out' (to women, to Latin@s, to working class people, to trans folk)." Cross explicitly appreciated and justified marginalized groups' righteous anger. Women, people of color, people with disabilities, trans people, the poor: all were unfairly stigmatized as "too angry," leading to negative stereotypes of "Angry Black Wo/Man," "Angry Tranny," "Feisty Latina," and so forth. Nonetheless, she argued that feminist online activism is hobbled by neoliberalism's emphasis on the individual, and thus on individual catharsis and anger—at the expense of the collective. Cross later emphasized that civility, "niceness" and "tone policing" were unnecessary. Forcefulness and robust advocacy, she said, "*must* attend any effort to challenge or change an ossified status quo . . . . Politics is not always nice" (2014b, emphasis in original).

The major divisions persisting among Blacks and feminists in the United States are especially evident in the Twitterverse; Black Twitter and Black feminist Twitter can be as hateful as sites positioned as serving feminists of all colors. Such toxicity surfaced, for example, after *Ebony* magazine senior editor Jamilah Lemieux, a Black woman who often com-mented on African American culture and feminism, dismissively referred to Raffi Williams, a Black Republican National Party executive, as White. As demanded by the RNC President, *Ebony* (#teamEBONY, 2014) imme-diately and effusively apologized for Lemieux's "lack of judgment."

Rebecca Carroll's (2014) online essay (which quickly drew 271 com-ments) decried the demonization of Lemieux as a Black woman; one mistaken comment can undo all of one's otherwise careful thoughtful writ-ing, she remarked sadly. "Because what you say online, specifically on Twitter, which operates at a breakneck and decidedly un-thoughtful pace, bears the weight of the world. And if you work in media, it serves as judge and jury of your career writ large, and its future." Recalling how Lemieux (and others) had addressed the deepening chasm between Black and White feminists, Carroll blamed social media, especially Twitter, for perpetuating the split. Lemieux had asserted that Black women are angry because they are in real pain, and are exhausted from doing so much emotional work for the feminist movement. Carroll praised Lemieux and her critique of the angry Black woman stereotype.

In the comments to Carroll's article, a couple of trolls repeatedly insulted Lemieux as racist and attacked "liberals" in even more extreme language; according to these trolls, Leftists are racist, whereas conservatives and Whites are "victims." Gender and feminism barely appeared in these exchanges, given the focus on race. Thus, Black and feminist Twitter face the same challenges of toxicity and division. Like feminism, Black cultural movements face intra-organizational strife as well as tensions across groups, lack of funding and other resources, and burnout. Noting that popular Black Twitter topics often reflect stereotypical and misogynistic messages, *Root* contributor Patrice Williams (2011) wondered whether African American social networks were doing more harm than good. Nonetheless, social media and Black Twitter are credited with publicizing the racially fraught shootings of Trayvon Martin, an unarmed Black Florida teenager, by a White man, as well as of other Black men (Michael Brown and Tamir Rice) by White men policeman and more recently, of Freddie Gray, who sustained fatal injuries while being transported in a police van. These events inspired passionate protest and activism, and the hashtag #BlackLivesMatter drove crucial attention to the underlying problems. If Twitter is the underground railroad of Black activism (Jones, 2013), what is the activist potential of feminist Twitter?

Scholars, pundits, and journalists, along with a majority of the U.S. public, tend to believe incivility in politics is increasing. Papacharissi (2004) is one of the few who defends incivility; she emphasized the democratic merit of robust heated discussion. Having found that most messages posted on political newsgroups are civil (albeit not polite), Papacharissi concluded that cyberspace promotes democratic emancipation and that the Internet may revive the public sphere. But an experiment regarding the so-called "nasty effect" (Anderson et al., 2013) found that civil comments posted to a technology blog were less persuasive than rude comments (with epithets or curse words), which polarized readers and often changed their minds. Even more problematic from both democratic and feminist perspectives is the proliferation of online misogyny and cyberbullying. Some scholars privilege free speech, treating flaming as relatively harmless and/or playful (see e.g. Lee, 2005). Proposing the term "e-bile" to describe sexualized threats and hyperbolic demands for violence, Jane (2014) claimed that mainstream media understand how the worsening problem of online vitriol and sexualized invective is silencing women and undermining the public cybersphere. She criticized theorists who trivialize the victimization of flame targets and scholars who ignore, downplay, defend, or celebrate e-bile.

## The Criticality of Intersectionality and
## Fluid Public Clusters

We suggest that the robust emergence of Black feminist Twitter is evidence of a problem for and within feminism. The relative weakness of a generalized feminism in achieving or maintaining leadership is presumably demonstrated by some Google search data, collected on September 15, 2014: plugging in "Black Twitter" produced 413,000 results whereas "feminist Twitter" produced only 7,910 and "Black feminist twitter" produced 2,060. Notably, Google's automatic fill-in also suggested, among others, the search terms "Black feminist Twitter war" and "feminist Twitter wars." Feminists define their movement as one intended to counter all oppressions and thus already and always intersectional and inclusive, or at least trying to be. By this token, the evidence that feminists of color feel alienated by "feminism"—feel unwelcome in "the feminist movement" and left out of "feminist Twitter"—speaks to a failure of feminism; this certainly challenges the idea of a single movement. Indeed, many women of color are establishing distinct online spaces. A Native American woman launched the #NotYourMascot hashtag, complaining that White feminists ignore violence perpetuated against indigenous women. #NotYourAsianSidekick emerged when Asian American feminists felt pushed to the margins of both mainstream feminism and Asian American race activism; 45,000 Tweets referenced it during its first weekend. On Black Girl Dangerous, a site for queer and trans women of color that regularly takes White feminists to task, a blog post titled "Toxicity: The True Story of Mainstream Feminism's Violent Gatekeepers" (Khan, 2014) mocked the White-centric feminist meme du jour about bullying.

Perhaps the reason the movement has not sufficiently worked to hear women of color is that feminists merely assume feminism's intersectionality, rather than assiduously and self-consciously working on it. Intersectionality is easily defined: it's "the interaction between gender, race, and other categories of difference in individual lives, social practices, institutional arrangements, and cultural ideologies and the outcomes of these interactions in terms of power" (Davis 2008, p. 68). But the viral dissemination of messages through Twitter and other social media highlight how feminists' promise to take intersectionality seriously has not become consistent practice. We propose expanding intersectionality theory by connecting it to the concept of fluid public clusters. To show how the combination of these two concepts help to theorize the expressions of (different) feminists online, we first describe the theory of intersectionality and then elaborate on the connection.

Originally, intersectionality evolved out of concern that the particular problems of women of color fell between the cracks of feminist and anti-racist discourses. Kimberlé Crenshaw argued that Black women cannot be understood through a "single-axis analysis" (1989, p. 139). Elsa Barkley Brown attributed the lack of research about differences among women to a false fear of weakening feminist politics. *Not* looking into differences arguably weakens feminism as much as it weakens the research: "uncomplicated discussions of universal women's experiences" (1992, p. 293) cannot address complex realities. Kathy Davis (2008) has emphasized how, precisely because of intersectionality's very vagueness and open-endedness, the concept highlights difference and diversity without denying the feminist ideal of addressing all women's concerns. Intersectional theorizing suggests that marginalization and oppression operate and are experienced differently by different groups—without undermining feminism's aims to critique, analyze, and undo oppressions.

Highlighting difference combats essentialism, the problematic implication that there is a correct way to be a member of a group (Yuval-Davis, 2006). Essentializing categories such as Black, woman or working class—the initial triangle of oppression that Crenshaw proposed—merely further marginalize people in a particular category. So whereas intersectionality gets at the multiple dimensions of identity, the concept of fluid public clusters underscores relatively messy constellations of people that emerge among people with shared interests and then may fade away. This notion, then, adds a dynamic character to intersectionality, acknowledging that women—and feminists—have divergent interests, agendas, projects, and concerns that are rooted in concrete experiences and specific identities; these often overlap, but not always or completely. Together, these constellations build an intersectional landscape of social media, albeit one that changes over time, sometimes quickly. As the many hashtags and exchanges on Twitter among feminists demonstrated, online platforms enable, sustain, and demonstrate the dynamism, plurality, and fluidity of clusters within feminisms, as well as conflicts across them (Eckert, 2014). Twitter users can participate in feminist Twitter *and* Black Twitter as well as other clusters that represent different—and changing—aspects of feminists' and women's identities and concerns such as ageism, ableism, motherhood, and sexuality. Twitter users do engage in selective exposure, following other users in their own relatively narrow cluster much more than users in other clusters, thereby participating in fragmented interactions and forming divided groups (see e.g. Himelboim, Smith, & Shneiderman, 2013). Still, the point is that social media can democratize access to tools that previously were restricted and even off-limits to marginalized groups; they can allow more individuals and clusters to produce and share content. Hashtags such as #YesAllWomen demonstrate how quickly groups can emerge and connect effectively to new or ongoing issues.

White feminists who are trying to be self-reflective about their commitment to intersectionality must therefore explicitly acknowledge feminisms of color and appreciate how Black feminist Twitter and other feminist Twitter users of color make visible the intersections of feminisms and race, as well as other social categories. All experiences are inevitably sexed, racialized, and classed—but the resulting epistemological positions are diverse and never static. Clusters may overlap, come together and share resources for certain projects but then separate to pursue interests that are not neatly shared or experienced with the same impact. Advocates of collective action may find this dynamic worrisome; but clusters may reunite in different variations when this is philosophically or strategically advantageous, and thereby grow stronger and more powerful. Consciously considering and tolerating the diverse experiences and backgrounds that feminists come from and the ways feminists choose or need to express themselves as well as acknowledging each other's good intentions will all help feminists return to working actively for social justice in a way that is consistent with intersectionality.

Martin and Valenti borrowed Kania and Kramer's (2011) account of the conditions required for successful collective impact: a common agenda or shared vision for change, shared systems for measuring success and holding each other accountable, mutually reinforcing coordinated activities with diverse groups of stakeholders in which each group does what it can do best, continuous communication, and a backbone that creates attention for issues. But this unified vision may be inappropriate and unworkable for the postmodern, fluid and networked age. Instead, a renewed effort for feminist collective action can build upon Chela Sandoval's (2001) proposal for a "differential consciousness" (p. 44) that flexibly responds to postmodernist challenges. According to Sandoval, feminists, especially women of color, have always switched among different forms of oppositional consciousness. These forms provide "tactical weaponry for intervening in shifting currents of power" (p. 58). Together they constitute a differential mode of consciousness, functioning "like the clutch of an automobile, the mechanism that permits the driver to select, engage and disengage gears in a system for the transmission of power" (p. 58). Fluid public clusters evident in social media are implementing Sandoval's approach by tackling issues of concern to different women in different ways. Feminists used Twitter's dynamic hashtags such as #NotYourAsianSidekick and #NotYourMascot to question power and privilege related to race; #SolidarityIsForWhiteWomen and #blacktransproud to highlight the intersections of race and gender (identification). When another gear was needed, feminists across different backgrounds joined for #YesAllWomen and #BlackLivesMatter. That is, different feminists merged online when seen as useful while not abandoning other interests in separate campaigns.

The notorious hostility of online platforms to women must also be acknowledged, although space constraints allow only a brief mention.

Women far more than men are targets of threats of sexualized violence, sexist jokes, revenge porn, non-consensual sexting, stalking, cybermob attacks, and cyberbullying (Citron, 2014; Pew Research Center, 2014). With social attitudes, laws, and law enforcement still mostly trivializing and/or not addressing and prosecuting online harassment (Citron, 2014), it becomes incumbent upon women to find resilience in themselves to respond to and deal with hostile situations. For instance, when trolls invaded #NotYourAsianSidekick, Jenn (2013), an Asian American feminist who blogs at Reappropriate (which covers Asian American activism, feminism, and pop culture), celebrated how #NotYourAsianSidekick centralized the narratives of Asian American women. But she also said the trolls proved: "Twitter is the wrong place to have this conversation. 140 characters isn't enough to express a lifetime of experiences—both oppressive and uplifting—and to be able to do it in a place where it can be heard and taken seriously."

But, right or wrong place, Twitter will continue. Individual sites can be subverted, but the Twitterverse will persist as a platform for the different gears for feminists, including by reclaiming hashtags and campaigns that get attacked. Twitter hashtags representing all sorts of feminisms have had enormous—if often short-term—impact. Social media do not need significant financial investment nor do their users seem to suffer the burnout that Martin and Valenti saw as threatening contemporary feminism. These hashtags, and the feminists who use them, represent how various fluid public clusters have embraced heterogeneity, with the hashtag #BlackTwitter continuing a Black linguistic tradition of signifyin' with wordplays, jokes, rules and indirect meanings (Florini, 2014). Such heterogeneity is expressed in multiple Blacktags, such as #atablackpersonfuneral, #ifsantawasblack or #onlyintheghetto, which work to disrupt Whiteness on Twitter (Sharma, 2013), and underscore the potential of Twitter and other online forums to express feminisms' democratic ethos, fluidity, and dynamism. To paraphrase the Black Power slogan of the 1960s, the revolution *will* be tweeted.

In sum, feminists will and should use social media to expose and respond to problems, in separate clusters if needed and jointly across clusters when possible. Trying to silence division is futile and counterproductive. Martin and Valenti's central presupposition about the enormous importance to feminists of social and online media was correct. However, our analysis shows that the #FemFuture worries about disunity and lack of a single well-funded backbone are essentially moot. Creativity and the cultivation of distinctive voices matter more than efficiency and a leadership pipeline. Fluid public clusters appear to be resilient. They merge, separate, re-form, and re-emerge to tackle the issues of concern of feminists with their different, specific locations, identities, and concrete experiences. The notion of one single online feminism as the central nervous system of a world-changing feminist body politic is unworkable. The efforts will be messy and uneven. Nonetheless, social media—and other technological innovations—must be taken seriously, and taken up, by progressive movements, and certainly by feminists.

## Notes

1 Black Twitter and black feminist Twitter are commonly used terms. Moreover, Black activists often—legitimately—mock racially insensitive feminism as "White feminism." Of course, some feminists are White. That said, we do not label feminist Twitter (i.e., that does not focus on some specific raced group) as White.
2 We have corrected spelling and punctuation in these quotations and eliminated last names to improve readability.

## References

Anderson, A., Brossard, D., Scheufele, D., Xenos, M., & Ladwig, P. (2013). The "nasty effect": Online incivility and risk perceptions of emerging technologies. *Journal of Computer-Mediated Communication, 1*(1), 1–15.

Bahadur, N. (2014). Why the problem of online toxicity is not the same thing as white feminists vs. fon-white feminists. *HuffPost Women*. Retrieved May 1, 2015, from http://www.huffingtonpost.com/nina-bahadur/why-the-problem-of-online-toxicity-feminism_b_4689113.html.

Barkley, E. B. (1992). "What has happened here?": The politics of difference in women's history and feminist politics. *Feminist Studies, 18*(2), 295–312.

Beetham, G. & Valenti, J. (Eds.) (2007). Blogging feminism: (Web)sites of resistance. *Scholar and Feminist Online, 5*(2). Retrieved June 15, 2016, from http://sfonline.barnard.edu/blogs/.

Carroll, R. (2014). Jamilah Lemieux is about more than her tweet to Raffi Williams. *xojane*. Retrieved May 1, 2015, from http://www.xojane.com/issues/jamiliah-lemieux-is-more-than-that-tweet-about-raffi-williams.

Citron, D. K. (2014). *Hate crimes in cyber space.* Cambridge, MA: Harvard University Press.

Crenshaw, K. (1989). Demarginalizing the intersection of race and sex: A black feminist critique of antidiscrimination doctrine, feminist theory and antiracist politics. *University of Chicago Legal Forum, 1*(8), 139–167.

Cross, K. (2014a). Words, words, words: On toxicity and abuse in online activism. *Nuclear Unicorn*. Retrieved May 20, 2015, from http://quinnae.com/2014/01/03/words-words-words-on-toxicity-and-abuse-in-online-activism/.

Cross, K. (2014b). Beyond niceness: Further thoughts on rage. *Nuclear Unicorn*. Retrieved May 20, 2015, from http://quinnae.com/2014/01/07/beyond-niceness-further-thoughts-on-rage/.

Davis, K. (2008). Intersectionality as buzzword: A sociology of science perspective on what makes a feminist theory successful. *Feminist Theory, 9*(1), 67–85.

Eckert, S. (2014). Digital rooms of their own: Women's voices online about the politics of women, family and maternity in four democracies. (Unpublished doctoral dissertation). University of Maryland, College Park.

Florini, S. (2014). Tweets, tweeps, and signifyin': Communication and cultural performance on Black Twitter. *Television & New Media, 15*(3), 223–237.

Franks, M. A. (2012). Sexual harassment 2.0. *Maryland Law Review, 71*(5), 655–704.

Fraser, N. (1990). Rethinking the public sphere: A contribution to the critique of actually existing democracy. *Social Text, 25/26,* 56–80.

Gitlin, T. (1998). Public sphere or public sphericules? In T. Liebes & J. Curran (Eds.), *Media, ritual, identity* (pp. 168–175). London: Routledge.

Goldberg, M. (2014, January 29). Feminism's toxic Twitter wars. *The Nation.* Retrieved June 15, 2016, from http://www.thenation.com/article/feminisms-toxic-twitter-wars/.

Grose, J. (2014). Is "toxic" online culture paralyzing feminism? *Slate.* Retrieved May 20, 2015, from http://www.slate.com/blogs/xx_factor/2014/01/31/_toxic_twitter_wars_is_online_culture_paralyzing_feminism.html.

Hall, S. (1975). Introduction. In A. C. H. Smith, with E. Immirizi & T. Blackwell (Eds.), *Paper voices: The popular press and social change 1935–1965* (pp. 11–24). London: Chatto and Windus.

Himelboim, I., Smith, M. & Shneiderman, B. (2013). Tweeting apart: Applying network analysis to detect selective exposure clusters in Twitter. *Communication Methods and Measures, 7*(3), 195–223.

Jane, E. A. (2014). "Your a ugly, whorish, slut." *Feminist Media Studies, 14*(4), 531–546.

Jenn. (2013) #NotYourAsianSidekick reveals the best—and worst—of Twitter. *Re-appropriate.* Retrieved May 20, 2015, from http://reappropriate.co/?p=3832.

Jones, F. (2013). Is Twitter the underground railroad of activism? *Salon.* Retrieved May 20, 2015, from http://www.salon.com/2013/07/17/how_twitter_fuels_black_activism/.

Kania, J. & Kramer, M. (2011). Collective impact. *Stanford Social Innovation Review, 69.* Retrieved May 20, 2015, from http://www.ssireview.org/articles/entry/collective_impact.

Kendall, M. (2013). "After #SolidarityIsForWhiteWomen: So you want to be an ally, now what?" *xojane.* Retrieved May 20, 2015, from http://www.xojane.com/issues/after-solidarityisforwhitewomen-so-you-want-to-be-an-ally.

Khan, A. (2014). Toxicity: The true story of mainstream feminism's violent gatekeepers. *Black Girl Dangerous.* Retrieved May 20, 2015, from http://www.blackgirldangerous.org/2014/02/toxicity-true-story-mainstream-feminisms-violent-gatekeepers/.

Martin, C. E. & Valenti, V. (2013). #FemFuture: Online revolution. *The Scholar and Feminist Online, 8.* Retrieved May 20, 2015 from http://bcrw.barnard.edu/wp-content/nfs/reports/NFS8-FemFuture-Online-Revolution-Report-April-15-2013.pdf.

Nussbaum, E. (2011). The rebirth of the feminist manifesto. *New York Magazine.* Retrieved May 20, 2015, from http://nymag.com/news/features/feminist-blogs-2011-11/index1.html.

Papacharissi, Z. (2004). Democracy online: Civility, politeness, and the democratic potential of online political discussion groups. *New Media & Society, 6*(2), 259–283.

Opam, K. (2013). Black Twitter's not just a group—it's a movement. *Salon*. Retrieved May 20, 2015, from http://www.salon.com/2013/09/03/black_twitters_not_just_a_group_its_a_movement/.

Pew Research Center. (2014). *Online harassment*. Retrieved June 1, 2015, from http://www.pewinternet.org/2014/10/22/online-harassment/.

Sandoval, C. (2001). US third world feminism: The theory and method of oppositional consciousness in the postmodern world. In K. K. Bhaveni, (Ed.), *Feminism and race* (pp. 261–280). Oxford: Oxford University Press.

Sharma, S. (2013). Black Twitter? Racial hashtags, networks and contagion. *New Formations, 78*, 46–64.

Smith, A. (2014). *African Americans and technology use: A demographic portrait*. Pew Research Center. Retrieved May 20, 2015, from http://www.pewInternet.org/files/2014/01/African-Americans-and-Technology-Use.pdf.

Squires, C. (2002). Rethinking the Black public sphere: An alternative vocabulary for multiple public spheres. *Communication Theory, 12*(4), 446–468.

Steiner, L. (1992). The history and structure of women's alternative media. In L. Rakow (Ed.), *Women making meaning: New feminist directions in communication* (pp. 121–143). New York, NY: Routledge.

#teamEBONY (2014). Diversity of thought. *Ebony*. Retrieved May 20, 2015, from http://www.ebony.com/news-views/diversity-of-thought#.U_4KIGNeI3H.

Williams, P. J. (2011). Black Twitter: Trending topics paint the wrong picture. *The Root*. Retrieved May 20, 2015, from http://www.theroot.com/articles/culture/2011/01/black_people_on_twitter_when_trending_topics_go_wrong.html.

Yuval-Davis, N. (2006). Intersectionality and feminist politics. *European Journal of Women's Studies, 13*(3), 193–210.

# 14

# PRODUCING SEXUAL CULTURES AND PSEUDONYMOUS PUBLICS WITH DIGITAL NETWORKS

*Ben Light*

Since the release of the Grindr app in 2009, interest in digitally mediated public sexual cultures concerning men who have sex with men has increased. Yet digital mediation of such public sexual cultures through apps had begun more than a decade before Grindr was released. For example, Squirt, a desktop and mobile hook up site for men who have sex with men, was launched in 1998 and has always functioned to facilitate public hook ups. Using Squirt as a case study, I will build on the work of Mowlabocus (2008) in relation to our understandings of digitally mediated public sex, employing a version of networked publics (boyd, 2008a; boyd, 2008b) and thinking regarding the real name web (Hogan, 2013). Through an actor-network theory (ANT) informed analysis of Squirt, I will demonstrate how, in a UK context, networked digital media inform and allow for the co-existence of a spectrum of gender and sexual politics, sexual preferences, and sexual practices. Such an analysis encourages further explorations of the theoretical potentials of networked publics, and in doing so, I present the concept of pseudonymous publics. Before I explain Squirt further, I discuss contemporary considerations of how networked media, particularly those seen as real name social media, are conceptualized as shaping our everyday experiences of the Web—especially considering concepts of pseudonyms and publics.

Discourses of being you on the Web via the use of your real name have long been seen as facilitating the establishment of trust, security, and protection in the face of digital harm and crime (Mansell & Collins, 2005). We also know that real names are necessary for online commercial interests where users are configured as a both a market and a generator of market data (Gerlitz & Helmond, 2013). Real names are requested by many sites and platforms; it is necessary to be you, so that others who know who you are can find and connect with you. Hogan (2013) argued that pseudonyms can be strategically deployed to mask identity in order to be treated in particular ways (e.g., some early western female authors used male pen names), to adopt a different persona (e.g., Indian call center workers adopting English sounding names) and for functional reasons (a long real name twitter handle might take up too many characters). Hogan also suggested several reasons for the rise of pseudonyms pre-Web 2.0—the Web at that time was textual (passing as someone else was easier when there were fewer visual images), sparsely connected (because it was rooted in interests, there was less of a chance of bumping into people one wanted to avoid), and strange (it was technically challenging and often seen as potentially dangerous). Therefore a culture of safety in pseudonyms emerged. Hogan argued that given the development trajectory of the Web, current discourses regarding the real name web are not surprising. He suggested that the Web is no longer as textual, sparsely connected and strange as it once was, and that such discourses were to varying degrees implicated in the Nymwars when the Google+ service in 2011 demanded users' real names as a condition of account creation. Other social media providers, such as Facebook, have adopted similar philosophical and policy positions though these have been subject to critique, debate and revision (Lingel & Golub, 2015; Statt, 2015). I argue that pseudonyms can operate, in a sanctioned fashion, with networked publics—with what I will term pseudonymous publics.

Publics have many conceptions, purposes, and uses. Publics can be regarded as centering on common understandings of a particular space (Livingstone, 2005); as deliberative spaces (Habermas, 1991); or sites of domination, exclusion, and regulation that can produce subaltern counterpublics (Fraser, 1990). Here, I see publics as spaces in which we do things alongside and with others without an expectation of complete privacy. I emphasize "without an expectation," because what we experience as public and private are not always mutually exclusive. I am interested in digitally networked publics, both as holding the capacity for articulating an assimilationist politic of what it means to be a gay man in the U.K., and as per Fraser's ideas of subaltern counterpublics—those parallel discursive arenas where members of subordinated groups circulate counter discourses and generate oppositional identities, interests and needs. I want to argue that Squirt challenges discourses regarding heteronormative assumptions associated with the real name web.

I am especially interested in the nature of digitally networked publics, or networked publics (boyd, 2008a; boyd, 2008b). As I have explained elsewhere, research pre-dating social media is helpful (Light, 2014). For example, Johnson (1997) articulated a framework for understanding the characteristics of communication in computer-based networks.

She suggested that communication in digital networks involves considerations of reproducibility (information can be observed, recorded, and is persistent), scope (greater reach than physical networks), and anonymity (individuals can use pseudonyms). Johnson's work can be read as a networked public prior to social media. boyd's (2008b) conceptualization of networked publics positioned them as incorporating properties both similar to and different from Johnson's. boyd's properties of networked publics included replicability (expressions can be copied verbatim), persistence (communications can be recorded), invisible audiences (we cannot fully know who may engage with content), and searchability (information can be found due to indexing and search facilities). In some iterations of her thinking, boyd (2008a) has also included the issue of scalability, which complements Johnson's (1997) concept of scope.

Johnson and boyd differ in how they approach anonymity and audience. Arguably, Johnson's work on anonymity in networks reflected the nature of contemporaneous digitally mediated networks where many informal spaces were based on pseudonyms, which early thinking often equated with anonymity. In contrast, with the rise of social media, the use of real names in public networks has increased and once-hidden audiences have become prominent. Both Johnson's and boyd's positions have resonance today: anonymity is possible and pseudonyms are used, even in social media which seek real name use. Of course, even where pseudonyms are used, this should not be conflated with anonymity (Hogan, 2013; Livia, 2002). We also know that users are adept at navigating networked publics through the articulation of private spheres of interaction (Papacharissi, 2010), selective use of sociotechnical arrangements (Light, 2014) and other means. However, at the same time, social media users can face context collapse when different aspects of their lives unexpectedly intersect.

Contemporary digitally mediated publics are sometimes conflated with context collapse and assumptions of a real name web. When articulated as such, the real name web and networked publics can be read as heteronormative. In terms of the real name web, there is an assumption that people are able, and would want to, use their real names. Whereas Facebook and Google+ say that it is more practical and safer to reveal ourselves in this way, such is not the case for those who do not identify as heterosexual, as shown by Brooklyn's drag queens (Lingel & Golub, 2015). Matters become more problematic in regions and cultures where not being heterosexual can lead to death. My critique of a particular articulation of networked publics as heteronormative rests upon a position where it is implicitly and explicitly associated with this figuration of the real name web.

I reassemble what we think networked publics might be, particularly where gender and sexuality are concerned, and in so doing reconsider our assumptions about what networked publics can do for and with us in a more politicized fashion. First, however, I offer a brief and partial historical and political context for Squirt as a pseudonymous public.

## Discourses of Digitally Mediated Public Sex Among Men

I draw on Sharif Mowlabocus' historical and political positioning of digitally mediated public sex between men. Mowlabocus (2008) studied a cybercottage, an unstable and difficult to find space within the public Web dedicated to facilitating public sex in toilets. Cottaging occurs in public toilets where men meet to have sex with other men, and cottages (so named because in the UK early stand-alone facilities resembled cottages), have had a significant role in the sex cultures of men who have sex with men, especially prior to the 1967 decriminalization of homosexuality in the UK. Such public sex locations are now found in parks, shopping malls, and universities. In the UK, cottaging is a criminal activity per the 2003 Sexual Offences act, but the criminality of sex between and among men in other public spaces—known as cruising grounds (parks, road side picnic areas, truck rest stops)—is less clear and considers whether the activity is visible to others. The cybercottage, although not illegal in itself, signals where illegal activity may take place. Mowlabocus argued that men of a variety of sexualities engage in such activities; importantly, this includes men who are open about their sexuality. Cottaging and cruising, as I will show, are activities undertaken by openly gay and bisexual men as well as by those identifying as straight, in the closet, or something else. What we see is a similar story to that portrayed in Humphreys' (1970) Tearoom Trade study: closeted straight identifying men frequenting public toilets for sex with other men were not deviants and led respectable family lives. Mowlabocus' analysis of the cybercottage suggested that gay men in particular may shun the so-called respectability of the gay scene and commercial sex venues (such as saunas) as espoused by assimilationist politics. He speculated that they are bored with being gay. As such, users of cybercottages favor older forms of hidden, queer sexual encounters that pre-date the decriminalization of homosexuality in the UK. Such encounters can be seen as not only potentially illegal, but also outside the boundaries of acceptable behavior as determined by both the gay community and the general public. As Mowlabocus stated, cottaging—and I would add cruising—are not generally celebrated lifestyle choices. Moreover, in Mowlabocus' work, the instability and invisibility of the cybercottage is set against highly visible and stable dating sites such as Gaydar (launched in 1999), which he and others (Light et al., 2008) implicated in the shaping of gay men's culture. Mowlabocus' conceptualization of the stability of Gaydar extends to newer developments such as the Grindr app, which although incorporating GPS for hooking up on the move, lacks any formal association with fluid public sex locations such as cottages and cruising grounds. I will examine another site/app, Squirt, which I think sits in a space that is between the cybercottage and mainstream gay dating and hook up sites/apps, and which operates as a pseudonymous public. Squirt is dedicated to public sexual cultures and hooking up in the same manner as cybercottages, but it shares the networked community elements (such as profiles and chat rooms) associated with Gaydar, and to some extent apps such as Grindr.

## Welcome to Squirt

Squirt is a site that self defines to prospective advertisers as "The online community where men hook up." The straplines on the home page of the desktop site reinforce such a positioning, communicating Squirt as concerned with "Hot 'n horny hook-ups" and suggesting to users "Horny—Hookup with local gay and bi men." Even though the latter strapline suggests a particular range of sexualities, others are present. For example, under the Hookups link, potential and current members are informed the site will enable you to "Find straight or married guys," and with the Communities link suggests that groups of "Bi, straight and married guys and just plain Businessmen in hot suits" are available. Squirt is a site where men can meet men for sex, regardless of their sexual orientation. The site also makes it very clear how much the digital matters because this page is illustrated with a range of devices, including smartphones, tablets, and laptops. These devices are strategically placed over the genitals of a range of models, further signifying the direct connections available between sex and contemporary communications technology.

In order to generate an interpretation of Squirt, I chose to employ a Latourian approach to building a sociology of associations. Latour (2005), in his presentation of ANT, argued for an interpretation of life where one lets situations reveal their associations and from this we assemble a social state of affairs. This is done by accounting for human and non-human actors who mediate a situation and in doing so engage in transformation work. In this instance, I was interested in the materiality of the digital in terms of interfaces, functions, devices, and infrastructures (see Light, 2014 for a fuller explanation of the digital as mediator). The sociology of associations that I assemble here is also necessarily partial. This is consistent with ANT's suggestion to not merely follow any actor, but follow those that are implicated in transforming arrangements.

To craft an interesting set of associations I first explored and documented the public-facing pages of Squirt, meaning those accessible without a user account. I then created an account on Squirt and documented the registration processes by taking screen grabs and describing the process of doing so, noting mediators such as particular language, drop down menus, exceptionally large and colorful buttons, registration functions, and optional and compulsory field completion requirements. I worked to establish mediators of the registration process—those actors that seemed to matter, rather than just carry me along my journey of registration. I spent 6 months in 2015 with Squirt examining its pages, content, interfaces, functions, uses, and the cultures of use it and its members co-generated. As with the registration process, I first documented the site via screen grabs and narrative description. Once I had a preliminary set of associations, I refined this by determining where the mediators acted. I was somewhat of a non-participant observer in that I did not interact directly with members within or outside of the site, but I did interact with Squirt. I accessed Squirt with desktop computers, a tablet, and a smart phone, via wi-fi, 3g/4g, and a fixed line cable modem. As I came to know Squirt I discovered theoretical links between ideas of networked publics, pseudonymity, the real name web, and, because of my prior work in the area, gendered discourses of digitally mediated public homosexual sex. This combined lens allowed me to revisit the site and uncover further associations being made with and beyond Squirt.

I now attend to the presence of features of networked publics in the processes of finding the site and registering an account as they interact with pseudonyms and as related to the movement of Squirt in the physical world.

### Finding and Joining Squirt

Locating Squirt is easy, that is, its searchability is high, if you know the terms to use. Using Google, the site is returned within the first few pages of results. These results are followed by links to entries on Yahoo Answers sites which name Squirt in response to questions regarding where men can find anonymous sex with men. In contrast to Mowlabocus' cybercottage research, finding Squirt, like a site such as Gaydar, does not necessarily need someone to show you the way, although as the Yahoo Answers example suggests, it might.

The registration process begins from the homepage, where you are informed you can sign up for free and will be given five days' Fan Club level access. The site has two levels of membership. Free accounts restrict such things as the number of profiles and videos that can be seen within a 24-hour period, whereas Fan Club members experience no such restrictions and gain additional features such as the ability to see who has looked at your profile. You are then invited to create a username and password, and your account is verified via email. The username and email need not include real name details. The site is based on the deployment of pseudonyms, which akin to Livia's (2002) study of the use of the French Minitel for hooking up, are often meant to be informative and seductive. Following this you are directed to a screen where you must provide location information including your postal code. False information can be provided if desired; it is not verified because normative rules of relationship making regarding the authenticity of being a real person associated with a real location are not enforced. You are then invited to select options for the kinds of things you are looking for, including when and where you can meet, sexual activities you want to engage in, the kinds of people you are seeking, and things that sexually arouse you. The only requirement is to state at least one form of desired sexual activity. Once this information is provided, you are directed to another page that is used as a framework to construct a profile.

The profile contains additional fields, but these—except sexual orientation, birth year, height and weight (which can be fabricated)—offer the option of "rather not say" from the drop down menu. A variety of disclosures about oneself is possible, ranging from the highly detailed to the minimal. My experience of the site is that members give details about their likes, dislikes, and physicality, but not much more. Photographs often focus on torsos, dick pics, people's behinds, or images of the member engaged in sexual activity on their own or with others, rather than on faces. In contrast to the usual uses of the real name web, face pics are often stored as private pics, made available only to those who are serious about hooking up. The reasons for this vary but include the facts that some men using the site are not open about their sexual preferences in everyday life, some are married to or in partnerships with other men and women, and of course the activities associated with the site are not necessarily socially and legally acceptable. As you leave this page a pop-up window reports to you that adding some photos to your account will increase your chances of being seen within the site. However, one is not required to upload facepics, and Squirt advises that you can make any added photos private if you require discretion. Finally, you are directed to screens where you have to indicate how you found out about Squirt and are presented with the option of purchasing an upgrade to Fan Club status. With this, registration is complete and you are directed to Squirt's welcome page.

From the welcome page members can upgrade their account; engage in chat and web camming; browse profiles; browse or cruising listings; read and contribute to message boards; read, rate, and contribute stories of their own sexual adventures and craft erotic fiction; watch member videos; update their profile; receive messages and chat invites; and, depending on their membership level, see who has looked at their profile and watch pornography for free. This is a significant landscape and I cannot possibly cover it all in this chapter, nor is it interesting to do so. In the following sections therefore I present the partial set of associations that has emerged which seems helpful in articulating the characteristics and workings of pseudonymous publics. These associations focus upon profiles and the cruising section. However, I refer to the network more broadly where mediators appear that are commonly associated with real name web networked publics that are normatively figured.

### Getting Noticed With Pseudonyms

As with other current social media, Squirt uses the device of the profile as one way for users to navigate the site, but the extent to which the profile is central depends on the situation. The profile is a way for members to find out about each other given that it holds the potential for information regarding sexual preferences, practices, and availability. But unlike many standard dating sites the profile is not only a device to peruse potential partners. The profile acts across the site and with other members. It is a mechanism for members to travel through and with Squirt. For example, in the "Cruising Tips" section, members are given the encouragement:

> If you want to get noticed more, use different areas of the site more often. On Squirt—guys who post to Message Boards, post or comment on Cruising Listings, and write Cocktales get noticed by others more often. Get your username out there and other guys will get in touch!

Getting your username out there with Squirt signals how pseudonymous profiles are attractive in network building. The idea of network building for the purposes of sexual play is hardly normative. Yet, in networked publics terms, for the purposes of being noticed, pseudonymous profiles are persistent, allow for scalability, and can attract hidden audiences. The purpose and process of being noticed with your profile is similar to what we might experience with other social media. Pseudonymous profiles allow for the development of social capital as has been argued in relation to sites such as Facebook (Ellison et al., 2011). In this case, though, such capital is not tied to claims of an authentic mainstream self as we might witness with Facebook; this capital can come from being a good citizen within the space, such as by not being a time waster when it comes to hook ups and by being polite when declining offers for or during a hook up. This capital is generated with the profile through at least two functions. The first, and most obvious, is via "Score Card" functionality; described by the site as follows:

> Every profile on Squirt has a Score Card section. It's an area where other guys can post comments about you for other guys to see . . . Sort of like a "testimonials" section! For example, if you hooked up with him and blew his mind, he can post a comment on your profile for other Squirters to see saying how hot it was. Then, when other guys look at your profile, they can see that other Squirters think you are fucking hot.

Therefore, members can engage with profiles to provide testimonials about each other. Squirt allows members to moderate their received testimonials, so they are, unsurprisingly, very positive where published. That said, Score Cards afford members the opportunity to display social cachet that brands them a good member. In this instance such capital is usually concerned with gendered interpretations of physical appearance and sexual prowess although sometimes a positive comment is made about the member's personality. Such commentary signals that this is someone to get involved with within the network, but as demonstrated on sites such as Gaydar, this can invoke discourses of homonormativity and hegemonic masculinity (Light, 2007). Importantly, even in a pseudonymous environment integrity and general politeness are valued and members can be criticized if they behave inappropriately. The "Cruising Tips" section advises:

> If you set up a meet, make sure you show up. If something comes up and you couldn't make it, let the guy know. Give him a call if you've exchanged numbers, or at least drop him an email to explain. Before the meet is scheduled is always better so he doesn't show up, but if that's not possible—at least after the fact to explain what happened. Remember—community members talk to each other, if you set up a bunch of meets and never show it'll take about five minutes for everyone to know not to hook up with you.

A further mode of the profile working to signal the value of the member in the network to others is where the functionality of connecting with "guys I do threesomes with" acts. This functionality allows members to consensually link profiles together to inform other users of those with whom they engage in group sex. Additionally, this function enables members to traverse connections in the network in a manner similar to, but less extensively than on, social networking sites. Travelling through the network on the basis of these connections, members can see with whom else another member engages, what those members' sexual interests are, and their associated gendered and sexualized social capital.

Pseudonymous profiles also allow members to travel the site and uncover hidden audiences. These audiences exist to be revealed and are perceived to have value. As the "Cruising Tips" section elaborates:

> if you have a specific want or need, post to the Message Boards in your area. Lots of guys think that their preferences or situations are unique, when really there are tons of guys within a few miles of them that have the same things going on!

Through this travel, Squirt also offers the chance for members not only to hook up but also to engage in any kind of desired sexual activity, whether in the privacy of a member's home or in a public space. Pseudonymous profiles allow for networking to take place through their ability to inform and connect via the potential to bring to bear anonymity while members get to know each other.

This travel or exploration also occurs through the crafting of user generated content such as photography, videography, and storytelling, which can be read as vernacular creativity (Burgess, 2006). In Squirt, one might see the photography (profile pics), videography (member videos), and storytelling practices (Cocktales) as entangled with erotic media, pornography, self-portraiture, and autobiographical writing, for example. This production, sharing, and rating of creative practice further articulates the gendered and sexualized networked public nature of the space where pseudonyms are involved. Such content is subject to scalability because it is available throughout the site. It is reproducible in that it can be favorited and added to profile pages, and shared with other members (even shared outside of the site to varying extents). These materials are also searchable with Squirt's interfaces, and are often subject to hidden audiences. For example, members not holding Fan Club status cannot see who has viewed their profile; similarly unless a member leaves a comment, Squirt does not inform a member who has read their Cocktale. Unlike the cybercottage described by Mowlabocus (2008), Squirt has associated gendered and sexualized networked public elements. Moreover, these can be inscribed with a higher degree of regulation in gender and sexual terms because of the more expansive range of the site, both technically and socioculturally.

### Pseudonymity, Physical Space, and Cruising With Squirt

The second matter I want to consider is the set of associations that emerges with Squirt in the physical world. The challenges presented by networked publics are often couched in terms of some kind of material impact not only on the Web but also in our physical dealings with others. That is, problems of searchability, persistence, scalability, replicability, and hidden audiences can be couched in terms of the problems arising when one's colleagues see, share, or like a picture of you, on Facebook for example, vomiting into the gutter after one too many drinks. Squirt increases the stakes in terms of context collapse beyond such mundane concerns even though its sharing features are much more limited.

A key feature of Squirt's existence is to facilitate hooking up in public places. The site's cruising section provides member generated listings of where such activity might take place, containing site photographs and GPS data. This GPS data connects with a map that feeds into apps such as Google maps that provide directions to the site on foot, and via public and private transport. These pages also contain information about the location: exactly where at the location one might meet people, the types of people who frequent such places, whether there is disabled access, and the best times to go. These listings include commercial sex venues such as saunas, sex clubs, and adult stores. Free to access listings include cruising grounds such as parks and canalsides, and cottages located at roadsides, in shopping malls, and town centers.

Cybercottages (Mowlabocus, 2008) mirror the invisibility and instability of cottages. Their function waxes and wanes in response to demand, time of the day, and police or some other presence (e.g., video surveillance equipment or security guards). Squirt is easier to find than cybercottages via search engines, and is more stable given the commercial investments made in the site and the millions rather than tens of men who engage with it. However, the cottages and cruising sites listed on Squirt are subject to stability issues. Members can never be sure that a public sex location will be accessible for sexual adventure. This is evident in the conversations attached to the cruising listings. Members visit these listings with their profiles and leave comments and questions in ways similar to those described by Mowlabocus. Such acts may be concerned with establishing who is at the site, or whether someone can make it later. But additionally, from time to time when no comments have been made, members arrive and ask whether the site is still used or what kinds of members it attracts. Yet although such spaces are subject to instability, at the same time, because the cruising listings have their own profile page which members collectively write in and out of being, their material existence within the site stabilizes matters and persistence is possible. These persistent listings are fully searchable within the site and can be ordered in a variety of ways, such as proximity to a user and recency of comments by other members. The listings can also be shared outside of Squirt and are consequently subject to scalability. Regarding hidden audiences, members do not know who has looked at a cruising listing unless a user leaves a comment. Indeed, there is much lurking in relation to the listings, signaled for instance when members who have not previously commented speak up and chastise others for publicly arranging a meet in the comment thread. Such organizing is problematized on the basis of hidden, and imagined audiences (Marwick & boyd, 2011). The assumption is that if other members can see these discussions so can the police, or people who live nearby a public sex location, who use such spaces for other purposes, and who might cause trouble for cruisers and cottagers. Such a discourse rests on a practice of "show the way, not show the when" (of course meets may be arranged using private chat and messaging functions). These functions of networked publics, combined with the legal status and lack of heteronormativity of the activities being planned, open the possibility for harms to occur should an unsympathetic user appropriate the app.

So far I have tacitly addressed associations that relate to mediated access with the desktop version of Squirt. There is more to be said if we switch to access with smartphones, particularly where cruising, cottaging and hooking up is concerned, and as related to other matters concerning digital infrastructure and software. The first mobile mediation that needs to be mentioned is that Squirt uses a HTML5 website optimized for such devices. Compared to the full site, Squirt Mobile has reduced functionality and focuses very much on hooking up. Once logged in, GPS-based grid sorting occurs and members are presented with online users, by default in order of geographical proximity. Messaging and chat functionalities are present and cruising listings are accessible—again with GPS functionality that links with mapping applications. It is also possible to upgrade an account, edit elements of a profile, and provide a status update (including whether you are looking for a hook up within the next 3 or the next 12 hours). Squirt Mobile is optimized for hooking up on the move and engages itself, and the user, into the pseudonymous public and physical space.

Despite the discourse of show the way, not show the when, members do engage with Squirt to communicate in real time that they are at or in close proximity to a given site. This is done purposefully by making comments on listing pages and by Squirt itself as the GPS locates a member in physical space. Members also advertise to cruisers that they live nearby and can accommodate those that have not hooked up at the cruising ground or cottage. This latter mode of appropriation shows how the networked public features of Squirt can be implicated in the navigation of public and private sexual encounters on the move, and further an engagement of it and its members with discourses of anti-assimilationist and assimilationist politics as related to what it means to be a responsible guy who has sex with guys (or more specifically a good gay man). Does one conform with normative standards of expected public behavior and have sex in the privacy of someone's home, or engage in deviant public sex?

The second point of mediation regarding Squirt as mobile actor is it is enmeshed with very particular digital infrastructures and software. When used with a smartphone, members can access the HTML5 site via 2g/3g/4g instead of a wi-fi network or LAN—meaning they can, to some extent, avoid friends, housemates, and family members knowing about their access to Squirt. Also, like Mowlabocus' (2008) cybercottage, Squirt operates with a browser even in mobile mode. Squirt, unlike sites and apps such as Gaydar and Grindr, does not offer members the option of downloading an app from the Apple App Store or Google Play. This is important because the HTML5 site creates a set of very particular associations. Squirt Mobile is completely uncensored (barring certain forms of imagery such as the inclusion of minors and bestiality). Gaydar and

Grindr are subject to app store rules prohibiting nudity and other forms of imagery deemed sexually suggestive on the public grid-sorting page (sexual imagery can shared in private chats). This seemingly slight difference is important in terms of the regulation of sex and gender in public. Squirt challenges heteronormative cultures of sex and sells itself as an anti-censorship alternative:

> Currently, apps that contain adult material are not allowed in the App Store or the Android Marketplace. Squirt does not believe in censorship. We are pro-sex, and we celebrate sexuality.

Additionally, members may browse Squirt using private browsing mode on their smartphones and thus readily conceal their network affiliation. They do not have to explain the presence of such an app on their phone, or in their App Store or Google Play purchase history.

## Networked Publics as Pseudonymous Publics

Whereas Mowlabocus' (2008) cybercottage is not so concerned with community, Squirt clearly is. However, in contrast to Gaydar, which has a significant sociality for its own sake operating alongside its dating and hooking up aims, Squirt emphasizes communities of sexual play. Such sexual play is concerned with cruising and cottaging, hooking up in hotels and at member's homes, sharing stories of sexual encounters, and the production of erotic fiction and visual media. Squirt is a site of multiple masculinities and sexualities, including those in the closet and those who identify as bi, gay, straight, or trans. In allowing for sex between men to take place in public and private Squirt enables a diversity of gendered and sexualized political stances with which members consciously and subconsciously engage. Although cybercottages may be seen as anti-assimilationist, and Gaydar and Grindr as somewhat assimilationist, I read Squirt as allowing a continuum between such competing positions. Of course I am not so naïve as to assume that people using Squirt are automatically interested in simultaneously consciously performing a particular gender or sexual politic. Hooking up in someone's home does not necessarily mark one as assimilationist any more than using a glory hole in a cottage makes one radical. Consciously and/or unconsciously, Squirt and the men who use it write into being "parallel discursive arenas where members of subordinated social groups invent and circulate counter discourses to formulate oppositional interpretations of their identities, interests, and needs" (Fraser, 1990, p. 67). It is matters such as this that make Squirt a public, particularly a subaltern counterpublic, and one that, along with the use of pseudonyms, allows for a challenge to the heteronormativity of the real name web.

243

Unlike normative dating sites, profiles on Squirt operate as travel companions and as enablers of pseudonymous publics that draw in characteristics of networked publics and earlier discourses regarding the anonymous and pseudonymous Web. Through Squirt we can see how gender—particularly sexual preference and sexual activity—become much more central to sexual relationships than many heteronormative dating sites would care to admit. Indeed, one could extend this claim to the ways that heteronormativity is written into the partnering possibilities of social media such as Facebook where polyamoury in the real name web is prohibited. Moreover, Squirt demonstrates how networked publics can be applied in non-normative ways to facilitate the development and operation of subaltern counterpublics where deeply gendered and sexual matters are concerned. Such is the non-normative potential of Squirt as a networked public: we see how even when members meet in the physical world, the pseudonyms are carried with them as they make posts at cruising sites and then transplanted back into Squirt through follow up testimonials on profile pages and cruising listings. The physical world does not necessarily break pseudonymous publics. It may, in fact, reinforce them.

Work on networked publics is implicitly gender-neutral and has the mainstream real name web in mind. I argue that the principles of networked publics (boyd, 2008a; boyd, 2008b), when combined with earlier theorizing about the characteristics of communication in computer based networks (Johnson, 1997) and Hogan's (2013) critique of the real name web, can be helpfully articulated into associations of what I see as pseudonymous publics. Pseudonymous publics are public spaces in which we do things alongside or with others, where there is no expectation of complete privacy but where the use of real names is not warranted. Pseudonymous publics can work akin to real name web networked publics but without a real name in place. Further, as seen with Squirt, these pseudonymous publics challenge what I see as the heteronormative configuring of the real name web.

The heteronormative configuration of networked publics is a problem because it seeks to black box an ordering of a social and cultural situation, and along with it, very particular assumptions of publicness that privilege normativity and subordinate outliers. It is not necessarily the capacity of the theorization of networked publics that is at fault here. The problem lies where tacit and explicit suggestions are made that we will use and are using our real names in these publics and that doing so in and of itself leaves us open to damage. In the context of this essay, this "damage" occurs when we are seen to do things that cross the line in terms of the heteronormative sexual ideals which have become inscribed in law, society, and culture. However, the idea of networked publics has further resonance if we extend it beyond the problems of context collapse and the real name web. Pseudonymous publics can simultaneously operate as apolitical and political when concerning questions of public and private sex between men. Pseudonymity, I argue, can allow for the generation of networked publics whether these are public in the sense of mainstream gay cultures or explicitly political as per Fraser's notion of subaltern counterpublics. On Squirt, replicability, persistence, searchability, and invisible audiences not only exist; they have practical, erotic, and political value.

# References

boyd, d. (2008a). *Taken out of context: American teen sociality in networked publics* (Unpublished Doctoral Dissertation). University of California, Berkeley, Berkeley, CA.

boyd, d. (2008b). Why youth ♥ Social network sites: The role of networked publics in teenage social life. In D. Buckingham (Ed.), *Youth identity and digital media* (pp. 119–142). Cambridge, MA: The MIT Press.

Burgess, J. (2006). Hearing ordinary voices: Cultural studies, vernacular creativity and digital storytelling. *Continuum: Journal of Media & Cultural Studies, 20*(2), 201–214.

Ellison, N. B., Steinfield, C., & Lampe, C. (2011). Connection strategies: Social capital implications of Facebook-enabled communication practices. *New Media & Society, 13*(6), 873–892.

Fraser, N. (1990). Rethinking the public sphere: A contribution to the critique of actually existing democracy. *Social Text, 25/26,* 56–80.

Gerlitz, C., & Helmond, A. (2013). The like economy: Social buttons and the data-intensive web. *New Media & Society, 15*(8), 1,348–1,365.

Habermas, J. (1991). *The structural transformation of the public sphere: An inquiry into a category of bourgeois society.* Cambridge, MA: The MIT press.

Hogan, B. (2013). Pseudonyms and the rise of the real-name web. In J. Hartley, J. Burgess, & A. Bruns (Eds.), *A companion to new media dynamics* (pp. 290–307). Hoboken, NJ: Wiley-Blackwell.

Humphreys, L. (1970). *Tearoom trade: Impersonal sex in public spaces.* London: Duckworth.

Johnson, D. G. (1997). Ethics online. *Communications of the ACM, 40*(1), 60–65.

Latour, B. (2005). *Reassembling the social: An introduction to actor network theory.* Oxford: Oxford University Press.

Light, B. (2007). Introducing masculinity studies to information systems research: the case of gaydar. *European Journal of Information Systems, 16*(5), 658–665.

Light, B. (2014). *Disconnecting with social networking sites.* Basingstoke, UK: Palgrave Macmillan.

Light, B., Fletcher, G., & Adam, A. (2008). Gay men, Gaydar and the commodification of difference. *Information Technology and People, 21*(3), 300–314.

Lingel, J., & Golub, A. (2015). In face on Facebook: Brooklyn's drag community and sociotechnical practices of online communication. *Journal of Computer-Mediated Communication, 20*(5), 536–553.

Livia, A. (2002). Public and clandestine: Gay men's pseudonyms on the French Minitel. *Sexualities, 5*(2), 201–217.

Livingstone, S. M. (2005). *Audiences and publics: When cultural engagement matters for the public sphere: Changing media, changing Europe*. Bristol, UK: Intellect Books.

Mansell, R., & Collins, B. S. (2005). Cyber trust and crime prevention. In R. Mansell & B. S. Collins (Eds.), *Trust and crime in information societies* (pp. 11–56). Cheltenham, UK: Edward Elgar Publishing.

Mowlabocus, S. (2008). Revisiting old haunts through new technologies: Public (homo)sexual cultures in cyberspace. *International Journal of Cultural Studies, 11*(4), 419–439.

Papacharissi, Z. (2010). *A private sphere: Democracy in a digital age*. Cambridge, UK: Polity Press.

Statt, N. (2015). Facebook to test tweaks to real name policy again after more criticism: Preventing the policy from being weaponized. *The Verge*. Retrieved November 15, 2015, from http://www.theverge.com/2015/10/30/9644066/facebook-real-name-policy-changes-criticism.

# 15

# ISLAMIC FASHION IMAGES ON INSTAGRAM AND THE VISUALITY OF MUSLIM WOMEN

*Kristin M. Peterson*

The extensive history of Muslim women's portrayal in Western visual culture has reached from the harem photography of the colonial period (Alloula, 2013) to the more recent post-9/11 photography of burqa-clad women in Afghanistan (Abu-Lughod, 2002). Through this imagery, the headscarf as a symbol has become fetishized as both an object of oppression and an item that covers the hyper-sexualized body of the Muslim woman. Over time, the representation of Muslim women has traditionally reflected a dichotomy: either covered and oppressed by Islam or naked and sexually liberated by Western culture.

Recent developments in Islamic fashion and social media have allowed young Muslim women opportunities to visually present themselves (in physical as well as digital spaces) in ways that may reflect alternatives to these dichotomies. In this chapter, I will analyze the Instagram pages of three prominent Muslim fashion gurus to examine how these women are using the style of Islamic fashion and the affordances of the social media to present the complexities of their lives and to resist over-simplified representations.

## Fashion and Intersecting Subject Positions

Fashion is not simply the trivial choice of what to wear each day or the elaborate, haute couture fashion of runway models and magazine spreads. Instead, fashion is a cultural and social process whereby individuals mark their positions in cultural groups and in turn produce and communicate meaning. Fashion theorist Malcolm Barnard argued that fashion is a form of communication, but he rejected the over-simplified concept that certain clothing items have inherent meanings that are transmitted from the wearer to the viewer. Barnard wrote that "the meanings of a piece of clothing are the result of a constantly shifting negotiation, and that they cannot escape the influence of differing positions of dominance and subservience" (2002, p. 33). For instance, the meaning of the Islamic headscarf is contested; it can be a sign of oppression, of liberation, of creativity, of sexual possibility, or of modesty. All of those meanings and more are present in the engagement with a simple piece of fabric.

Clothing plays a significant role in forming individual subjects within larger cultural groups: "It is the social interacting, by means of the clothing, that produces the individual as a member of the group rather than vice-versa" (Barnard, 2002, p. 32). Through the wearing of certain clothes, a woman is marked and constituted as a Muslim. Fashion also creates and communicates "not only things like feeling and mood, but also the values, hopes and beliefs of the social groups of which they are members" (p. 39). Although fashion often reinforces dominant ideologies by restricting how people can dress, individuals can use fashion as what Barnard called "ideological weapons" to subvert dominant power structures (p. 44) and contest dominant ideologies, as Dick Hebdige (1979) illustrated in his seminal study of subcultures. Islamic fashion is not as extreme as the punk fashion of interest to Hebdige, but many young Muslim women still resist dominant ideologies around beauty, modesty, and sexuality through their fashion.

People can also use fashion to engage with multifaceted and overlapping subject positions. Susan Kaiser advocated for an approach that explores fashion's intersections, complexities and ambivalences. To Kaiser, fashion "highlights the multiple intersections and entanglements among gender, race, ethnicity, national identity, social class, sexuality and other facets of our identities" (2012, p. 4). Young Muslim women in the West can use fashion to represent their intersecting subject positions, but although fashion grants women the agency to articulate their intersecting subject positions, Kaiser argued that these subjects still exist within structures that regulate fashion, such as formal dress codes and informal cultural norms. Kaiser explained the tension between individual agency and structure: "people create their own 'fashion statements' but are ultimately constrained by what is available in the marketplace, by dress codes and social conventions, by political regimes, and the like" (2012, p. 31). Subjects have more or less agency depending on their positions and cultural forces, and Kaiser argued for fashion theory to focus on the "overlapping or 'in-between' spaces" in which individuals (such as the Muslim women considered in this chapter) negotiate and articulate multiple subject positions (p. 37).

The movement of Islamic fashion revolves around the complex and ambivalent spaces inhabited by Muslim women who wear fashionable

Western styles while adhering to the Islamic principle of modesty. The term Islamic fashion refers to the fast-growing international industry of modest fashion styles that is estimated to be worth around $100 billion annually (Bint-Abubaker, 2015). Islamic fashion follows general rules of modesty prescribed by the religion: wearing long and loose-fitting clothing that reveals only a woman's hands, feet, and face. However, Islamic fashion is about more than simply wearing modest clothing for religious reasons; it is about fashion. It is a movement of Muslim women who want to maintain their religious convictions yet dress in contemporary fashion styles. Islamic fashion has been a highly contested area, with some critics arguing that Muslims should not focus on fashion and external appearances and defenders asserting that fashion presents Islam in a positive light.

When Muslims' clothing choices are discussed outside the Islamic community, the focus tends to lean toward the rights of Muslim women to wear the headscarf in public situations, such as in identification photos, in courts, in public schools, and while working. Much has been written about the "headscarf debates" in Europe and North American, but Tarlo and Moors shifted the focus to examine how Muslim women use fashion as a political tool. They argued that through Islamic fashion, Muslim women are able to "disrupt and challenge public stereotypes about Islam, women, social integration and the veil even if their voices are often drowned out in political and legal debates on these issues" (2013, p. 3). The physical presence of (mostly young) Muslim women wearing fashionable yet modest clothing in Western public spaces asserts that these women have the right to exist and to speak publicly. Islamic fashion also works against stereotypes, according to Tarlo and Moors, that view Muslim women as "dull, downtrodden, oppressed and out of sync with modernity" (p. 20). Muslim women—even when modest—can be hip and fashionable.

The Islamic fashion industry has grown alongside the expansion of digital technologies and social media, so that online boutiques, fashion blogs, Instagram images, and YouTube videos are all popular venues to share the latest fashion styles. Muslim lifestyle gurus are now some of the most popular Muslims on social media sites, offering fashion tips while also presenting an alternative to the dominant visuality of Muslim women as oppressed and lacking individuality. Instead, these Muslim women create images that represent themselves as independent, creative, and assertive; they present their beauty in ways that are fashionable but still modest. Building on the work of Tarlo and Moors, which showed that fashion and images can provide Muslim women with political tools, I explore how the Instagram pages of three Islamic lifestyle gurus go beyond empowering women through an alternative form of representation to show how the women use the visual space of Instagram to navigate their positions as Muslim women in a contemporary neoliberal Western culture.

## The Pressures of Postfeminism

All young women using social media spaces face particular pressures to display their bodies, personalities, and identities in specific ways; postfeminism can help explain the pressures for women in the neoliberal context to be hyper-focused on their appearances and behaviors. According to Angela McRobbie postfeminism assumes that feminism has achieved equality between the sexes; feminism is viewed as "common sense" (2009, p. 6) and as a "spent force" (p. 12) that is no longer necessary to achieve gender justice. This plays out in culture when women accept equality between the sexes as obvious but simultaneously reinforce an assumption that women must perfectly embody a particular form of femininity. The resulting demand for constant self-work on one's appearance is not questioned or seen as restricting women to an inferior and dependent status. As McRobbie explained, postfeminism appears to give women the power to represent themselves in new ways, but bolsters gender inequalities and capitalist structures. This false sense of power functions to limit women's power.

Postfeminism is closely tied with the assumed liberation of women through consumption, entrepreneurship, and constant self-work. Tasker and Negra explained that postfeminism accepts certain aspects of feminism such as individual freedoms, but that "it also works to commodify feminism via the figure of woman as empowered consumer" (2007, p. 2). In postfeminism, a woman is granted a false sense of freedom to buy ever more products to reflect her body and social image. Women are also expected to embrace the freedom to promote and sell commodities that will benefit other women. This path can allow women, especially women in minority positions, to become successful entrepreneurs, or what McRobbie called, "economically active female citizens" (2009, p. 58).

In addition to the pressure for women to constantly monitor their bodies in order to appear as perfect objects of sight, women must also monitor their inner selves. Indeed, how a woman manages her interior life will be reflected in her external appearance. A woman who doesn't wear makeup and goes out in her pajamas, for instance, is assumed to have a disastrous personal life. Gill explained, "the self has become a project to be evaluated, advised, disciplined and improved or brought 'into recovery'" (2007, p. 156). McRobbie (2009) argued that women are expected to have life-plans and be self-reflexive about their personal choices. Every aspect of a woman's life is always up for scrutiny.

The postfeminist context places women in a conflicting position. They can become public entrepreneurial figures and share their experiences with a larger audience, but at the same time their labor is exploited by the neoliberal capitalist system and they are expected to meet impossible feminine beauty standards. The solution to these contradictions lies not in celebrating the liberatory potential of social media or in dismissing all social media work as exploited labor, but rather in focusing on what Sarah Banet-Weiser (2013) terms the "ambivalences" of the current neoliberal culture. The emphasis should be on how women produce meaning within these conflicting and ambivalent spaces.

Muslim women are under particular pressures because in addition to achieving postfeminist goals, they also must present their bodies in ways that resist dominant representations of Muslim women while meeting the modesty requirements of Islam. Social media provide new public spaces for Muslim women to share their experiences, but these spaces are infused with postfeminist pressures for women to do constant self-work to scrutinize their bodies and interior selves and to consume products in a quest for perfection. The Instagram images of Muslim fashion gurus illustrate these intersecting demands and ambivalences that are specific to Muslim women in the West.

## The Ambivalences of the Veiled Muslim Woman

In addition to the pressures of postfeminism, young Muslim women in the West are confronted with a long visual history of portraying the female Muslim body as either hyper-sexualized objects or oppressed victims. As will be shown, these categories are not mutually exclusive. Malek Alloula explored the harem photography of the early 1900s, noting Western colonizers' fascination with getting under the veil of Muslim women to access the "phantasm" of the harem space (2013, p. 510). Models were hired to enact sexual fantasies of lifting the veil for the camera. Created for the sexual pleasure of the colonizers, these photos solidified the connection between the veil and sexual desire. Beverly Weber (2013, p. 85) explained that the veiled was "a deeply eroticized symbol of the unavailability and desirability of Muslim women."

The veiled Muslim body also symbolizes the presumed oppression of Islam and the violence of Muslim men. Lila Abu-Lughod (2002) astutely pointed out that the West uses the narrative of saving Muslim women from the oppression of Islam in order to position Western liberalism as superior to Islam and to ignore the ways that Western countries have contributed to social oppression in Muslim-majority contexts. Despite Abu-Lughod's evidence that for many Muslim women wearing a headscarf is an individual decision, Westerners often assume that the veil is a symbol of oppression and a lack of agency. As Dina Siddiqi noted, the only way for Muslim women in the West to embrace the freedoms of Western society is to distance themselves from Islam and appear unveiled and sexually liberated: "exercising the 'right' to bare the body signifies an act of empowerment for the Muslim woman whose 'natural' state is understood to be covered or behind the veil" (2014, p. 5). In other words, the visual

251

imagery of the veiled body presents only two options for Muslim women: to be veiled and oppressed or exposed and sexually liberated.

## Dominant Ways of Seeing Muslim Women

In recent years, young Muslim women in the West have taken to social media as spaces to discuss lifestyle topics, share their faith, and find a supportive community. Because of their specific positions, these women are faced with two distinct but often overlapping forces: the postfeminist pressures to appear as the perfect embodiment of the feminine ideal and the stereotypes of Muslim women as either hyper-sexualized or oppressed. Both of these tensions represent what Amelia Jones (2010) called visualities, because they promote dominant ways of seeing others. Visuality reflects "the conditions of how we see and make meaning of what we see" and "is one of the key modes by which gender is culturally inscribed in Western culture" (Jones, 2010, p. 1). Through visualities, hegemonic ideas about gender, race, religion, and other forms of identification are naturalized. Visuality works alongside dominant discourses to apply hegemonic meaning to certain visual codes. For instance, Edward Said (1978) explained how the European projection of Orientalism became a dominant discourse to make sense of the "other" or more specifically Islam. Through Orientalism, Muslim men were presented in Western literature and scholarship as backwards, violent, and angry, and Muslim women were presented as exotic and oppressed. These dominant discourses are also reinforced through visual codes such as the veil.

Mirzoeff wrote that people in positions of power use visuality to make coherent narratives of the social world in order to maintain the power structures, and that visuality "ordered and narrated the chaotic events of modern life in intelligible, visualized fashion" (2009, p. 91). Stuart Hall also examined how ideologies get encoded into media discourses and visuality, but he pointed to the ability of individuals to decode a message and the potential for an "oppositional reading" of a text or image (2000, p. 61). Although all viewers of an image are able to decode an image in their own ways, visuality focuses on how the dominant visual codes and stereotypes permeate society. People in positions of power use visuality to make sense of the world in a way that supports their domination. European colonizers created visualities of Muslim women as either oppressed or eroticized, and today the dominant social group perpetuates this visuality to assert the superiority of the West and its power to liberate these veiled Muslim bodies.

Additionally, the ideologies of postfeminism are represented by another type of visuality that promotes dominant codes of femininity; women should appear beautiful, perfect, successful, and positive. Muslim women are also under pressure to fulfill the visuality of modesty. In Islam, modesty rules structure what women may wear, what parts of their body must be covered, and how they should act in public. In this chapter, I analyze the Instagram pages of three Muslim women to examine how the women negotiate these multiple visualities. Through an examination of their images, I explore whether there may be an ambivalent space in between these tensions that might facilitate a new and different way of seeing young Muslim women in the Western context.

## Islamic Fashion Gurus on Instagram

The expansion of social media spaces has led to an increase in the popularity of fashion gurus on sites such as Instagram, YouTube, and Tumblr. Hundreds of thousands of self-appointed lifestyle experts, mostly women, have taken to social media to share tips about fashion styles, makeup, and beauty products. Fans consume numerous videos and images of trends, such as outfit of the day (OOTD), shopping hauls, makeup tutorials, get ready with me, do-it-yourself (DIY), and lists of seasonal "faves" or favorite products. Although most of these creators will never make a name for themselves through social media, a handful have become celebrities among teenage girls and young women, such as Michelle Phan, Hannah Hart, Mamrie Hart, Grace Helbig, and Jenna "Marbles" Mourey. These women have also become financially successful with advertisers clamoring to reach the millions of followers who regularly visit these sites.

Instagram has become a particularly popular space for up and coming fashion designers and stylists to post images of innovative outfits, as well as makeup and beauty tips. Although YouTube can let women develop their personalities and act in character, Instagram allows for creators to quickly compose and upload a photo and for followers to scan through a feed of images. Instagram users can post a single photo along with a written caption. Small thumbnail images are arrayed on the profile page, allowing viewers to easily scroll through photos.

As do mainstream fashion gurus, young Muslim women post images on Instagram featuring fashion styles, lifestyle advice, and makeup tips. Muslim women frequently display elements of their religious identity in their images. As with the mainstream lifestyle gurus, some Muslim women have been financially successful through product promotions, advertising revenue, and the sale of clothing and accessories. For this study, I analyzed the Instagram sites of two of the most popular Islamic lifestyle gurus, Amena Khan and Dina Torkia, as well as the images of Nye Armstrong, a less successful but still influential figure in this online community. I conducted a visual analysis of images posted to their Instagram pages from 2014–2015 and focused on images that displayed the blending of and negotiations between postfeminist pressures and Islamic concerns about modesty and piety.

Amena Khan and Dina Torkia were selected for this study because they are by far the most popular (based on views and followers) Muslim fashion gurus on social media sites such as YouTube, Instagram, and Facebook. Amena initially attracted followers through her YouTube hijab tutorials, demonstrating multiple ways to tie a headscarf. As of July 2016, her videos have been viewed more than 29 million times. She has more than 450,000 followers on Instagram where she posts images of her outfits, makeup tips, and previews of her twice-weekly videos. She has designed her own version of a headscarf, called a hoojab, which she sells along with other modest clothing items in her online boutique, Pearl Daisy. Dina is a successful fashion designer with her own clothing line, and a top Muslim fashionista on Instagram with more than a million followers. She also posts regular videos on YouTube, garnering more than 50 million total views. Both Dina and Amena are British.

I included Nye Armstrong in this study because her images provide a useful counterpoint to the online work of Amena and Dina. Nye is an American convert to Islam. She started a YouTube channel several years ago to document her experiences as a convert. Nye is not part of the fashion industry, although she is loosely connected by her friendship with Amena. Most of Nye's images and videos highlight her bubbly personality, and she devotes a lot of time to providing helpful information for fellow converts. Nye has more than 10,000 Instagram followers.

## *Amena Khan: Perfection of the Feminine Ideal*

In every one of her Instagram photos, Amena presents herself as beautiful and absolutely perfect: she is wearing gorgeous outfits, she has impeccable makeup, and she is confident and positive. She practically glows in her photos, such as the one captioned, "Happy Sunday," in which Amena is taking what may appear to be a casual selfie in her house. She has a slight grin on her face and is wearing a pink top, black headscarf, and a headband of pink flowers on top of her scarf. The flattering lighting emphasizes Amena's perfect skin and beautiful makeup. Even when Amena is not feeling well, such as in the image captioned "My 'sick day' makeup essentials," she still appears just slightly less than perfect. Large prescription glasses hide her puffy eyes, and we can see a few small blemishes on her skin. Despite that, Amena is smiling and looks presentable in public. She even offers tips for what she calls "sick day makeup," indicating that women must always appear perfect and beautiful.

Looking through Amena's photos on Instagram, it's difficult to find one image where she doesn't look flawless. Even when outside of her amateur home studio, Amena still looks gorgeous. In one image, captioned "I love traveling on the train," Amena is sitting on a train, staring out the window. She's wearing a brown headscarf and a white faux-fur jacket;

with minimal makeup, the sunlight on her face makes it look like Amena is naturally beautiful, no matter the setting. Amena also posts photos such as the one captioned, "Met some fab viewers in Birmingham!" taken with fans that she happens to meet in public. This image was taken at a mall, with Amena clutching a bag from one of the stores. Even though Amena's outfit isn't fancy, she clearly planned and prepared her outfit and makeup for the shopping excursion. Her fan, in a flannel shirt and jeans, is distinctly less fashionable and by implication less attractive.

Amena has mastered many of the ideals of femininity in the postfeminist moment; she does constant work on her body in order to appear as a perfect object of sight. John Berger was prescient when he wrote in 1977 that a woman "has to survey everything she is and everything she does because how she appears to others, and ultimately how she appears to men, is of crucial importance for what is normally thought of as the success of her life" (Berger, 1977, p. 46). Amena's images reinforce that the only way to be a successful woman is to be perfect and beautiful, inside and out. For her Muslim followers, Amena asserts that Muslim women can be successful in the postfeminist context while still maintaining their faith.

Berger focused on women as sexual objects of the male gaze, but more recently, Gill explained, "Women are not straight-forwardly objectified but are portrayed as active, desiring sexual subjects who choose to present themselves in a seemingly objectified manner because it suits their liberated interests to do so" (2007, p. 151). Postfeminism has been charged with granting women an inauthentic form of freedom to present their bodies in sexualized ways for the pleasure of the male viewer. In actuality, the presumed freedoms of postfeminism offer Amena and other Muslim women the chance to control their images and present their bodies as attractive but not overly sexualized. In one photo, "I had my hand on my hip," Amena takes a snapshot with her husband. This photo reinforces some of the gender codes that Erving Goffman (1979) traced in advertisements: Amena's delicate hand caresses her husband's chest and her tilted head signifies a sense of physical instability. Amena's husband is grounded, strong and in control. Amena's caption indicates that she thinks the photo is a little awkward, but although the pose is somewhat unnatural, given her other posts, she presumably would not have posted this image if she were truly embarrassed by it. Seemingly, Amena has control over her images because she selects which images to display, even though her images could be decoded in different ways. Although other women in the postfeminist context may be empowered by the presumed sexual freedom, Amena resists the dominant visualities that display liberated Muslim women as uncovered and sexually liberated. Instead, she is empowered by her capacity to protect her sexuality and to remain covered.

Amena's Instagram images constantly reinforce both that she is beautiful and perfect, and that she spends a lot of time surveying and improving herself. This perpetuates a particular way not only of being a woman, but also of being a perfect Muslim subject. Berger (1977) argued that women are pressured to monitor their appearances, but more recent feminist scholars have seen this pressure as integral to post-feminist culture: "The body is presented simultaneously as women's source of power and as always unruly, requiring constant monitoring, surveillance, discipline and remodeling (and consumer spending) in order to conform to ever-narrower judgments of female attractiveness" (Gill, 2007, p. 149). Every aspect of a woman's appearance is up for constant scrutiny, but this never-ending form of labor must appear to be "fun, pampering, or self-indulgence and must *never* be disclosed" (p. 155). When Amena posts images of her daily routines, such as cleaning up her eyebrows, caring for her skin, and applying foundation, these are certainly never shown as labor but rather as fun activities. For example, Amena posts "get ready with me" videos or makeup tutorials that turn the tasks of getting dressed and applying makeup into carefree and enjoyable pastimes. She also posts images of makeup or skin care products that viewers can use to improve their own appearances, and images of her teeth before and after straightening them with invisible braces. These images reinforce as normative the constant work required to perfect one's appearance. Amena also posts an image of her open dresser drawers, displaying all of her headscarves folded and perfectly organized. Amena is perfect in both her appearance and her ability to organize and manage her life, thus illustrating the postfeminist assumption that a successful exterior presentation reflects success in one's interior, personal life.

Although most of Amena's images focus on fashion and makeup, they illustrate her success at negotiating the tensions between the postfeminist context and her identity as a Muslim. Her images challenge the stereotype that the only way for Muslim women to be empowered is to abandon Islam, take off the headscarf and embrace sexual liberation. Amena shows that Muslim women can be quite successful in contemporary Western society while still following their faith and dressing modestly. Amena has posted a few images that highlight her faith and exhibit the productive potential of the ambivalent spaces between the pressures of postfeminism and the stereotypes of the oppressed Muslim woman. For instance, the image captioned "Stunned by the tranquility of the Ortakoy Mosque" shows Amena in an identifiably Islamic setting, a mosque in Turkey. This is one of the few images of Amena that exhibits a practice of Islam (prayer), without allusion to consumption or fashion. This image appears to be staged because Amena is located in a position that perfectly frames her body in light from the window. Amena's head and hands are illuminated as she kneels and prays in the ornately decorated mosque. Her facial expression is serene with closed eyes. Amena's pious and serious expression is atypical, although it is consistent with her overall visual theme: presenting herself as calm, competent, attractive, and positive, but not too assertive or exuberant. This image is notable because it focuses on Amena's faith and not her fashion. The grandeur of the mosque is more prominent than is Amena, whose body is positioned in one corner of the image. Amena does not need to abandon her faith in order to be an empowered woman.

### Dina Torkia: Successful Entrepreneur

The images on Dina Torkia's Instagram page reinforce, as do Amena's, the ideal form of femininity, but Dina's images also cement her identity as an effective entrepreneur, another important element of postfeminism. For instance, in "Its shoot day for @dinatorkia collection," we see Dina in front of a mirror preparing for a fashion photo shoot. She is surrounded by her makeup gear, and in the background her husband prepares some outfits. She is showing viewers the behind-the-scenes aspects of her work. Her expression is calm and competent; everything is clearly under control. Another photo, "@theworldmuslimah pageant begins as of tomorrow," also provides an insider look at Dina's busy life. She is being interviewed by a film crew, and the camera angle shows two images of Dina: one of her sitting on a coach and another through the lens of the video camera. This image visually reinforces her popularity—she is being featured in a BBC documentary. Again, Dina looks confident and sophisticated; she is comfortable on camera. Another image shows the #bts (behind-the-scenes) of another photo shoot, "Love this #bts shot by @slegamma from our @dinatorkia debut shoot!" It features Dina carefully arranging a scarf on the neck of a mannequin. Her face is serious and focused. She is not just a pretty face, but a competent and successful fashion designer and business owner.

In addition to images of Dina working as a fashion designer, most of her Instagram page features photographs of Dina's clothing line. Dina herself poses in most of these images, which serve as fashion lookbooks of her recent collections. Although some of Amena's images do reinforce Western codes of gender, such as the photo of her with her hand caressing her husband's shoulder, the vast majority of Dina's fashion images employ the set of gestures and poses common in Western fashion photography and advertisements. These gendered codes solidify the dominant ways of seeing women as perfect objects of sight. For example, Dina commonly poses with one hand up by her face, gently touching her hijab, such as in the images "Loving my kimono" and "Feeling that ELEGANCE in my paisley abbaya." Goffman argued that the "feminine touch" in advertisements symbolizes passivity and delicacy in women (1979, p. 29). The woman is represented as having a soft touch that just grazes over the surface but is not strong or in control. It is also notable that Dina's hand frequently touches her headscarf, which may evoke the gesture in harem photography when the Muslim woman would remove her veil and become sexually available. In her effort to present an image of Muslim women as modern and beautiful, some of these images and Dina's gestures harken back to the visual history of the sexualization of the Muslim female body. In another photo, "ZARA. Todays look," Dina appears in a two poses wearing the same outfit: a long tunic with jeans and a neutral-colored headscarf. The clothes hide the form of Dina's body and reflect modest fashion, but her poses engage with mainstream fashion and reinforce powerlessness. In one, she stands with her legs crossed, which Goffman argued presented women as weaker, unstable, and less able to respond. Dina's expression is common to her (and indeed mainstream) fashion photographs: aloof and staring off into space. Goffman argued that this appearance of "mentally drifting" as if in a dream or trance reinforces the subjects' weakness (1979, p. 65). In the companion image, showing only Dina's torso and legs, she clasps her arms across her chest— not in the defiant and strong folded arms stance of a male authority figure but as a scared and powerless woman. Dina is a successful fashion entrepreneur, but the gestures in these fashion shots might reinforce for some viewers that Dina is just another passive female body that becomes the object of the gaze. Still, the headscarves and modest clothing in the images prevent viewers from gawking at the contours of Dina's body. Dina may be employing gestures from mainstream fashion photography not to highlight her sexuality but rather to display the beauty and legitimacy of Islamic fashion. Her photos demonstrate that Islamic fashion, as well as Islam's focus on modest beauty standards, can be seen on the same level as other forms of fashion.

Besides the fact that Dina wears the headscarf and modest clothing in her images, few of her photos emphasize other aspects of her Islamic identity. She does post the occasional image to celebrate religious holidays, such as one titled "Happy Ramadan everyone!" This image features the Blue Mosque in Turkey with "Happy Ramadan" written in Arabic across the sky. This picture is different from most of her pictures because Dina is not in it and it is not about fashion. Dina posted "Another piccy with The Blue mosque!," and although it includes a mosque, this image is different from Amena Khan's photo discussed above. Dina stands in front of the famous mosque, positioned in the lower left corner of the image. She has turned her head to reveal her profile. She stares off into the distance, with no indication that she is pondering her faith, and her left hand lightly touches her neck. She wears a flowered, turban-style headscarf, a black and white striped blouse, and purple hoop necklaces. Between Dina and the mosque, numerous tourists and souvenir kiosks are visible. There is no direct connection between Dina and the religious experiences of going to the mosque. The mosque seems a backdrop for her fashionable outfit; it is her headscarf, not the mosque, that identifies her faith.

### Nye Armstrong: Flawed but Trying

Individuals such as Amena and Dina set a high standard for how young Muslim women are expected to behave and appear in public, but Nye Armstrong offers a more balanced take on the struggles of living in the postfeminist context. Among the three Instagram pages, Nye's images go the furthest in displaying the ambivalences of life as a Muslim woman in the West. Several of her images focus on Islam and not fashion, but Nye often posts images illustrating her attempts to be a successful postfeminist subject. For example, Nye overtly seems to monitor her body, appearance, and actions, and she is open about how difficult it is to achieve the beauty ideals. She is far from the flawless and carefree Amena or the confident and successful Dina. In postfeminism, every aspect of a woman's life is always up for scrutiny. Nye represents the opposite end of the spectrum—someone constantly struggling with her life. Even though Nye is the only one who openly struggles, all three women engage in the same self-work and self-monitoring expected of all women in the postfeminist culture.

Nye's Instagram page is littered with images of her personal failings: spilled tea on the carpet, her carpal tunnel injured hand, a screen shot of a computer error, and a "meals for one" sign at Target, which highlights Nye's status as a 30-something divorcee. Nye frequently posts silly selfies, which illustrate her personality and are often unflattering. For example, in "Mannequins need hugs too," Nye grins while hugging a mannequin during one of Amena's fashion shows. This image exhibits Nye's sense of humor and is a far cry from the gorgeous images that Amena posts. Nye wears a simple headscarf, a plain white shirt, and maybe a little bit of makeup. There is nothing glamorous about her appearance. She awkwardly hugs the mannequin, her head nestled in the breasts and her arms wrapped around the butt. It is an unnatural pose that also highlights that Nye is twice as wide as the stick-thin mannequin. Even though this image shows Nye's personality, the postfeminist eye is trained to see that she has failed both at maintaining a healthy body weight and at always looking beautiful.

Many of Nye's images document her work to try to improve herself, both inside and out. She posts images of her exercise routines, of eating healthy food one day and junk food the next, and of herself after getting a makeover at the mall. A photo captioned "Just changed into outfit 4" allows the viewer to relate to the frustration of not finding an outfit that fits or looks just right. Nye's face expresses her frustration; she is about to exhale a large sigh, and her eyes seem angry. This image would never appear on Amena's page. Nye, on the other hand, is almost expected to post these images to show that she is *trying* and that living within this postfeminist context is exhausting. In "Rate the jacket 1–10," Nye asks for her followers' feedback on a jacket she is trying on at the store. Obviously, many women get feedback when shopping with friends, but in this social media context, it is almost as if Nye asks her followers to rate her and how well she wears this jacket. Again, Amena and Dina would never ask their viewers to decide on their clothing. Amena and Dina are fashion experts who know what to wear, but Nye seems to seek constant approval that she is successful at (or at least trying to be) living in this culture.

Unlike Dina and Amena's Instagram pages, Nye posts many images that reflect her personal religious beliefs and practices. Perhaps because Nye works for an Islamic education organization, she posts many images promoting lectures and online resources. She also posts photos of her personal work to gain Islamic knowledge: attending lectures with prominent scholars, learning Arabic, and praying at the mosque. Nye posts a picture of a scholar recording a video. Reminiscent of Dina Torkia's image of her documentary shoot, this also shows the scholar speaking and the camera crew recording him. Nye is not present in this image, signifying that the religious beliefs are more important than her own image. The caption also highlights the religious experience, "Blessed to be able to watch this in person. Alhumdulillah [praise be to God]!"

In "Softening my heart," Nye takes a photo in a mosque while the imam is giving the sermon. The quality of this photo is nothing compared to the dramatic beauty of Amena Khan's mosque image. In Nye's photo, the room is dark and bland. The carpet is dull green, the wall is white, and the low ceiling is covered in acoustic tiles. A large pole in the center of the picture is wrapped in a tangle of black wires. Men are arranged on the floor in front of the imam, who is barely visible. Nothing about the image is visually appealing, but the existence of this image on Nye's page emphasizes her religious values and the caption highlights her faith, "Alhumdulillah for every opportunity to get closer to our creator." This image is one of many on Nye's page that are not about her successes or failures at living in the postfeminist context, but rather reflect how Nye's religion helps her to live a more fulfilling life.

## Ambivalences and the Political Potential
## of Islamic Fashion Images

Through an examination of the Instagram images of Amena Khan, Dina Torkia, and Nye Armstrong, this chapter has explored the ways that these women represent their lives as Muslims in the West. Although it may be easy to dismiss the women's online work, especially the work of fashion gurus Amena and Dina, as just reinforcing the postfeminist emphasis on appearances, the presence of Islam within these images signifies more complexity. These women are under constant pressure to visually present their lives in ways that contradict traditional Western visualities of the Muslim woman as hyper-sexualized or oppressed, and consequently, the women engage with visual elements of postfeminism in many images by presenting themselves as embodying a beautiful and impeccable form of femininity, constantly surveying their bodies and actions to maintain perfection, and consuming and selling products to achieve success.

On the other hand, several of the images on Nye's page as well as the image of Amena praying in the mosque complicate the argument that the women are just falling into the postfeminist trap with no avenue for liberation. The fact that this image of Amena praying at a mosque appears among her lifestyle images illustrates the ambivalences of the contemporary culture and the productive potential of ambivalences. It is possible for Amena to be a successful consumer, a fashionable dresser, and a pious Muslim. Amena is doing something distinct in this image: she is using her body to exhibit the beauty of Islam. Consumption, self-work, makeup, and beauty routines did not produce the subject pictured in this image; the photo presents Islam as bearing the sole responsibility for this beauty. The presence of this image on Amena's Instagram page does not take away from the ambivalences and tensions present throughout her images, but Amena may be attempting to negotiate elements of her intersectional identity: to practice her faith and maintain modesty, to appear as the perfect and beautiful postfeminist subject, and to resist stereotypes about the oppression and hyper-sexuality of Muslim women.

Instead of just focusing on dichotomies between Islam and Western culture or between authentic public engagement and the exploitation of postfeminism, it is more productive to examine the multifaceted tensions arising as various elements of Muslim women's identities intersect. For instance, the Islamic values of modesty, piety, and humility are subtly present in these Instagram images and complicate the ideals of postfeminism. Postfeminism has been useful in reflecting on how neoliberalism has pressured women to value their physical appearance and sexuality, but postfeminism can be overly simplistic in its judgment of women, such as these lifestyle gurus, as falling for a false sense of liberation through an empty focus on beauty, fashion, and consumption. The images that Amena, Dina, and Nye post on Instagram reflect the ambivalences of their lives as Muslim women in the West. These women carefully walk a line between practicing Islamic ethics of modesty and piety without appearing oppressed or controlled by the religion, and participating in mainstream fashion trends without being subsumed by a focus on appearances.

Through their Instagram images, Amena, Dina, and Nye engage with what Sarah Banet-Weiser (2013, p. 14) called the "ambivalence" of the contemporary brand culture because they live within tensions between the pressure to represent Islam in a positive light and the expectations that young women brand themselves online as beautiful, perfect, and successful. Banet-Weiser argued that these ambivalent spaces are not necessarily shallow spaces where, for example, people falsely believe they can solve social problems through Facebook. Instead, the ambivalences of brand culture are productive spaces in which people can construct identities, cultural activities, and political actions. Ambivalences have potential and generative power, Banet-Weiser wrote, "for it is within these spaces that hope and anxiety, pleasure and desire, fear and insecurity are nurtured and maintained" (2013, p. 218). In these Instagram images we can see glimpses of the negotiation between the authenticity of Islam and the market demands to consume and brand oneself. Just because these young women exhibit an interest in consumption does not mean that their work should be disregarded as inauthentic.

The one element of these images that signifies the unique experiences of these three women is the incorporation of Islam. All of these images are marked as distinctly Islamic because of the presence of modest clothing and headscarves. Nye's images go furthest in emphasizing Islam's impact on her daily life and spreading Islamic values and teachings. Returning to Tarlo and Moors's work on Islamic fashion, these women have produced a nuanced picture of Islamic femininity that fights against both the visuality of Muslim women as oppressed and the visuality of women as sexualized objects of sight. Their photos show them women as fashionable and independent while still maintaining modesty and Islamic piety. Tarlo and Moors explained that because of the headscarves, Muslim women are aware that "as a marked category, they can never escape the burden of representation," and therefore they want to portray Islam in a positive light (2013, p. 20). Tarlo discussed how Muslim women deal with what she called the "representational challenge" of their visibility in public while wearing the headscarf: "through experimenting with style and adopting mainstream fashions, innovative young hijabi women develop and project assertive and attractive self-images which correspond to their complex backgrounds, interests and concerns whilst simultaneously challenging and combating dominant negative stereotypes of Muslims" (2010, p. 74). Similarly, these three young Muslim women use Instagram as a space to display the complexity and ambivalences of their lives. To simply dismiss these images as vacuous and meaningless misses the real political potential of the ambivalences within these images. These Muslim women are able to use their images to resist dominant stereotypes of Muslim women as oppressed and hyper-sexualized by showing themselves as individuals with creative fashion styles who maintain modesty in dress and behavior.

# References

Abu-Lughod, L. (2002). Do Muslim women really need saving? Anthropological reflections on cultural relativism and its others. *American Anthropologist, 104*(3), 783–790.

Alloula, M. (2013). From *The Colonial Harem*. In N. Mirzoeff (Ed.), *The visual culture reader* (pp. 510–515). London: Routledge.

Banet-Weiser, S. (2013). *Authentic* ™: *The politics of ambivalence in a brand culture*. New York, NY: New York University Press.

Barnard, M. (2002). *Fashion as communication*. London: Routledge.

Berger, J. (1977). *Ways of seeing*. London: BBC and Penguin Books.

Bint-Abubaker, R. (2015, July 3). The rise of the Muslim fashion industry. *Huffington Post Style UK*. Retrieved October 8, 2015, from http://www.huffingtonpost.co.uk/romanna-bint-abubaker/muslim-fashion_b_3045171.html.

Gill, R. (2007). Postfeminist media culture: Elements of a sensibility. *European Journal of Cultural Studies, 10*(2), 147–166.

Goffman, E. (1979). *Gender advertisements*. Cambridge, MA: Harvard University Press.

Hall, S. (2000). Encoding/Decoding. In P. Marris & S. Thornham (Eds.), *Media studies: A reader* (pp. 51–61). New York, NY: New York University Press.

Hebdige, D. (1979). *Subculture: The meaning of style*. London: Metheun.

Jones, A. (2010). Introduction: Conceiving the intersection of feminism and visual culture, again. In A. Jones (Ed.), *The feminism and visual culture reader* (pp. 1–8). London: Routledge.

Kaiser, S. B. (2012). *Fashion and cultural studies*. London: Berg.

McRobbie, A. (2009). *The aftermath of postfeminism: Gender, culture and social change*. London: Sage.

Mirzoeff, N. (2009). *An introduction to visual culture*. London: Routledge.

Moors, A. & Tarlo, E. (2013). Introduction. In E. Tarlo & A. Moors (Eds.), *Islamic fashion and anti-fashion: New perspectives from Europe and North America* (pp. 1–30). London: Bloomsbury.

Said, E. W. (1978). *Orientalism*. London: Routledge & Kegan Paul.

Siddiqi, D. (2014). Sexuality as liberation? The work of salvation narratives in neoliberal times. *Alal O Dulal*. Retrieved October 8, 2015, from http://alalodulal.org/2014/03/13/sexuality-as-liberation/.

Tarlo, E. (2010). *Visibly Muslim: Fashion, politics, faith*. Oxford: Berg.

Tasker, Y. & Negra, D. (2007). Introduction: Feminist politics and postfeminist culture. In Y. Tasker & D. Negra (Eds.), *Interrogating postfeminism: Gender and the politics of popular culture* (pp. 1–25). Durham, NC: Duke University Press.

Weber, B. M. (2013). *Violence and gender in the "new" Europe*. New York, NY: Palgrave Macmillan.

# Part III

# CULTURE
## Media Industries, Policy, Production

# 16

# WOMEN'S ACCESS TO MEDIA

## Legal Dimensions of Ownership and Employment in the United States

*Carolyn M. Byerly and Alisa Valentin*

Historically women have recognized the importance of media access as a condition for equality, yet in the United States women have owned or controlled few major media companies. Recently, women have also experienced glass ceilings in media employment, where they are stuck in middle management and severely under-represented on boards of directors. Women's structural relationship to the media that enables women's media access, as defined by regulations, laws, and legal cases, remains an understudied area of feminist communication scholarship. In this chapter, we help fill this gap by reviewing legal developments in the United States related to women's ability to own their own companies, and to be treated equally alongside men in hiring, compensation, and promotion in media professions. Because the women-and-media relationship has been a dynamic one brought about through feminist action over the years, we also examine women's agency in challenging exclusion and discrimination since the 1970s in order to expand ownership and employment.

The broadcast media (by law a public resource) are the only mass communications media whose ownership has historically been regulated; however, as media companies have become increasingly consolidated, their ownership practices have come under federal purview. Media companies have also come under federal scrutiny for their employment practices, which (like other workplaces) are regulated by national labor laws on equality and discrimination.

Many parties are involved with the activities and processes surrounding women's media access. With regard to federal regulation, the main administrative agencies of concern in this chapter will be the Federal Communications Commission (FCC), which is responsible for licensing broadcast stations and determining ownership limits (among other things), and the Equal Employment Opportunities Commission (EEOC), which adjudicates complaints. The federal courts have also been important in determining women's access to media. Beyond the formal political and legal apparatus are women media professionals and women within the broader citizenry, both of whom have a vested interest in media access. This broader context of women's interest in media access grounds the chapter in a critical feminist theory of women's right to communicate.

We focus on statutes, regulations, and court decisions affecting women's media ownership and employment, as well as women's agency in trying to bring about greater access to the media through employment and ownership. Many of the barriers to women's access to media have also blocked racial and ethnic access; therefore, gender and race will sometimes be intertwined in the discussion.

## The Problem of Women's Media Access

Women's media access in this discussion refers to women's ability to own or to hold positions of decision making in media companies, or to otherwise achieve positions of authority such as to determine the direction and content of information disseminated by media companies (Byerly, 2014).

According to Byerly (forthcoming), women in the United States in 2012 owned 50% or more of the voting shares in only 7.8% of the 3,830 full-powered AM stations, 6.7% of the 5,611 full-powered FM stations, and 6.8% of the full-powered television stations. Their representation on the boards of the largest diversified media companies is also low: 8% on Comcast, 14% on CBS, 17% on Time Warner Cable, and 25% on News Corp's boards. Even in media companies where women have slightly higher representation on boards of directors (e.g., Disney at 30% and Viacom at 31%), that representation is still well under parity with men (Byerly, forthcoming). Although women own 30% of all privately-owned firms in the US, these are mainly small enterprises, employing only 6% of the country's workforce and contributing only 4% of all business revenues (American Express, 2014, p. 2).

Women's employment in news media industries has been unable to rise above these low percentages. Women's journalism employment has suffered as the number of jobs has declined due to conglomeration and other shifts in the industry. Women's newsroom employment fell from 20,323 full-time journalism positions in 1999 to only 14,971 in 2012 (Women's Media Center, 2013, p. 10). In both traditional newspapers and online news sites, women journalists also face gender discrepancies and are relegated to covering soft news stories such as health and entertainment rather than economics, government, and politics.

Women's progress in securing supervisory positions in journalism is similar to their slow progress in other sectors. Nationally, women in managerial and professional occupations increased by just over 6%—from 33.2% to 39.9%—in the 12 years between 2001 and 2013 (IWPR, 2015, p. xvii). It bears noting that in the same approximate period, women's representation increased by equally small numbers in both houses of Congress—from 14 to 20 (20%) in the Senate and 60 to 84 (18%) in the House of Representatives (IWPR, 2015, p. xvii). Presently, three of the U.S. Supreme Court's nine justices are women; however, historically the court has been all or nearly all male. Thus, women have also been severely under-represented in the legal structures where they might advocate more actively for women's equal access in media through legislation and high court action.

Our study of legal developments affecting women's access to media through ownership and employment is situated within the literatures on women's right to communicate, women's media employment, and women's media ownership.

## Women's Right to Communicate

Women's right to free expression in the United States is guaranteed by the First Amendment to the Constitution, which provides freedom of speech and of the press. However, most research on women and the First Amendment has studied women's right to express their opinions (on issues such as abortion or pornography), rather than women's right to expression as facilitated by media employment or ownership.

The international feminist literature does address the latter concerns. Gallagher (1981) and Rush and Allen (1989) identified women's universal media concerns as media representation, professional marginalization, and women's ability to control content. Rush and Allen (1989) laid theoretical ground by problematizing the second and third of these as constituting a "question of who has constructed and continues to construct social reality" (1989, p. 17). They challenged communication scholars to see the First Amendment as one that should encompass women's access to media in order to speak. Without access to the channels of communication, they said, women were silenced, and argued that abundant evidence pointed to media industries as "a closed marketplace" that routinely denied participation—that is, access—by those who held aberrant beliefs (1989, p. 17).

Thus, access to media (through greater control of production and messaging) is essential for women to exercise their right to communicate. McLaughlin (1993) expanded the conceptual space related to access by invoking Habermas's notion of a public sphere—or more accurately, she said, a masculine public sphere in which political discourse might lead to social and political policy formation. Byerly and Ross (2006) adopted that reasoning when constructing their Model of Women's Media Action to illustrate how women's media activism had contributed to creating a feminist public sphere, or a communicative space where women articulated a politics of equality and advancement.

More recently, Gallagher linked media policy to women's free expression. She observed that "the apparent impregnability of 'freedom of expression' discourse in the gender equality domain gives rise to an inevitable question: Whose freedom, defined by whom?" (2011, p. 457). She said that "a radical re-balancing of gender determined rights and freedoms may seem unrealistic, at least at this point," but emphasized that women's right to freedom of expression and information is severely limited by "layers of structural, economic, and cultural constraints" (p. 457). Thus, structural constraints may be understood to include women's ownership. Gallagher (2012) observed that gender-based censorship, such as that occurring in the news media, results in women's relative invisibility and silence, and obscures the reality of women's lives. The role of women journalists then must be understood as key to women's right to communicate about men's violence and all other things in women's interests.

## Women's Media Employment

Many studies have focused on women's employment in media, particularly journalism professions. Most specifically is Strategic Objective J—the program for action in the Beijing Women's Conference of 1995, which recognized that the media sector represented a cross-national network with the power to influence "public policy, private attitudes and behavior, especially of children and young adults" (UN Women, 1995). It acknowledged "the potential for the media to make a far greater contribution to the advancement of women," but that women had "attained few positions on [media] governing boards and bodies that influence media policy," hence "gender-based stereotyping" continued in media at local, national, and international levels, thereby reinforcing the barriers to women's social advancement (UN Women, 1995). The strategic objective set forth the mandate to move women into media decision-making roles and to create alternative non-mainstream communication channels using new media to enable women "to participate fully in their growth and impact" (UN Women, 1995).

Two recent international studies responding to these principles demonstrate the extent to which women have—and have not—advanced in media professions. The *Global Report on the Status of Women in News Media* (Byerly, 2011) was a 59-nation, 522-company study revealing male domination in the news industry: men held three quarters of the positions on boards of directors and in top management, and two thirds (74%) of reporting jobs. Women were best represented in the newsrooms of Eastern and Nordic Europe. A European Institute for Gender Equality-funded study (EIGE, 2013) showed that women in Europe had progressed only marginally in media professions since the mid-1990s, with results closely paralleling those of Byerly's *Global Report*. Women held only 24% of the positions on boards of the 99 companies surveyed, and only 16% of top management positions. Those studies illustrated a pervasive pattern of glass ceilings for women at mid-management in the media industries.

In the US, the Women's Media Center (2015) found a significant gender gap in employment, with women holding about only one third of the jobs in print news, evening news broadcasts, and news agency wire services, and 42% of Internet news site jobs.

Laws have had much to do with women's ability to challenge exclusion and sexism in media, as shown by Crichton (2014), who noted that the 1970s saw numerous seminal legal challenges to sex discrimination by women at *Newsweek* and other companies that used the Equal Pay Act of 1963 and Title VII of the Civil Rights Act of 1964 as the bases for their complaints. Women were able to make "meteoric advances" (Crichton, 2014, p. 55) in media companies after these equality laws were passed, but then faced glass ceilings, marginalization by masculine traditions of gender-stereotyping and sexual harassment. Crichton noted that restrictions to women's advancement persist even today, due to what she called a "resurgence of 'gendered news categories'" cloaked in a "'new' journalism tradition" (p. 102) emphasizing style over substance, and with feature soft-news reporting typically assigned to women while men retain their hold on hard news. The problem for women journalists today, she said, is that they are less likely to file discrimination lawsuits than their predecessors were in the 1970s—an issue to be probed in more depth below.

## Women's Media Ownership

Women's media ownership is generally understood as women owning 51% or more of a company's voting stock. Byerly (1995, 2014, forthcoming) has demonstrated that women's problems with employment and control over content lie in the macro-level of media policy, finance and ownership. She has argued that women's media activism should focus on developing interventions to reform federal ownership policies in order to break up media conglomerates. She also favors supporting lawsuits (e.g., the *Prometheus* cases discussed below) challenging further deregulation of ownership, in order to protect women's access to ownership. Byerly and Ross (2006) showed that women's media activism has been a key element in changing women's relationship to media industries, and that women-owned media enterprises give women the greatest control over employment and content.

Feminist media scholars in the United States have rarely focused on women's ownership in the larger industry or policy content. An exception is Byerly's qualitative study of women's broadcast ownership in which she interviewed 40 female owners of radio and television stations as well as experts on women's ownership. She found that women who own and operate stations do so in a hostile regulatory environment and in an industry that "blocks women from gaining experience and access to capital to prepare and successfully compete" for station ownership (2011, p. 24).

Women's media ownership has also been problematized and examined by researchers in governmental and non-governmental agencies. The first major study of female broadcast ownership was based on a statistical analysis of FCC Form 323 reports (ERLA Group, 1982). The researchers measured gender in ownership of AM, FM, and TV stations by size of community. The study established that 24% of the stockholders of AM stations, 20% of FM stations and 17% of TV stations were female (ERLA Group, 1982). The FCC-commissioned study also revealed that more than 85% of the females owning stock in broadcast stations were related to the male owners, most commonly as wife or mother. More recently, the advocacy group Free Press (Turner & Cooper, 2006; Turner, 2007) conducted studies on women's broadcast ownership, finding percentages of female station ownership in the low single digits.

## Impact of Legal Cases

Our feminist critical approach examines structural aspects of women's marginality and advancement in communications industries and considers women's efforts to remove barriers to media ownership and employment. Our approach involved analyzing the history of laws, court rulings, and FCC policies relevant to gender in employment and assessing the implications thereof. We sought to learn which event(s) prompted the adoption of key laws affecting women's relationships to the media, how women have used those laws to gain access to media through ownership and employment, and how the courts have ruled when women have used laws to challenge discrimination.

To locate relevant case law we searched the LexisNexis database using keyword combinations such as "women and media" and "women's media employment." We also identified laws and policies cited in relevant and formal FCC comments submitted by feminist-oriented groups such as the National Organization of Women and the Institute for Public Representation. We tracked the year of the event, determined who was president, identified the parties involved (plaintiffs, etc.), and noted the implications for women. An abbreviated version of this information is provided in chronological order in Table 16.1 (see pp. 281ff.).

Women's agency in effecting changes in law and policy was of particular interest, and thus we took note of feminist advocacy, as well as coalition advocacy, such as when women's groups joined with civil rights groups to challenge cases involving sex and race discrimination.

## Impact of Civil Rights and Feminist Movements

Both civil rights and feminist movements have engaged in legal activism to increase access in employment and ownership for racial minorities and women in the United States. What is often called "second wave feminism" began in 1966 with the founding of the National Organization for Women (Rosen, 2000). NOW's existence owed much to the civil rights movement that preceded it and whose legal agendas were relevant to women. For example, women's employment relationship to the media was greatly enhanced by the passage of Title VII, amending the 1964 Civil Rights Act to prohibit workplace discrimination on the basis of sex, race, color, national origin, and religion. In 1972, the Equal Employment Opportunity Commission (EEOC) was formed to administer the provisions of the act and its amendments, and was authorized to investigate and conciliate charges of discrimination.

A major EEOC case concerning women's advancement was brought against *Newsweek* magazine in 1970. On the day that 46 female employees began to protest the magazine for job discrimination, the cover of *Newsweek* read "Women in Revolt" with a caricature of a woman raising her fist in the air (Beasley & Gibbons, 2003). The magazine's reporting on the women's uprising within its ranks marked a historic moment—it brought a major news focus to women's challenge to employment discrimination in its own newsroom, but it caricatured (and therefore trivialized) that challenge. The lawsuit at *Newsweek* was, nevertheless, a spark that ignited women journalists' fights for equal wages and career advancement in U.S. companies. In 1972, led by Catherine Mackin, women at WRC-TV, an NBC-owned station in Washington, DC, filed a lawsuit challenging sex discrimination. According to *The New York Times* (1982), Mackin was the first woman to work as a television reporter on the floor of the Democratic and Republican National Conventions. Mackin and several of her female colleagues raised questions about inequality in pay for men and women and the lack of opportunities for advancement (Beasley & Gibbons, 2003). The women won, with the court requiring the television station to alter its hiring and promotion practices. The ruling directly affected female and Black employees (Beasley & Gibbons, 2003).

Unfortunately, there have also been cases in which the courts did not rule in favor of the plaintiffs, as in *New York City Chapter of National Organization for Women v. FCC*, in 1972. The Center for Constitutional Rights (CCR) represented NOW in challenging the license renewal of WABC-TV in New York City on the grounds of sexual discrimination. The case is seen as the first sweeping challenge to the treatment of women in the media. CCR's attorneys, who claimed sex discrimination in both employment and programming, built their legal case on evidence gathered by NOW members in what the CCR described as "extensive monitoring studies" of WABC-TV (Center for Constitutional Rights, 2007). The petition to deny the license renewal said that the station had presented a distorted, one-sided image of women, employed fewer women than did any other local station and had refused to consult with women's groups on programming. The parties negotiated for months but were unable to work out their differences, and the FCC eventually ruled that the station had not discriminated against women in either employment or programming. In its appeal to the DC District Court of Appeals, NOW and other grassroots groups joined to challenge the license renewal of a second station, WRC-TV (a local ABC affiliate), in conjunction with the WABC-TV case. In 1977, the court affirmed the FCC's original decision. Although these cases were not successful, they had two important outcomes. According to the Center for Constitutional Rights (2007), this case was later used as a national model for similar challenges to TV stations for sex discrimination. The second outcome was encouragement for stations to hire more women, particularly as camera operators, and to improve programming to meet women's needs. In other words, although women's legal challenges in these two companion cases did not have a direct positive effect, they had an important indirect effect of motivating stations to adopt measures before women challenged their practices.

Institutionalized sexism continued to hold women back, however, and, in 1991, Part II of the Civil Rights Act of 1991 created the Glass Ceiling Commission. Some of the recommendations in the commission's report, *Solid Investment: Making Full Use of the Nation's Human Capital* (1995) included selecting, promoting, and retaining qualified individuals who can assist in bettering the organization, and preparing minorities and women for senior decision-making positions. These recommendations were especially applicable to women in the media industry. Additional recommendations included proposals for improved data collection and disclosure of diversity data.

## Using the Law for Access

When women have used laws to petition the courts for remedies to employment discrimination, it has not always been just to provide a way for individual women to redress immediate grievances, but sometimes to establish case law (i.e., precedence) and policies or mechanisms to improve conditions for others. These broader goals were seen, for example, in a 1972 court case in which an EEOC ruling against *The Washington Post* found that female employees were restricted from upward mobility and preference had often been given to males. Following the case, the newspaper established a scholarship and sabbatical program for women employees; these enabled women to advance and by 1986, *The Washington Post* reported that 40% of its reporters, assignment editors, and critics were women (Palmeira, 2012).

More recently, women saw some hope for success in what would be called the *Prometheus I* and *II* federal court decisions. In 2003, FCC Chairman Michael Powell and the commission's Republican majority—all appointed by President George W. Bush—had proposed further relaxation of regulations governing the number of radio and television stations and newspapers that a single company could own. The Prometheus Radio Project, a Philadelphia-based non-profit organization that helps community groups establish low-power radio stations, sued the FCC, charging that further media consolidation would threaten smaller broadcast companies (Prometheus Radio Project, 2011). Represented by Andrew Schwartzman and Cheryl Leanza of the Media Access Project, the Prometheus Radio Project case served to coalesce a range of feminist and other activist groups to prevent what they saw as discriminatory practices by the FCC. The Third Circuit Court of Appeals' 2004 landmark 2-to-1 ruling agreed with the plaintiffs, mandating that the FCC retain the previous ownership rules until commissioners could provide a rationale for changes. More relevant to the present discussion, the court ruled that the commission would have to consider ways to address the low rates of broadcast ownership by women and minorities (Byerly, Park, & Miles, 2011; Prometheus Radio Project, 2011).

Seven years later, the FCC still had not complied with the 2004 ruling by undertaking studies or adopting mechanisms to address the low levels of media ownership by minorities and women. Moreover, the commission was again poised—this time under a Democratic majority—to relax ownership rules that would have overturned a 35-year ban on allowing companies to own both a newspaper and broadcast stations in a single market. This time the legal case was led by attorney Angela Campbell of the Georgetown Law Center's Institute for Public Representation (which included National Organization for Women among the clients it represented in the case). Plaintiffs again succeeded in arguing that allowing cross-ownership would thwart competition and harm small broadcast owners, particularly women and minorities. In its second landmark ruling, the Third Circuit Court of Appeals' affirmed its earlier requirement that the FCC address minority and women's ownership (Free Press, 2011). The court thus created the legal space for gender- and race-conscious regulation and for remedies for low levels of ownership by women and minorities in broadcast. However, as of early 2016, the commission has still failed to respond, and the situation has worsened in terms of both women's and minorities' broadcast ownership (see Byerly, Park, & Miles, 2011; Byerly, forthcoming).

## Settling Without Admitting Fault

At times, media companies have settled out of court or implemented company policies to assist in the upward mobility of plaintiffs, even without acknowledging responsibility for discriminatory practices against women.

This occurred in the 1973 case filed on women employees' behalf by the EEOC against the Associated Press (AP). An out of court settlement was reached, and the company developed an affirmative action plan for women and minorities (Beasley & Gibbons, 2003); as a result, the number of women working at AP doubled in the next five years, from 22% in 1983 to 44% in 1988. An increase of women's employment also occurred in the 1975 case of *Women's Committee for Equal Employment Opportunity v. National Broadcasting Co, Inc.*, when the court allowed the EEOC to intervene on women's behalf. The two parties entered a consent decree, which had various "utilization goals," including a specific percentage of women to be in certain positions.

The *Reader's Digest* (1973) case, in which eight female employees sued the magazine on the basis of promotion, hiring, and reporting assignments, among other issues, provided plaintiffs with a $1.5 million out-of-court settlement and set important legal precedent in securing back pay, raises, and mechanisms to advance more women into top editorial jobs (Beasley & Gibbons, 2003, "Readers Digest Settles," 1977).

## Gender, Race, and the FCC

As noted earlier, women's progress in the communication industry was often influenced by the efforts of racial minorities. In the *TV 9, Inc. v. FCC* (1973) decision, the court reasoned that merit should be given to racial minorities in order to diversify viewpoints. That same reasoning would be extended to women through several cases, including, for example, the 1975 *Rosemore Broadcasting Co., Inc. v. FCC* decision in which female applicants advanced the notion that, as with race, the gender of owners would increase the diversity of content for its female viewers. The company's use of gender as a basis for its argument led to a victory in gaining the broadcast license it had originally sought through a comparative hearing (FCC, 2000).

Soon after these decisions, the FCC released its *Statement of Policy on Minority Ownership*, explaining minority merits in the comparative hearing process and describing two programs—the tax certificate policy and the distress sale policy—which were designed to facilitate minority ownership of broadcast stations (FCC, 2000). Reinforcing the merit of minority ownership, the U.S. Supreme Court upheld the distress policy:

> [M]inority ownership policies bear the imprimatur of longstanding congressional support and direction and are substantially related to the achievement of the important governmental objective of broadcast diversity.
>
> (*Metro Broadcasting Inc. v. FCC*, 1990, as cited in Cornell University Law School Legal Information Institute, n.d.)

However, this decision ignored the merits of sex. Gender preferences in ownership policies had been introduced with the *Gainesville Media, Inc.* Review Board (1978) case. An applicant argued reconsideration for the awarding of a license, claiming she should not be subjected to punishment because of an employee's conduct. It was at this time the Review Board addressed items not raised in the pleading, but rather items that needed to be clarified, including the "additional point" one received for being a female shareholder.

Although the Board had once decided there was no evidence that female ownership would be of benefit to the public, it now claimed the better course would be to consider female ownership and participation, despite the absence of recorded evidence on ownership situations at other stations. For a moment in time it appeared as though there would be a gender preference applied in comparative hearings to assess applicants' suitability. Then the Review Board revisited that decision in the *Mid-Florida Television Corp. v. FCC* (1978) ruling. In this decision, the Review Board acknowledged that women had suffered as a result of discriminatory practices, but said it viewed women's suffering as less significant than that of racial minorities. Thereafter, any consideration of applicants' sex, the Board said, would be limited and secondary to that of race in the hearings process.

### Women's Progress Stalled by the FCC

The progress of women in media was also slowed a decade later in the *Steele v. FCC* (1989) ruling by the DC Circuit Court. The court noted that programming choices by women and minorities would differ from those of White males (Hunter, 2012). However, the court remanded the case to the FCC, which at the time had a Republican chairman who had already led the commission toward greater deregulation. Later, Congress attempted to prevent the FCC from completely abolishing preference policies by simply closing the discussion on the issue. This demonstrates the ways in which women's interests in media can become fodder for partisan battles that are largely controlled by male decision makers (Hunter, 2012).

*Pappas v. FCC* (1986) concerned a female applicant, Stella Pappas, who sought licensing for a multi-channel, multi-point distribution service (MMDS, a transmission system allowing for the distribution of television programming). The comparative process for gender preference was expected to provide grounds for significant assistance to individuals underrepresented in the communication industry—in this case females. Due to the large number of applicants, however, the FCC now called the term "minorities" into question in its application to women. The court agreed, ruling that the FCC had acted reasonably when declining to award license preferences to women.

The court again ruled against women in *Lamprecht v. FCC* (1992). Lamprecht, a male applicant, argued that the sex preference in the awarding of licenses violated his constitutional rights, after he lost a bid for a radio station to Marmet, a female applicant. The court held that in granting the license to Marmet on the basis of her gender status, the commission had violated Lamprecht's constitutional right to equal protection. The ruling emphasized that the FCC had failed to demonstrate how gender preference would help achieve greater diversity in the public airwaves (*Lamprecht v. FCC*, 1992).

A few months later came the D.C. Circuit panel's ruling in *Bechtel v. FCC* (Bechtel I, 1992). In this case, a female applicant argued that some criteria for ownership used in comparative hearings did not serve the FCC's original objectives. The panel then remanded the case to the commission for further explanation of how "integration" is of public interest. The FCC had previously defined integration as the full-time participation by owners of a radio station in its management but the *Bechtel I* case prompted the FCC to seek comment on larger rulemaking processes including minority and gender preferences. During the height of the rulemaking process, a second and related ruling by the D.C. Circuit Court—*Bechtel v. FCC* (Bechtel II, 1993)—halted the integration credit, which had given preference to applicants who planned on managing and operating a station individually. The following year, the commission suspended comparative hearings altogether in order for issues raised in *Bechtel* to be addressed.

## Women's Access Hindered by Deregulation

Women were also negatively affected by the first major communications statute overhaul in decades: the Telecommunications Act of 1996, which deregulated the telecommunications industry and abolished many of the restrictions on the number of media outlets companies could own. The Act allowed wealthy individuals and corporations to consolidate their media holdings, creating what has become a media oligopoly landscape. Two years later, FCC Chairman William E. Kennard expressed concern for women's status in that landscape, saying:

> As you all know, promoting opportunities for those underrepresented in the communications industry is a high priority for me. Whether increasing the levels of women-owned television and radio stations, or increasing employment opportunities for women at all levels of the broadcast and cable industries, I believe that this challenge is central to the public interest. But as you know, the challenge for government to adopt remedies is challenging in these times. Courts have struck down our licensing measures to assist women in getting broadcast licenses. Consolidation in the broadcast industry has limited the ownership opportunities for new entrants.
>
> (Kennard, 1998)

His comments were prescient. Nearly two decades later, women make up over 50% of the U.S. population but own less than 7% of TV and radio licenses (Free Press, n.d.; Byerly, forthcoming). Activist groups such as the Prometheus Radio Project, the Center for Media Justice, Women's Institute for Freedom of Press, the Media Action Project, the Institute for Public Representation, the Free Press, and the Minority Media Telecommunications Council, among others, have responded to women's low ownership levels by expanding public awareness and lobbying for structural means to increase minority and women's media ownership.

Feminist groups bringing more specific attention to gender disparities in ownership include National Organization for Women, Association for Women in Communication, Alliance for Women in Media, and American Women in Radio and Television. These groups have a long and sustained history of advocating for women's entry into and advancement in media professions.

Similarly, women's employment in media—both journalism and other media formats—lags substantially behind that of men, as discussed above. Crichton (2014) observed that women journalists are much less likely today to file lawsuits against their employers for discrimination in hiring and advancement than were their counterparts in the 1970s. The reasons for this reluctance are unknown but raise empirical questions for feminist media scholars' research agendas.

Even in successful legal challenges such as the *Prometheus I* and *II* (2004, 2011) rulings, the individuals central to the cases have seen little in the way of material results. These victories have shown that marginalized populations can win in courts, but that little may change in the aftermath. The most successful outcomes have often taken years of legal action on the part of large numbers of activist groups with strong and experienced lawyers having deep knowledge of discrimination, labor laws and the communications industries.

## Women's Right to Communicate Thwarted

We have traced U.S. laws, policies, and court rulings related to women's media employment and ownership with an overarching goal of determining how these have shaped women's right to communicate in a nation that guarantees free expression through its Constitution, and that more than 60 years ago voted for adoption of the United Nations' *Universal Declaration of Human Rights*, whose Article 19 guarantees free expression. Although the statutory framework exists for women to seek the means to communicate through the media, the nation's laws, regulatory bodies, and courts have done little to facilitate that. Such has been demonstrated, for example, with the FCC's less-than-eager response to implement policies to ensure women's ability to communicate. Nor have media companies been concerned with women's participation in the communication professions, as seen, for example, in their decisions to award monetary compensation and on-site programs without admission of wrongdoing when charged with discrimination.

Over the years, Congress has addressed women's rights to equal employment in communication and other industries and even created the Equal Employment Opportunities Commission to help achieve gender equality in these and other workplaces. Women have thus been able to file grievances and lawsuits to force employers to hire, train, and promote them, and in some cases their efforts were successful. Congress also created a Glass Ceiling Commission to recommend ways to dismantle sexist practices holding back qualified women in the workplace.

At the structural level, however, the Federal Communications Commission has not always affirmed women's efforts to own broadcast stations. When the FCC abandoned its comparative hearings process in favor of bidding as the means for awarding licenses, it essentially assured that the wealthiest companies would buy out smaller ones thereby creating a conglomerated industry. Because women have tended to own smaller and fewer stations, in smaller markets, their revenues have been less secure and their futures less certain (Byerly, 2011)—in other words, they are vulnerable to buyout and takeover. The commission has twice failed to respond to rulings from the U.S. Third Circuit Court of Appeals (*Prometheus I* and *II* ) requiring it to seek remedies to low media ownership levels by women and racial minorities. Refusal and inaction are where that agency presently stands in its commitment to equality of diversity in communication. Court rulings in women's favor in cases related to broadcast licenses have been few over the years; instead, rulings have systematically reduced the ability for women to have gender considered as they attempt to own and operate broadcast stations. There is at present no organized feminist legal strategy to challenge the FCC's behavior emanating from women media professionals or feminist advocacy organizations (Byerly, forthcoming). Such is clearly warranted given the commission's continued failure to comply with federal court rulings, and the courts' tendency to squeeze women from access to media ownership.

We emphasize that laws and regulations matter to women's right to communicate, because they provide the framework within which women can make legitimate demands. However, women must use them if they are to have meaning beyond their inherent potential. Thus, we urge leaders of feminist movements and women's professional organizations to refocus on the legislative process, and we urge women media professionals and feminist activists working in advocacy roles to revisit complaints and litigation. In the academic world, there is a complementary case to be made for media studies and journalism programs to incorporate into the curriculum the sex and race discrimination issues evident in professional practice. In so doing, future professionals can be prepared to take action when they encounter discrimination. We also encourage feminist scholars in the academy and beyond to continue tracking the relevant structural issues and advancing theoretical arguments for women's right to communicate through employment and ownership.

Table 16.1 Selected Legal Events Affecting Women's Relationship to Media in the United States

| Event | Category | Year | Description |
|---|---|---|---|
| The Equal Pay Act of 1963 | Legislation | 1963 | Made it illegal for employers to discriminate on the basis of sex when compensating employees performing similar jobs. |
| United Church of Christ v. Federal Communications Commission | Court Ruling | 1965 | Court held that television viewers were allowed to intervene in FCC hearings on the renewal of station licenses. Although this case was brought on the basis of racial discrimination in programming, it would enable women to similarly challenge license renewals a few years later on the basis of sex. |
| Office of Communication of the United Church of Christ v. Federal Communications Commission | Court Ruling | 1966 | Court ordered the FCC to hold a comparative hearing as to who should be the new station owner; however, it did not disqualify WLBT-TV (current license holder) from seeking a new license. |
| ACLU v. ABC News | Court Ruling | 1970 | ACLU filed on the behalf of Sharon Niederman and other women employees. Niederman applied for a position as a writer or news producer, but was hired as a secretary to the news division's director of public relations. Niederman noted that she was laughed at or ignored when she asked to be promoted to writer or another news position. The court supported the discrimination claim and noted that only 50 of ABC News' 250 employees were women, and a majority (33 of those) were at the bottom of the hierarchy as secretaries or researchers. |
| National Organization for Women v. WRC-TV | Court Ruling | 1971 | Catherine Mackin and other female employees complained about unbalanced pay scales and lack of upward mobility. The lawsuit was settled in favor of the women and required the station to change hiring and promotional practices. |

(continued)

Table 16.1 *(continued)*

| Event | Category | Year | Description |
|---|---|---|---|
| Title VII (amending the Civil Rights Act of 1964) | Legislation | 1972 | Prohibits employment discrimination based on race, sex, religion, and national origin. Created the Equal Employment Opportunities Commission. |
| Equal Employment Opportunity Act of 1972 | Legislation | 1972 | The law added six amendments to Title VII, including litigation authority for the EEOC. In addition, educational institutions, federal, state, and local governments were made subject to Title VII. Also, the number of employers covered by Title VII increased, and the complaining parties were given a longer period to file charges. |
| EEOC v. *Newsweek* Magazine | Settlement | 1972 | 46 female employees had accused *Newsweek* magazine of discriminatory practices in hiring and promotion. The case, which was settled outside of court, sparked other women to fight for equal wages and career opportunities. |
| TV9, Inc. v. FCC | Court Ruling | 1974 | Case involved the issuing of a permit to construct a commercial television station in which the principal applicants for TV 9 were two Black men with civic involvement in a community with a 25% Black population. Initially, the FCC examiner wrote that the Communications Act is color blind and that Black ownership could not be an independent comparative factor. The D.C. circuit court disagreed and held that a comparative license proceeding helps broaden community representation and gave merit to racial minorities in order to diversify viewpoints. |
| Equal Employment Opportunity Commission v. *The Washington Post* | Settlement | 1974 | The *Post* did not admit to discrimination in its agreement to compensate 567 women who had charged sex discrimination. The *Post* also established scholarship and sabbatical programs for women to support their development and advancement. |

| National Organization for Women, New York City Chapter *v.* FCC (WABC-TV and WRC-TV) | FCC ruling (1975) Court Ruling (1977) | 1975 (and 1977) | In 1975, FCC ruled that the station had not discriminated against women in employment or programming as NOW's lawyers had claimed in their petition challenging the station's license renewal. In appealing the ruling to the DC District Court of Appeals, NOW joined this case with a similar case against local WRC-TV. In 1977, the court affirmed the FCC ruling but these cases would become a model for similar license challenges. They also helped increase women's employment in television. |
|---|---|---|---|
| Women's Committee for Equal Employment *v.* National Broadcasting Co, Inc. | Settlement | 1977 | NBC settled the case without admitting to charges of salary discrimination on the basis of sex, but the company agreed to pay female employees back wages and revamp policies that affected women specifically in relation to employment and promotion. |
| Women's Committee for Equal Employment Opportunity *v.* National Broadcasting Co, Inc. | Court Ruling | 1977 | The EEOC intervened on behalf of female employees who accused the National Broadcasting Co, Inc., of discrimination. The parties were ordered to enter into a consent decree, which included goals to be reached by NBC. Those goals included identifying positions to be held by women. The ruling also mandated women's ability to create or update forms with career goals and experience which were to be reviewed when vacancies became available. |
| Susan Smith *v. Reader's Digest* | Settlement | 1977 | While working at *Reader's Digest*, Susan Smith became the plaintiff spokesperson for a case brought by 8 women employees in a class action suit against Reader's Digest Assn. The magazine did not acknowledge discriminatory practices, but its executives agreed to a $1.5 million settlement, which was noted as the highest payment per capita for a sex discrimination case based on equal employment rights during that time. The agreement included back pay and salary increases for female employees. |

*(continued)*

Table 16.1 (continued)

| Event | Category | Year | Description |
|---|---|---|---|
| Elizabeth Wade Boylan, Louise Carini, Joan Cook, Nancy Davis, Grace Glueck, and Andrea Skinner v. *The New York Times* | Settlement | 1978 | Female employees sued *The New York Times* charging they were being paid less than male employees for the same work. A $385,000 out-of-court settlement was reached. Additionally, the settlement outlined specific goals and timetables for hiring and promotion of women. The company paid $223,500 in back pay to women in news and commercial departments. |
| Gainesville Media, Inc. v. FCC | Court Ruling | 1978 | Gainesville Media, Inc. (GMI) was an unsuccessful broadcast applicant, and the station's owners argued they should not be penalized for the conduct of an employee. The Board had not previously weighed the comparative merit of two of GMI's female employees. This did not change the Board's GMI's application; however, upon further reflection the FCC Review Board called for female ownership and participation to be under the same consideration as Black ownership and participation. For a short time, it appeared that a gender preference in comparative hearings would be allowed. |
| Mid-Florida Television Corporation v. FCC | Court Ruling | 1978 | Mid-Florida Television argued that women should be included as minorities and argued that the Commission's failure to include women was not aligned with the Board's previous decision to give women merit in comparative hearings. The court altered the decision made in Gainesville Media, Inc. v. FCC and held that the merit for female ownership and participation is warranted upon essentially the same basis as the merit given for Black ownership and participation, but that it is a merit of lesser significance. This gave women a limited preference. |

| | | | |
|---|---|---|---|
| National Black Media Coalition v. Federal Communications Commission | Court Ruling | 1978 | The National Black Media Coalition sought review of the FCC's Commission Report and Order, because the Commission had declined to have "quantitative program standards for television broadcasters involved in comparative renewal proceedings" (*National Black Media Coalition v. FCC*). The court held that the FCC's consideration of the licensee's post term improvements was not consistent with its own established policies and that the FCC's justifications for failing to follow its precedents were unpersuasive. |
| Mary Lou Butcher v. *The Detroit News* | Settlement | 1983 | Mary Lou Butcher and other female employees filed a class action lawsuit against *The Detroit News*. Butcher initially experienced upward mobility in her newsroom until a male editor was hired and she was demoted to the weekend shift despite having higher qualifications; this became the foundation for the case. Butcher was later transferred from the city newsroom to the suburbs and filed her EEOC complaint soon after. The plaintiffs in this case sought compensation and equal rights for future women in the field. Following an 8-year legal battle, the paper paid $330,000 to nearly 90 female employees. |
| Equal Employment Opportunity Commission v. Associated Press | Settlement | 1983 | In 1973 women at AP had claimed that the company did not have the same hiring and promotion practices for women as for men. In addition, they said, women's salaries were significantly lower than men's. In 1978 the EEOC claimed AP had violated the Civil Rights Act of 1964. AP agreed to a $2 million out-of-court settlement for relief and to implement an affirmative action plan to increase the number of women, Blacks, and Hispanics in news, editorial, and news-photography positions. |

*(continued)*

Table 16.1 *(continued)*

| Event | Category | Year | Description |
|---|---|---|---|
| Steele v. FCC | Court Ruling | 1985 | In the initial case the FCC gave preferential treatment to female applicants for FM stations. James U. Steele, who planned to construct an FM station in St. Simons Island, appealed, saying that gender preferences violated the constitution. In its opinion, the court made a distinction between preferences for minorities and women. Distinction meant there were separate needs and interests for specific groups. This case was sent back to the FCC, which initiated an inquiry. Congress froze that inquiry in 1988 and it remained frozen till 1994. |
| Pappas v. FCC | Court Ruling | 1986 | Plaintiff Stella Pappas had argued she would have had a better chance for a license if the gender preference had been given to her when she applied. The FCC did not apply this preference to the lottery system used in the selection of license recipients. The D.C. Circuit Court concluded that the FCC's decision not to award lottery licensing preferences to women was a reasonable interpretation of the law. |
| Kathleen Neville v. Taft Broadcasting Company and WGR-TV | Court Ruling | 1987 | Kathleen Neville, an employee of Taft Broadcasting Company, sued the company for violations of Title VII and the New York Human Rights Law after she reported the sexual harassment she experienced and was fired. Neville lost the case, and the district court ruling said that the Taft company had had legitimate business reasons for terminating her. She had to appear in court to pay her part of the company's fees despite already being in debt. |
| Metro Broadcasting, Inc. v. FCC | Court Ruling | 1990 | Metro Broadcasting and Shurburg Broadcasting argued that the FCC's minority preference was unconstitutional. In a 5-to-4 decision, the Supreme Court held that the FCC's minority preference policies were constitutional. |

| | | | |
|---|---|---|---|
| The Civil Rights Act of 1991 | Legislation | 1991 | This act expanded provisions of the original Civil Rights Act of 1964 to allow plaintiffs suing their employers for discrimination to request a jury trial, to request attorney's fees for expert witnesses, and if successful, to receive compensatory damages. It enabled employees to sue for emotional distress damages, while limiting the amount a jury could award. It also prohibited employment decisions based on sex and allowed employees to challenge an established seniority system. |
| The Glass Ceiling Act of 1991—Part II of the Civil Rights Act of 1991 | Legislation | 1991 | This important provision of the Civil Rights Act of 1991 established the Glass Ceiling Commission, which was charged with making recommendations to remove the "artificial barriers" that prevent women and minorities upward mobility. |
| Lamprecht v. FCC | Court Ruling | 1992 | Jerome Thomas Lamprecht argued that the FCC's policy, which gave Barbara Driscoll Marmet an extra credit for being a woman, deprived him of his right to equal protection of the law in his bid for a station license. The Court ruled that the FCC's gender preferences were a violation of equal protection because the commission had not shown that its sex-preference policy was "substantially related to achieving diversity on the airwaves." |
| Bechtel v. FCC (Bechtel I) | Court Ruling | 1992 | A judge rejected the application of Susan M. Bechtel who argued that certain ownership criteria used in comparative hearings for awarding broadcast licenses did not serve the FCC's objectives. The Court remanded the case to the FCC for further explanation as to why its focus on integration was still in the public interest. This case prompted the FCC to seek comment on larger rulemaking processes including minority and gender preference. |
| Bechtel v. FCC (Bechtel II) | Court Ruling | 1993 | Bechtel appealed the FCC's remand decision. The D.C. Circuit Court struck down the FCC's integration credit giving preference to license applicants to who intended to personally manage and operate a station. At the same time the Commission suspended all comparative hearings as a method for awarding station licenses to applicants and moved to a lottery system. |

*(continued)*

Table 16.1 (continued)

| Event | Category | Year | Description |
|---|---|---|---|
| Garrett Broadcasting Service (WEUPEP), v. FCC | Court Ruling | 1995 | This appeal was prompted by the FCC's denial of an application to Garrett Broadcasting Service which was owned by a Black man, Leroy Garrett. The court said that WEUP had urged that its Black ownership and Black operation were factors deserving careful attention. Using *TV 9 Inc. v. FCC* as a precedent, the court decided that merit should be awarded when a station is able to provide evidence of minority ownership. |
| Adarand Constructors, Inc. v. Pena | Court Ruling | 1995 | The 1990 Metro Broadcasting Inc. v. FCC ruling, in which FCC policies were reviewed with intermediate scrutiny, was overruled in this construction industry case in which Adarand filed suit against the Department of Transportation. Plaintiff argued that the company lost a subcontracting job to a minority company despite being the lowest bidder. The court decided any federal program which uses race or ethnicity as a basis for its decision making would be subject to strict scrutiny by the courts. |
| Telecommunications Act of 1996 | Legislation | 1996 | This act represented the first major overhaul of telecommunications law in 62 years. According to the FCC, which was charged with implementing it, the goal was to allow "anyone to enter any communications business—to let any communications business compete in any market against any other." In fact, the law created the statutory basis for mergers and acquisitions with few limits to ownership, even within markets. The era of media conglomeration in the US dates from passage of this law. |

| | | | |
|---|---|---|---|
| EEOC v. *The New York Times* Co. and New York Newspaper Printing Pressmen's Union No. 2 | Court Ruling | 1998 | The EEOC discovered that the Times and Union discriminated against racial minorities and women and violated Title VII of the Civil Rights Act of 1964. Initially, in 1995, the parties entered a consent decree, which would include that the *Times* would increase the representation of minorities and women as junior pressman to 25% as well as a training program for minorities. In 1997, the *Times* agreed to a transfer of 15 outside pressman, none of whom were women or minorities. The EEOC claimed this was a violation of the decree and the court agreed. |
| Jones v. WDAS FM/AM Radio Stations | Court Ruling | 1999 | Lillian Jones filed suit against WDAS FM/AM radio stations on claims of sex and age discrimination and hostile work environment. The Court ruled in favor of the company because the plaintiff had failed to file with the EEOC within 300 days from when those adverse employment actions occurred. |
| Prometheus Radio Project v. the FCC (Prometheus I) | Court Ruling | 2004 | Lawyers for Media Action Project and other groups representing Prometheus Radio Project asked the court to block implementation of proposed FCC rules allowing further deregulation of media industry saying it would threaten small stations' survival. In 2004, the majority of the Third Circuit Court of Appeals ruled 2-1 in favor of Prometheus. Court remanded the case to FCC with the directive it must consider low levels of female and minority broadcast ownership. |
| Prometheus Radio Project v. the FCC (Prometheus II) | Court Ruling | 2011 | Lawyers for Prometheus Radio Project again petitioned the court on behalf of small station owners. The Third U.S. Circuit Court of Appeals rejected the FCC's rules that would have allowed one company to own a newspaper and broadcast stations in the same market. Overall, the Court agreed with Prometheus and other public interest groups that the FCC had failed to consider the impact of its rules on women and people of color. |

# References

Beasley, M. H., & Gibbons, S. J. (2003). *Taking their place: A documentary history of women and journalism*. State College, PA: Strata Pub Co.

*Bechtel v. FCC*. (1992). 957 F.2d 873.

*Bechtel v. FCC*. (1993). 10 F.3d 875.

Byerly, C. M. (1995). News, consciousness and social participation: The role of Women's Feature Service in world news. In A. Valdivia (Ed.), *Feminism, multiculturalism and the media* (pp. 105–122). Thousand Oaks, CA: Sage.

Byerly, C. M. (2011). Behind the scenes of women's broadcast ownership. *Howard Journal of Communications, 22*(1), 24–42.

Byerly, C. M. (2014). Women and media control: Feminist interrogations at the macro-level. In C. Carter, L. Steiner, & L. McLaughlin (Eds.), *The Routledge companion to media and gender* (pp. 105–115). New York, NY: Routledge.

Byerly, C. M. (forthcoming). Feminist activism and U.S. communications policy. In B. Zelizer (Ed.), *Media activism*. New York, NY: Routledge.

Byerly, C. M. & Ross, K. (2006). *Women and media: A critical introduction*. Malden, MA: Blackwell.

Byerly, C. M., Park, Y. J., & Miles, R. D. (2011). Race- and gender-conscious policies: Toward a more egalitarian communications future. *Journal of Information Policy 1*, 425–440.

Center for Constitutional Rights. (2007). *Historic cases: National Organization of Women (NOW) v. WABC-TV, FCC, and WRC-TV*. Retrieved March 30, 2015, from https://ccrjustice.org/home/what-we-do/our-cases/national-organization-women-now-v-wabc-tv-fcc-and-wrc-tv.

*Civil Rights Act of 1964 § 7, 42 U.S.C. § 2000e et seq (1964)*.

Comstock, D. (1982). A method for critical research. In E. Bredo & W. Feinberg (Eds.), *Knowledge and values in social and educational research* (pp. 370–390). Philadelphia, PA: Temple University Press.

Crichton, S. N. L. (2014). The incomplete revolution: Women journalists—50 years after Title VII of the Civil Rights Act of 1964, we've come a long way baby, but are we there yet? *Howard Law Journal, 58*(1), 49–112.

EIGE. (2013). *Advancing gender equality in decision-making in media organizations* (Report of the European Institute for Gender Equality). Luxembourg: European Union.

ERLA Group, Inc. (1982, May). *Female ownership of broadcast stations*. East Lansing, MI: ERLA Group, Inc.

Federal Communications Commission. (2008). *The public and broadcasting: How to get the most service from your local station*. Retrieved October 31, 2015, from https://www.fcc.gov/guides/public-and-broadcasting-july-2008#ACT.

Federal Communications Commission. (1996). *Telecommunications Act of 1996*. Retrieved March 14, 2015, from http://www.gpo.gov/fdsys/pkg/PLAW-104publ104/html/PLAW-104publ104.htm.

Federal Communications Commission. (2000). *History of the broadcast license application process*. Retrieved July 27, 2015, from https://transition.fcc.gov/opportunity/meb_study/broadcast_lic_study_pt1.pdf.

Free Press (2011). *Court rejects FCC attempt to weaken media ownership rules*. Retrieved October 30, 2015, from http://www.freepress.net/press-release/2011/7/7/court-rejects-fcc-attempt-weaken-media-ownership-rules.

Free Press. (n.d.). *Diversity in media ownership*. Retrieved March 14, 2015, from http://www.freepress.net/diversity-media-ownership.

*Gainesville Media, Inc.*, 70 F.C.C.2d 143, 149 (Rev. Bd. 1978)

Gallagher, M. (1981). *Unequal opportunities: The case of the media*. Paris: UNESCO.

*Glass ceilings: Women and men in Southern African media*. (2009). Johannesburg, South Africa: Gender Links. Retrieved March 15, 2014, from www.genderlinks. org.za/page/media-glass-ceiling-research.

Hunter, L. (2012, April). *Feats, foibles and failures: Minority ownership policy and FCC's inability to enact long-term change*. Paper presented at the Broadcast Education Association Conference. Las Vegas, Nevada.

IWPR. (2015). *The status of women in the states 2015*. Washington, DC: Institute for Women's Policy Research. Retrieved June 10, 2015, from http://www.iwpr.org.

Kennard, W. E. (1998, September). *Remarks by William E. Kennard, Chairman, Federal Communications Commission to American Women in Radio and Television*. Retrieved March 15, 2015, from https://transition.fcc.gov/Speeches/ Kennard/spwek826.html.

*Lamprecht v. FCC*. (1992)., 958 F.2d 382.

*Metro Broadcasting, Inc. v. FCC*. (1990). *497 U.S. 547, 110 S. Ct. 2997, 111 L. Ed. 2d 445.*

*Mid-Florida Television Corp. v. FCC*, 70 F.C.C.2d 281, 326 (Rev. Bd. 1978).

McLaughlin, L. (1993). Feminism, the public sphere, media and democracy. *Media, Culture & Society, 15*(4), 599–620.

Palmeira, A. 2012. *Suing their way into the newsroom: How women at the* Detroit News *changed journalism*. Retrieved February 10, 2015, from http://etd.fcla. edu/CF/CFH0004306/ Palmeira_Amanda_N_201212_BA.pdf.

*Pappas v. FCC*. (1986). 807 F.2d 1019).

Prometheus Radio Project. 2011. *Federal court rejects media consolidation in* Prometheus vs. FCC. Retrieved October 31, 2015, from http://www. prometheusradio.org/content/federal-court-rejects-media-consolidation- prometheus-vs-fcc.

*Prometheus Radio Project v. FCC*. (2004). 373 F.3d 372.

*Prometheus Radio Project v. FCC*. (2011). 652 F.3d 431.

Reader's Digest settles bias suit—women workers to get $1.5 million. (1977, November 5). *Daytona Beach Morning News*, p. 10A. Retrieved November 6, 2015, from https://news.google.com/newspapers?nid=1873&dat=1977110 5&id=3dEpAAAAIBAJ&sjid=P8oEAAAAIBAJ&pg=2965,1486238&hl=en.

Rosen, R. (2000). *The world split open: How the modern women's movement changed America*. New York, NY: Penguin Books.

Rush, R. R. & Allen, D. (Eds). (1989). *Communication at the crossroads: The gender gap connection*. Norwood, NJ: Ablex.

*Steele v. FCC, 770 F.2d 1192 (DC Cir. 1989).*

*The New York Times*. (1982, November 21). *Catherine Mackin, 42, Reporter for* ABC News, The New York Times. Retrieved March 10, 2015, from http:// www.nytimes.com/1982/11/21/obituaries/catherine-mackin-42-reporter-for- abc-news.html.

Turner, S. D. & Cooper, M. (2006). *Out of the picture: Minority & women's TV ownership in the United States*. Retrieved October 31, 2015, from http://www. freepress.net/sites/default/files/fp-legacy/out_of_the_picture.pdf.

Turner, S. D. (2007). *Off the dial: Minority & women's radio ownership in the United State*s. Retrieved October 31, 2015, from https://www.freepress.net/sites/default/files/stn-legacy/off_the_dial.pdf.

*TV 9, Inc. v. FCC*, 495 F.2d 929 (D.C. Cir. 1973).

UN Women. (1995, September). *Platform for action*. Women and the media. The United Nations fourth world conference on women. Beijing, China. Retrieved October 31, 2015, from http://www.un.org/womenwatch/daw/beijing/platform/media.htm.

Women's Media Center. (2013). *Status of women in the U.S. media*. Retrieved March 8, 2015, from http://wmc.3cdn.net/51113ed5df3e0d0b79_zzzm6go0b.pdf.

Women's Media Center. (2015). *Status of women in the U.S. media*. Retrieved March 8, 2015, from http://www.womensmediacenter.com/pages/2015-divided-media-gender-gap-infographic.

# 17

# SECOND CLASS NETIZENS
## Race and the Emerging Mobile Internet Underclass

*Philip M. Napoli and Jonathan A. Obar*[1]

An important question to pose as digital divide challenges evolve is the extent to which mobile devices close gaps in Internet access among demographic groups. Race has traditionally been a prominent dimension of the digital divide, with African Americans and Latinos consistently demonstrating lower levels of Internet access than Whites (NTIA, 2011). These disparities are of particular significance given the centrality of Internet access and usage to full and effective participation in economic, political, and cultural life. For this reason, the digital divide has been described as "one of the most important civil rights issues facing our modern information economy" (Carvin, 2000, p. 56).

Policies addressing these disparities have been implemented (see Choemprayong, 2006; Federal Communications Commission, 2012; Parker, 2000); however, the rapid diffusion of mobile devices among minority populations is perhaps the most effective means of reducing these access gaps. The lower prices of mobile devices relative to PCs and laptops, and the fact that usage does not require a home broadband subscription, are key factors in mobile's rapid diffusion (Horrigan, 2009; James, 2009).

These developments suggest that, for segments of the population, mobile devices represent the primary—or only—means by which individuals access the Internet. A recent study by the Pew Research Center (2015) examined the demographics of smartphone dependence—when individuals rely primarily or exclusively on their smartphones to access the Internet. According to Pew (2015), 7% of Whites lack a broadband connection in their home, compared with 17% of Hispanics and 21% of African Americans. Four percent of Whites are completely smartphone dependent, compared with 12% of African Americans and 13% of Latinos. For younger generations, these patterns appear to be more pronounced. Recent research by comScore (2013), for instance, found that two out of five Hispanic millennials access the Internet exclusively via their mobile device. These patterns suggest reliance on mobile devices to access the Internet is more common in minority populations in the United States.

The question that arises from these patterns—one receiving relatively little discussion or empirical attention—is whether mobile Internet access is an adequate form of access when compared with traditional forms. That is, should we consider the digital divide problem solved once mobile devices have effectively equalized Internet-adoption across all sectors of the population?

It may be tempting to think so, because the idea of successfully connecting everyone to the grid would seem a laudable public interest victory, realizing current iterations of longstanding universal service goals (see White House, 2015), and ending the digital divide conversation on a seemingly positive note. The goal here is to question this assumption and to highlight a more nuanced analysis of mobile/PC-internet divides. We present an alternative, more critical perspective on mobile Internet access than is typically found in digital divide policy discourse. Drawing upon recent research across a range of disciplines, we illustrate that mobile Internet access represents, in many ways, a form of Internet access considerably inferior to PC-based access.[2] Moreover, this disparity is likely to be even greater for the growing population of mobile-only or mobile natives (i.e., those who abandon or leapfrog traditional forms of Internet access for mobile; see Boyera, 2007; Chircu & Mahajan, 2009; Napoli & Obar, 2014; Napoli & Obar, 2015). Furthermore, as the Pew Research Center (2015) data discussed above illustrates, these mobile onlys and mobile natives are more likely to come from minority populations; thus any meaningful disparities in the utility of mobile forms of Internet access relative to PC-based forms will disproportionately affect minority populations.

## A Comparative Assessment of Mobile- and PC-based Internet Access

Most research to date on mobile Internet access has failed to assess and compare the characteristics or usage patterns of mobile platforms relative to PCs. There are, however, a number of findings scattered across different fields that can begin to inform our understanding of their differences. The goal here is to focus on gaps between PC and mobile Internet access that represent fundamental, and perhaps difficult to change, differences between the platforms. Thus, certain disparities that could diminish rapidly over time (e.g., pricing differences, download allowances) will not be a point of focus, although these too have been raised in the few extant discussions about the possible shortcomings of mobile Internet access (e.g., Southwood, 2011). In what follows, differences in technological capability, content availability, network platform/architecture, and usage patterns will be discussed to emphasize the considerable Internet access divides that remain.

## Technological Capabilities

At the most basic level, it is important to consider the technological capabilities of mobile devices relative to PCs. Whereas both categories of devices provide gateways to the Internet (although, as discussed below, not an identical Internet), the mechanisms by which users engage with the Internet are fundamentally different in significant ways—ways that often have a direct bearing on whether the platforms represent equivalent opportunities for users to take full advantage of the opportunities for social, political, and economic development that the Internet provides. As Rice and Katz (2003) noted in an early comparative analysis of PC and mobile device usage, an important dimension of the multi-faceted digital divide is the potential gap between those who have advanced functionality and services and those who have technologies with lesser capabilities.

## Memory, Storage Capacity, and Speed

Mobile devices differ from PCs on fundamental characteristics as basic as available memory and storage capacity. Mobile devices simply cannot store or process as much data as a PC (Kim & Hwang, 2012). Their capacity relative to PCs is described as "intrinsically limited" (Finamore, et al., 2011, p. 345). As Table 17.1 indicates, smartphones continue to lag between popular PCs/laptops in terms of processor speed, memory, and storage.

Although we will certainly see mobile devices improve in all of these areas over time, our concern is with their performance *relative to* PCs. In this regard, the significant speed differences between fixed and mobile broadband services will likely persist into the foreseeable future. As Noam (2011) compellingly demonstrated through a detailed comparative analysis of the capacities and traffic management of cell sites, fiber, cable, and DSL services, "fiber and cable are 20 to 100 times as fast as optimistically projected 4G rates, and DSL is about twice as fast" (p. 475). He concluded that "wireless is not going to catch up with wireline," given that, over time, "wireline seems to stay roughly two orders of magnitude ahead, i.e., about 100 times as fast, while actually accelerating over wireless in recent years" (Noam, 2011, p. 476).

Table 17.1 Technical Specifications for PCs and Smartphones

| Specs | iMac | Dell Inspiron | iPhone 6 | iPhone 6 Plus | Samsung Galaxy S5 mini | Samsung Galaxy S5 | HTC One mini | HTC One M8 |
|---|---|---|---|---|---|---|---|---|
| Processor | 3.1GHz | 3.4GHz | 1.4GHz | 1.4GHz* | 1.4GHz | 2.5GHz | 1.4GHz | 2.45GHz |
| Memory | 16GB | 8GB | 1GB | 1GB | 1.5GB | 2GB | 1GB | 2GB |
| Storage | 1TB | 1TB | 64GB | 64GB** | 16GB | 16GB*** | 16GB | 32GB*** |
| Screen Size | 21.5 inch | 22 inch | 4.7inch | 5.5 inch | 4.5 inch | 5.1 inch | 4.3 inch | 5.0 inch |

*Note:* *It is possible that the A8 may have capabilities above 2.0GHz. **Apple was offering a 128GB version, but as of this writing, only 64GB versions are available. This may be due to some reported concerns with the 128GB models. ***128GB with memory card, but this is sold separately.

Certainly, mobile broadband does—and will continue to—operate at speeds that facilitate many applications, but from a relative standpoint, it remains inferior to what is available to users of wireline service, providing the latter with significantly better performance and better ability to utilize high capacity services and content. This is particularly important given that we should expect applications to continue to grow rapidly in terms of their need for speed (Noam, 2011).

Such differences affect the quality and nature of access to Internet services. For instance, a comparative analysis of YouTube's functionality across mobile and PC platforms found that YouTube performed far better on the PC largely due to the challenges associated with coping with "the tighter constraints in terms of storage availability for mobile devices" (Finamore et al., 2011, p. 347).

In an analysis of South African Internet users' attitudes and behaviors in relation to the mobile platform, Hyde-Clark and Van Tonder (2011) found that mobile devices' memory and storage limitations were among the most frequently articulated reasons why mobile devices could not effectively replace PCs. Respondents felt that mobile devices could replace PCs for various online social activities, but not for a range of more rigorous business activities.

### Content Availability

Certainly some of these memory and storage shortcomings affect the availability and display of mobile Internet content. Considering the technological capabilities of PCs versus mobile devices, we must also consider how content is delivered on each platform (MacKay & Watters, 2003).

Of course, the smaller screens of mobile devices limit how much information can be displayed on a screen and how that information is displayed. Consequently, the history of the mobile Internet has been one in which three different approaches to displaying and accessing web content have been employed. The first involves accessing full web sites (designed for PC interface) via Internet-enabled mobile devices. The second involves what Rampton (2014) termed adaptive design, in which mobile-tailored web sites are developed to parallel traditional web sites, reflective of the limitations of mobile devices (Kaikkonen, 2009). A third option involves the use of mobile apps for bypassing the Web (discussed below).

Indeed, mobile-based interactions with web sites designed for PCs can prove difficult, and in some cases, impossible (Kaasinen et al., 2009), leaving mobile users at a distinct disadvantage. This is of particular relevance when we consider the less sophisticated mobile devices being adopted in developing nations and among low-income populations, which have a lower capacity than sophisticated smartphones in terms of displaying standard web pages. According to a 2012 estimate, less than 10% of the

Web was "mobile-ready" (Martin, 2012), a number that has certainly increased in recent years, though to what extent remains speculative.[3] A focus group study of nearly 100 early adopters of mobile devices in Kenya found that users had very little access to locally-produced mobile-ready content, and users spent most of their time with international platforms such as Facebook, Wikipedia, and YouTube (Souter, 2011). Thus, even as users in developing nations gain access to the Internet via mobile devices, they still suffer from a relative lack of mobile-ready content that directly addresses their specific needs and interests.

Another content availability issue to consider is that mobile-ready web sites often present streamlined or watered down versions of standard web sites (Fisch, 2012; Meunier, 2012). Thus, users of sites designed for mobile access typically have access to less information and less functionality than PC-based users do. Search engines designed specifically for mobile devices offer a more streamlined (one might say less information-rich) user experience than do traditional search engines, reflecting the designers' assessment that in the mobile context "the use case is more for messing around" rather than focused and directed information-seeking (Miller, 2013, p. 1).

## Network/Platform Architecture

In considering the technological capabilities and characteristics across both means of Internet access, it is also important to consider the structure and operation of the networks and platforms through which access is obtained. Southwood (2011) emphasized, "the very nature of the networks over which the Internet and mobile Internet are delivered differs" (p. 6). Of particular importance is the relative openness of mobile versus PC-based Internet access. This issue arose in a session of the 2011 Internet Governance forum devoted to the impact of the mobile Internet on Internet governance in Africa, which began with the recognition that "the Internet in general is open, transparent and accessible. However, in contrast [the] mobile Internet . . . is relatively limited" (IGF, 2011). In particular Apple's strategy in the mobile space has been described as one directed at creating a "vertically integrated, closed system," in which the company "maintains high levels of control over the entire product ecosystem" (Kenney & Pon, 2011, p. 252).

These differences in openness are reflected in the re-emergence of the walled garden model in mobile Internet access (Isomursu et al., 2007; Kenney & Pon, 2011). The walled garden metaphor characterized the early days of dial-up Internet access, when Internet Service Providers (ISPs) such as America Online (AOL) sought to contain users within their own proprietary content, rather than positioning the ISP as a gateway to the full expanse of the Web (Aufderheide, 2002). The walled garden model in the mobile Internet context is reinforced by the explosion in mobile apps which bypass the Web. Apps are designed, in part, as specific compensations for the various shortcomings of mobile-based web access (Anderson & Wolff, 2010). Although apps certainly can provide an efficient and user-friendly experience, in the context of assessing mobile Internet access and usage against PC-based access and usage, the mobile apps model represents a much less open Internet ecosystem than the Web (see, e.g., Anderson & Wolff, 2010; Sigal, 2012). For instance, the major app stores (e.g. iTunes App Store and Google Play) play a powerful gatekeeping role in comparison to the Web model in which content and applications can bypass such intermediaries. This is a fundamental change in the dynamics of content and application dissemination. Constraining the range of available content sources and applications, may, according to some critics, throttle innovation (Sigal, 2012). The point is that although there are tremendous end-user benefits accompanying the migration to mobile applications, there are significant detriments as well.

The devices themselves are also fundamentally different in terms of openness. Mobile handheld devices (including tablets) are a much less open platform for engaging with the Internet than are PCs (for detailed discussions of this issue, see Wu, 2007; Zittrain, 2008). As Horner (2011) noted, "unlike personal computers (PC), mobile handsets are primarily closed, proprietary technologies that are difficult for people to adapt and programme for different uses" (p. 13). Users who go online via more closed, less programmable devices such as tablets and smartphones do not have the same capacity to enhance the Internet and its offerings or to reap the benefits of doing so. These efficacy challenges are only the beginning of a host of potential "re-passification" concerns associated with Internet audiences (as opposed to prosumers) that connect via mobile devices (Napoli & Obar, 2015).

### Usage Patterns

The technological characteristics of different communications platforms inevitably contribute to varied behavioral patterns and tendencies among users. Consequently, assessing the extent to which mobile devices represent an effective substitute to PC-based Internet access should be grounded in a detailed understanding of the use of newer platforms, and whether usage patterns differ in significant ways from the old platforms. More specifically, do any of these differences in usage patterns relate to disparities in the ability to access, produce, and disseminate information having significant social, political, and economic ramifications?

Traditionally characterized by siloed lines of inquiry, the research on PC and mobile Internet usage reveals few comparative or integrated analyses (Cui & Roto, 2008; for recent exceptions, see Humphreys, Von Pape, & Karnowski, 2013; Pearce & Rice, 2013). Yet one can see findings from disparate strands of research that, together, raise legitimate concerns about whether mobile Internet users are able to use the Internet in ways that put them on anything close to an even playing field with their PC-based counterparts. In what follows, differences in information-seeking behaviors, content creation, and skill sets across platforms are discussed.

### Information Seeking Behaviors

At the most basic level, it seems reasonable to question whether the depth of a user's engagement with the Internet is comparable across PC and mobile platforms. Are mobile Internet users capable of engaging in as rigorous and engaged information seeking as those who have PC-based access? Humphreys et al. (2013) conducted in-depth interviews with U.S. and German Internet users, and characterized PC-based Internet usage as primarily "immersive" and mobile Internet usage as primarily "extractive" (i.e., purposeful engagements of a shorter duration). Similarly, Isomursu et al., who examined the dominant metaphors for the mobile Internet that emerged in a series of user studies, concluded that an appropriate metaphor for PC-based Internet access is scuba diving, in which individuals can "dive deep into their areas of interest and be totally immersed with the experience" (2007, p. 262). Mobile Internet access, on the other hand, is analogous to snorkeling, because "Environmental factors and equipment are optimized for 'skimming the surface' or 'dipping in and out'" (p. 262). Isomursu et al concluded that "*Passive forms of content consumption* . . . often work better in this kind of situation because they take up less cognitive energy" (pp. 262–263, emphasis in original; see also Nielsen & Fjuk, 2010).

Supporting this perspective is a growing body of comparative research examining the dynamics of searching and information seeking. A study of mobile users in six countries concluded that information gathering was not a common task (Cui & Roto, 2008). A large-scale survey of Japanese Internet users found that PC users habitually accessed an average of 8.64 categories of web sites, whereas mobile users habitually accessed an average of 3.58 categories when seeking information (Ishii, 2004). At the time this study was conducted, 65% of mobile Internet users also accessed the Internet via PC ("mobile only" Internet users were not subjected to separate analysis). A more recent study comparing user behavior across tablets and smartphones found that users viewed 70% more pages per web site visit when using a tablet than when using a smartphone (O'Malley, 2013).

Along related lines, research suggested that the average number of characters in mobile search queries was significantly lower than in PC search queries, with mobile searches utilizing a significantly more limited search vocabulary (Baeza-Yates, Dupret, & Velasco, 2007; Church, Smyth, Cotter, & Bradley, 2007). Mobile searches also were significantly less likely to utilize advanced search features such as Boolean operators or query modifiers.[4] Such tendencies may help explain why unsuccessful search queries (as measured by no click-throughs of the search results) were more common in an earlier study of mobile queries than PC-based queries (Church, Smyth, Cotter, & Bradley, 2008). Mobile searchers also exhibited a significantly greater tendency to rely on the first few search returns than PC-based searchers. Newer research suggests that perhaps usage behaviors have not necessarily changed all that dramatically with the growing popularity of smarter phones, as ranking effects (the extent to which placement in search returns affects content selection) have been shown to be significantly more powerful in mobile than in PC search contexts (Ghose, Goldfarb, & Han, 2013).

Although some of these findings are dated by Internet research standards, they do suggest that patterns related to finding and accessing information on mobile devices are considerably more constrained than on PCs—search costs are, essentially, higher on mobile platforms (Ghose et al., 2013). Considering the process of mobile device adoption in developing nations or lower-income populations, it is important to remember that these populations are unlikely to possess the most advanced devices (e.g., Nielsen, 2013). As a result, findings that reflect five-to-eight-year-old technological features and capabilities are likely to reflect the technological features and capabilities available to a significant proportion of the mobile-only population.

Accessing information and services on mobile devices has been described as "inherently difficult" (Harding, Storz, Davies, & Friday, 2009, p. 1). Certainly, as devices and services improve, such a blanket statement may become more difficult to support. However, it does seem reasonable to assume that mobile Internet access and usage will remain inherently *more* difficult than PC-based access and usage. Human-computer interaction researchers have found that, given the range of usage contexts, mobile users can sustain their attention to mobile activities for only four to eight second intervals, leading to the conclusion that "the same social, physical, and artefactual resources and goals that make us desire and enjoy mobility also cause resource-depletion from the point of view of human-computer interaction [that] . . . seriously constrain mobile interaction" (Oulasvirta et al., 2005, p. 8).

Findings such as these may explain why mobile usage tends to be weighted much more heavily than PC usage toward leisure and entertainment (Hyde-Clark & Van Tonder, 2011). For instance, a study of mobile users in Kenya found that "non-recreational uses of the Internet, in particular professional activities, rank more highly in PC use . . . than on mobile phones, while the opposite is true for pure leisure uses such as playing games" (Souter, 2011, p. 15).

## Content Creation

Users' abilities to create and disseminate content, applications, and software online, rather than simply being able to access, retrieve, and consume information, have increasingly been recognized as vital dimensions of the opportunities for social, political, and economic advancement afforded by Internet access (Schradie, 2011). The associated notion of participation divides, in which the distribution of online content creation activities conform to, and thus potentially reinforce, existing social stratifications (Blank, 2013), has become an increasingly prominent dimension of both academic and policy discussions of digital divides (Brake, 2014; Hargittai & Walejko, 2008).

In the realm of content creation, mobile access also falls short of PC-based access. Despite celebrated examples of best-selling novels being written on smartphones (Onishi, 2008), entering significant amounts of information is still easier on a PC-sized keyboard (Yesilada, Harper, Chen, & Trewin, 2010). Not surprisingly, typing speeds are significantly higher on PC keyboards than on smartphone keypads (Bao et al., 2011).

Such differences ultimately cast the mobile device as more of an information retrieval device than an information creation and dissemination device. This is not to say that creating and distributing substantial amounts of content via mobile devices is impossible (e.g., VozMob Project, 2011), only that creating content of significant scope, complexity, and depth is easier on a PC than on a mobile. Certainly, if we follow this line of thinking into the realm of complex large-scale applications and services, the gap between the two modes of access likely can never be overcome (consider, for instance, whether a Facebook or a Google could be created and maintained on a set of smartphones).

This perspective is supported by findings that the creation of large and complex documents are uncommon on mobile devices (Cui & Roto, 2008; Yesilada et al., 2010). The Wikimedia Foundation has found that Wikipedia participants who transition from PCs/laptops to tablets contribute significantly less after the transition, because tablets "are better for watching videos and surfing the Internet than for typing text" (Walker, 2013, p. 1). It would seem reasonable, then, to expect an even more pronounced disparity between PC- and smartphone-based contributors. In that vein, Cohen (2014) found that only 1% of changes to Wikipedia articles are made via mobile devices.

Kaikkonen (2011) compared mobile versus PC findings across two time periods (2007 and 2010), and found that considerable differences persist, particularly in terms of production and dissemination-oriented activities such as writing email and participating in online discussions. For instance, in 2010, 35% of mobile subjects reported writing emails on their devices, compared with 57% of PC users. Similarly, 24% of mobile users reported participating in online discussions, compared with 51% of PC users (Kaikkonen, 2011). Similar patterns were found in a PC deprivation study in which PC users were allowed only mobile Internet access for four days (Hinman, Spasojevic, & Isomursu, 2008). Participants used the device to read email, but cut back on composing and sending emails due to the difficulties associated with composition on a mobile device (Hinman et al., 2008; see also Bao et al., 2011).[5]

A study in South Korea, a country with high levels of Internet and mobile penetration, found considerable interactions between content creation and content consumption activities (Ghose & Han, 2011). Specifically, through time-lagged analysis of data on content uploading and downloading activities (obtained from nearly 200,000 3G mobile users), the authors found a negative causal relationship between the two. In effect, content consumption activities appear to displace content creation activities. These findings are from a country with high levels of digital literacy; the negative effect of mobile platform usage on content creation in other populations could be even greater.

These studies appear to reflect broader patterns emerging in macro-level multi-national research indicating that "as new users get online, fewer and fewer of them appear to be content producers" (Pimienta, 2008, p. 31). Although this pattern may reflect intrinsic differences between earlier and later Internet adopters, and may diminish over time, it also seems reasonable to ask whether such patterns might suggest differences in the characteristics of the devices utilized.

### Skill Sets Across Platforms

As noted above, many mobile only users are accessing the Internet for the first time via mobile devices. It is essential that we understand that the experiences and resulting opportunities of mobile natives differ considerably from those afforded to individuals who first accessed the Internet via PC and later migrated to the mobile device (either exclusively or in conjunction with the PC). The difference in these processes has import because the PC-initiated Internet user may have developed related digital literacies and skills that transfer to the mobile context, thereby allowing a PC-initiated user of a mobile device to make more effective and advanced use of the platform than a mobile native (Hyde-Clark & Van Tonder, 2011). For instance, a multi-national study of mobile users in developing nations found that the single best predictor of usage of Internet services on smartphones is whether the individual already uses the Internet through a PC (Zainudeen & Ratnadiwakara, 2011). Similarly, Hargittai and Kim (2010) found consistent evidence that the amount of prior Internet experience and the range of Internet-related skills developed in the context of PC-based Internet access is positively related to the range of functionalities afforded by mobile devices. On the basis of these findings, they raise the concern that the spread of mobile devices could exacerbate existing digital inequalities, and feed into increasing disparities in the knowledge and skill sets necessary to use the Internet effectively.

In a rare study of the challenges faced by mobile natives, Gitau, Marsden, and Donner (2010) found that low-income residents of Cape Town, South Africa faced a variety of technical challenges related to issues such as device set-up, security settings, menu navigation, and the dearth of mobile-ready online content in their native language (see also Donner, Gitau, & Marsden, 2011). These findings suggest that "many elements of the mobile Internet have been deployed with the assumption that would-be users would have access to a PC, and/or previous experience with the PC-based Internet" (Gitau et al., 2010, p. 3). Similarly, a study of novice and low-literacy mobile users in India, the Philippines, and Kenya found a wide range of usage barriers related to "understanding or utilizing hierarchical structures, soft keys, scroll bars, nonnumeric inputs, and specialized terminology" (Medhi et al., 2011, p. 2). Wijetunga (2014) found that underprivileged youths in Sri Lanka utilized a much narrower range of their smartphones' capabilities (in many cases not moving beyond traditional voice functionality) than did youth of higher socio-economic status, due largely to a lack of relevant competencies.

Of course, PC usage would pose similar challenges to novice and low literacy users. Nonetheless, it is important to recognize that mobile Internet access represents an instance in which the skill sets associated with the previous technology are relevant to the effective use of the new technology. Such findings mean that a lack of PC-based Internet experience contributes to digital skill set disparities between mobile natives and those who have had PC-based Internet access (Steinmueller, 2001).

Findings such as these reflect the increasing recognition among scholars and policy advocates (and to a lesser extent, policymakers) of what has been termed the second-level digital divide (Hargittai, 2002; see also Epstein et al., 2011)—gaps in technology usage skill sets that persist even after disparities in access are addressed. As Campbell and Kwak warn, "the rapid evolution of mobile communication technology creates new affordances for people to be connected and informed, however it also poses new challenges for those with lower levels of technological fluency, and this can have a detrimental effect on one's ability to maximize benefits of mobile communication technology" (2010, p. 548).

## Calling Attention to the Marginalization
## of Second Class Netizens

This critique of mobile Internet access is offered as a counterpoint to the more prominent discourse focusing on the benefits of mobile, and the ways in which mobile diffusion is helping to alleviate the digital divide, in an effort to highlight the potentially negative implications of the relative prominence of mobile natives and mobile onlys in minority populations. The impetus behind our current effort is to shine a light on yet another area of ICT access and opportunity where minority populations have consistently, over many years, been marginalized (see for example Turner, 2006; Turner, 2007).

We recognize that the diffusion of mobile devices is, in many ways, an incredibly positive development. For many users, mobile Internet access is the only viable means of going online. In such cases, some form of Internet access certainly is better than none. Further, we recognize the compelling evidence across a variety of contexts that mobile Internet access can provide those without traditional forms of Internet access opportunities to become better integrated into social, economic, and political life (Castells et al., 2007; Chigona et al., 2009; Chircu & Mahajan, 2009; Fong, 2009; Schejter & Tirosh, 2012; Wareham, Levy, & Shi, 2004). That said, we feel it is important that all stakeholders involved in addressing the digital divide have as clear a sense of the potential detriments associated with mobile forms of Internet access as they do of the potential benefits. Thus our goal has been to address this other, relatively neglected, side of the equation.

As we have pointed out, although mobile Internet diffusion may effectively address the basic issue of getting individuals online, the differences between mobile and PC-based forms of Internet access can reinforce, and perhaps even exacerbate, inequities in digital skill sets, online participation, and content creation. Consequently, mobile-only Internet users become, in many ways, second-class netizens, or even a mobile Internet underclass (Napoli & Obar, 2014).

It is important to emphasize that we do not oppose efforts to support mobile adoption and usage. Rather, the aim is to inject into the policy dialogue a more comprehensive and nuanced recognition of the socially, economically, and politically significant shortcomings associated with the transition to mobile-based forms of Internet access, particularly for mobile-only users. There are significant compromises arising from policy approaches to addressing the digital divide that focus on mobile access and largely abandon any emphasis on PC-based access. Moving forward, a policy approach that maintains an emphasis on both forms of access, and that recognizes the complementarity or supplementarity in the relationship between PC and mobile Internet access, is recommended.

If promoting mobile access and diffusion does become the default policy solution to persistent digital divides, then such efforts should be accompanied by policy initiatives that maximize mobile Internet access that is functionally equivalent to PC-based Internet access across as many of the areas of disparity identified herein as possible. Such efforts might include digital readiness/digital literacy training to ensure that mobile users are able to make the most out of their device's functionality, as well as subsidies to support the creation of mobile-ready web sites and mobile applications for certain content categories deemed particularly vital to individuals' and communities' information needs, or for marginalized user segments whose needs and interests are not well served by the market (e.g., Leber, 2014). Ultimately, policymakers need to make sure that newer platforms don't replicate or exacerbate the information inequalities that have characterized the past.

## Notes

1 This research was conducted with the support of the New America Foundation's Media Policy Program.
2 For the sake of simplicity, the term "PC" will be used to encompass not only traditional desktop personal computers, but also laptop and notebook computers.
3 More recent research, offering a more up-to-date estimate, could not be located.
4 These results come from an analysis of mobile usage data gathered from over 600,000 European mobile Internet users.
5 The small scale of this study, which focused on eight U.S. college students and the data derived from online diaries that they kept of their activities via their mobile devices, should be noted.

## References

Anderson, C., & Wolff, M. (2010, August 17). The Web is dead. Long live the Internet. *Wired*. Retrieved October 19, 2015, from http://www.wired.com/magazine/2010/08/ff_webrip/.

Aufderheide, P. (2002). Competition and commons: The public interest in and after the AOL-Time Warner merger. *Journal of Broadcasting & Electronic Media, 46*(4), 515–532.

Baeza-Yates, R., Dupret, G., & Velasco, J. (2007, May). *A study of mobile search queries in Japan*. Paper presented at the WWW2007 Conference, Banff, Canada. Retrieved October 22, 2015, from http://www2007.org/workshops/paper_50.pdf.

Bao, P., Pierce, J., Whittaker, S., & Zhai, S. (2011, September). *Smart phone use by non-mobile business users*. Paper presented at the MobileHCI Conference, Stockholm.

Blank, G. (2013). Who creates content? *Information, Communication & Society, 16*(4), 590–612.

Boyera, S. (2007, May). *The mobile Web to bridge the digital divide?* Sophia-Antipolis, France: World Wide Web Consortium. Retrieved October 19, 2015, from http://www.w3.org/2006/12/digital_divide/IST-africa-final.pdf.

Brake, D. R. (2014). Are we all online content creators now? Web 2.0 and digital divides. *Journal of Computer-Mediated Communication, 19*(3), 591–609.

Campbell, S. W., & Kwak, N. (2010). Mobile communication and civic life: Linking patterns of use to civic and political engagement. *Journal of Communication, 60, 536–555.*

Carvin, A. (2000). Mind the gap: The digital divide as the civil rights issue for the new millennium. *Multimedia Schools, 7*(1), 56–58.

Castells, M., Fernandez-Ardevol, M., Qiu, J. Linchuan, Sey, A. (2007). *Mobile communication and society: A global perspective.* Cambridge, MA: The MIT Press.

Chigona, W., Beukes, D., Vally, J., & Tanner, M. (2009). Can mobile Internet help alleviate social exclusion in developing countries? *Electronic Journal on Information Systems in Developing Countries, 36*(7), 1–16.

Chircu, A. M., & Mahajan, V. (2009). Revisiting the digital divide: An analysis of mobile technology depth and service breadth in the BRIC countries. *Journal of Product Innovation Management, 26, 455–466.*

Choemprayong, S. (2006). Closing digital divides: United States' policies. *Libri, 56, 201–212.*

Church, K., Smyth, B., Cotter, P., & Bradley, K. (2007). Mobile information access: A study of emerging search behavior on the mobile Internet. *ACM Transactions on the Web, 1*(1), 1–38.

Church, K., Smyth, B., Cotter, P., & Bradley, K. (2008). A large scale study of European mobile search behavior. In *Proceedings of the 2008 Mobile HCI Conference* (pp. 13-22). New York: ACM.

Cohen, N. (2014, February 9). Wikipedia v. the small screen. *The New York Times.* Retrieved October 19, 2015, from http://www.nytimes.com/2014/02/10/technology/wikipedia-vs-the-small-screen.html.

comScore (2012). Mobile future in focus. Retrieved October 19, 2015, from http://www.comscore.com/Insights/Presentations_and_Whitepapers/2012/2012_Mobile_Future_in_Focus.

comScore (2013). Two out of five Hispanic Millennials are mobile-only internet users. *comScore Insights—Data Mine.* Retrieved October 19, 2015, from http://www.comscore.com/Insights/Data-Mine/Two-Out-of-Five-Hispanic-Millennials-are-Mobile-Only-Internet-Users.

Cui, Y., & Roto, V. (2008, April). *How people use the Web on mobile devices.* Paper presented at the International World Wide Web Conference, Beijing.

Donner, J., Gitau, S., & Marsden, G. (2011). Exploring mobile-only Internet use: Results of a training study in urban South Africa. *International Journal of Communication, 5, 574–579.*

Epstein, D., Nisbet, E. C., Gillespie, T. (2011). Who's responsible for the digital divide? Public perceptions and policy implications. *The Information Society, 27, 92–104.*

Federal Communications Commission. (2012). *National broadband plan.* Retrieved October 19, 2015, from http://www.broadband.gov.

Finamore, A., Melia, M., Munafo, M. M., Torres, R., Rao, S.G. (2011). YouTube everywhere: Impact of device and infrastructure synergies on user experience. In *Proceedings of the 2011 ACM SIGCOMM Internet Measurement Conference*, pp. 345–360. New York, NY: ACM.

Fisch, M. (2012). Mobile friendly Web sites turn visitors into customers. *Google Mobile Ads Blog*. Retrieved October 19, 2015, from http://googlemobileads.blogspot.com/2012/09/mobile-friendly-sites-turn-visitors.html.

Fong, M. W. (2009). Technology leapfrogging for developing countries. *Electronic Journal of Information Systems in Developing Countries, 36*(6), 1–12.

Ghose, A., Goldfarb, A., & Han, S. P. (2013). How is the mobile Internet different? Search costs and local activities. *Information Systems Research, 24*(3), 613–631.

Ghose, A., & Han, S. P. (2011). An empirical analysis of user content generation and usage behavior on the mobile Internet. *Management Science, 57*(9), 1,671–1,991.

Gitau, S., Marsden, G., & Donner, J. (2010). After access: Challenges facing mobile-only Internet users in the developing world. In *Proceedings of the 28th International Conference on Human Factors in Computing Systems* (pp. 2,603–2,606). New York: ACM.

Harding, M., Storz, O., Davies, N. & Friday, A. (2009, February). *Planning ahead: Techniques for simplifying mobile service use.* Paper presented at the HotMobile Conference, Santa Cruz, CA.

Hargittai, E. (2002). Second-level digital divide: Differences in people's online skills. *First Monday, 7*, 1–16.

Hargittai, E., & Kim, S. J. (2010). *The prevalence of smartphone use among a wired group of young adults (Working Paper).* Evanston, IL: Institute for Policy Research, Northwestern University. Retrieved October 19, 2015, from http://www.ipr.northwestern.edu/publications/docs/workingpapers/2011/IPR-WP-11-01.pdf.

Hargittai, E., & Walejko, G. (2008). The participation divide: Content creation and sharing in the digital age. *Information, Communication & Society, 11*(2), 239–256.

Hinman, R., Spasojevic, M., & Isomursu, P. (2008, April). *They call it "surfing" for a reason: Identifying mobile Internet needs through PC deprivation.* Paper presented at the Computer Human Interaction Conference, Florence, Italy.

Horner, L. (2011). *A human rights approach to the mobile Internet.* Melville, South Africa: Association for Progressive Communications. Retrieved October 19, 2015, from https://www.apc.org/en/system/files/LisaHorner_MobileInternet-ONLINE.pdf.

Horrigan, J. B. (2009). *Wireless Internet use.* Washington, DC: Pew Internet and American Life Project.

Humphreys, L., Von Pape, T., & Karnowski, V. (2013). Evolving mobile media use: Uses and conceptualizations of the mobile Internet. *Journal of Computer-Mediated Communication, 18*, 491–507.

Hyde-Clark, N. & Van Tonder, T. (2011). Revisiting the leapfrog debate in light of current trends of mobile phone usage in the greater Johannesburg area, South Africa. *Journal of African Media Studies, 3*(2), 263–276.

IGF (2011). Internet governance forum. *EI workshop 63: SWOT analysis of the impact of mobile internet on internet governance in Africa.* Retrieved October 19, 2015, from http://www.intgovforum.org/cms/component/content/article/71-transcripts-/896-ei-workshop-63-swot-analysis-of-the-impact-of-mobile-Internet-on-Internet-governance-in-africa.

Ishii, K. (2004). Internet use via mobile phone in Japan. *Telecommunications Policy, 28,* 43–58.

Isomursu, P., Hinman, R., Isomursu, M., Spasojeciv, M. (2007). Metaphors for the mobile Internet. *Knowledge, Technology & Policy, 20*(4), 259–268.

Kaasinen, E., Roto, V., Roloff, K., Vaananen-Vainio-Mattila, K., Vainio, T., Maehr, W., Joshi, D., & Shrestha, S. (2009). User experience of mobile Internet: Analysis and recommendations. *International Journal of Mobile Human Computer Interaction, 1*(4), 4–23.

Kaikkonen, A. (2009). Mobile Internet: Past, present, and the future. *International Journal of Mobile Human Computer Interaction, 1*(3), 29–45.

Kaikkonen, A. (2011, November). *Mobile Internet, Internet on mobiles or just Internet you access with a variety of devices.* Paper presented at the OZ Computer Human Interaction Conference, Canberra, Australia.

Kenney, M., & Pon, B. (2011). Structuring the smartphone industry: Is the mobile Internet OS platform the key? *Journal of Industry, Competition, & Trade, 11,* 239–261.

Leber, J. (2014, February 4). Now that everyone's got a smartphone, we need apps that serve low-income groups. *Fast Company.* Retrieved October 19, 2015, from http://www.fastcoexist.com/3025472/now-that-everyones-got-a-smartphone-we-need-apps-that-serve-low-income-groups.

MacKay, B., & Watters, C. (2003). The impact of migration of data to small screens on navigation. *IT & Society, 1*(3), 90–101.

Martin, M. (2012, February 20). Less than 10% of the Web in 2012 is mobile ready. *Search Engine Land.* Retrieved October 19, 2015, from http://searchengineland.com/less-than-10-of-the-web-in-2012-is-mobile-ready-112101.

Medhi, I., Patnaik, S., Brunskill, E., Nagasena, G., Nagasena, S.N., Thies, W., & Kentaro, T. (2011). Designing mobile interfaces for novices and low-literacy users. *ACMS Transactions on Computer-Human Interaction, 18*(1), 2:1–2:28.

Meunier, B. (2012) 14 differences between mobile search and desktop search results. *Search Engine Land.* Retrieved October 19, 2015, from http://searchengineland.com/14-differences-between-smartphone-search-desktop-search-results-74687.

Miller, C.C. (2013, January 8). A search engine made for mobile devices. *New York Times.* Retrieved October 19, 2015, from http://bits.blogs.nytimes.com/2013/01/08/a-search-engine-made-for-mobile-devices/.

Napoli, P. M., & Obar, J. A. (2014). The mobile internet underclass: A critique of mobile internet access. *Information society, (30)*5, 323–334.

Napoli, P. M., & Obar, J. A. (2015). The mobile conversation, Internet regression, and the re-passification of the media audience. In R. A. Lind (Ed.), *Produsing theory in a digital world: The intersection of audiences and production in contemporary theory, 2.0. Volume 2* (pp. 125–140). New York, NY: Peter Lang.

Nielsen (2013, January 17). *Smartphones: Still room to grow in emerging countries*. Retrieved October 19, 2015, from http://blog.nielsen.com/nielsenwire/consumer/smartphones-still-room-to-grow-in-emerging-countries/.

Nielsen, P., & Fjuk, A. (2010). The reality beyond the hype: Mobile Internet is primarily an extension of PC-based Internet. *The Information Society, 26*(5), 375–382.

Noam, E. (2011). Let them eat cellphones: Why mobile wireless is no solution for broadband. *Journal of Information Policy, 1*, 470–485.

O'Malley, G. (2013, November 19). Consumers consider phones primary mobile device. *MediaPost*. Retrieved October 19, 2015, from http://www.mediapost.com/publications/article/213847/consumers-consider-phones-primary-mobile-device.html.

Onishi, N. (2008, January 20). Thumbs race as Japan's bestsellers go cellular. *New York Times*. Retrieved October 19, 2015, from http://www.nytimes.com/2008/01/20/world/asia/20japan.html?pagewanted=all&_r=0.

Oulasvirta, A., Tamminen, S., Roto, V., & Kuorelahti, J. (2005, April). *Interaction in 4-second bursts: The fragmented nature of attentional resources on mobile HCI*. Paper presented at the Conference on Human Factors in Computing Systems, Portland, Oregon.

Parker, E. B. (2000). Closing the digital divide in rural America. *Telecommunications Policy, 24*, 281–290.

Pearce, K. E., & Rice, R. E. (2013). Digital divides from access to activities: Comparing mobile and personal computer Internet users. *Journal of Communication, 63*, 721–744.

Pew Research Center (2015). *U.S. smartphone use in 2015*. Retrieved October 19, 2015, from http://www.pewinternet.org/2015/04/01/us-smartphone-use-in-2015/.

Pimienta, D. (2008). Accessing content. In A. Finlay & L. Nordstrom (Eds.), *Global Information Society Watch 2008* (pp. 31–33). Melville, South Africa: Alliance for Progressive Communications, Hivos, and ITeM.

NTIA (2011). *Digital nation: Expanding internet usage. NTIA research preview*. Retrieved October 19, 2015, from http://www.ntia.doc.gov/files/ntia/publications/ntia_internet_use_report_february_2011.pdf.

Rampton, J. (2014, March 24). The future of design is adaptive. *Forbes*. Retrieved October 19, 2015, from http://www.forbes.com/sites/johnrampton/2014/03/24/adaptive-design/.

Rice, R. E., & Katz, J. E. (2003). Comparing Internet and mobile phone usage: Digital divides of usage, adoption, and dropouts. *Telecommunications Policy, 27*, 297–623.

Schejter, A., & Tirosh, N. (2012). Social media new and old in the Al-'Aarakeeb conflict: A case study. *The Information Society, 28*(5), 304–315.

Schradie, J. (2011). The digital production gap: The digital divide and Web 2.0 collide. *Poetics, 39*(2), 145–168.

Sigal, M. (2012, December 19). Why the mobile web vs. apps debate is a false dichotomy. *Gigaom*. Retrieved October 19, 2015, from http://gigaom.com/2012/12/19/why-the-mobile-web-vs-apps-debate-is-a-false-dichotomy/.

Souter, D. (2011). Mobile Internet usage and demand in Kenya: The experience of early adopters. In *Making broadband accessible for all* (Vodaphone Policy Paper Series), pp. 12–20. Newbury, UK: Vodaphone Group.

Southwood, R. (2011). *Policy and regulatory issues in the mobile Internet.* Melville, South Africa: Association for Progressive Communications.

Steinmueller, W. E. (2001). ICTs and the possibilities for leapfrogging by developing countries. *International Labour Review, 140*(2), 193–210.

Turner, S. D., & Cooper, M. (2006). *Out of the picture: Minority & female TV station ownership in the United States.* Free Press. Retrieved October 19, 2015, from http://azcmf.org/uploads/out_of_the_picture.pdf.

Turner, S. D., & Press, F. (2007). *Off the dial: Female and minority radio station ownership in the United States.* Retrieved October 19, 2015, from http://www.freepress.net/sites/default/files/stn-legacy/off_the_dial.pdf.

VozMob Project (2011). Mobile voices: Projecting the voices of immigrant workers by appropriating mobile phones for popular communication. In P. M. Napoli & M. Aslama (Eds.), *Communications research in action: Scholar-activist collaborations for a democratic public sphere* (pp. 177–196). New York, NY: Fordham University Press.

Walker, R. (2013, March 4). Are smartphones and tablets turning us into sissies? *Yahoo! News.* Retrieved October 19, 2015, from http://news.yahoo.com/are-smartphones-and-tablets-turning-us-into-sissies--175359859.html.

Wareham, J., Levy, A., & Shi, W. (2004). Wireless diffusion and mobile computing: Implications for the digital divide. *Telecommunications Policy, 28,* 439–457.

White House (2015). *Connecting America: What high speed internet means in the 21st century.* The White House: President Barack Obama. Retrieved October 19, 2015, from https://www.whitehouse.gov/connect-america.

Wijetunga, D. (2014). The digital divide objectified in design: Use of the mobile telephone by underprivileged youth in Sri Lanka. *Journal of Computer-Mediated Communication, 19*(3), 712–726.

Wu, T. (2007). Wireless Carterfone. *International Journal of Communication, 1,* 389–426.

Yesilada, Y., Harper, S., Chen, T., & Trewin, S. (2010). Small-device users situationally impaired by input. *Computers in Human Behavior, 26,* 427–435.

Zainudeen, A., & Ratnadiwakara, D. (2011). Are the poor stuck in voice? Conditions for adoption of more-than-voice mobile services. *Information Technologies & International Development, 7*(3), 45–59.

Zittrain, J. (2008). *The future of the Internet: And how to stop it.* New Haven, CT: Yale University Press.

311

# 18

# "DAMSELING FOR DOLLARS"
## Toxic Technocultures and Geek Masculinity

*Adrienne L. Massanari*

In 2012, media critic Anita Sarkeesian of Feminist Frequency launched a Kickstarter campaign to fund a video series called *Tropes vs. Women in Video Games*. An extension of earlier work in which she critiqued how women were portrayed in pop culture (*Tropes vs. Women*), the campaign received considerable press coverage when it generated a barrage of harassment and threats from a segment of the video gaming community. Much of the vitriol directed at Sarkeesian was rooted in a misogynistic view of gaming culture—where men are considered the real audience for video games, and women and minorities are viewed as unwelcome interlopers or not real gamers (Consalvo, 2012; Shaw, 2013).

In this chapter, I consider the ways in which geek masculinity (Kendall, 2011; McArthur, 2009) often works to marginalize women and people of color, using the ongoing harassment of Anita Sarkeesian as a case study. Michael Kimmel argued that many White men see gains in gender and racial equity coming at the cost of their own privilege, to which they feel entitled, calling this concept "aggrieved entitlement" (2013, p. 18). I argue that this feeling is at the root of the misogynistic, anti-feminist actions directed at Sarkeesian and others. A certain vocal segment of the gaming community (mostly White men) perceives the increasing diversity of gaming content and audiences as fundamentally threatening their social identity as gamers and are expressing their anger (Shaw, 2013). This case also highlights the mutability of new media—both its potential to encourage organization and coordination globally (as evidenced by Sarkeesian's use of the crowd-funding site Kickstarter)—as well as the ease with which these same technologies can be leveraged as efficient tools for coordinated bullying and harassment.

By focusing on one case, and one person, I do not mean to suggest Anita Sarkeesian's experience is anything new; women have long been targeted for public shaming in online spaces (Anderson, 2015; Citron, 2014; Nussbaum, 2010). In particular, prominent women working in technology organizations or affiliated with geek-friendly communities are often the recipients of abuse (Liebelson & Raja, 2013; Sierra, 2014; Watson, 2012). Likewise, online harassment has always had a distinctly gendered bent, as Julian Dibbell's (1999) discussion of the virtual rape of a participant in an early online community, and as Susan Herring's (Herring, 1999; Herring, Job-Sluder, Scheckler, & Barab, 2002; Herring & Stoerger, 2014) large body of research aptly demonstrates. Still, investigating how *Tropes vs. Women in Video Games* has been received is important, not just because of the significant press it has generated,[1] but because of the confluence of issues it represents: contemporary public discourse around feminism and media; geek masculinity in gaming and technology; and the ways in which platforms such as YouTube, Reddit, and Twitter serve to promote the kind of toxic cultures that target Sarkeesian and others. Understanding the convergence of these factors can provide activists, policy makers, and individuals a better understanding of how they might combat future harassment and provide a better space for productive discourse around these complex issues.

## Geek Masculinity

The terms "geek" and "nerd" are gradually losing their pejorative nature. Both traditionally were used as insults to indicate someone was socially awkward, preoccupied with unpopular interests in technology or science, and sexually frustrated (Eglash, 2002; Kendall, 1999). But geek culture has become increasingly mainstream. Young Silicon Valley millionaires helm the most popular media/communication companies (such as Twitter and Facebook), fandom communities (a long time home of the geek) are courted by media executives, and a DIY/hacker ethos permeates everything from content creation to political activism (Andrejevic, 2008; Coleman, 2013; Jenkins, 2006). At the same time, geek culture remains tied to hegemonic masculinity (Connell & Messerschmidt, 2005); even if it repudiates some elements, it still remains largely White, cisgendered, heterosexual, and male-dominated (Kendall, 2011). Likewise, the rise in the so-called "brogrammer" stereotype (a portmanteau of the term "bro" and "programmer")—as a socially successful, image and body-conscious White young man who just happens to code—demonstrates both the changing nature of geek culture and its continuing tendency to marginalize women and people of color (MacMillan, 2012).

However, geek masculinity remains in conflict with other aspects of hegemonic masculinity. Heterosexual male geeks in particular may perceive themselves as perpetually marginalized because in their youth, their interests made them a target for bullies and invisible to the objects of their sexual desire. The suggestion that they hold immense amounts of social and cultural capital is often met with incredulity, because it does not match their lived experiences (Tufekci, 2014). Thus, discussions of the implicit marginalization of women and people of color in technology and geek communities are often met with skepticism or outright hostility, because some members see themselves completely at odds with the more pernicious aspects of hegemonic masculinity.

Much of the rise and acceptance of geek culture is intertwined with the simultaneous rise of new media technologies. The traditional one-way media producer to consumer role has been transformed, and a new class of "produsers" (producer-consumers) has emerged (Bruns, 2008). The increasing penetration of network technologies into everyday life, and the rise of user-generated content, offers new possibilities for political activism and deliberative discourse. However, the same features that make spaces such as Twitter, 4chan, and Reddit popular for sharing user-generated content also make them effective platforms for coordinated harassment and misogynistic activism. In other work (Massanari, 2015), I have suggested we might refer to these kinds of cultures which are both enabled by and publically accessible through these platforms as "toxic techno-cultures." This is a particularly salient concept in light of the *Tropes vs. Women in Video Games* series and the harassment campaign it generated. Geek culture and toxic technocultures often overlap in their valorization of free speech as a foundational principle, even if this results in tolerating offensive or potentially criminal behavior. Likewise, both cultures often embrace technolibertarianism, embracing meritocratic structures, neoliberal politics, and individualism over other ideals (Borsook, 2001; Turner, 2006).

## Feminist Frequency and *Tropes vs. Women*

*Tropes vs. Women in Video Games* grew out of Sarkeesian's previous work for Feminist Frequency (the non-profit media organization she founded to produce the videos) that examines the role of women in all forms of popular culture. Entitled *Tropes vs. Women* (*TvW*), the original series discussed six common tropes used in popular culture to portray women, particularly in science fiction and fantasy media. For example, the video for the Evil Demon Seductress trope features clips from geek-friendly television series *Battlestar Galactica* and *Buffy the Vampire Slayer*. Although video games are briefly mentioned in the *TvW* series, they are subsumed within a larger context of popular media—movies, comics, television series, and so forth. Each video deconstructs the trope under consideration, suggesting that it can easily become a cliché and is problematic because of its tendency to perpetuate offensive stereotypes about women, and ends with a brief message asking Hollywood writers to create roles that more fully portray the complexity of female experience. Sarkeesian is the on-screen narrator for both series.

Although the original *Tropes vs. Women* series did result in some harassment, it was relatively minimal. In an interview when *TvW* was released, Sarkeesian said she received harassing comments, but they were mostly along the line that she should, "get back into the kitchen" (Angyal, 2011). Soon after the *TvW* videos were released, a popular sociology blog linked to one describing the Straw Feminist trope in popular media. Although some commenters disagreed with Sarkeesian's perspective, the discussion thread is mostly civil and on-topic (Wade, 2011).[2] Contrast this to the reaction to Sarkeesian's later videos even before their release: after her Kickstarter campaign was announced, someone created an interactive web game in which one could "beat up Anita Sarkeesian" by clicking on her photo (Lewis, 2012). Despite the videos' feminist approach, it seemed to be the examination of game texts (and by extension, gaming culture) that inspired the most vitriol.

Sarkeesian's second set of videos, *Tropes vs. Women in Video Games* (*TWVG*), launched on crowd-funding site Kickstarter in May 2012. The campaign's goal was $6,000 to fund a set of five videos exploring how women were portrayed in video games, specifically to "explore, analyze and deconstruct some of the most common tropes and stereotypes of female characters" (Sarkeesian, 2012). The modest goal was met within a day, and Sarkeesian eventually raised over $158,000 to produce the series, which expanded to 12 videos as a result of the increased funding. Within days of the project's debut on Kickstarter, however, Sarkeesian was subjected to repeated misogynistic harassment through comments on her YouTube channel, Twitter feed, and website. In addition, her Wikipedia entry was repeatedly vandalized at times featuring pornography, racial slurs, and rape and death threats (Feminist Frequency, 2012a, 2012b). Gaming forums and geek-friendly communities such as Reddit and 4chan became awash in memes, videos, and pornographic images featuring Sarkeesian and lambasting her (still-unreleased) videos. Sarkeesian used the opportunity to publically discuss the harassment, giving talks at conferences such as TEDxWomen to highlight the issues women often face from their membership in gaming and technology communities. After the videos were released the harassment intensified; eventually, Sarkeesian disabled comments on her YouTube channel to stem the torrent of death and rape threats. She also faced accusations of swindling Kickstarter backers and misusing funds from the campaign (Baker-Whitelaw, 2013).

## #Gamergate and Gaming Identity

Although the Kickstarter campaign for *TWVG* began the first wave of harassment against Anita Sarkeesian, each subsequent video release led to a new storm of harassment, mostly through Twitter and on anonymous image boards such as 4chan. 4chan in particular became a spot for sharing anti-Anita memes (detractors refer to Sarkeesian by her first name only), often trading in pornographic and violent imagery. However, a more virulent strain of attack against Sarkeesian and others began later in the form of a hashtag activism movement called #GamerGate.

In February 2013, game developer Zoe Quinn released a game to her website called *Depression Quest*. Players embody a character struggling with chronic depression in an interactive story setting. The game was met with mostly positive reviews. However, Quinn received a spate of death and rape threats after releasing it to Steam's Greenlight service (an offshoot of the popular PC gaming platform specifically for independent games) (Parkin, 2014). In August 2014, a lengthy blog posting was linked to several forums, including 4chan's /v (video game) board. In it a developer named Eron Gjoni accused Quinn of a long list of transgressions, most of which centered on her purported infidelity during their relationship. In particular, Gjoni insinuated that Quinn had received favorable press coverage for *Depression Quest* because of her ongoing sexual relationship with a games journalist (despite the fact that it was later revealed that the journalist never reviewed her game). This in particular caught the attention of 4chan and later Reddit, where accusations centered on the idea that Quinn's actions were indicative of larger problems in the independent gaming community and its relationship with the gaming press, which was perceived by some as too cozy (Stuart, 2014). Under the banner of demanding greater transparency and encouraging ethical games journalism, people started using Twitter to discuss the accusations against Quinn. This led to a groundswell of harassment directed at Quinn, other independent game developers, and journalists perceived as supporting Quinn and social justice causes. Later, conservative actor Adam Baldwin, who appeared on geek fan favorite Joss Whedon's short-lived television series *Firefly*, coined the term "#Gamergate" to describe the movement and suggested it was further proof of a liberal bias in the media and disturbing evidence of political correctness run amuck (Kaufman, 2014).

People rallied around the hashtag, insisting that #Gamergate was a consumer campaign to raise awareness about ethics in games journalism. However, #Gamergate effectively became a harassment campaign enacted via Twitter, Reddit, 4chan (and 8chan after 4chan's owner banned discussion about Quinn from the boards after her personal information was repeatedly shared by users). It also gained public attention, when it became a popular topic on Twitter—over 316,000 tweets using the hashtag were sent over the course of three days in mid-October 2014 (Baio, 2014). Of course, not all tweets using the #Gamergate hashtag supported the movement; some decried the harassment. For supporters, however, the hashtag became an effective way to swarm the mentions of

users perceived as not sharing their views, which became known colloqui-
ally as "sea lioning" (Malki, 2014). This made it difficult to determine
who was using the #Gamergate hashtag in earnest, and who was using
it to harass. When confronted, #Gamergate supporters often responded
that harassment was done by people unaffiliated with the grassroots
movement. But this argument became difficult to justify, because people
publicly demonstrating affinity for the perspective of #Gamergate often
spouted misogynistic and retrograde views about women and people of
color, and rarely discussed the underlying ethical issues of games journalism in their numerous tweets, videos, and blog posts (Alexander, 2014b;
McCormick, 2014; Quinn, 2014). And then there were the very real
threats of physical violence against Anita Sarkeesian, Zoe Quinn, and
Brianna Wu (another independent game developer who spoke out against
#Gamergate), which caused each of them to leave her home for safety.
That same month (October 2014), Sarkeesian canceled an appearance
at Utah State University after someone threatened a massacre and police
were unable to ensure the safety of Sarkeesian and audience members
(Wingfield, 2014).

So why did #Gamergate gain traction among the gaming community?
One answer has to do with the diversification of gaming content and players. As digital distribution has enabled a rise of independent developers,
the gaming industry has expanded its production, moving beyond hard-
core and expensive franchises such as *Call of Duty* and *Grand Theft Auto*
(Martin & Deuze, 2009). Increasingly, casual and independent games
have dominated the marketplace and attracted a new, more diverse gaming audience. An Electronic Software Association (2015) report described
the gaming public as 44% female with an average age of 35. #Gamergate
is a direct response to this change, because Gamergaters (GGs) often
opine that just as certain gamers are not really gamers, these kinds of
games are not really games.[3] They also vehemently disagree with journalists such as Leigh Alexander (2014a) who argued that the social category
"gamer" is no longer relevant or useful because games and game culture
have moved beyond the image of the young, White male as its primary
player/audience. More specifically, they lament the inclusion of what they
disparagingly term "social justice warriors" (SJWs) in industry and journalism ranks and who they claim are pushing a feminist agenda in how
games are made and covered. The rise of independent developers and
casual gaming have altered gaming culture in ways perceived as a direct
threat to what Derek Burrill (2008) called a "digital boyhood" imaginary
(p. 15), challenging the idea that gaming culture is somehow immune to
critique or is a space only for boys or men (Shaw, 2013).

Ironically, the increasing sophistication of games (in terms of both
narratives and mechanics) has rendered moot the question of whether
games are legitimate cultural forms—even as their increasing relevance

and sophistication has drawn the ire of many GGs. Most journalists, players, and developers consider games an art form—and thus deserving of critical consideration. Contemporary journalism and innovative game development reflect this stance, but also challenge the received notion that games are unimportant, just for fun, or separate from the world of the everyday (Consalvo, 2009). These are precisely the underpinnings of the digital boyhood identity to which many GGs cling. To explain the presence of women in gaming communities, some #Gamergate supporters rely on the popular stereotype that they are merely "fake geek girls," there just to gain the attention of the opposite sex (Edidin, 2012). Conservative columnist and GG supporter Milo Yinnopoulos demonstrated this way of thinking:

> There is a platoon of irritants in the media whose talents are vanishingly slight, but who generate column inches by the thousand for victimising innocents and manipulating their way around an over-sensitive industry. Some of them, such as Anita Sarkeesian, have no discernible higher purpose in life, except to bother innocent games developers.
>
> These women purposefully court—and then exploit—boisterous, unpleasant reactions from astonished male gamers and use them to attract attention to themselves. What's remarkable is how deeply unpleasant the skeletons lurking in their own closets often are, how completely those skeletons give lie to their public image, and how uncritically their claims are repackaged by credulous games journalists.
>
> (Yiannopoulos, 2014)

According to this logic, GGs are the victims here—they are the ones subject to the machinations of nefarious, talentless women (such as Sarkeesian) who victimize "innocent games developers" in their quest to destroy gaming, while also manipulating players and journalists into doing their bidding. This logic also suggests that women in games (as developers, journalists, critics, and players) should have no expectation of a private life. It would be easy to dismiss these claims, because they sound remarkably close to those expressed by conspiracy theorists—and there is significant overlap between the two communities on Reddit for example (RedditAnalysisBot, 2014)—if the implications of this line of thinking were not so serious. Using this logic, it is an easy leap to suggest that any doxxing (the distribution of private information) of Quinn, Sarkeesian, and others targeted by #Gamergate is fair play—they are public figures and are therefore, to use the odious phrase associated with rape culture, simply "asking for it."

Yiannopoulos' words and those of other Gamergate supporters are prime examples of "aggrieved entitlement" (Kimmel, 2013, p. 18), in which White men may view their position of privilege as both immutable and above reproach. Michael Kimmel argued that this results in ". . . a personal sense of self that is defined always in relationship to some perceived injury and whose collective politics mixes hatred and envy of those who we believe have injured us" (2013, p. 38). GG attacks often suggest this duality, with Zoe Quinn and Anita Sarkeesian characterized as swindlers who somehow are able to curry favor with the press and public in a way that the #Gamergate community envies. Instead of believing that Sarkeesian's Kickstarter campaign was popular because supporters agreed that women are often poorly represented in mainstream gaming and thought the project was worthwhile, GGs suggested that she received attention because of conspiratorial connections between independent game developers and gaming journalists.

Coupled with Yiannaopoulos' belief that Sarkeesian is merely interested in gaining publicity for herself is the common GG complaint that the video series is flawed simply because Sarkeesian is not a gamer. This suggests that being a gamer confers some special legitimacy to critique, but that it also requires fully embracing the "digital boyhood" identity mentioned above. It also presupposes that those who consider themselves gamers will not engage in larger discussions of games' cultural impact or meaning. To be fair, part of this reluctance to consider games worthy of in-depth cultural critique has much to do with moral panics that continue to flourish about the relationship between violent videogames and real world violence (Critcher, 2008; Squire, 2002). For the gamer any possible suggestion that video games matter, that they reflect and possibly influence the ways we think about the world outside games, becomes a kind of slippery slope argument—one that might lead to attempts to censor or suppress gaming content. Thus, dismissing Sarkeesian as "not a gamer" allows some in the gaming community to distance themselves from acknowledging that games, in fact, matter.

A YouTube video posted by Sargon of Akkad (2014), a popular figure in the #Gamergate community, demonstrates these ideas. The video juxtaposes professionally produced clips from an interview with Sarkeesian and from her Kickstarter campaign, in which she declares herself a gamer, with grainy, black-and-white footage taken from a 2010 academic presentation in which she suggests she "is not a fan of video games" and "had to learn a lot about video games in the process of making this [remix video]." It finishes with a screenshot of the Wikipedia entry for "confidence trick" paired with a voiceover asking the viewer to consider which declaration "sounded like a candid moment of honesty, and which one sounded like a scripted lie" (Sargon of Akkad, 2014). Clearly, we are meant to view these moments as fundamentally irreconcilable and conclude that Sarkeesian is lying when she says she is a gamer. What gets discounted and left out in this interpretation is manifold. Sarkeesian is likely downplaying her video gaming experience in the 2010 presentation, possibly as a rhetorical strategy to deflect critiques of the video remix she is presenting for the first time. More likely, her statement about "not being a fan of video games" is meant to signal her dislike of certain genres of video games, specifically, first-person shooters. At one point she clarifies her statement, saying, "I don't want to go around shooting people and ripping off their heads . . . it's just gross." Because the video is merely an incomplete excerpt of the 2010 presentation, it is difficult to contextualize both its purpose and what, exactly, she meant by deflecting her experience playing video games.

## Anita Sarkeesian as Feminist Critic

Attacks on Sarkeesian's videos were not limited to those within the gaming community. The founder of men's rights activism/anti-feminist blog *A Voice for Men*, Paul Elam, joined the multitude of voices suggesting that Sarkeesian's "arguments are poorly articulated, boring, constructed like slop, highly biased, and completely, excruciatingly stupid" and that her videos were attempts to swindle overly sensitive feminists and white knights.[4] She was, in his words, "damseling for dollars" (Elam, 2014). Elam further suggested that although Sarkeesisan did not deserve the rape and death threats, she was profiting from them—profits that he suggested he might receive for his own work but, "I don't have a vagina and the sociopathic acumen to be profitably distressed and empowered at the same time" (Elam, 2014). Besides the troubling biologically essentialist invective Elam uses, what seems to bother him (and other anti-feminists) most is not just that Sarkeesian used her voice to speak out about how games often marginalize and stereotype female characters, but that she did so from an openly feminist perspective.

Importantly, Sarkeesian's feminist stance does not align with the post-feminism ideals that characterize today's popular discourse. As scholars have argued, post-feminism substitutes individual choice, consumer demand, and neoliberal ideals for systemic critiques of patriarchal power structures (Anderson, 2015; McRobbie, 2004; Tasker & Negra, 2007). Sarkeesian's videos present infrastructural critiques about video games and gaming culture. For example, in framing her videos as discussions of tropes across multiple games series, she implies that these are ongoing patterns and the culture of mainstream game design. At the same time, she prefaces each by suggesting that we still might enjoy playing such games even as we attend to how which women are represented in them. As she said in her first video, "This series will include critical analysis of many beloved games and characters. But remember—it's both possible, and even necessary, to simultaneously enjoy media while also being critical of its more problematic or pernicious aspects" (Feminist Frequency, 2013). Sarkeesian's statement echoes a familiar dialectical tension is of media/cultural studies work. Few individuals would willingly devote the amount of time that cultural critics do to consuming and analyzing media if they did not at some level actually enjoy said media. However, the concomitant ability to both enjoy and critique media seems lost on many of Sarkeesian's detractors. GGs and others rely on oversimplified explanations for troubling content in games. They either suggest that players who are bothered by the portrayal of women in games just should not buy them, or because "it's just a game" these things do not matter.[5]

Another complaint levied by #Gamergate supporters is that SJWs will not hear or respond to their critiques. Feminist Frequency videos on YouTube have comments disabled (as are blog entries on the non-profit's website) as a result of the harassment Sarkeesian continues to receive. What appears to outsiders as a reasonable choice (disabling at least some of the channels by which individuals can publically shame and threaten) is perceived by her detractors as proof that she is unwilling and unable to debate the issues. As one Tumblr user argued,

> She says she wants to "create a dialogue" or "force video games into open debate", except she turns off both comments and even ratings on her videos. Wanting to hear your own voice in an echo chamber is the total opposite of "open debate". You cannot have "debate" in a vacuum, and she very clearly wants to critique video games in a vacuum from her educated-liberal upper-middle-class white Jewish Canadian-American woman without input from other point of views. It's posturing. That's all it is.
>
> (robbiebaldwin, 2013)

The question becomes: what kind of dialogue can be had when harassment becomes the language through which individuals express their displeasure at Sarkeesian's findings?

This environment also creates another, more insidious problem. As cultural critiques, Sarkeesian's videos are not perfect. They neither fully acknowledge audience agency in terms of resistive readings (Hall, 1992), for example, nor address the complexities of how individuals (especially marginalized ones) engage with issues of representation and identification in video games (Shaw, 2014). Nor do they engage with the political-economic realities of video game production (Martin & Deuze, 2009). They fail to address the even more problematic realities of representation of people of color in games (Williams, Martins, Consalvo, & Ivory, 2009). One could even say that at moments, Sarkeesian's critiques lack nuance or academic rigor (even though this was not her goal). However, the ongoing harassment she receives makes it difficult for anyone to engage legitimately in a dialogue about these issues without, as some say, "feeding the trolls"—by providing further evidence for would-be harassers to claim that Sarkeesian doesn't know what she's talking about. So, the complaint that SJWs close ranks and refuse to acknowledge the limitations of her work is not entirely unfounded. But what harassers refuse to acknowledge is that their actions demonstrate a complete lack of respect for her personhood and her right even to exist in what they see as their space. As Sarkeesian wrote in a letter to supporters in Feminist Frequency's 2014 annual report, "Back in 2012, when I announced the *Tropes vs Women in Video Games* project, I received an enormous amount of abusive harassment. Unfortunately, this vitriol is still a daily occurrence, making it impossible to separate our media criticism work from the reception of that work" (Feminist Frequency, 2015, p. 5). This aspect of the case is also troubling—harassment of Sarkeesian and anyone else targeted under the #Gamergate banner has effectively shut down productive conversation about these issues. Neither are academic conversations immune; #Gamergate has also targeted the Digital Games Research Association's members, suggesting that a vast conspiracy exists between academic gaming research and feminist concerns (Chess & Shaw, 2015).

## Moving Forward

The case of Anita Sarkeesian and #Gamergate remind us that participatory culture (Jenkins, 2006; Jenkins, Ford, & Green, 2013)—a culture which has been frequently lauded for undermining an earlier era of mass media characterized by a one-way relationship between media producers and consumers—can as easily serve non-democratic as democratic purposes. In this case, Anita Sarkeesian's harassment utilized the same platforms that encourage the sharing of remixes, videos, games, memes, tweets, blog posts, and so on. Toxic technocultures such as #Gamergate flourish on platforms including YouTube, Reddit, 4chan, and others for many reasons: users remain semi- or fully anonymous; moderation policies often favor freedom of speech over other concerns; and the public nature of the services makes it easy for others to see harassing statements and perhaps join in (as GGs did by swarming mentions). However, these platforms provide an unequal playing field for participants. Because they are built by and reflective of technolibertarian ideals, and because their creators are unlikely to be targets of systemic campaigns such as #Gamergate, tools to prevent harassment of other users tend to be secondary design concerns.

But why Anita Sarkeesian in particular? Underlying many of the insults hurled her way (and at others who speak out against #Gamergate) are retrograde notions about women and their right to speak—in particular, their right to critique the institutions and infrastructures that serve patriarchy. Sarkeesian's refusal to be quiet about her harassment, and her unwillingness to embrace post-feminism ideology, which substitutes a language of individual choice and empowerment for larger critiques of systemic, infrastructural inequalities, makes her a tantalizing target (McRobbie, 2009). In addition, her critique of gaming cuts to the core of geek masculinity—questioning the unstated assumption that gamers and their pastime are culturally marginal, and thus ineligible for critique. By challenging the "digital boyhood" imaginary that has characterized a strain of gaming culture understood by media producers and some audience members, Sarkeesian (along with others targeted by #Gamergate) directly challenge the validity of "gamer" as a meaningful social category.

Video games are no longer special, nor are they relegated to the margins of media cultures. One would think that this diversification of the gaming industry and its audience would lead to more conversation, not less, about its importance as a cultural form—particularly by those who are most invested in consuming games. But #Gamergate supporters and others who target Anita Sarkeesian too often rely on a language not of inclusion, but exclusion, thus effectively shutting down any meaningful dialogue that could and should be had about ethics in games journalism and likely prevents individuals from even wanting to make games—a loss for everyone.

## Notes

1 The high-profile nature of Anita Sarkeesian's harassment (and ensuing media coverage) led to her being named as one of *Time*'s "The 100 Most Influential People" for 2015 (Wheaton, 2015).

2 It is possible that the blog's status as an academic space would attract more civil commentary. Likewise the blog's moderation policies may have eliminated any personal attacks made by readers. However, the tenor and intensity of online discussion around Sarkeesian subsequently makes that unlikely—and suggests that something changed after her first videos were released.

3 See, for example, the comments on Metacritic from users about Zoe Quinn's *Depression Quest* ("Depression Quest—user reviews," 2015) or The Fullbright Company's *Gone Home* ("Gone Home—user reviews," 2015). Many users suggested that these should not even be considered games at all—ostensibly because they were more narratively driven than many games, but more likely because they foregrounded characters which were unlikely to be seen in many more popular titles (a person experiencing significant clinical depression in the former, and a young woman who was coming out to her family in the latter).

4 White knight is a popular pejorative term for men who defend women on the internet, presumably for romantic rewards (Don, 2013).

5 A sampling of this kind of thinking can be seen in the comments on a video entitled "Anita Sarkeesian-BUSTED!" by YouTube blogger Thunderf00t: https://www.youtube.com/watch?v=WuRSaLZidWI.

# References

Alexander, L. (2014a, August 28). "Gamers" don't have to be your audience. "Gamers" are over. *Gamasutra*. Retrieved October 17, 2015, from http://www.gamasutra.com/view/news/224400/Gamers_dont_have_to_be_your_audience_Gamers_are_over.php.

Alexander, L. (2014b, October 3). *List of ethical concerns in video games (partial)*. Retrieved October 17, 2015, from http://leighalexander.net/list-of-ethical-concerns-in-video-games-partial/.

Anderson, K. J. (2015). *Modern misogyny: Anti-feminism in a post-feminist era*. New York, NY: Oxford University Press.

Andrejevic, M. (2008). Watching television without pity: The productivity of online fans. *Television & New Media, 9*(24), 24–46.

Angyal, C. (2011, March 12). The Feministing five: Anita Sarkeesian. *Feministing*. Retrieved October 17, 2015, from http://feministing.com/2011/03/12/the-feministing-five-anita-sarkeesian/.

Baio, A. (2014, October 27). 72 Hours of #Gamergate. *Medium*. Retrieved October 17, 2015, from https://medium.com/message/72-hours-of-gamergate-e00513f7cf5d.

Baker-Whitelaw, G. (2013, August 1). Anita Sarkeesian faces backlash for disabling YouTube comments. *The Daily Dot*. Retrieved October 17, 2015, from http://www.dailydot.com/society/anita-sarkeesian-feminist-frequency-backlash/.

Borsook, P. (2001). Cyberselfish: Ravers, guilders, cyberpunks, and other Silicon Valley life-forms. *Yale Journal of Law & Technology, 3*(1). Retrieved October 25, 2015, from http://digitalcommons.law.yale.edu/yjolt/vol3/iss1/1.

Bruns, A. (2008). *Blogs, Wikipedia, Second Life, and beyond: From production to produsage*. New York, NY: Peter Lang.

Burrill, D. A. (2008). *Die tryin': Videogames, masculinity, culture*. New York, NY: Peter Lang.

Chess, S., & Shaw, A. (2015). A conspiracy of fishes, or, how we learned to stop worrying about #GamerGate and embrace hegemonic masculinity. *Journal of Broadcasting & Electronic Media, 59*(1), 208–220.

Citron, D. K. (2014). *Hate crimes in cyberspace*. Cambridge, MA: Harvard University Press.

Coleman, E. G. (2013). *Coding freedom: The ethics and aesthetics of hacking*. Princeton, NJ: Princeton University Press.

Connell, R. W., & Messerschmidt, J. W. (2005). Hegemonic masculinity: Rethinking the concept. *Gender & Society, 19*(6), 829–859.

Consalvo, M. (2009). There is no magic circle. *Games and Culture, 4*(4), 408–417.

Consalvo, M. (2012). Confronting toxic gamer culture: A challenge for feminist game studies scholars. *Ada: A Journal of Gender, New Media, and Technology, 1*(1). Retrieved October 25, 2015 from http://adanewmedia.org/2012/11/issue1-consalvo/.

Critcher, C. (2008). Making waves: Historical aspects of public debates about children and mass media. In K. Drotner & S. Livingstone (Eds.), *The International handbook of children, media and culture* (pp. 91–104). London: Sage.

Depression Quest—user reviews (2015). *Metacritic*. Retrieved October 17, 2015, from http://www.metacritic.com/game/pc/depression-quest/user-reviews.

Dibbell, J. (1999). *My tiny life: Crime and passion in a virtual world*. New York, NY: Henry Holt and Company.

Don (2013). White knight. *Know Your Meme.* Retrieved October 17, 2015, from http://knowyourmeme.com/memes/white-knight.

Edidin, R. (2012, November 15). Geek masculinity and the myth of the fake geek girl. *Comics Alliance.* Retrieved October 17, 2015, from http://comicsalliance. com/geek-masculinity-and-the-myth-of-the-fake-geek-girl/.

Eglash, R. (2002). Race, sex, and nerds: From Black geeks to Asian American hipsters. *Social Text, 20*(2), 49–64.

Elam, P. (2014, August 28). Damseling for dollars. Anita Sarkeesian scores again. *A Voice for Men.* Retrieved October 17, 2015, from http://www.avoiceformen. com/feminism/damseling-for-dollars-anita-sarkeesian-scores-again/.

Electronic Software Association (2015). *Essential facts about the computer and video game industry.* Retrieved October 17, 2015, from http://www.theesa. com/wp-content/uploads/2015/04/ESA-Essential-Facts-2015.pdf.

Feminist Frequency (2012a, June 10). *Harassment via Wikipedia vandalism.* Retrieved October 17, 2015, from http://feministfrequency.com/2012/06/10/ harassment-and-misogyny-via-wikipedia/

Feminist Frequency (2012b, June 7). Harassment, misogyny and silencing on YouTube. Retrieved October 17, 2015, from http://feministfrequency. com/2012/06/07/harassment-misogyny-and-silencing-on-youtube/.

Feminist Frequency (Producer) (2013). Damsel in distress: Part 1. *Tropes vs Women in Video Games.* [Video] Retrieved October 25, 2015, from https:// www.youtube.com/watch?v=X6p5AZp7r_Q.

Feminist Frequency. (2015, January 23). *Feminist Frequency's 2014 annual report.* Retrieved Retrieved October 17, 2015, from http://feministfrequency. com/2015/01/23/feminist-frequencys-2014-annual-report/.

Gone Home—user reviews. (2015). *Metacritic.* Retrieved October 17, 2015, from http://www.metacritic.com/game/pc/gone-home/user-reviews.

Hall, S. (1992). Encoding/decoding. In S. Hall, D. Hobson, A. Lowe & P. Willis (Eds.), *Culture, media, language* (pp. 128–138). New York, NY: Routledge.

Herring, S. C. (1999). The rhetorical dynamics of gender harrassment on-line. *The Information Society, 15*, 151–167.

Herring, S. C., Job-Sluder, K., Scheckler, R., & Barab, S. (2002). Searching for safety online: Managing "trolling" in a feminist forum. *The Information Society, 18*, 371–384.

Herring, S. C., & Stoerger, S. (2014). Gender and (a)nonymity in computer-mediated communication. In S. Ehrlich, M. Meyerhoff, & J. Holmes (Eds.), *The handbook of language, gender, and sexuality* (pp. 567–586). Chichester, UK: Wiley-Blackwell.

Jenkins, H. (2006). *Convergence culture: Where old and new media collide.* New York, NY: NYU Press.

Jenkins, H., Ford, S., & Green, J. (2013). *Spreadable media: Creating value and meaning in a networked world.* New York, NY: NYU Press.

Kaufman, S. (2014, November 10). Actor Adam Baldwin: #GamerGate defeated the left, but there will be no parade. *Raw Story.* Retrieved October 17, 2015, from http://www.rawstory.com/2014/11/actor-adam-baldwin-gamergate-defeated-the-left-but-there-will-be-no-parade/.

Kendall, L. (1999). Nerd nation: Images of nerds in US popular culture. *International Journal of Cultural Studies, 2*(2), 260–283.

Kendall, L. (2011). "White and nerdy": Computers, race, and the nerd stereotype. *The Journal of Popular Culture, 44*(3), 505–524.

Kimmel, M. (2013). *Angry White men: American masculinity at the end of an era.* New York, NY: Nation Books.

Lewis, H. (2012, July 6). This is what online harassment looks like. *New Statesman.* Retrieved October 17, 2015, from http://www.newstatesman.com/blogs/internet/2012/07/what-online-harassment-looks.

Liebelson, D., & Raja, T. (2013, March 22). Donglegate: How one brogrammer's sexist joke led to death threats and firings. *Mother Jones.* Retrieved October 17, 2015, from http://www.motherjones.com/politics/2013/03/pycon-2013-sexism-dongle-richards.

MacMillan, D. (2012, March 1). The rise of the "brogrammer". *Bloomberg Business.* Retrieved October 17, 2015, from http://www.bloomberg.com/bw/articles/2012-03-01/the-rise-of-the-brogrammer.

Malki, D. (2014, September 19). #1062; The terrible sea lion. *Wondermark.* Retrieved October 17, 2015, from http://wondermark.com/1k62/.

Martin, C. B., & Deuze, M. (2009). The independent production of culture: A digital games case study. *Games and Culture, 4*(3), 276–295.

Massanari, A. L. (2015). #Gamergate and The Fappening: How reddit's algorithm, community, and culture support toxic technocultures. *New Media & Society.* Retrieved October 25, 2015, from http://nms.sagepub.com/content/early/2015/10/07/1461444815608807.

McArthur, J. A. (2009). Digital subculture: A geek meaning of style. *Journal of Communication Inquiry, 33*(1), 58–70.

McCormick, R. (2014, November 4). Gamergate: A misogynist harassment campaign disguised as consumer revolt. *The Verge.* Retrieved October 17, 2015, from http://www.theverge.com/2014/11/4/7153549/gamergate-campaign-video-game-ethics-feminism-harassment.

McRobbie, A. (2004). Post-feminism and popular culture. *Feminist Media Studies, 4*(3), 255–264.

McRobbie, A. (2009). *The aftermath of feminism: Gender, culture and social change.* Thousand Oaks, CA: Sage.

Nussbaum, M. C. (2010). Objectification and internet misogyny. In S. Levmore & M. C. Nussbaum (Eds.), *The offensive Internet: Speech, privacy, and reputation* (pp. 68–87). Cambridge, MA: Harvard University Press.

Parkin, S. (2014, September 9). Zoe Quinn's *Depression Quest. The New Yorker.* Retrieved October 17, 2015, from http://www.newyorker.com/tech/elements/zoe-quinns-depression-quest.

Quinn, Z. (2014, December 4). Gamergate is about ethics in games journalism—but not in the way you think. *The Daily Dot.* Retrieved October 17, 2015, from http://www.dailydot.com/opinion/zoe-quinn-gaming-journalism/.

RedditAnalysisBot (2014, October 21). */r/KotakuInAction Drilldown October 2014.* Retrieved October 17, 2015, from http://www.reddit.com/r/SubredditAnalysis/comments/2jvrdl/rkotakuinaction_drilldown_october_2014/.

robbiebaldwin (2013). *Anita Sarkeesian.* Retrieved October 17, 2015, from http://robbiebaldwin.tumblr.com/post/44832850970/anita-sarkeesian.

Sargon of Akkad (Producer) (2014). *Anita Sarkeesian debunked in under a minute #GamerGate #NotYourShield.* [Video] Retrieved October 17, 2015 from https://www.youtube.com/watch?v=FW-69xXD734.

Sarkeesian, A. (2012). Tropes vs. women in video games. *Kickstarter*. Retrieved October 17, 2015, from https://www.kickstarter.com/projects/566429325/tropes-vs-women-in-video-games/description.

Shaw, A. (2013). On not becoming gamers: Moving beyond the constructed audience. *Ada: A Journal of Gender, New Media, and Technology, 1*(2). Retrieved June 17, 2016, from http://adanewmedia.org/2013/06/issue2-shaw/.

Shaw, A. (2014). *Gaming at the edge: Sexuality and gender at the margins of gamer culture*. Minneapolis, MN: University of Minnesota Press.

Sierra, K. (2014, October 8). Why the trolls will always win. *Wired*. Retrieved October 17, 2015, from http://www.wired.com/2014/10/trolls-will-always-win/.

Squire, K. (2002). Cultural framing of computer/video games. *Game Studies, 2*(1). Retrieved October 25, 2015, from http://gamestudies.org/0102/squire/.

Stuart, K. (2014, December 3). Zoe Quinn: "All Gamergate has done is ruin people's lives". *The Guardian*. Retrieved October 17, 2015, from http://www.theguardian.com/technology/2014/dec/03/zoe-quinn-gamergate-interview.

Tasker, Y., & Negra, D. (2007). Introduction: Feminist politics and postfeminist culture. In Y. Tasker & D. Negra (Eds.), *Interrogating postfeminism* (pp. 1–25). Durham, NC: Duke University Press.

Tufekci, Z. (2014, March 19). No, Nate, brogrammers may not be macho, but that's not all there is to it. *Medium*. Retrieved October 17, 2015, from https://medium.com/technology-and-society/2f1fe84c5c9b.

Turner, F. (2006). *From counterculture to cyberculture: Stewart Brand, the Whole Earth Network, and the rise of digital utopianism*. Chicago, IL: University of Chicago Press.

Wade, L. (2011, October 6). Anita Sarkeesian on the straw feminist. *Sociological Images*. Retrieved October 17, 2015, from http://thesocietypages.org/socimages/2011/10/06/anita-sarkeesian-on-the-straw-feminist/.

Watson, R. (2012, October 24). It stands to reason, skeptics can be sexist too. *Slate*. Retrieved October 17, 2015, from http://www.slate.com/articles/double_x/doublex/2012/10/sexism_in_the_skeptic_community_i_spoke_out_then_came_the_rape_threats.html.

Wheaton, W. (2015, April 16). Anita Sarkeesian. *Time: The 100 Most Influential People*. Retrieved October 17, 2015, from http://time.com/3822727/anita-sarkeesian-2015-time-100/.

Williams, D., Martins, N., Consalvo, M., & Ivory, J. D. (2009). The virtual census: representations of gender, race and age in video games. *New Media & Society, 11*(5), 815–834.

Wingfield, N. (2014, October 15). Feminist critics of video games facing threats in "GamerGate" campaign. *The New York Times*. Retrieved October 17, 2015, from http://www.nytimes.com/2014/10/16/technology/gamergate-women-video-game-threats-anita-sarkeesian.html.

Yiannopoulos, M. (2014, September 1). Feminist bullies tearing the video game industry apart. *Breitbart*. Retrieved October 17, 2015, from http://www.breitbart.com/Breitbart-London/2014/09/01/Lying-Greedy-Promiscuous-Feminist-Bullies-are-Tearing-the-Video-Game-Industry-Apart.

# 19

# THIS WEEK IN BLACKNESS AND THE CONSTRUCTION OF BLACKNESS IN INDEPENDENT DIGITAL MEDIA

## *Sarah Florini*

A listener once suggested to Elon James White, founder and CEO of This Week in Blackness (TWiB!), that TWiB!, given its broad appeal across racial groups, would be more aptly named "This Week in Humanness." White rejected the deracialization of TWiB!, clarifying his vision for the project: "I made a very conscious decision, when I created This Week in Blackness . . . I wanted it to be clear that you can come from and embrace a position of 'Blackness' and racial identity and self-identification and yet still all these [different] things are still things that are of interest to you and in your background" (*TWiB! Radio*, 2013d). White's statement, which centers Blackness while simultaneously highlighting the diversity of Black[1] people, encapsulates a tension at the center of TWiB!'s work.

Started as a web video series in 2008, by 2015 TWiB! had grown into a multi-media content producer. Independently run and funded, TWiB! has maintained the freedom to operate outside of media industry logics that commonly underrepresent and misrepresent Black people and Black perspectives. TWiB! introduced its first podcast *Blacking It Up!* in 2011 (since renamed *TWiB! Prime*) and now produces seven podcasts which cover a range of topics including politics, popular culture, sex positivity, and sports. Additionally, TWiB! publishes an electronic magazine *Valid* on its website and has produced an eight episode run of *A Black Show* for Free Speech TV. *TWiB! Prime* remains TWiB!'s flagship program, covering news and current events, and averaged 1–1.5 million downloads a month in 2015 (E. J. White, personal communication, April 8, 2015).

TWiB! operates in a complex socio-cultural context characterized by two problematic and polarized racial logics—colorblindness and persistent regimes of racist representations. Contemporary U.S. racial politics are dominated by notions of colorblindness, a discourse conflating the erasure of difference with the achievement of racial equality, seemingly the impulse behind the listener's suggestion that race be extracted from TWiB!'s brand identity. Yet, contradictorily, the dominance of colorblindness has not resulted in the disappearance of the longstanding practice of constructing Black Americans as a monolith, one usually defined through racist stereotypes. White's comment represents both TWiB!'s refusal to erase racial identity (a rejection of colorblindness) and the ongoing struggle to define Blackness in ways that recognize the fullness and diversity of Black humanity.

This chapter explores how TWiB! negotiates the contentious process of rejecting colorblindness and reasserting the social importance of race without reifying constructions of Blackness that have long served to justify racist policies and practices. My analysis is based on thousands of hours of TWiB! content and derived from ongoing ethnographic work with TWiB!, which includes both on- and offline participant observation and interviewing. Drawing on frameworks from critical/cultural media studies and critical race theory, I argue that TWiB!'s work reflects the complexities and the contradictory demands of representing race in the twenty-first-century US.

I begin with a brief description of TWiB! and its operation. Next I outline the discourse of colorblindness that forms the dominant racial logic in the US. I then move on to examine how TWiB! creates media that center Black voices and experiences, foregrounding racial identity in direct conflict with the edicts of colorblindness. Finally, I examine how TWiB!, in centering race, works to prevent Blackness from becoming flattened out and homogenized by asserting Black heterogeneity and diversity.

## This Week in Blackness

TWiB! began as a small-scale operation, with the video series and podcasts produced out of White's Brooklyn apartment. Initially, White had attempted to form partnerships with existing media outlets such as SiriusXM and Interactive One, but was unsuccessful largely because he refused to relinquish creative control and because the outlets were skeptical of whether there was an audience for TWiB!'s content. In mid-2013, TWiB! formed a partnership with progressive media outlet *The Daily Kos* and relocated to the Kos building in Berkeley, CA, where TWiB! built a fully equipped digital production studio. In the summer of 2014, TWiB! implemented the "TWiBularity," a freemium distribution model combining free and subscription-only content that now provides TWiB!'s primary revenue stream.

Between 2011 and 2014, TWiB! relied on listener donations and the donated labor of its hosts and staff to stay afloat. This arrangement has resulted in frequent shifts in the make-up of the team hosting *TWiB! Prime*.

White was joined by Aaron Rand Freeman shortly after the launch of *Blacking It Up!* and the duo had four different co-hosts between 2011 and 2015—poet Bassey Ikpi, political strategist L. Joy Williams, academic and educator Dacia Mitchell, and lawyer and reproductive rights advocate Imani Gandy. Each of these women balanced co-hosting *TWiB! Prime* with busy careers, an arrangement that is difficult to maintain long-term.

TWiB!'s technological structure is best thought of as a network in the dual sense of the term. First, TWiB! can be characterized as an independent broadcast-style media network producing and distributing programming. Black communities have long and rich histories of producing alternative media, from Black newspapers to radio to film (Barlow, 1999; Diawara, 1993; Vogel, 2001), and TWiB! certainly must be understood as embedded within this history. TWiB! uses the broadcast model to intervene in hegemonic commercial media representations of Blackness, allowing for self-representation and self-definition. In addition to functioning as a broadcast-style network, the interactive digital environment in which TWiB! operates allows it to operate as a network of people and technologies. TWiB! exploits the affordances of digital and social media to create an interactivity and geographical reach unavailable to previous generations of Black media producers. TWiB! has a strong social media presence, particularly on Twitter, and prioritizes community and audience interaction.

In addition to *TWiB! Prime*, TWiB! as of early 2016 produces six other podcasts covering a range of topics: *TWiB! After Dark*, *We Nerd Hard*, *SportsBall*, *Historical Blackness*, *Academic Shade*, and *This Tastes Funny*. Although TWiB!'s content varies greatly and moves across multiple platforms, one constant is its blend of complex analysis with irreverent humor. The hosts of *TWiB! Prime*, who collectively go by "Team Blackness," have joked that they are not "CNN Negro" or "N(egro)PR," thus freeing themselves from the conventions of traditional journalism and political analysis. They swear, joke, and offer off-color commentary. Despite their humorous approach, TWiB! is not satire. The team produces carefully researched analyses of the topics covered, often bringing in experts such as academics, lawyers, politicians, and activists to provide context for discussion. For example, Gandy's legal analysis, grounded in her professional knowledge as a licensed attorney, is frequently laced with humor and profanity. This juxtaposition was evident in her explication of the federal Religious Freedom Restoration Act. After explaining that the law "prevents a government from substantially burdening a person's exercise of religious freedom without a compelling interest to do so," she provided a humorous and irreverent example: "A person can go and sue the government and say 'Hey, you're fuckin' with my shit. I'd rather you not fuck with my shit. I'm gonna sue you under this law'" (*TWiB! Prime*, 2015b). This commentary by Gandy is characteristic of TWiB!'s work in both content and tone.

To fully understand the strategies and stakes of TWiB!'s work, one must understand the socio-cultural context in which the organization operates. Post-Civil Rights Movement racial politics in the US have been shaped by the ascendency of neoliberalism and the emergence of color-blindness as the dominant racial discourse. Colorblind discourses have redefined racial equality as the erasure of difference, as simply not seeing race, thus thwarting discussion of racial injustice and creating a cultural landscape where the assertion of racial difference is perceived as inherently problematic. Within this context, TWiB! works to recuperate and celebrate Blackness.

## Foregrounding Blackness in a Colorblind Culture

In the latter half of the twentieth century, colorblindness emerged as the dominant racial discourse in the US. By rearticulating race as personal trait irrelevant to public life, colorblindness has foreclosed discursive space for addressing racial injustice. Consequently, discourses making race visible as an important social or political category have been cast as a source, rather than a reflection, of racial inequality. TWiB! violates the tenets of colorblindness by centering Blackness and racially marking its output. Beyond simply foregrounding Blackness, TWiB! also constructs Blackness as a collective social identity and emphasizes the shared experiences of Black Americans living as racialized subjects in U.S. society.

Neoliberalism, the dominant cultural paradigm in the US, combines the values of liberal humanism, such as individualism, egalitarianism, and meritocracy, with free market logics and the prioritization of individual freedom and autonomy. Refracted through neoliberalism's emphasis on individual rights, Civil Rights Movement language and discourses—such as Martin Luther King Jr.'s admonition that people should be judged "not by the color of their skin, but by the content of their character"—have been rearticulated in support of neoliberal individualism. Imbricated with a prioritization of the individual, the egalitarianism advocated by King has been transformed into a means of sustaining white privilege and power in seemingly race-neutral ways (Bonilla-Silva, 2010; Delgado & Stefancic, 2001). Policies meant to ameliorate racial inequalities can now be opposed because they are "group based" rather than "case by case" (Delgado & Stefancic, 2001, pp. 35–36) and racism and discrimination have been recast as "problems to be confronted *only* at an individual level" (Omi & Winant, 1986, p. 129, emphasis orginal). The neoliberal racial regime asserts "the insignificance of race as social force," and "aggressively roots out any vestige of race as a category at odds with an individualistic embrace of formal legal rights" (Giroux, 2003, p. 200). Thus, race has become divorced from politics, histories of oppression, and

331

economic opportunities, and transformed into an individual characteristic (Gallagher, 2003).

The denial of race as anything more than a personal characteristic has become the foundation of colorblindness, which sociologists have found to be the dominant racial logic among white Americans since the 1990s (Gallagher, 2003). As a result, using race to assert collective identity or to articulate group demands "violates the cherished notion that as a nation we recognize the rights of individuals rather than group rights" (Gallagher, 2003, p. 9). Thus, the obscuration of difference has become conflated with the realization of racial equality, positioning any who assert race as an important social or cultural category as the true proponents of oppression. Simultaneously, whiteness functions as the invisible norm of U.S. culture (Dyer, 1997), creating a media landscape in which white Americans are positioned as universal and white representations and perspectives as race neutral. Thus, colorblindness functions not as the absence of race, but as the reification of the hegemonic normalization of whiteness. TWiB! deliberately rejects colorblindness, and its accompanying unspoken whiteness, and instead centers Black experiences and voices.

Everything TWiB! does is explicitly racially marked by the brand name This Week in Blackness, a fact that has frequently garnered criticism. As the exchange in the opening paragraph demonstrates, TWiB! founder and CEO Elon James White has always been clear about the centrality of race to TWiB! and all of its projects. The violation of the tenets of colorblindness and the demarcation of TWiB! as an unapologetically Black space is often met with disapproval or even hostility. White routinely receives comments via email and Twitter asserting that TWiB!'s name is inherently racist. For example, one self-described conservative Twitter user with the handle @LibertyForUSA, tweeted to White,

"This Week in Blackness" Cool! I want to create "This Week in Whiteness"! #racist (December 29, 2011)

White has received similar reactions from (predominantly white) progressives, such as Internet radio host Nicole Sandler who, during a public disagreement with White, criticized TWiB!'s name in a blog post saying, "way to make white people feel welcome there" (Sandler, 2015).

The responses from White, TWiB! staff, and TWiB! listeners to these criticisms have highlighted the unspoken, largely unmarked, and naturalized whiteness of mainstream corporate media. White has responded with statements on Twitter such as,

I get letters and comments "What if i [sic] made "This Week in WHITENESS huh? or WHITING IT UP?!!?" Um, it already exists. Its called CNN. (April 15, 2011)

White, exasperated with this recurring criticism, once tweeted,

> I've heard 1 too many "What if there was a This Week in Whiteness?" Ya want it? Here ya go: http://ThisWeekInWhiteness. com. (February 22, 2014)

The link redirected users to the Fox News website. Thus, White asserts, via sarcasm and humor, the need for Black media spaces by literally linking mainstream news outlets to whiteness, revealing them to be as racialized as TWiB!. Their whiteness simply remains unnamed.

One of the most notable strategies for marking TWiB! as a Black space is *TWiB! Prime*'s theme, "Enter the Blackness," a hip hop song produced by Willi Evans Jr. and featuring rapper Jasiri X. The song begins with the sound of trumpets and Jasiri declaring that the horns demarcate the point at which the listening audience "enters" Blackness. The lyrics then provide a series of metonyms representing Blackness, including soul food and Black historical icons such as Martin Luther King Jr. and Malcolm X. Thus, TWiB!'s particularity as a separate Black space is announced with a fanfare that serves as a metaphorical sonic gateway through which listeners enter the Black space of *TWiB! Prime*.

In addition to refusing to obscure Blackness, TWiB! violates the edicts of colorblindness by constructing race as a social identity, rather than solely as an individual personal characteristic. *TWiB! Prime* frequently reports on studies providing evidence of racial disparities across social arenas such as education, incarceration, and healthcare, and frames those reports in a manner emphasizing the impact of race on the lives of Black Americans. For example, after reporting on a study finding that Black Americans disproportionately experience physical and emotional stress, resulting in poorer physical and mental health, co-host Dacia Mitchell recognized how the social construction of race shapes the lives of Black Americans, concluding, "Apparently, racism is bad for you" (*TWiB! Radio*, 2013a). Similarly, after reporting a study revealing medical professionals' implicit biases caused them to treat Black and white patients differently (recommending less aggressive treatment if they believed patients to be Black), co-host Imani Gandy explained, that white racial biases "might actually be killing Black people" (*TWiB! Prime*, 2014). In defiance of neoliberal colorblind logics, TWiB! reasserts race as a salient social category, one with group-based experiences and outcomes and, by implication, in need of group-based solutions.

Perhaps the most overt and powerful way TWiB! centers the shared experience of living as a racialized subject is through recurring discussions of how state-sanctioned violence structures Black Americans' lives. Discussions of the anxiety many Black Americans experience during interactions with police have been frequent topics of conversation on the podcasts. In 2011, White, Freeman, and guest host Kriss (host of the *Insanity Check* podcast) shared their experiences, as did listeners calling in to the open phone lines. Freeman shared that he had been raised "never to say anything to police officers," and even to avoid eye contact when possible. One caller, longtime TWiB! listener P-Funk, explained the difference between Black and non-Black experiences of law enforcement saying, "That's the one thing I wish I could convey to most people who are not Black. It's just that, even to this day, I feel uncomfortable walkin' down the street with my hood up . . . Because you look like 'that type of Negro' walking down the street like that" (*Blacking It Up!*, 2011c). The phrase "that type of Negro," referencing stereotypical images of criminal and suspicious Black men wearing hoodies, is notable given that the conversation predates the February 2012 death of unarmed Black teenager Trayvon Martin by nearly a year.

TWiB! heavily covered Martin's murder by a self-appointed neighborhood watch member, George Zimmerman, foregrounding another Black collective experience: "the talk" parents of Black children must given them explaining racial profiling and the precautions it necessitates in their day-to-day lives. TWiB! hosted an unscheduled call-in show the night Zimmerman's acquittal was announced (*TWiB! Radio*, 2013e), taking 21 calls over the course of three hours. Both hosts and many of the callers expressed the difficult experience of having to talk to their children about the case. Co-host Dacia Mitchell described the event saying,

> It's moments like this that there are people all over the country . . . having to explain this to their kids . . . and it's not white folks that are explaining this to their white kids . . . They're not getting a talk that's like, uh, you know, "You will not be safe." They're not getting that talk tonight.
>
> (*TWiB! Radio*, 2013e)

Monika from Oakland, a longtime TWiB! listener, called to discuss raising a Black teenage boy, saying, "Most parents know that we have to tell our kids early. I had to tell my son 'People are going to call you nigger even though you're awesome,' in the first grade when he was first called that" (*TWiB! Radio*, 2013e). She went on to talk about the experience of having to tell Black children about the adversity they will face and the difficulty of trying to encourage them to excel anyway. White responded, noting this as a longstanding aspect of Black American life,

> That's something that's been said for years, the idea that you have to be awesome . . . The Black community is considered very tough on our kids. It's like, why is that? Because they had to be. Because if your kid did something, it wouldn't be simply they'd

get in trouble. Your kid would be dead. Your kid would be in prison. So . . . this is a conversation that has happened for years.

(*TWiB! Radio*, 2013e)

White's comments both highlight a shared experience of parenting in Black communities and position that experience as an ongoing historical commonality, undermining distinctions between the racist past and the ostensibly colorblind present.

TWiB! not only rejects colorblindness, foregrounding Blackness in all it does, but also asserts the important ways in which racial identity shapes Black Americans' lives. Through discussion of shared Black experiences of racism, TWiB! makes a case for the group based understandings of race that neoliberal colorblindness seeks to dismantle. However, in asserting the collective shared experience of Black Americans, TWiB! risks reducing Blackness to a fixed homogenous category that may not only erase the complexity and diversity of Black experiences but also make representations of Blackness vulnerable to negative racist stereotypes.

## Disrupting Constructions of Blackness

Although asserting Black collective experience undermines the individualism that allows colorblind discourses to erase structural causes of racial inequality, doing so risks fixing and homogenizing the identities of Black Americans. To guard against this, TWiB! is committed to constructing Blackness as heterogeneous. Though its programming, TWiB! both serves and represents a diverse Black audience by avoiding and critiquing essentialist discourses of Black authenticity and by embracing intra-group diversity. This disrupts regimes of representation by both resisting the homogenization of Blackness and undermining racist tropes.

By foregrounding Blackness, TWiB! enters into a struggle for the meaning of what Herman Gray has referred to as the "sign of Blackness" (2005, p. 15): the socially constructed set of meanings and concepts attached to Blackness. The sign of Blackness, like any sign, is inherently polyvocal and multi-accentual. Stuart Hall (1996b) has argued that race is a floating signifier, which has no true referent but is continually used to refer to a signified in flux and under contestation. Hegemonic forces work to make signifiers mono-accentual, seeking to control meaning and reify social hierarchies (Voloshinov, 2003/1929). TWiB! preserves the multi-accentuality of the sign of Blackness, representing its heterogeneity.

A key arena for the struggle over the sign of Blackness is media representation. Media studies and cultural/critical studies scholars have long pointed to the importance of representation as a constitutive element in social and political life (Hall, 1996a, p. 443). Since the minstrel shows of the nineteenth century, representations of Blackness in U.S. culture have served to construct Black people as inferior, thereby justifying racist ideologies and practices (Bogle, 2001; Collins, 2000; Lott, 1993). Representations of Black Americans as lazy, hyper-sexual, violent, criminal, and of low intelligence can be traced from the minstrel shows to the present day (Bogle, 2001; Collins, 2000). These problematic representations of Blackness still populate the U.S. media landscape and serve to reinscribe boundaries between racial groups, allowing for the rejection and exclusion of Black Americans as Other, as "what does not belong" (Hall, 1997, p. 258). When combined with the "burden of representation," the notion that one Black voice or image represents the entire group (Hall, 1997, p. 262; Mercer, 2008), these negative images become projected onto Black people at large, reducing them to a monolith deliberately crafted to be disparaged, feared, and loathed, thereby naturalizing race-based social inequities.

TWiB! works to disrupt these regimes of representation, showing Black Americans in ways that both undermine negative stereotypes and disrupt discourses that flatten out and homogenize Black people into an undifferentiated mass. White's decision to use the name This Week in Blackness not only eschews colorblind logics, but also claims the label "Black" for content containing a range of non-normative, diverse, often contradictory representations of Blackness. White has been clear that the relationship between TWiB!'s name and content is deliberate and strategic, functioning as a means of "shattering the stereotypes around what is 'Black'" (*TWiB! Radio*, 2013d). In TWiB's programming, Blackness becomes not one or even a handful of perspectives and experiences, but a complex polyphony of Black voices that preserves the multi-accentuality of Blackness and denies racist stereotypes a unified signifier onto which to map.

From its inception, TWiB! has sought to serve a diverse Black audience. In 2011, White and then *TWiB! Prime* co-host L. Joy Williams described the significant, heterogeneous, and largely erased Black audience they see themselves as both speaking to and representing. Williams highlighted TWiB's goal of undermining the myth that Black people "are this monolith that all watch BET, drink Kool-aid, and occasionally go to jail," emphasizing that TWiB! simultaneously targets both the homogenization and the misrepresentation of Blackness. She argued for the necessity of independent media to "break down that myth and say that you can program differently because we have a different audience within our people" (*Blacking It Up!*, 2011d). According to White, the goal of TWiB! is "to prove a point," that there is a clear and strong audience for the programming offering complex representations of Blackness. He described TWiB!'s audience as comprised of people,

Who [are] smart, who [are] politically engaged, who [are] technologically engaged, who can enjoy the ratchet[2] just right alongside intelligent shit. Who can quote 50 Cent and Nietzsche within the same sentence.

*(Blacking It Up!*, 2011d)

Additionally, TWiB's mere existence challenges hegemonic constructions of Blackness, particularly those coding technology as white. The persistent myth of Black "technophobia" and a "general presumption of black nonparticipation" in technology allows recursive racist assumptions of Black inferiority "to find new means of cultural currency" (Everett, 2009, p. 19) in the twenty-first century. Governmental policies regarding Internet infrastructure and access were formed during the 1990s, at "the premillennial neoliberal moment, when race was disappeared from public and governmental discourse," allowing neoliberal values to shape understandings of emerging technology (Nakamura, 2008, p. 202). This, combined with discourses asserting cyberspace as a raceless, genderless, placeless space, naturalized the erasure of people of color, ultimately reifying the whiteness of digital technologies and constructing Blackness as the non-technological Other. TWiB!, as an elaborate trans-platform multi-media project, disrupts the conflation of technology with whiteness.

TWiB!'s programming also reflects a commitment to constructing a heterogenic understanding of Blackness. Besides *TWiB! Prime*, TWiB! also provides programming focusing on a range of topics. TWiB!'s *We Nerd Hard* covers technology, video games, and media fandom. It represents and gives voice to Black nerds who are often erased because of the common conflation of nerdiness with whiteness and the ways nerdiness's opposite, coolness, is often constructed as synonymous with Blackness (Bucholtz, 2001; Eglash, 2002; Kendall, 2011). *We Nerd Hard* disrupts racial categories by positioning nerd tastes and practices squarely within the realm of Blackness. TWiB!'s premium content service, the TWiBularity, also includes the podcast *Black Girl Nerds*, which similarly repositions nerd culture—typically coded as not only white but also masculine—explicitly at the intersection of Blackness and femininity.

In asserting and foregrounding Blackness, TWiB! must also work to avoid essentializing or reifying discourses of authenticity limiting possible performances of Black identity. TWiB! created a term "Black checking" to shorthand the problematic practice of fixing and bounding Blackness. Black checking is the act of evaluating and policing Black authenticity by designating some behaviors, and thereby some people, as "Black" or "not Black (enough)." White summarized his objection to Black checking saying,

> The fact is if you're Black, you're Black. I'm not going to rip your "Black card" from you. Even if you're doing something that I

think might be harmful to Black people. I'm going to call you an a-hole and say "Never talk to me." You're still Black. You're just a Black a-hole.

(*TWiB! Prime*, 2015a)

Black checking and the negative impact of policing Black authenticity has remained a recurring topic since the first month of *TWiB! Prime* (then *Blacking It Up!*). In 2011, then co-host Bassey Ikpi described herself saying, "I'm Nigerian. I was born in Africa. I figured that was as Black as you could get" (*Blacking It Up!*, 2011a). However, she explained that, during her childhood, her Blackness was routinely questioned when her family moved from Oklahoma to Washington DC, where the kids at her school teased her for what they perceived as her "white" speech patterns and musical tastes. That same year, *TWiB! Prime* devoted an entire episode to playing music the three hosts—White, Freeman, and Ikpi—liked but that wasn't typically considered "Black." As White introduced the show topic, he noted, "Weirdly, we're Black and we're not a monolith. We actually have . . . different thoughts and ideas and likings-of-things that people wouldn't expect" (*Blacking It Up!*, 2011b). Over the course of the episode, Team Blackness played music including Bjork, Keith Urban, Yes, John Williams film scores, and the musical *Rent*, all of which are not commonly associated with Blackness, disrupting the racialization of musical taste cultures.

Discussions of Black checking commonly arise in stories about President Barack Obama, whose Black authenticity has been frequently challenged. For example, in May 2011, *TWiB! Prime* discussed the increasingly harsh criticism of the president from well-known Black academic Cornel West. West had criticized Obama for not focusing on poverty or doing enough to help Black communities, stating that Obama was "afraid of free Black men" and seemed to be more comfortable around white and Jewish people. Co-host Ikpi argued that West was "taking shots" at Obama's Blackness: "He's trying to define Blackness, based on negating who the president and what the president is . . . he's teasing the president the way I was teased in middle school . . . for not being Black enough" (*Blacking It Up!*, 2011b).

When it comes to interrogating essentialism, even *TWiB! Prime*'s theme song is not above reproach. In an interview with Jasiri X shortly after the song's premiere, White expressed his concern that the song may convey too narrow an image of Blackness. The ensuing discussion negotiated the signifiers of Black racial identity and asserted the particularity and reality of Black American culture while attempting to prevent it from becoming too tightly bounded (*TWiB! Radio*, 2013c). The question was again raised by an audience member who challenged the same lyrics as stereotypical and one step away from "chicken and watermelon." The response from Team Blackness in both cases sought balance between recognizing the particularity of Black culture (e.g., the cultural importance of soul food) without reducing it to a fixed set of characteristics or practices.

TWiB! seeks to destabilize constructions of Blackness by embracing intersectionality, a framework recognizing individuals inhabit multiple intersecting subject positions (Crenshaw, 1991). To this end, significant attention is given to Black women and LGBTQI members of the community. Often, media spaces marked as "Black" privilege racial identities and discourses over those of gender, sexuality, or class, which reifies rather than challenges social hierarchies and power relations (Crenshaw, 1991). Although marked as a Black space, TWiB!'s Blackness remains fluid, complex, and multi-dimensional, invoking Black racial identities as inseparable from gender identities, sexuality, and class, and colliding these discourses to disrupt these categories without diminishing their importance.

Black women's voices are prominent in TWiB!'s programming. All of TWiB!'s podcasts have at least one female co-host, and shows routinely deconstruct problematic representations of Black women. Although mainstream media often portray Black women through a variety of what Patricia Hill Collins (2000) dubbed controlling images—dutiful mammies, welfare queens, angry Black women—TWiB! shows a range of Black women who challenge these images. This is not just a matter of undermining the stereotype by representing its opposite, a move that equally controls Black women by demanding they constantly police their behavior so as not to reinforce problematic representations. The women on TWiB! reject controlling images by refusing to perform either the stereotype or its opposite. For example, Imani Gandy, a former attorney who is now the Senior Legal Analyst for both TWiB! and the reproductive rights advocacy group RH Reality Check, is intellectually formidable and professional accomplished, placing her in stark contrast to Collin's controlling images. Yet, Gandy has an online presence under the moniker "Angry Black Lady" as both the title of her personal blog and her Twitter handle (@AngryBlackLady). Rather than erase her anger to avoid reinforcing the controlling image of the angry Black woman, she instead refuses to calibrate her performance of self in relation to the framework at all.

The clearest examples of TWiB!'s intervention into normative representations of Black femininity are Feminista Jones and N'Jaila Rhee, co-hosts of TWiB! *After Dark, TWiB!*'s sex positive show. Jones and Rhee undermine the longstanding binary of Black women as either respectable or hypersexualized (Collins, 2000). Jones is a mental health social worker, writer, and mother. Rhee, who identifies as a Black and Asian biracial woman, is a journalist and BBW (Big Beautiful Woman) model, who also co-hosts TWiB!'s *We Nerd Hard*. Both Jones and Rhee represent Black women who are simultaneously and unapologetically intelligent, professional, and sexy, and who act as sexual subjects rather than sexual objects. Jones has explicitly stated that the goal of intervening in representations of women of color is a major component of *TWiB! After Dark* and of TWiB! more broadly (*TWiB! After Dark*, 2014).

TWiB! also resists the conflation of Blackness with Black masculinity, offering considerable coverage of issues affecting women. TWiB! addresses gender oppression and male privilege with increasing frequency, parsing out the axes of power at the intersection of race and gender. Perhaps most notable are the ongoing discussions about the rollback of women's reproductive rights and the epidemic of sexual assault in the US. TWiB!'s characteristic sarcasm and humor at times give way to serious and pointed discussions, such as those regarding the Stubenville rape case. This case, in which two Stubenville, Ohio high school football players carried an unconscious sixteen-year-old girl with them from one party to another, repeatedly sexually assaulting her throughout the night, received national news coverage. TWiB! simultaneously modeled a rhetorical approach grounded in feminist discourses about rape and critiqued mainstream news outlets for reinforcing problematic tropes about sexual assault.

TWiB!'s coverage of the Stubenville trial and verdict in March 2013 focused on the prevalence of sexual violence in U.S. society and myriad ways women are taught to avoid rape, discourses that *TWiB! Prime*'s co-hosts argued served to justify problematic assumptions about victims' culpability in their own assaults. TWiB!'s coverage repeatedly asserted a progressive feminist approach to rape prevention, arguing that society should focus on teaching men about getting clear consent from their sexual partners. Additionally, TWiB! critiqued mainstream corporate news coverage of the case. The day the two perpetrators were found guilty, CNN's coverage was sympathetic to the young men. CNN's Poppy Harlow described the young men as "star football players" and "very good students" and emphasized how tragic it was to watch as the teens "believed their life fell apart." White criticized the coverage in disbelief that anyone could frame a story in this way, "Forget the fact that there was a girl who was dragged around unconscious and used as a rape doll. Forget that part. Let's talk about the fact that these, these dudes, 'Man, they, their life is over . . . their promising life.'" Mitchell pointed out, "For CNN, this is the most appropriate way to talk about this . . . There was no one there to problematize it. That means that there is a vast amount of all kinds of privilege in regards to sexual violence and gender violence, rape, in the CNN copy room that allowed that to make it to air." Privilege, she argued, that allowed CNN's staff to "ignore the significance of getting the story right about rape . . . It's not important enough to make sure that the angle is depicted accurately" (*TWiB! Radio*, 2013b).

TWiB! also works to be inclusive of LQBTQI people, simultaneously challenging both homophobia and pervasive discourses framing Black

Americans as more homophobic than their white counterparts. After the 2008 elections, media popularized the narrative that the high Black voter turnout resulting from Obama's candidacy led to the passage of California's Proposition 8 banning same sex marriage (Grad, 2008). More recently, celebrities have asserted the prevalence of homophobia in Black communities, such as when director Lee Daniels argued publicly that homophobia is "rampant" in Black communities. Referring to the openly gay character on Daniel's hit television show *Empire*, he stated, Black men are afraid to come out, "because your priest says, your pastor says, mama says, your next-door neighbor says, your homie says, your brother says, your boss says [that homosexuality is wrong] . . . So I wanted to blow the lid off more on homophobia in my community" (Manuel-Logan, 2015). Regardless of whether these discourses about Black communities' homophobia are true, the narrative is prominent in the media landscape in which TWiB! operates. TWiB! both critiques and rejects homophobic discourses and practices while also undermining the assumption that Black spaces are unwelcoming to LBGTQI people.

TWiB! frequently reports about LGBTQI rights, critiquing both the legal and cultural mechanisms oppressing LGBTQI people. For example, in the aforementioned discussion of *TWiB! Prime*'s coverage of the Religious Freedom Restoration Act, TWiB! condemned the version of the bill passed by Indiana state legislature in 2015. Gandy explained how the Indiana bill had a far more reaching impact than other religious freedom laws at the federal or state level. She outlined how the law allowed for the use of religious freedom as a defense in individual civil laws suits—in effect, critics claim, legalizing discrimination against LGBTQI people. Gandy asserted, "It literally permitted bigots to say 'Homosexuality is a sin,' if a homosexual individual sued them because they were denied services or denied entrance to a place or whatnot" (*TWiB! Prime*, 2015b).

TWiB! has also been vocal about transgender issues, addressing discrimination and injustice. For example, after trans activist and author Janet Mock appeared on Peirs Morgan's evening talk show, conflict emerged between Mock and Morgan because Morgan used the offensive phrase "used to be a man" to refer to Mock, a trans woman. In response to the criticism he received, Morgan claimed he was the victim of "cisphobia." The notion of cisphobia deploys the neologism "cis," a term created to refer to individuals whose gender identity matches the gender they were assigned at birth, to position cisgendered people as oppressed. On *TWiB! Prime*, White, Freeman, and guest host Dara Wilson derided the very notion of cisphobia. They asserted cisphobia was analogous to "reverse racism" and "men's rights," terms created by dominant social groups as a means of reframing themselves as disempowered. Freeman asked incredulously, "I don't even understand how that can be a thing. People are terrified of embracing the dominant norm that overwhelms everyone else's way of life? I don't understand" (*TWiB! Prime*, 2014). White asked, "Cisphobia? Really? Are you ignoring the LGBT community completely? Are you ignoring the record amount of violence toward trans folks, especially trans women of color?" (*TWiB! Prime*, 2014). TWiB! also works to create an inclusive space by both welcoming trans and gender non-conforming people and providing resources for educating cis people on trans issues. For example, a *TWiB! After Dark* episode titled "A Practical Guide to Trans-life," featuring Errol Lynn, a trans man, covered the appropriate terminology and how to be respectful of how people identify (*TWiB! After Dark*, 2013), thus serving a pedagogical function for audience members.

## Visibility and Multiplicity

White created TWiB! to offer diverse representations of Blackness and nuanced political and cultural criticism privileging Black perspectives. TWiB! was deliberately designed as a space in which to challenge the rhetorics of colorblindness that often function to obscure ongoing racism and to problematize the dominant representations of Blackness that homogenize Black communities. In doing this, TWiB! navigates a terrain in which claiming and celebrating Blackness is often perceived as problematic and even racist act, while still fighting the homogenizing stereotypical images of Blackness that operate in U.S. culture.

TWiB!'s work is characterized by a seemingly irreconcilable demand to both foreground and interrogate the construction of Blackness. Within these contradictory discourses TWiB! constantly negotiates representations and performances of Blackness. TWiB!'s content is characterized by consistent tensions between asserting both the individuality and the collectivity of Black people, and between constructing Blackness as heterogeneous while asserting commonality. At a moment when colorblind logics seek to erase race from public discourse, TWiB!'s assertion of Black identity not only garners criticism, but also risks inadvertently feeding into persistent misrepresentations of Blackness that have long served to justify the racism colorblindness seeks to obscure.

## Notes

1 I capitalize Black but not white based on how the constructs of whiteness and Blackness operate differently in society, and my desire to draw attention to those socially constructed differences.
2 "Ratchet" is a term from Black vernacular English that is used to refer to the practices, tastes, and aesthetics commonly characterized by dominant cultures as excessive, improper, and inappropriate. The term is often used as a derogator description of ways of being common among low-income Black women. TWiB! has since stopped using the term because of its sexist and classist implications.

# References

Barlow, W. (1999). *Voice over: The making of Black radio*. Philadelphia, PA: Temple University Press.

*Blacking It Up!* (2011a, January 19). Ep. 16 Haters are like teabags [podcast episode]. Retrieved January, 2011, from https://itunes.apple.com/us/podcast/twib!-prime-w-elon-james-white/id302330739?mt=2.

*Blacking It Up!* (2011b, March 4). Ep. 38 Biggie, MJ, John Williams [podcast episodes]. Retrieved March, 2011, from https://itunes.apple.com/us/podcast/twib!-prime-w-elon-james-white/id302330739?mt=2

*Blacking It Up!* (2011c, April 18). Ep. 63 The barbershop [podcast episode]. Retrieved April, 2011, from https://itunes.apple.com/us/podcast/twib!-prime-w-elon-james-white/id302330739?mt=2.

*Blacking It Up!* (2011d, June 28). Ep. 102 Question everything [podcast episode]. Retrieved June, 2011, from https://itunes.apple.com/us/podcast/twib!-prime-w-elon-james-white/id302330739?mt=2.

Bogle, D. (2001). *Toms, coons, mulattoes, mammies, and bucks: An interpretive history of Blacks in American film* (6th ed.). New York, NY: Continuum.

Bonilla-Silva, E. (2010). *Racism without racists: Color-blind racism and racial inequality in contemporary America* (3rd ed.). New York, NY: Rowman & Littlefield.

Bucholtz, M. (2001). The whiteness of nerds: Superstandard English and racial markedness. *Journal of Linguisitic Anthropology, 11*(1), 84–100.

Collins, P. H. (2000). *Black feminist thought* (2nd ed.). New York, NY: Routledge.

Crenshaw, K. (1991). Mapping the margins: Intersectionality, identity politics, and violence against women of color. *Stanford Law Review, 43*(6), 1,241–1,299.

Delgado, R., & Stefancic, J. (2001). *Critical race theory: An introduction*. New York, NY: New York University Press.

Diawara, M. (1993). *Black American cinema*. New York, NY: Routledge.

Dyer, R. (1997). *White: Essays on race and culture*. New York, NY: Routledge.

Eglash, R. (2002). Race, sex, and nerd: From Black geeks to Asian American hipsters. *Social Text, 20*(2), 49–64.

Everett, A. (2009). *Digital Diaspora: A race for cyberspace*. Albany, NY: State University of New York Press.

Gallagher, C. (2003). Color-blind privilege: The social and political functions of erasing the color line in post race America. *Race, Gender, and Class, 10*(4), 1–17.

Giroux, H. (2003). Spectacles of race and pedagogies of denial: Anti-black racist pedagogy under the reign of neoliberalism. *Communication Education, 52*(3/4), 191–211.

Grad, S. (2008). *L.A. Now Blog*. Retrieved October 28, 2015, from http://latimes-blogs.latimes.com/lanow/2008/11/70-of-african-a.html.

Gray, H. (2005). *Cultural moves: African Americans and the politics of representation*. Berkeley, CA: University of California Press.

Hall, S. (1996a). Cultural studies and its theoretical legacies. In D. Morley & K.-H. Chen, (Eds.), *Stuart Hall: Critical dialogues in cultural studies* (pp. 262–275). New York, NY: Routledge.

Hall, S. (1996b). *Race: The floating signifier*. Video. Produced and directed by Sut Jhally. Northampton, MA: Media Education Foundation.

Hall, S. (1997). The spectacle of the "Other". In S. Hall (Ed.), *Representations: Cultural representations and signifying practices* (pp. 223–279). London: Sage and The Open University.

Kendall, L. (2011). "White and nerdy": Computers, race and the nerd stereotype. *Journal of Popular Culture, 44*(3), 505–524.

Lott, E. (1993). *Love and theft: Blackface minstrelsy and the American working class.* New York: Oxford University Press.

Manuel-Logan, R. (2015). Lee Daniels uses "Empire" to shine light on homophobia in Black community. *News One.* Retrieved October 28, 2015, from http://newsone.com/3083439/lee daniels-uses-empire-to-shine-light-on-homophobia-in-black-community/.

Mercer, K. (2008). Black art and the burden of representation. *Third Text, 4*(10), 61–78.

Nakamura, L. (2008). *Digitizing race: Visual cultures of the Internet.* Minneapolis, MN: University of Minnesota Press.

Omi, M., & Winant, H. (1986). *Racial formation in the United States: From the 1960s to the 1980s.* New York, NY: Routledge.

Sandler, N. (Host) (2015, February 24). *Nicole Sandler Show: They sure told me*! Retrieved October 28, 2015 from http://radioornot.com/blog/2-24-15-nicole-sandler-show-they-sure-told-me/

*TWiB! After Dark* (2013, November 7). Ep. 16 A practical guide to trans-life [podcast episode]. Retrieved November, 2013, from https://itunes.apple.com/us/podcast/twib!-afterdark-twibnation/id977325287?mt=2.

*TWiB! After Dark* (2014, January 8). Ep. 20 #NotYourRescueProject [podcast episode]. Retrieved January, 2014, from https://itunes.apple.com/us/podcast/twib!-afterdark-twibnation/id977325287?mt=2.

*TWiB! Prime* (2014, February 19). Ep. 504 All cars are real [podcast episode]. Retrieved February, 2014, from https://itunes.apple.com/us/podcast/twib!-prime-w-elon-james-white/id302330739?mt=2.

*TWiB! Prime* (2015a, January 6). Ep. 623 An evening with a revolutionary [podcast episode]. Retrieved January, 2015, from https://itunes.apple.com/us/podcast/twib!-prime-w-elon-james-white/id302330739?mt=2.

*TWiB! Prime* (2015b, April 2). Ep. 669 Indiana issues [podcast episode]. Retrieved April, 2015, from https://itunes.apple.com/us/podcast/twib!-prime-w-elon-james-white/id302330739?mt=2.

*TWiB! Radio* (2013a, March 12). Ep. 387 Define "riot" [podcast episode]. Retrieved March, 2013, from https://itunes.apple.com/us/podcast/twib!-prime-w-elon-james-white/id302330739?mt=2.

*TWiB! Radio* (2013b, March 18). Ep. 390 Humans rape [podcast episode]. Retrieved March, 2013, from https://itunes.apple.com/us/podcast/twib!-prime-w-elon-james-white/id302330739?mt=2.

*TWiB! Radio* (2013c, March 27). Ep. 396 Spit right or go home [podcast episode]. Retrieved March, 2013, from https://itunes.apple.com/us/podcast/twib!-prime-w-elon-james-white/id302330739?mt=2.

*TWiB! Radio* (2013d, April 4). Ep. 401 How not to be a pundit [podcast episode]. Retrieved April, 2013, from https://itunes.apple.com/us/podcast/twib!-prime-w-elon-james-white/id302330739?mt=2.

344

*TWiB! Radio* (2013e, July 13). Ep. 447 #Zimmerman verdict [podcast episode]. Retrieved July, 2013, from https://itunes.apple.com/us/podcast/twib!-prime-w-elon-james-white/id302330739?mt=2.

Vogel, T. (2001). *The Black press: New literary and historical essays.* New Brunswick, NJ: Rutgers University Press.

Voloshinov, V. (2003/1929). From V.N. Volosinov, Marxism and the philosophy of language, 1929. In P. Morris (Ed.), *The Bakhtin reader: Selected writings of Bakhtin, Medvedev, Voloshinov* (pp. 50–61). New York, NY: Oxford University Press.

# 20

# PROBLEMS AND PROSPECTS OF SPANISH LANGUAGE TELEVISION BROADCASTING IN THE UNITED STATES

*Alan B. Albarran and Nicole Warncke*

"*La vida es como un arca inmensa llena de posibilidades.*"
[Life is like an immense ark full of possibilities.] Amado
Nervo (1870–1919)

One of the most important poets of the nineteenth century, Amado Nervo died in 1919, and never experienced television broadcasting. If one substituted "Spanish language television broadcasting" for "life" in the quotation above, it would offer a good way to describe the medium in the twenty-first century. Spanish language television broadcasting has immense potential, but will it be able to become all that it is capable of being?

This chapter offers an examination of the state of Spanish language television broadcasting in the United States from an industry perspective. We begin with an overview of the number of stations and networks, their ownership, programming content, audiences, and advertising revenues found in Spanish language television. From there we present an analysis of the problems and prospects facing Spanish language broadcasting, along with ideas for future research and investigation.

Spanish language television broadcasting in the United States is one of the fastest growing sectors of the larger television broadcasting industry. Starting with a single TV station in 1955 (Wilkinson, 2009), Spanish language television broadcasting consists of hundreds of local full- and low-power television stations, several national broadcasting networks, and numerous digital channels targeting Latinos, the fastest growing ethnic group in the United States. Despite—or perhaps because of—its growth, Spanish language television broadcasting in the twenty-first century is challenging to define. Although most of the content is presented in Spanish, some channels offer a combination of Spanish and English language programming to appeal to audience members who may be Spanish-dominant or English-dominant in terms of language. Other networks and services targeting Latinos[1] program only in English, attempting to reach a combination of English-dominant Latinos and younger, bicultural Latinos who speak Spanish but are also very comfortable with English. Thus, a broad definition of Spanish language broadcasting is utilized for this chapter because it is an evolving medium, with many different approaches and perspectives.

Like the larger English language television market—referred to as the general market—Spanish language television functions in a multiplatform environment involving traditional broadcasting, digital channels, mobile-based programming services, and social media. Spanish language broadcasting is financed by local and national advertising. Companies that own Spanish language networks also receive revenues from cable, satellite, and IPTV (telco) services in contract negotiations for their channels to appear in various subscription packages. In this chapter, our primary focus is on the traditional broadcast component of Spanish language television.

## Ownership

As of November 2015, there is a total of 1,371 over-the-air commercial television broadcasting stations in the United States, according to the Federal Communications Commission (see https://www.fcc.gov/encyclopedia/television for updated figures). Approximately 238 of these stations (17.3%) are self-identified as Spanish language stations (Category: Spanish language television stations, n.d.); Texas (51), California (50), and Florida (22) have the most Spanish language TV stations in the country.

Based on analysis of FCC data and additional research by the authors, approximately 65% of full-power Spanish language television stations are owned by groups or conglomerates. The two largest owners of television stations in terms of revenue and market share are Univision and Comcast. Univision owns a total of 56 Spanish language television stations and is controlled by a group of private equity firms known as Broadcast Media Partners Inc. (this includes Madison Dearborn Partners, Providence Equity Partners, TPG, Thomas H. Lee Partners, and Saban Capital Group, none with discernable Hispanic representation). Univision is a privately-held company, but is considering an initial public offering (IPO) to become publicly-traded. Comcast, a publicly-held conglomerate, owns 26 Spanish language stations. Entrevision (58 stations), Liberman Broadcasting (nine stations), and Spanish Broadcasting Systems (six stations) are the other significant owners.[2] Entrevision is a public company owned in part by Univision (10%). Liberman calls itself the largest privately held Hispanic-owned media company in the United States (Liberman Broadcasting, 2014); Spanish Broadcasting System claims it is the largest publicly held Hispanic-owned media company in the US (Spanish Broadcasting System, 2014). The remaining 35% of stations are owned either by independent broadcasters or by general market groups that have added Spanish language stations to their portfolios (e.g., Sinclair, Tegna, Raycom). In addition to these full power commercial stations, there are numerous low power TV stations and digital sub-channels that carry some type of Spanish language broadcasting service, although these channels have smaller audiences due to technical and distribution limitations.

The growth of Spanish language television stations has been facilitated by the growth of Spanish language broadcast networks, which provide important sources of programming and news for their local affiliates. Univision, Comcast, and RCN Television Group are the top three Spanish language broadcast network owners. Univision operates two national networks: Univision (featuring novellas and other traditional programming) and UniMás (featuring movies and programs appealing to younger audiences; no news). Comcast also operates two national networks: Telemundo (novellas and other traditional programming) and NBC Universo (formerly Mun2, available to cable and satellite audiences). RCN is now the sole owner of MundoMax, formerly known as MundoFox. The network began as a joint venture between 21st Century Fox and RCN, but Fox sold its investment in July 2015 (Lafayette, 2015). MundoFox is a full-service network in terms of programming, except for news.)

Regarding ownership, none of the three largest (Univision, UniMás and Telemundo) Spanish language networks is U.S. Hispanic-controlled. The only Spanish language network controlled by Hispanics—the Estrella network—is operated by Liberman Broadcasting and is one of the smallest networks with only about 40 affiliates, many located on digital sub-channels with limited distribution and availability.

More detail on the state of ethnic ownership is available from the *Federal Communications Commission Quadrennial Review* of broadcast ownership (Federal Communications Commission, 2014). The state of Hispanic-owned broadcast media is woeful, as the FCC report demonstrated:

> *Broadcast ownership and ethnicity.* Hispanic/Latino persons collectively or individually held a majority of the voting interests in 571 broadcast stations, comprised of 42 full power commercial television stations (3.0 percent) of 1,386 stations; 155 low power television stations, including Class A stations (9.4 percent) of 1,651 stations; 194 commercial AM radio

stations (5.2 percent) of 3,737 stations; and 180 commercial
FM radio stations (3.2 percent) of 5,714 stations.
(Federal Communications Commission, 2014, p. 3)

There are two main reasons for these dismal numbers. One is the long-term failure of regulatory policies in the United States to provide for more ethnic ownership, detailed in previous research on the subject (see Albarran & Fender, 2006 for a comprehensive review). The second reason is the lack of capital available for minority owners, who are often unable to garner funding from lenders. Although deep consideration of these and other factors affecting minority ownership of broadcast facilities is beyond the scope of the present chapter, we note that the lack of ethnic ownership is a major concern for the television industry and beyond.

## Content

Spanish language television both mirrors and differs from its general market counterparts in regard to programming. In terms of similarities, one will find news and sports programming, reality programs, talk shows, game shows, dramas, comedies, variety programs, and movies. Prime-time programming blocks perform especially well in Spanish language television ratings. Univision and Telemundo typically outperform other networks. Two major content categories are news and public affairs, and entertainment.

### News and Public Affairs Programming

News programming is as vital to Latinos as it is to general audiences; issues such as immigration, education, health, the economy (jobs), and news from Latin America where many audience members may have extended family are particularly relevant. News has also been an important source of cultural assimilation and understanding for older audiences, especially those who have immigrated to the United States. However, news content is costly to produce, and unless a station is affiliated with a network or is in a major market, its audiences may not be as well-served as could be. For example, many stations in small markets offer limited local news unless they are owned by Univision or Telemundo, and for many small-market stations there is only the Univsion or Telemundo national news—which is better than no news at all, but does not serve the local audience particularly well.

Television news helps empower audiences to engage in democracy, especially around presidential elections. Spanish-speaking audiences, just like their English-speaking counterparts, rely heavily on television news coverage of national politics. Latinos depend on the media to learn where candidates stand on relevant issues and topics. Spanish language stations that have local newscasts tend to address local and regional concerns and better serve the Spanish speaking community, just as English language local news serves the local general market.

## Entertainment Programming

Although some news and public affairs content airs during prime time, and, as will be noted below sports programming can be a ratings juggernaut, the success of telenovelas drives prime time.

Sports, notably futbol (soccer), is wildly popular on Spanish language television and skews towards male viewers, but futbol is also enjoyed by women and children. The quadrennial World Cup typically brings the highest audience ratings for Spanish language television, but broadcasts of Mexican, Latin America, and European leagues are also heavily viewed. Live broadcasts of American sports such as football, baseball, and basketball attract Latino viewers to general networks. Most of these games air during prime-time and weekends, but as do many sports broadcasts, tend to attract more male than female viewers.

The greatest content difference between Spanish language and general market outlets is in prime-time, where the telenovela—Spanish language soap opera—dominates the program schedule. Whereas general market soap operas can last for decades (e.g., *General Hospital*, 1963–present; *The Young and the Restless*, 1973–present), telenovelas rarely last more than a year—most of them of even shorter duration. Telenovelas have historically been produced in Latin American countries (Mexico, Colombia, Brazil, Argentina); in recent years more domestic production of telenovelas has taken place in the United States. The most successful telenovela to date has been *Yo soy Betty, la fea* (*Ugly Betty*), a romantic comedy that has been reproduced in several countries including a successful run in the United States (2006–2010).

Telenovelas are often criticized for both their content and their casting. Much like general market soap operas, telenovela content is rife with sex and violence. Some of the increase in violence and concerns about violence are associated with the increasing popularity of narconovelas—telenovelas featuring stories about crime and the drug trade. Narconovelas are performing well and opening the genre beyond the traditionally female audience, garnering male viewership as well (Bauder, 2015). Viewers also lament the long-held telenovela tradition of casting Anglo, blonde, and other actors who do not reflect the physical characteristics of most of the people in the shows' home country. Light-skinned actors are cast in the majority of roles on telenovelas; in addition, when darker-skinned actors are cast, their characters are typically portrayed as more sexual and violent than their lighter-skinned counterparts (Rivadeneyra, 2011).

Although telenovelas are criticized for their casting as well as their sensational content that misrepresents and stereotypes Latinos, they out-perform other Spanish language broadcast content in terms of ratings. Despite criticism, viewers are still tuning in. The ratings success may be partially attributed to their place in the prime-time schedule. The only Univision programming that comes close to performing as well as its prime-time block of telenovelas is the Sunday night block containing *Aqui y Ahora* (*Here and Now*), a national level public affairs program, and *La Banda* (*The Band*), a reality show and singing competition (Media Life, 2015). The future of novelas may be affected, however, as Telemundo and Univision are beginning to air reduced numbers of episodes of each series. Traditionally, a novela such as Univision's *Lo Imperdonable* may have run for up to 150 episodes, but upcoming novelas, including Univision's *Pasion y Poder* and *El Gran Hotel* have been slated to run for about half as long (Bauder, 2015). We have yet to see how this will affect viewership as these time slots cycle through new programming more frequently.

## Audiences

The population of the United States is approximately 318 million. The number of Hispanics living in the United States is estimated at 54 million, or 17.4% of the total population (Matsa, 2015; State and Country Quick Facts, 2014), not including the undocumented population, which according to Krogstan and Passel (2015) is approximately 11.3 million people.

The Latino audience is large and growing, and it is quite young. The "new Latino," (Cobo, 2006, p. 1026) is defined as young, bicultural, and digitally connected. According to Nielsen (2012), the Latino population has a median age of 27, compared to 37 years for non-Latinos. Further, U.S.-born Latinos (65% of all Latinos) are even younger, with a median age of 18, and are heavy users of technology and digital content. In contrast, foreign-born Latinos (median age of 40) have different prefer-ences and needs regarding language, content, and digital media (Nielsen, 2014a). In short, the audiences for Spanish language television are seg-mented by age and immigration status, and have very different needs that correspond to their lifestyle (Nielsen, 2014a).

The audience for Spanish language television tends to be segmented by language preference. This creates three distinct groups of audiences: Spanish-dominant, or individuals who demand content in Spanish; English-dominant, or audiences who want their content in English; and bilingual, referring to people who are comfortable with both Spanish and English content. Of all Latinos in the United States, 65% self-report either that they speak only English at home, or speak English very well (Motel & Patten, 2012); this means almost two-thirds of Latinos are communicat-ing in both Spanish and English. The way that broadcasters incorporate a bilingual approach creates segmentation, especially across age or degree of assimilation/acculturation.

According to Tsai and Li (2012, p. 316), "acculturation must be recognized as a useful and important market segmentation variable," especially because assimilation/acculturation occur at varying levels and results in the creation of subgroups with differing preferences and needs. For instance, young bilingual/bicultural Latino consumers may be adept at code switching, vacillating between cultural identities without forsaking the other. Accordingly, they may seek both mainstream English language content and Spanish language media. They may also be more comfortable with Spanish language programming surrounded by advertisements that utilize English or a mix of English and Spanish commonly referred to as Spanglish. Meanwhile, older Latinos may be less familiar with the bicultural approach to programming and advertisements and may find such content juxtapositions "confusing or bizarre" (Tsai & Li, 2012, p. 317). Switching back and forth between languages can be confusing for older Latinos or recent immigrants who rely almost exclusively on Spanish. Part of this confusion may also be attributed to the assimilated consumer's expectation for a binary delineation of mainstream or dominant culture advertisements in English and more Hispanic-specific content in Spanish.

## Advertising

The Latino population and its growing economic clout, estimated at $1.5 trillion in 2015, long ago caught the interests of advertisers wanting to target this explosive market (Bookman, 2015; Nielsen, 2014a). Overall Hispanic media spending increased 8.1% to $8.3 billion from 2012 to 2013, compared to just 0.9% in general market media spending (Advertising Age, 2015). Of this, Spanish language television captured $6.01 billion—or about three-quarters of the total.

Over the years marketers and advertisers have become increasingly sophisticated in their approach to the Spanish television market. At first, advertisers simply hired Spanish-speaking actors to overdub the original English language recording, thus essentially using the same ads as in the general market. This approach proved ineffective. Television ads were next adapted to Hispanic audiences, meaning that the ads were produced in Spanish language, featuring Latino actors in the same situations as general market ads. However, these were still essentially direct translations of the same advertising campaigns. Advertisements that are culturally sensitive, reflecting Latino cultural values and traditions, and created specifically for the Hispanic market, are deemed the most effective (Tindle, 2011).

Latino audiences are as likely as any group to be critical of or find fault with the kinds of products and services being advertised. Spanish language television advertising, like that of the general market, raises concerns about promoting fast food and poor diets that contribute to health issues such as obesity and diabetes, especially in children. Fleming-Milici, Harris, Sarda, and Schwartz argued that Hispanic audiences are of special concern because obesity is more common among Hispanic youth, which is made worse considering "food companies' stated intentions to increase marketing to Hispanics" (2013, p. 723).

These authors also found Spanish language television offered fewer food advertisements than English language television did, but that Spanish language television was more likely to direct advertisements for unhealthy foods and restaurants at both children and adult women. These findings are especially important considering that adult women tend to hold purchasing power in households, and can be influenced by requests from children who are also viewing a large number of advertisements for nutrient-deficient foods. Because Hispanic children tend to watch more television per day than non-Hispanic children, we can assume that the negative effects of such content may be amplified for Hispanic youth (Fleming-Milici, Harris, Sarda, & Schwartz, 2013).

## Problems and Prospects of Spanish Language Broadcasting

Having reviewed the state of Spanish language television broadcasting in the United States, we now turn to a discussion of the problems and prospects facing this sector of the media. Our hope is that this section will spur the industry (and audiences, as applicable) to action to address these challenges.

### Problems

In terms of problems, our intent is to present advice to the industry on how it can do a better job of serving the growing Hispanic audience. Some of these problems will also need policy actions to help remedy the situation.

### Limited Latino Ownership of Spanish Language Television Stations

A huge disparity exists between the nation's largest ethnic group and its ownership of television stations. Hispanics represent approximately 17.4% of the population (Matsa, 2015) yet own only 3% of the full power commercial TV stations (Federal Communications Commission, 2014). The lack of minority ownership of broadcast stations in the United States is a long-term problem. Several policy initiatives were established over the course of the past four decades to try to improve minority ownership. These included policies such as distress sales applicable in certain situations when transferring ownership of stations to minorities; establishment of tax credits and certificates for potential station sales to minorities; establishment of a capital fund for prospective minority owners; comparative hearings and policy statements, and establishment of low power television with preference to minority applicants (Albarran & Fender, 2006).

However, none of these efforts has improved minority ownership, especially among Hispanics. Incentives must be created for potential Hispanic owners; these must be constitutionally sound and not subject to elimination by the courts, as in the case of some of the options detailed above. The lowering of capital requirements would help, as would new funding to support Hispanic acquisition of television properties. It will take a combination of new ideas and approaches among politicians in Washington, the FCC, Latino entrepreneurs, and activists to find solutions to this long-term problem.

### Under- and Poor Representation of Latinos on Spanish Language Television

Content analyses and audience reception studies conducted over the past decade have pointed out that modern audiences are frustrated with representations of Latino characters on Spanish language television (Rojas, 2002, 2004). Although telenovelas garner some of the highest ratings, their content leaves much to be desired. Audiences are especially critical of the representations of traditional gender roles, occupational roles, class stereotypes, and race relationships in telenovelas that help reinforce dominant ideology (Rivadeneyra, 2011). This is especially problematic considering the lack of Latino ownership in the industry, and the outsider perspective this imposes upon a niche, ethnic audience. The presentation of sexuality and violence is especially problematic. Although many programs have been criticized for objectifying and over-sexualizing female characters, the emergence of narconovelas in particular reinforces stereotypes of both male and female Latino characters as criminals.

As in the general market, producers' reliance upon stereotypes—good and bad—must be replaced by new, diverse representations of Latino characters. For example, simply increasing the number of female characters with an identifiable occupation would allow female characters to focus on more than merely their domestic roles, physical appearance, and sexuality (Rivadeneyra, 2011). Additionally, the casting of Latino characters should be more inclusive and focus less on light-skinned actors. Even if the goal of future programming is not to be more realistic or reflect viewers' tastes, there is a wide range of identities and storylines that have yet to be explored. As the Hispanic audience continues to grow, future content should be more reflective of the range of skin tones, body types, identities, sexualities, and cultural values among the Hispanic population.

### Focus on Latino Audiences as Consumers Rather Than as Citizens

Since the 1990 census the Hispanic population has mushroomed, and advertisers have discovered a new, growing audience segment in which to market their products and services. The Hispanic audience is an important commodity in the twenty-first century. At the same time, Spanish language television can do more for its audiences than simply selling them to sponsors. Stations and networks can do a much better job informing and educating the audience with more news and public affairs programs dealing with issues and topics important to Hispanic households. Expanding news coverage will be expensive, especially at the local level, but it is needed in areas of high-density Hispanic population that receives little television news. It is important that Spanish language television be not just ratings-driven, but also public service-driven.

For example, political coverage is key; Latinos play an increasingly important role in elections at all levels of democracy (Fowler, Hale, & Olson, 2009). Political debates must be made available, and presented in Spanish for voters who are Spanish-dominant. However, in the primary campaign leading up to the 2016 presidential election, there were no debates presented in Spanish on any network; indeed there were no debates (English or Spanish) aired on any Spanish language network. A debate on February 26, 2016 had been scheduled to air live on Telemundo, but a controversy between Comcast-owned NBC and the Republican National Party resulted in its removal from the broadcast schedule (Wofford, 2015). Clearly, such a decision only serves to hurt voters and democracy in general, and is short-sighted in terms of the political parties and their efforts to inform the electorate.

### Prospects

Regarding prospects, our focus is on opportunities available to the Spanish language television market.

### The Latino Population Is Young and Growing

According to the 2010 census, more than half of the Hispanic population is under 30, with a mean age of 28.1 years, compared to the general population mean age of 37.6 years (Advertising Age, 2015). Brown and Patten (2014) found that Hispanics have the second largest number of three or four-person households (behind Whites) and the largest number of households with five or more persons.

These data, reflecting current population trends, suggest that the Hispanic population will continue to grow and to expand over the next several decades. Growth in terms of sheer numbers will be complemented by an expansion in terms of the diversity of the Hispanic people, including but not limited to their geographic dispersion, educational level, and occupations. This means more potential consumers of all types of Spanish language media, including television—and suggests the potential of not only bigger audiences, but also larger advertiser revenues. Some of these additional revenues should be used to expand programming options, help encourage greater Latino ownership of television properties, and better serve the Spanish speaking citizens in our democracy.

## The Spanish Language Television Audience Can Expand

Although there is fragmentation in Spanish language television broadcasting, television remains a heavily used medium. As Spanish language television continues to adopt more English language programming it will likely entice English-dominant audience members to sample more programs. This could result in larger aggregate audiences moving forward, although broadcasters will no doubt want to appeal to the needs of their Spanish-dominant viewers.

Despite the need to be sensitive to Spanish-dominant viewers, however, we can expect more stations to offer programming entirely in English, as more second-, third-, and fourth-generation households (which are increasingly likely to be comfortable with the English language) emerge (Nielsen, 2014a). Fusion, an English-language programming network operated by Disney-owned ABC, is one of the earliest channels to target English-dominant Latinos. We can expect to see more broadcast channels move toward an English language lineup. This may not mean the end of Spanish language broadcasting as we know it, but simply another form of audience fragmentation along language lines.

## Spanish Language Television Can Capitalize on Emerging Technologies

Although broadcast television will continue to be an important medium for Hispanics, the rise of digital sub-channels and new Internet-based platforms hold great promise for Spanish language television. There is already a strong digital presence in terms of satellite-delivered channels, streaming options and social media platforms.

Previous research has shown Hispanics to be heavy users of technology, who are using mobile devices and social media sites at higher levels than other ethnic groups (Lopez, Gonzalez-Barrera, & Patten, 2013). This is helping to mitigate some of the concerns of the digital divide by making content available to everyone despite language, cultural status, or screen preference.

*Shorter Runs of Telenovelas May*
*Increase Content Diversity*

Although telenovelas maintain successful ratings across Spanish language television outlets, the recent decrease in the number of episodes for upcoming Univision and Telemundo telenovelas may mean that loyal viewers could consume more programs throughout the year. This approach toward future programming may produce a more flexible and timely response to changes in the industry and the changes in viewer preferences. Spanish language broadcasters have the opportunity to tell new stories, using new storytelling methods and fresh characters, which may satisfy the needs of the ever-evolving modern Latino audience.

## Spanish Language Media at a Crossroads

Our examination of the state of Spanish language television broadcasting reveals a number of questions and topics that deserve ongoing examination and research by scholars interested in Latino audiences and the media they consume. From a structural standpoint, Latinos are a true minority when it comes to ownership, especially of full power broadcast stations. This is an ongoing challenge for the industry, because more ownership by Latinos should result in an increase of entertainment and information content that truly serves the audience rather than simply offers audiences as a commodity to advertisers.

There are issues with programming, especially the popular prime time telenovelas. Telenovelas tend to offer sensational storylines, and are cast with beautiful and violent characters who often perpetuate gender and ethnic or racial stereotypes. There is a need for ongoing content analysis of telenovelas to track trends and patterns, and to observe any changes to typical formulaic plot and character development. It will also be interesting to see how shorter forms of telenovelas fare in terms of ratings and audience appeal.

We know the Latino audience is becoming more segmented in terms of language and culture (Nielsen, 2014a, 2014b), with those groupings operating alongside the usual gender and life cycle categories used by advertisers to separate audiences. How will segmentation affect future

357

programming decisions? At what point will more English language content be integrated with Spanish content? How will this affect the evolution of Spanish- and English-language television? Here a variety of audience studies are warranted beyond traditional demographic analysis. Panel designs and longitudinal research in particular could observe how younger audiences respond to a shifting environment in Spanish language television. Surveys can also look at the uses and gratifications of Spanish language broadcasting as a content platform compared to other new digital platforms.

Advertisers and advertising for Spanish language television is another area warranting further research. Advertising is the financial base of broadcast television, and advertisers wanting to reach Hispanic audiences need television and other platforms to introduce their products and services. Studies are needed both on advertising content targeting Hispanics, and trends as to where advertising dollars are being directed by marketers. Advertisers must also assess how their messages will be affected in a growing media environment that includes segmentation along language and cultural lines.

In its short history, Spanish language broadcasting in the United States has emerged as a dynamic medium. Yet Spanish language broadcast television is approaching a crossroads presenting challenges regarding ownership, programming, audience base, and advertising. Our hope is this review will spur other research on Spanish language media to track the trends and evolution of the industry, its ownership and management, the consumers it seeks, and the citizens it serves.

## Notes

1 We use both "Latino" and "Hispanic" to refer to the cultural group being considered in this chapter; the literature we cite tends to uses one or the other of terms. For example, the U.S. census uses the term "Hispanic," although "Latino" is recognized as a broader and more inclusive (if gender-specific) label.

2 For comparison, in the general market, the top five owners own 440 stations, or approximately 32% of all TV stations (Matsa, 2014).

## References

Advertising Age (2015, July 29). *11th annual Hispanic fact pack*. Retrieved November 2, 2015, from http://gaia.adage.com/images/bin/pdf/Hispanic_Fact_Pack_2014_web.pdf.

Albarran, A. B., & Fender, D. (2006). Behind the numbers: The impact of government preferences and non-preference on minority broadcast ownership. In A. Tait & G. Meiss (Eds.). *Ethnic media In America. Book 1: Building a system of their own* (pp. 219–238). Dubuque, IA: Kendall Hunt Publishing.

Ang, I. (1991). *Desperately seeking the audience*. New York, NY: Routledge.

Bauder, D. (2015, October 27). *Telemundo rising in competition with Univision for Spanish-language viewers.* Retrieved November 26, 2015, from http://www. usnews.com/news/business/articles/2015/10/27/telemundo-closing-gap-on-spanish-language-leader.

Bookman, S. (2015, February 4). *Hispanic audiences, and $1.5T in buying power, trend toward OTT.* Retrieved November 1, 2015, from http://www. fierceonlinevideo.com/special-reports/hispanic-audiences-and-15t-buying-power-trend-toward-ott.

Brown, A., & Patten, E. (2014). *Statistical portrait of Hispanics in the United States, 2012.* Pew Research Center. Retrieved November 3, 2015, from http:// www.pewhispanic.org/2014/04/29/statistical-portrait-of-hispanics-in-the-united-states-2012/#households-by-family-size-race-and-ethnicity-2012.

*Category: Spanish language television stations in the United States by state.* Retrieved October 19, 2015, from: https://en.wikipedia.org/wiki/Category:Spanish-language_ television_stations_in_the_United_States_by_state.

Cobo, L. (2006). Targeting the new Latino. *Billboard, 118*(10), 26.

Federal Communications Commission. (2014). *Report on ownership of commercial broadcast stations.* Retrieved November 26, 2015, from https://www.fcc. gov/document/report-ownership-commercial-broadcast-stations-0.

Fleming-Milici, F., Harris, J. L., Sarda, V., & Schwartz, M. B. (2013). Amount of Hispanic youth exposure to food and beverage advertising on Spanish- and English-language television. *JAMA Pediatrics, 167*(8), 723–730.

Fowler, E., Hale, M., & Olsen, T. (2009). Spanish- and English-language local television coverage of politics and the tendency to cater to Latino Audiences. *International Journal of Press/Politics, 14*(2), 232–256.

Lafayette, J. (2015, July 16). *Fox sells interest in MundoFox network.* Retrieved November 16, 2015, from http://www.broadcastingcable.com/news/currency/ fox-sells-interest-mundofox-network/142605.

Liberman Broadcasting (2014). About us. *Liberman Broadcasting.* Retrieved January 10, 2015, from http://www.lbimedia.com/.

Lopez, M. H., Gonzalez-Barrera, A., & Patten, E. (2013, March 7). *Closing the digital divide: Latinos and technology adoption.* Retrieved November 16, 2015, from http://www.pewhispanic.org/2013/03/07/closing-the-digital-divide-latinos-and-technology-adoption/.

Lotz, A. (2007). *The television will be revolutionized.* New York, NY: New York University Press.

Matsa. K. (2014). *The acquisition binge in local TV.* Retrieved November 16, 2015, from http://www.pewresearch.org/fact-tank/2014/05/12/the-acquisition-binge-in-local-tv/.

Matsa, K. (2015). *Hispanic media: Fact sheet.* Retrieved October 19, 2015, from http://www.journalism.org/2015/04/29/hispanic-media-fact-sheet/.

Media Life Magazine. (2015, November 15). *This week's broadcast ratings.* Retrieved November 15, 2015, from http://www.medialifemagazine.com/this-weeks-broadcast-ratings/.

Motel, S., & Patten, E. (2012). *The 10 largest Hispanic origin groups: Characteristics, rankings, top counties.* Pew Hispanic Center. Retrieved February 2, 2014, from http://www.pewhispanic.org/files/2012/06/The-10-Largest-Hispanic-Origin-Groups.pdf.

Nielsen (2014a). *A fresh view of Hispanic consumers.* Retrieved August 20, 2015, from http://www.nielsen.com/us/en/insights/news/2014/a-fresh-view-of-hispanic-consumers.html.

Nielsen (2014b). *Engaging the evolving Hispanic consumers: A look at two distinct sub-groups.* Retrieved February 2, 2015, from http://www.nielsen.com/us/en/insights/news/2014/engaging-the-evolving-hispanic-consumers.html.

Nielsen. (2012). *The state of the Hispanic consumer: The Hispanic market imperative.* Retrieved February 10, 2014, from http://es.nielsen.com/site/documents/State_of_Hispanic_Consumer_Report_4-16-FINAL.pdf.

Rivadeneyra, R. (2011). Gender and race portrayals on Spanish-Language television. *Sex Roles, 65*(3), 208–222.

Rojas, V. (2002, July). *Do I see myself represented on Spanish television? Latinas "Talk Back" to Univision and Telemundo.* Paper presented to the International Association for Media and Communication Research conference, Barcelona, Spain.

Rojas, V. (2004). Gender and Latinidad: Latinas speak about Hispanic television. *The Communication Review, 7*, 125–153.

Spanish Broadcasting System (2014). Station directory. *Spanish Broadcasting System.* Retrieved January 10, 2015, from http://www.spanishbroadcasting.com/station_directory.html.

*State and county quick facts* (2014). United States Census Bureau. Retrieved December 6, 2014, from http://quickfacts.census.gov/qfd/states/00000.html.

Tindle, T. (2011, October 26). *Advertising strategies for targeting U.S. Hispanics.* Retrieved November 2, 2015, from https://www.comscore.com/ita/Insights/Blog/Advertising-Strategies-for-Targeting-U.S.-Hispanics.

Tsai, W & Li, C. (2012). Bicultural advertising and Hispanic acculturation. *Hispanic Journal of Behavioral Sciences, 34*(2), 305–322.

Wilkinson, K. (2009). Spanish language media in the United States. In A. B. Albarran (Ed.), *Handbook of Spanish Language Media* (pp. 3–16). New York, NY: Routledge.

Wofford, T. (2015, October 30). *RNC cancels only debate to air on Spanish-language TV.* Retrieved November 3, 2015, from http://www.newsweek.com/rnc-cancels-telemundo-debate-388815.

# 21

# ETHICAL SENSITIVITY ASSESSMENT IN EDUCATIONAL SETTINGS

## Examining Awareness of Ethical Issues Related to Media and Diversity

*Rebecca Ann Lind and Tammy Swenson-Lepper*

From the use of the word "thug " by journalists to describe #BlackLivesMatter protesters, to calling trans women such as Caitlyn Jenner "he/she" or even "it," to seemingly mundane stories about urban food deserts, coverage of matters that explicitly or implicitly reflect issues of socially constructed differences present ethical concerns for journalists and audiences alike. Covering stories highlighting issues of race, ethnicity, gender identity or sexual orientation, and so forth is challenging because of the many ethical issues that arise. Yet ethical issues related to diversity or socially constructed differences may occur in nearly any news story.

In this chapter, we argue that the concept of ethical sensitivity can provide a worthwhile tool in the education of not only future and current media professionals but also media audiences. We begin by describing ethical sensitivity (ethsen) and reviewing ethsen research before focusing on ethsen in contexts involving race, gender, and other areas of socially-constructed difference. Finally, we turn to how assessing ethsen may contribute to both undergraduate education and the ongoing professional development of journalists.

## Ethical Sensitivity

Moral decision-making about the presentation of the news is complex; especially as our cultures become global and emerging media facilitate citizen journalism, the variety of potential ethical issues, their ramifications, and the number of stakeholders affected by journalists' decisions increases. Thus, we need a suitably sophisticated model to guide our thinking about moral decision making in contemporary journalism. For that, we turn to James Rest's (1986a, 1986b) Four Component Model of moral behavior.

Rest's Component One, moral or ethical sensitivity, represents an individual's ability to notice that a situation has a moral or ethical dimension. This involves interpreting and comprehending the situation. Component Two, moral judgment, focuses on an individual's ability to make the most moral decision. The individual may balance competing goals and values, apply elements of an ethical system or theory, and use some decision criteria. In Component Three, moral motivation, people are confronted with choices between conflicting values, both moral and non-moral. People may balance their moral evaluations with all other pertinent situational factors, and may decide that some action is called for. In Component Four, moral action, people enact (or do not enact) the moral decision they have made. Perhaps setbacks or obstacles cause an individual to abandon an attempt to carry out an intended behavior, or perhaps no attempt will be made.

Although each component offers insight into a significant aspect of moral behavior, and we have conducted research into each of the components over the last two decades,[1] our program of research has focused primarily on ethical sensitivity, which we argue is key; before one may solve a moral problem, one must first recognize it as such. Our work is guided by Bebeau, Rest, and Yamoor's definition of ethical sensitivity: "the perception that something one might do or is doing can affect the welfare of someone else either directly or indirectly (by violating a general practice or commonly held social standard)" (1985, p. 226). The process of recognizing that an ethical issue exists is distinct from the process of its resolution. Ethical sensitivity is a precursor to moral judgment, in that a person must acknowledge the presence of an ethical issue or problem before it can be evaluated and potentially resolved. Lacking the ability to notice that a situation includes moral or ethical characteristics, people are unlikely to make thoughtful, defensible moral decisions.

Many scholars (including Rest, Bebeau, and others) have approached ethical sensitivity as we do: ethsen is a cognitive ability or skill, which with practice may be improved. Thus, ethsen—like any other ability—can benefit from educational interventions which may occur in a classroom, a workshop, or another setting. Bebeau argued that individuals "can learn to see things as others see them, to reason more carefully, to rethink their priorities and to change communication habits that undermine their goals" (2002, p. 288).

Our research team has studied ethsen in a variety of contexts, including media (Lind, 1997; Lind & Rarick, 1995; Lind & Rarick, 1999), organizational communication (Swenson-Lepper, 2005), and classroom settings

(Lind, Rarick, & Ibrahim, 1996). Although some of our prior work based on the ethical sensitivity construct has articulated analogous constructs such as sensitivity to research misconduct or RMsen (Lind & Swenson-Lepper, 2007) and sensitivity to conflicts of interest or COIsen (Lind & Swenson-Lepper, 2013), we believe it is most appropriate to frame sensitivity to ethical issues involving race and other issues of socially constructed differences—such as gender, social class, able-bodiedness, religious or faith community affiliation, and more—in the broad context of ethical awareness. Our position is consistent with work studying "ethical sensitivity to acts of racial and gender intolerance" (Brabeck et al., 1998, p. 3).

Brabeck et al. noted that intolerance need not "involve physical conflict or be maliciously motivated to be hurtful and/or harmful"; it may take the form of "disapproving and distrustful attitudes" which—whether intentional or unintentional—may "prevent individuals from treating persons different from themselves with respect and dignity" (1998, p. 3). Such attitudes may be rooted in stereotypes or ignorance and may be conveyed subtly or explicitly through verbal or nonverbal communication. Brabeck et al., whose work focused on secondary schools, argued that intolerant acts can "adversely affect the way students feel about themselves, their peers and their schools. This, in turn, will affect their adjustment to school and academic success" (1998, p. 3). The ramifications of intolerance are not limited to the educational setting, however; aversive racism (Gaertner & Dovidio, 2005) and microaggressions or "brief and commonplace daily verbal, behavioral, or environmental indignities, whether intentional or unintentional, that communicate hostile, derogatory, or negative racial slights and insults toward members of oppressed groups" (Nadal, 2008, p. 23) may occur in any social interaction.

### *Ethical Sensitivity and Professional Obligations*

According to Brabeck et al., "educators and other professionals have the responsibility to acquire the knowledge and skills to respond to intolerant behavior in ways that are ethically defensible and consistent with the ethical codes of their profession" (1998, p. 3). Indeed, Brabeck et al. noted that "ethical concerns related to racial and gender intolerance clearly cut across professional disciplines and it is fair to say that there is a core set of ethics that is common to different helping professions" (p. 6). Besides addressing the crucial issue of intolerance, therefore, Brabeck et al. have foregrounded the relevance of professional codes of ethics, with clear applicability to the practice of journalism.

To Bebeau, "professional practice is predominantly a moral enterprise. Consequently, professional schools are concerned with the ethical development of their students" (2002, p. 271). She described ethical sensitivity in professional practice as involving the ability to see things from the perspective of other individuals and groups (including other cultural and socio-economic groups) and more abstractly, from legal, institutional and national perspectives. Thus, it includes knowing the regulations, codes and norms of one's profession, and recognising when they apply.

(Bebeau, 2002, p. 283)

She argued that "understanding that one is responsible provides the bridge between knowing the right thing to do and doing it" and that "in professional contexts, moral motivation and commitment has to do with the importance given to professional values in competition with other values" (p. 285).

The need to understand diverse other social and economic groups is evident in the guiding codes of many professional organizations, including but not limited to those affiliated with journalism. For example, the American Society of Newspaper Editors has—since its *Canons of Journalism* were first adopted in 1922—articulated journalists' professional and moral obligations:

The First Amendment, protecting freedom of expression from abridgment by any law, guarantees to the people through their press a constitutional right, and thereby places on newspaper people a particular responsibility. Thus journalism demands of its practitioners not only industry and knowledge but also the pursuit of a standard of integrity proportionate to the journalist's singular obligation.

(ASNE, 1975)

The Accrediting Council on Education in Journalism and Mass Communications (ACEJMC) presents "commitment to diversity and inclusiveness" among its nine principles of accreditation (2009), stating among other things that "the professions of journalism and mass communications should understand and reflect the diversity and complexity of people, perspectives and beliefs in a global society and in the multicultural communities they serve," and that "Programs seeking accreditation should develop curricula and instruction that educate faculty and prepare students with the multicultural knowledge, values and skills essential for professional practice." ACEJMC's nine accrediting standards (2013) include "diversity and inclusiveness"; in addition, diversity-related "core values" and competencies are also evident in the "curriculum and instruction" standard.

The Society of Professional Journalists' *Code of Ethics* (2014) includes in its primary exhortation to "Seek truth and report it" the following specific obligations for journalists to be sensitive to issues of difference and diversity: "Boldly tell the story of the diversity and magnitude of the human experience. Seek sources whose voices we seldom hear," and "Avoid stereotyping. Journalists should examine the ways their values and experiences may shape their reporting."

Indeed, these seem to suggest not mere sensitivity to but active engagement with issues of socially constructed difference and multiculturalism—a position consistent with Fowers and Richardson's description of multiculturalism as "a moral movement that is intended to enhance the dignity, rights, and recognized worth of marginalized groups" (1996, p. 609).

## Assessing Ethical Sensitivity

As we have described in prior work (Lind & Swenson-Lepper, 2013), scholars have used three types of tasks to measure ethsen: production tasks, recognition tasks, and self-assessment tasks.

First, production tasks generally ask participants to respond to open-ended questions about a scenario. For example, Sanders and Hoffman (2010) asked participants to detail ethical issues in a social work scenario. Livingston et al. (2006) and Dotger (2010) asked participants to describe racial and ethical issues in scenarios about education. Myyry and Helkama (2002) studied ethical sensitivity in social psychology students and asked about ethical issues in the professional lives of social psychologists. Lohfeld et al. (2012) asked undergraduate medical students to provide brief paragraphs about the ethical issues they noticed in 12 different vignettes about health care. More recently, Martinov-Bennie and Mladenovic (2015) measured students' ethical sensitivity based on whether they identified two specific ethical issues related to an environment and human rights case. Although we believe production tasks are likely the most effective way to measure ethsen, and, as described below, we use such tasks in our research, many studies using production tasks have failed to encompass the entirety of Rest's conceptualization of ethical sensitivity, and some have primed participants that the scenario contains an ethical issue. Our approach has attempted to avoid these shortcomings.

Second, in recognition tasks, participants complete surveys after reading short ethical dilemmas. Participants may be asked to select the ethical theory that they believe best fits a scenario, provide a rating of whether the situation has ethical components, or choose an action they might take in that situation (Cohen, Pant, & Sharp, 1993; Ozdogan & Eser, 2007; Shawver & Sennetti, 2009). However, forcing (or at least inviting) people to engage an ethical issue in a survey may not be the most effective way to evaluate their ethical sensitivity, because they may not have perceived any ethical issues until confronted with them as survey options. We concur fully with Schlacter's argument that: "Researchers who seek to study the ethical sensitivity of their subjects and use leading questions will tend to prejudge outcomes . . . If ethical consciousness is the object of study, a procedure like this will bias the inquiry at the outset, and that data which result will only indicate a sensitivity to the experimenter's demand" (1990, p. 848).

Finally, self-assessment tasks measure ethsen by having respondents review descriptions of behaviors and rate how ethical the behaviors are. For instance, Simga-Mugan et al. defined ethical sensitivity as "the tendency to judge the conduct unethical" (2005, p. 147), and based on their self-assessment method, people who rank specific behaviors as more unethical are said to have higher ethical sensitivity. The Ethical Sensitivity Scale Questionnaire (ESSQ) by Tirri and Nokelainen (2007, 2011) asks people to evaluate themselves based on statements such as "When I am working on ethical problems, I consider the impact of my decisions on other people" and "I ponder on different alternatives when aiming at the best possible solution to an ethically problematic situation" (p. 593). Szabó, Németh, and Kéri (2013) and Gholami, Kuusisto, and Tirri (2015) have also used the ESSQ. We note that this type of self-assessment examines respondents' reported perceptions of their ethical sensitivity, not their actual ability to notice ethical issues and the consequences of those issues to various stakeholders in a particular situation. Yet this is but one of several limitations of the ESSQ—in addition, it is both vulnerable to the problem of social desirability bias inherent in all self-report data and prone to distorted self-perceptions such as may be influenced by narcissism or the positive illusory bias.

Again, we believe production tasks are usually the most appropriate to use when assessing ethical sensitivity, and we have relied on them almost exclusively in our work.

### Ethical Sensitivity Indicators

Consistent with the perspective that ethsen is a cognitive ability which can be taught and with practice improved, our view of ethical sensitivity has been influenced by an information processing approach, which "focuses on processes of attending to, selecting and storing, integrating, and evaluating information" (Lind & Swenson-Lepper, 2013, p. 45). We see ethical sensitivity as a knowledge structure as defined in the fields of social and organizational cognition: "a mental template that individuals impose on an information environment to give it form and meaning" (Walsh, 1995, p. 281). According to Swenson-Lepper (2005), knowledge structures are developed through "a recursive process of social involvement, reflection, and experience" (p. 208). Informed by work in organizational cognition, we examine *integration*, defined as "the degree of interconnectedness among the knowledge structure dimensions" (Walsh, 1995, pp. 298–299) and *differentiation*, defined as "the number of dimensions within a knowledge structure" (p. 298).

We argue that people's knowledge structures can be reflected in their encoding of messages, such as verbalizations during an interview, written responses to open-ended questions, or creation of media content. In our program of research, ethical sensitivity is evidenced by any number of what we call "indicators," operationally defined as verbalizations of discrete relevant concepts or the relationships among these concepts. Ethsen indicators may take many forms, and represent at least four content domains (and linkages among them) and three dimensions. The content domains and indicators represent differentiation, or the dimensions of a knowledge structure; linkages among these represent integration, or the interconnectedness of the information in the knowledge structure.

The four content domains are situational characteristics, ethical issues, consequences, and stakeholders. Combined, these content domains encompass the sum of Bebeau, Rest, and Yamoor's (1985) definition of ethical sensitivity. The domain of *situational characteristics* refers to acknowledging relevant elements, actions, or contextual features of the situation with which one is presented. The *ethical issues* domain shows understanding that an action may fall along a right-wrong continuum, or may affect the welfare of others positively or negatively. The domain of *consequences* is illustrated through referencing effects of the ethical issue on people, situations, actions, or ideas. The *stakeholders* domain reflects individuals, groups, or institutions that may feel the consequences of an ethical issue. The three dimensions of ethsen include *time* (how quickly or spontaneously ethsen indicators are exhibited), *breadth* (the range of different ethsen indicators exhibited), and *depth* (the amount of thought or detail evident in the ethsen indicators).

## Conducting Interviews to Assess Ethical Sensitivity

Our preferred method of assessing ethsen involves a production task relying on open-ended, semi-structured interviews using a funnel sequence. We have also had success adapting this method to an open-ended written survey in which questions are revealed, one at a time, after the response to the prior question is complete. A production task, as described above, requires participants to generate their own responses to the situations with which they are faced. Open-ended questions allow respondents to state whatever they wish, so their responses may or may not contain any ethsen indicators. A semi-structured funnel sequence, which presents general questions early in the interview and targeted questions near the end of the interview, allows respondents to discuss ethical issues at any time, even before being specifically asked to do so. It also allows respondents to state that the situation does not present any ethical issues.

In the typical application of our method, we begin by presenting a situation (e.g., a TV news story) to a participant, followed by the interview (or written survey). The early questions solicit only description, not evaluation (asking participants to describe the situation; to highlight what stood out in the situation), although the open-ended questions fully allow for evaluative comments to be made. Later in the interview the questions do solicit evaluation (asking participants whether the story should have been aired and to discuss negative and positive aspects of the participant's decision [to air or not to air the story]), but do not introduce the concept of ethical issues—although ethical issues can be raised by the subject, if desired. Only after subjects respond to these questions are they explicitly asked whether the situation presents any ethical issues—and if so, what they are, who might be affected by them, and how these stakeholders might be affected.

### Analyzing the Interviews: Cognitive Maps, Coding, and Scoring

After the recorded interviews are transcribed, we code the transcripts using cognitive mapping techniques (Axelrod, 1976) adapted from a procedure developed by Wrightson (1976). A cognitive map presents characteristics of a subject's thinking. In our work, the cognitive maps represent ethsen indicators in each of the four content domains (situational characteristics, issues, stakeholders, and consequences) as well as the linkages a subject makes between indicators. The more ethsen indicators that are present in the subjects' maps, the greater the subjects' ethical sensitivity. For a more in-depth discussion of how Axelrod's work has been adapted to ethical sensitivity, including excerpts of maps resulting from the application of our methods, see Lind (1997) and Lind, Rarick, and Swenson-Lepper (1997).

The number of indicators present in subjects' responses reflects the breadth dimension of ethsen. To factor the time dimension into ethsen, interview or survey responses may be divided into units based on the increasingly targeted focus of the questions. Although we believe that assessments of ethical sensitivity do not always require a calculated ethsen score, we have presented several methods for doing so. The basic method described by Lind, Swenson-Lepper, and Rarick (1998), which reflects the breadth dimension, involves simply summing the number of unique indicators present over the entire interview. An alternative and more sophisticated method is the weighted-additive scoring method, presented in our work assessing sensitivity to conflicts of interest (Lind & Swenson-Lepper, 2013). By giving more value to indicators presented earlier in the interview, the weighted-additive scoring method incorporates both the breadth and the time dimensions of ethical sensitivity.

## Applicability to Instructional Contexts

Because our open-ended interview and survey approaches are production tasks, they are especially well-suited to educational contexts. Our funnel-type interview or survey approach (or variants thereof) may be used as the foundation for in-class exercises or formal assignments. Educators—whether at the secondary or tertiary level, or involved in facilitating workshops for the ongoing professional development of working journalists—may use ethsen assessment as a qualitative or quantitative diagnostic tool. For example, responses to stimuli may be used to identify individuals' relative areas of strength and weakness, which then allows instructors to focus educational efforts on areas in need of improvement. Variants of the method—such as using the funnel sequence to direct a class discussion—may be applied for impromptu assessments of students' sensitivity to ethical issues such as those arising in any particular current event. Should quantitative assessments be desired in the instructional context, the basic method of summing the number of indicators present in the response will often suffice (Lind, Swenson-Lepper, & Rarick, 1998), although the weighted-additive method (Lind & Swenson-Lepper, 2013) may be preferable in research applications.

We believe that educators and facilitators may also use ethsen assessment techniques when evaluating media content produced by participants in their classrooms or workshops. For example, media texts or artifacts produced by participants may be evaluated according to the extent to which it reflects (or lacks) indicators of ethical sensitivity. These indicators may be encoded in the media content verbally (statements by the reporter/student or an interviewee), visually (actions, framing of shots, textual on-screen identifiers, and so forth), aurally (voiceover, sound on tape, music, sound effects), through editing, and more. Indicators may also be present in the student/reporter's verbal (written or spoken) self-reflections on the process of and decisions related to creating any given media artifact or set thereof (e.g., a media portfolio).

One of the perhaps unintended benefits of conceptualizing ethical sensitivity as a cognitive ability or skill is that doing so may reduce some attitudinal barriers to participation, which may be especially evident among professionals. Although students are accustomed to producing work for evaluation in a classroom context, media practitioners may not approach the process as eagerly. When ethsen is approached as a skill, however, as Bebeau argued, "because criteria for judgement are grounded in professional expertise, and because norms are available to help an individual compare his/her ability to others, the assessment is viewed as authentic, and professionals are willing to submit to the learning process" (2002, p. 288). A skills approach may also ameliorate some of the negative responses to being associated with lapses in moral judgment or moral failings. Bebeau wrote that "when practitioners are referred by a licensing board for ethics instruction, they often assume that they are viewed as people who lack integrity" (2002, p. 288), but "helping them to see that they have deficiencies in one or more abilities related to ethical decision-making has restorative power" (p. 288).

## Using Ethical Sensitivity Assessment as an Educational Tool

Instructors interested in using ethsen assessment in the classroom or workshop setting must first select an appropriate stimulus and then begin to identify the potential indicators of ethical sensitivity likely to appear in participants' discourse related to that text. Although, as noted above, we believe that ethsen may be used as a tool when evaluating media texts produced by students or workshop participants, in this section we focus on our traditional interview or survey methods.

### *Selecting Stimuli*

Instructors and others wishing to assess sensitivity to ethical issues involving racial or gender intolerance using the open-ended, funnel-type interview or survey method described above must first select stimulus material and then identify the ethsen indicators it is most likely to generate. Stimuli may be created by the instructor or researcher (see Brabeck et al., 1998), or existing media artifacts (e.g., news stories) may be used (Lind, 1997; Lind & Rarick, 1999; Lind, Swenson-Lepper, & Rarick, 1998). For instance, a scenario could be developed around how #BlackLivesMatter—a movement arising in response to the 2014 shooting of an 18-year-old unarmed African-American man by a White police officer—is portrayed in a news story. A story about this issue (whether in a print, audio, video, or online format) could be selected or generated as a stimulus.

### *Potential Indicators of Ethical Sensitivity and Intolerance*

Following stimuli selection or creation, potential ethsen indicators must be considered. Although the ethsen dimensions defined above are consistent across multiple contexts, as are the conceptual definitions of each of the four content domains and the linkages across content domains, identifying the individual ethsen indicators contained within each of the four content domains is situation-specific. In practice, the ethsen indicators associated with a story about #BlackLivesMatter will be very different from those associated with a story about marriage equality. Lists of ethsen indicators discovered in some of our prior research using actual news stories as stimuli may be seen in Lind (1997), Lind, Rarick, and Swenson-Lepper (1997), and Lind, Swenson-Lepper, and Rarick (1998). For example, Lind, Swenson-Lepper, and Rarick (1998) used open-ended funnel-type inter-viewers with 104 individuals who viewed a story about a young Latina who was injured by a hit-and-run driver, and identified in the participants' discourse 10 unique story characteristics or relevant facts about the situa-tion (e.g., an African American "Good Samaritan" who helped the victim was interviewed), 11 ethical issues (e.g., the appropriateness of depicting certain content—blood, stretcher, victim), 11 consequences (e.g., it may have a positive outcome—help find the criminal, driver may turn him- or herself in, witnesses may come forward), and six stakeholders (e.g., the people directly affected—the victim, her family, friends, and neighbors).

The process of identifying potential ethsen indicators may be guided by relevant scholarly literature, *a priori* knowledge of the phenomenon of interest, review of the stimuli by professionals, interview or survey pretests, professional codes and standards, and more. However, until the assessments are conducted, the potential indicators are just that—potential, possible, or likely indicators. Creating the actual list of ethsen indicators is done when the evaluative discourse is analyzed. In doing so, we advocate the use of inductively-derived content-analytic systems. Whether applied formally (for research purposes) or informally (for pedagogical purposes), inductively-derived systems are grounded in the discourse itself (e.g., interviews or written responses to media stimuli) rather than created out of context and then imposed on the discourse. Generating a list of the potential indicators of racial or gender intolerance relevant to the particular stimulus material is a helpful starting point, and we agree with Jordan (2007) that linking back to professional codes of ethics enhances content validity. However, as Jordan noted, "Using a code of ethics to define moral issues . . . is not ideal for predicting how individuals would identify moral issues that arise in professional interac-tions because a profession's explicit ethics (or legal) code may not contain all important moral issues" (2007, p. 349).

Once created, the list of potential indicators of sensitivity to racial or gender intolerance should be continually supplemented by whatever additional indicators appear in the discourse being evaluated. The initial list—which will likely contain both broadly-applicable (e.g., discrimina-tion is unethical) and situation-specific (e.g., Ms. X crossed the line when she said Y to Mr. Z) indicators—can be enhanced by a review of the stimulus material by members of the profession. For example, prior to analyzing audience evaluations of ethical issues in a TV news report, Lind (1997) asked media ethics experts (ethics scholars, news council mem-bers, and journalists) to identify the ethical issues in the story.

A number of sources provide starting points for identifying indicators of ethical sensitivity to issues relating to socially constructed difference.

Many of these may inform analyses of student/reporter discourse or media texts created by course or workshop participants. As with the open-ended interviews, media artifacts created by students or reporters may contain multiple ethsen indicators reflecting relevant decision-making processes and thought structures.

In generating a list of potential ethical issues, one may refer to the six ethical principles presented by Brabeck et al. (1998) based on their review of a number of professional codes of ethics: competence, integrity, professional and scientific responsibility, respect for others' rights and dignity, concern for others' welfare, and social responsibility. However, generic ethical principles in and of themselves do not necessarily function as what we call "indicators" of ethical sensitivity – ethsen indicators must be applied to the specific situation at hand. Although Brabeck et al. did not present the specific ethical issues recognized by participants as ethsen indicators in their study, we believe they qualify as such – these include recognizing that individuals in a scenario had engaged in making stereotypic comments or gendered slurs, differential treatment of individuals, racial bias, modeling racism, seeing diversity as a strength, and more.

Additional guidance regarding principles linked to potential ethsen indicators may be found in the competencies presented in the American Counseling Association's *Multicultural and Social Justice Counseling Competencies* (Ratts et al., 2015), *Competencies for Counseling with Lesbian, Gay, Bisexual, Queer, Questioning, Intersex and Ally Individuals* (Harper et al., 2012), and *Competencies for Addressing Spiritual and Religious Issues in Counseling* (American Counseling Association, 2009). The American Psychological Association's (1990) *Guidelines for Providers of Psychological Services to Ethnic, Linguistic, and Culturally Diverse Populations* may also be of value. The Association of American Colleges and Universities' program promoting the personal and social responsibility of students includes detailed lists of character traits (AAC&U, n.d.) and numerous potentially relevant rubrics for multiple dimensions of personal and social responsibility (Value Rubric Development Project, n.d.), some of which are directly applicable to issues of tolerance and ethical sensitivity.

Each of these resources considers attitudes and beliefs, knowledge, skills, or actions which not only reflect awareness of diversity, but also acknowledge its fundamental role in the professional's interactions with members of a community of diverse others. The detailed nature of many of these competencies makes them attractive for modification and application to the assessment of ethical sensitivity. However, despite the value of these resources in helping direct attention to the relevant ethical issues, most focus on the content domain of ethical issues. Indicators reflecting situational characteristics of necessity can only arise from the stimulus itself; stakeholders and consequences are somewhat less context-bound but remain significantly context-restrained.

## Moving Forward

Our work developing ways for students, faculty, and other professionals to assess ethical sensitivity, and our interest in ethical issues relating to race, gender, and other areas of socially-defined difference, reflect national trends urging attention to multicultural awareness, tolerance, and personal and social responsibility. The various professional competencies referenced above have much to offer in terms of educating our students, although in some cases the need may be more clearly felt by journalism educators and professional workshop facilitators. However, we must also highlight the AAC&U's work to promote and assess students' personal and social responsibility of students. Although what Reason (2013) called the "Herculean task" of identifying and assessing the relevant learning outcomes is still in progress, two of the five dimensions of personal and social responsibility are particularly relevant to us: "taking seriously the perspectives of others" and "developing competence in ethical and moral reasoning and action." The first is defined as "recognizing and acting on the obligation to inform one's own judgment; engaging diverse and competing perspectives as a resource for learning, citizenship, and work"; the second is defined as "developing ethical and moral reasoning in ways that the incorporate the other . . . dimensions; using such reasoning in learning and in life" (Reason, 2013). The connection between dimensions such as these has been noticed by scholars including Narvaez and Endicott, who argued that multicultural experiences "can lead to an adjustment in thinking, a broadening of perspective, and greater cognitive flexibility" (2009, p. 43). Further, Narvaez and Endicott stressed that "cognitive flexibility and similar capacities of ethical sensitivity are critical for ethical behavior in professionals and lay alike" (p. 43).

We believe that the concept of ethical sensitivity should receive more overt attention in the classroom. All too often, when engaging in ethics instruction, we emphasize asking students to analyze the ethical issues we place before them. Perhaps we hope that by discussing these ethical issues in the classroom, students will become more sensitive to the ethical issues in the communication situations all around them. However, although such a practice can help encourage students to approach the ethical decision making process in a logical fashion (e.g., via the Potter Box), it does not necessarily increase ethical sensitivity. Bebeau (2002) reminded us that "studies typically report low to very low correlations between ethical sensitivity and moral judgement" (p. 288). As part of assessing our students' relative strengths and weaknesses to identify where our educational interventions will have the most impact, we should strive first to understand how sensitive students are to ethical issues in communication situations, and then try to increase their sensitivity to those issues.

Our work in assessing ethical sensitivity, based on more than two decades of research, is founded in real-life situations and presents a method to measure how well students or practitioners understand relevant situations, detect ethical issues, recognize who may be affected by those ethical issues and how, and make connections among those content domains. Our method, therefore, reflects two crucial components of ethsen training as presented by Bebeau, who argued that "profession-specific measures" are "key to helping an individual identify personal shortcomings," as is "the analysis of verbatim dialogues offered in response to real-life professional problems" (2002, p. 288) or scenarios. Continued efforts in this realm might focus on developing stimuli related to media coverage of stories involving or invoking issues of socially constructed difference or diversity and incorporating cognitive mapping as an educational strategy for training current and future journalists about covering those stories and issues.

Scenarios could be based on current events, to help make their relevance more clear to participants. They must include realistic ethical issues, stakeholders, and consequences so that participants have the opportunity to develop knowledge structures related to these issues, increasing the likelihood that participants will begin to engage in more complex ways of thinking about diverse others. Alternatively, as discussed above, the very act of creating media content about stories involving matters of race, gender, or other forms of socially constructed difference can be used to teach and assess ethical sensitivity. However, we have not yet tried this approach. What is the best way to incorporate such a method? Does the resulting media text on its own provide sufficient evidence of indicators of ethical sensitivity, or is an accompanying self-analysis required? What are this method's unique strengths and weaknesses, and what do educators need to be aware of when using this method?

The cognitive mapping techniques discussed here could be used in a multitude of ways. They could be used to gather data about students' and practitioners' levels of ethical sensitivity using a pre-test, post-test study design or they might be used by the participants themselves. For instance, after participants have written responses to the scenarios, they could be taught to map the connections they have made. Such active engagement with their responses to the stimuli would not only reinforce the relevance of all four of the content domains of ethsen indicators, but also provide the opportunity for self-reflection about participants' hidden attitudes, beliefs, and assumptions of multiculturalism. Such experiential and self-reflective learning opportunities can be powerful, especially when taking place in a context involving group discussion. As Rest (1986a) found three decades ago, discussion groups are a particularly valuable way for people to improve their ethical decision making skills because they provide "concentrated practice in moral problem-solving, stimulated by peer give-and-take (challenging one another's thinking, reexamining assumptions, being exposed to different points of view, building lines of argument, and responding to counter argument)" (Rest, 1986a, pp. 79–80).

Finally, in the particular context of sensitivity to ethical issues related to diversity or socially constructed differences, the robust preparation of future media professionals is imperative. As students move into and eventually become the standard-bearers of their professions, a lack of multiculturalism can hurt their clientele (e.g., Spindler & Spindler, 1994)—even to the extent of pathologizing those who exhibit different cultural patterns (Sue & Sue, 2013).

Ethical sensitivity as a construct has important theoretical, heuristic, pragmatic, and pedagogical applications. Its conceptual core is robust yet sufficiently flexible that it may be applied to vast array of contexts, including, as we have done here, those involving diversity. As we approach a quarter-century of working with what Rest presented as the first of four components of moral behavior, we remain enthusiastic about its possibilities for guiding our work as educators and researchers.

## Note

1 The authors dedicate this chapter to their mentor, collaborator, and friend David L. Rarick (University of Minnesota), in grateful acknowledgment of his pivotal role in and many contributions to this ongoing program of research.

## References

Accrediting Council on Education in Journalism and Mass Communications, The (2009). *Principles of accreditation*. Retrieved November 8, 2015, from http://www2.ku.edu/~acejmc/program/principles.shtml.

Accrediting Council on Education in Journalism and Mass Communications, The (2013). *ACEJMC Accrediting Standards*. Retrieved November 8, 2015, from https://www2.ku.edu/~acejmc/PROGRAM/STANDARDS.SHTML#std3.

American Psychological Association (1990). *Guidelines for providers of psychological services to ethnic, linguistic, and culturally diverse populations*. Retrieved November 15, 2015, from http://www.apa.org/pi/oema/resources/policy/provider-guidelines.aspx.

American Society of Newspaper Editors (n.d.) *Statement of principles*. Retrieved November 8, 2015, from http://asne.org/content.asp?pl=24&sl=171&contentid=171.

Association of American Colleges and Universities (n.d.). *Character traits associated with the five dimensions of personal and social responsibility*. Core Commitments: Educating Students for Personal and Social Responsibility. Retrieved November 15, 2015, from http://www.aacu.org/sites/default/files/CharacterTraitsofthe5Dimensions.pdf.

Axelrod, R. (Ed.) (1976). *Structure of decision: The cognitive maps of political elites*. Princeton, NJ: Princeton University Press.

Barry, N. H., & Lechner, J. V. (1995). Preservice teachers' attitudes about and awareness of multicultural teaching and learning. *Teaching and Teacher Education, 11*(2), 149–161.

Bebeau, M. J. (2002). The Defining Issues Test and the Four Component Model: Contributions to professional education. *Journal of Moral Education, 31*(3), 271–295.

Bebeau, M. J., Rest, J. R., & Yamoor, C. M. (1985). Measuring dental students' ethical sensitivity. *The Journal of Dental Education, 49*(4), 225–235.

Brabeck, M. M., McCubbin, L., Rogers, L. A., Ting, K., Warner, C. Sirin, S., & Weaver, M. (1998). *Increasing ethical sensitivity to racial and gender intolerance in schools: Development of the REST (Racial Ethical Sensitivity Test)*. Boston, MA: Boston College. Retrieved from ERIC database. (ED423354)

Cohen, J., Pant, L., & Sharp, D. (1993). A validation and extension of a multidimensional ethics scale. *Journal of Business Ethics, 12*(1), 13–26.

Dotger, B. H. (2010). "I had no idea": Developing dispositional awareness and sensitivity through a cross-professional pedagogy. *Teaching and Teacher Education, 26*, 805–812.

Fowers, B. J., & Richardson, F. C. (1996). Why is multiculturalism good? *American Psychologist, 51*, 609–621.

Gaertner, S. L., & Dovidio, J. F. (2005). Understanding and addressing contemporary racism: From aversive racism to the Common Ingroup Identity Model. *Journal of Social Issues, 61*(3), 615–539.

Gholami, K., Kuusisto, E., & Tirri, K. (2015). Is ethical sensitivity in teaching culturally bound? Comparing Finnish and Iranian teachers' ethical sensitivity. *Compare: A Journal of Comparative and International Education, 45*(6), 886–907.

Harper, A., Finnerty, P., Martinez, M., Brace, A., Crethar, H. . . ., & Lambert, S., (2012). *Competencies for counseling with lesbian, gay, bisexual, queer, questioning, intersex and ally individuals*. The Association for Lesbian, Gay, Bisexual, and Transgender Issues in Counseling. Retrieved November 8, 2015, from http://www.counseling.org/docs/default-source/competencies/algbtic-competencies-for-counseling-lgbqqia-individuals.pdf?sfvrsn=8.

Jordan, J. (2007). Taking the first step toward a moral action: A review of moral sensitivity measurement across domains. *The Journal of Genetic Psychology: Research and Theory on Human Development, 11*(2), 323–359.

Lind, R. A. (1997). Ethical sensitivity in viewer evaluations of a TV news investigative report. *Human Communication Research, 23*(4), 535–561.

Lind, R. A., & Rarick, D. L. (1995). Assessing ethical sensitivity in television news viewers: A preliminary investigation. *Journal of Mass Media Ethics, 10*(2), 69–82.

Lind, R. A., & Rarick, D. L. (1999). Viewer sensitivity to ethical issues in TV coverage of the Clinton-Flowers scandal. *Political Communication, 16*(2), 169–181.

Lind, R. A., & Swenson-Lepper, T. (2007). Sensitivity to research misconduct: A conceptual model. *Medicine and Law, 26*(3), 589–599.

Lind, R. A., & Swenson-Lepper, T. (2013). Measuring sensitivity to conflicts of interest: A preliminary test of method. *Science and Engineering Ethics, 19*(1), 43–62.

Lind, R. A., Rarick, D. L., & Ibrahim, B. (1996). A demonstration of ethical sensitivity assessment in a college media ethics course. *Paper presented at the National Communication Ethics conference*. Gull Lake, MI.

Lind, R. A., Rarick, D. L., & Swenson-Lepper, T. (1997). Cognitive maps assess news viewer ethical sensitivity. *Journal of Mass Media Ethics, 42*(4), 133–147.

Lind, R. A., Swenson-Lepper, T., & Rarick, D. L. (1998). Identifying patterns of ethical sensitivity in TV news viewers: An assessment of some critical viewing skills. *Journal of Broadcasting & Electronic Media, 42*. 507–519.

Livingstone, G., Derryberry, W. P., King, A., & Vendetti, M. (2006). Moral developmental consistency? Investigating differences and relationships among academic majors. *Ethics & Behavior, 16*(3), 265–287.

Lohfeld, L., Goldie, J., Schwartz, L., Eva, K., Cotton, P., Morrison, J., . . . & Wood, T. (2012). Testing the validity of a scenario-based questionnaire to assess the ethical sensitivity of undergraduate medical students. *Medical Teacher, 34*, 635–642.

Martinov-Bennie, N., & Mladenovic, R. (2015). Investigation of the impact of an ethical framework and an integrated ethics education on accounting students' ethical sensitivity and judgment. *Journal of Business Ethics, 127*(1), 189–203.

Myyry, L., & Helkama, K. (2002). The role of value priorities and professional ethics training in moral sensitivity. *Journal of Moral Education, 31*(1), 36–50.

Narvaez, D., & Endicott, L. (2009). *Ethical sensitivity: Nurturing character in the classroom*. Notre Dame, IN: ACE Press.

Nadal, K. (2008). Preventing racial, ethnic, gender, sexual minority, disability, and religious microaggressions: Recommendations for promoting positive mental health. *Prevention in Counseling Psychology: Theory, Research, Practice and Training, 2*, 22–27.

Ozdogan, F. B., & Eser, Z. (2007). Ethical sensitivity of college students in a developing country: Do demographic factors matter? *Journal of Teaching in International Business, 19*(1), 83–99.

Ratts, M. J., Singh, A. A., Nassar-McMillan, S., Butler, S. K., & McCullough, J. R. (2015). *Multicultural and social justice counseling competencies*. Association for Multicultural Counseling and Development Executive Council, Division of American Counseling Association. Retrieved November 8, 2015, from http://www.counseling.org/docs/default-source/competencies/multicultural-and-social-justice-counseling-competencies.pdf?sfvrsn=20.

Reason, R. D. (2013, Winter). *Creating and assessing campus climates that support personal and social responsibility*. Retrieved November 8, 2015, from American Association of Colleges & Universities: https://www.aacu.org/publications-research/periodicals/creating-and-assessing-campus-climates-support-personal-and-social.

Rest, J. R. (1986a). *Moral development: Advances in research and theory*. New York: Praeger.

Rest, J. R. (1986b). Morality. In J. H. Flavell, & E. M. Markman (Eds.), *Handbook of child psychology: Cognitive development* (4th ed.) (Vol. 3, pp. 556–629). New York: Wiley.

Rogers-Sirin, L. (2008). Approaches to multicultural training for professionals: A guide for choosing an appropriate program. *Professional Psychology: Research and Practice, 39*(3), 313–319.

Sanders, S., & Hoffman, K. (2010). Ethics education in social work: Comparing outcomes of graduate social work students. *Journal of Social Work Education, 46*(1), 7–22.

Schlacter, P. J. (1990). Organizational influences on individual ethical behavior in public accounting. *Journal of Business Ethics, 9*(11), 839–853.

Shawver, T. J., & Sennetti, J. T. (2009). Measuring ethical sensitivity and evaluation. *Journal of Business, 88*(4), 663–678.

Simga-Mugan, C., Daly, B. A., Onkal, D., & Kavut, L. (2005). The influence of nationality and gender on ethical sesnitivity: An application of the issue-contingent model. *Journal of Business Ethics, 57*(2), 139–159.

Sirin, S. R., Brabeck, M. M., Satiani, A., & Rogers-Sirin, L. (2003). Validation of a measure of ethical sensitivity and examination of the effects of previous multicultural and ethics courses on ethical sensitivity. *Ethics & Behavior, 13*(3), 221–235.

Spindler, G., & Spindler, L. (Eds.) (1994). Pathways to cultural awareness: Cultural therapy with teachers and students. Thousand Oaks, CA: Corwin Press.

*SPJ Code of Ethics* (2014). Retrieved November 7, 2015, from Society of Professional Journalists: http://www.spj.org/ethicscode.asp.

Sue, D. W., & Sue, D. (2013). Counseling the culturally diverse: Theory and practice (6th ed.). Hoboken, NJ: John Wiley & Sons.

Swenson-Lepper, T. (2005). Ethical sensitivity for organizational communication issues: Examining organizational differences. *Journal of Business Ethics, 59*(3), 205–231.

Szabó, C., Németh, A., & Kéri, S. (2013). Ethical sensitivity in obsessive-compulsive disorder and generalized anxiety disorder: The role of reversal learning. *Journal of Behavior Therapy and Experimental Psychiatry, 44*, 404–410.

Tirri, K., & Nokelainen, P. (2007). Comparison of academically average and gifted students' self-rated ethical sensitivity. *Educational Research and Evaluation, 13*(6), 587–601.

Tirri, K., & Nokelainen, P. (2011). Ethical Sensitivity Scale. In K. Tirri, P. Nokelainen, F. Oser, & W. Veugelers (Eds.), *Measuring multiple intelligences and moral sensitivities in education* (Vol. Series: Moral Development and Citizenship Education, pp. 59–75). Rotterdam, Netherlands: Sense Publishers.

Value Rubric Development Project. (n.d.). Retrieved November 8, 2015, from Association of American Colleges & Universities: https://www.aacu.org/value/rubrics.

Walsh, J. P. (1995). Managerial and organizational cognition: Notes from a trip down memory lane. *Organizational Science, 6*(3), 280–321.

Wrightson, M. T. (1976). The documentary coding method. In R. Axelrod (Ed.), *Structure of decision: The cognitive maps of political elites* (pp. 291–331). Princeton, NJ: Princeton University Press.

# INDEX